Leadership in the Digital Enterprise:
Issues and Challenges

Pak Yoong
Victoria University of Wellington, New Zealand

BUSINESS SCIENCE REFERENCE

Hershey · New York

Director of Editorial Content:	Kristin Klinger
Senior Managing Editor:	Jamie Snavely
Managing Editor:	Jeff Ash
Assistant Managing Editor:	Michael Brehm
Publishing Assistant:	Sean Woznicki
Typesetter:	Jeff Ash
Cover Design:	Lisa Tosheff
Printed at:	Yurchak Printing Inc.

Published in the United States of America by
 Business Science Reference (an imprint of IGI Global)
 701 E. Chocolate Avenue
 Hershey PA 17033
 Tel: 717-533-8845
 Fax: 717-533-8661
 E-mail: cust@igi-global.com
 Web site: http://www.igi-global.com/reference

Library of Congress Cataloging-in-Publication Data

Leadership in the digital enterprise : issues and challenges / Pak Yoong, editor.
 p. cm.

Includes bibliographical references and index.
Summary: "This book presents a comprehensive collection of the most current research on various aspects, roles, and functions of digital enterprises"--Provided by publisher.

ISBN 978-1-60566-958-8 (hardcover) -- ISBN 978-1-60566-959-5 (ebook) 1. Knowledge management. 2. Leadership. 3. High technology industries. I. Yoong, Pak, 1945- II. Title.

 HD30.2.L427 2010
 658.4'092--dc22

2009012908

British Cataloguing in Publication Data
A Cataloguing in Publication record for this book is available from the British Library.

All work contributed to this book is new, previously-unpublished material. The views expressed in this book are those of the authors, but not necessarily of the publisher.

List of Reviewers

Mahfooz A.Ansari, *University of Lethbridge, Canada*
Traci A. Carte, *University of Oklahoma, USA*
Petros Chamakiotis, *University of Bath, UK*
Charlie C. Chen, *Appalachian State University, USA*
Brian Corbitt, *RMIT University, Australia*
Jocelyn Cranefield, *Victoria University of Wellington, New Zealand*
Mohamed Daassi, *IUT-GEA, France*
Gert-Jan de Vreede, *University of Nebraska at Omaha, USA*
Marc Favier, *University of Grenoble, France*
Jo Hanisch, *University of South Australia, Australia*
Albert L. Harris, *Appalachian State University, USA*
Sid Huff, *Victoria University of Wellington, New Zealand*
Annick Janson, *Victoria University of Wellington, New Zealand*
Rod Jarman, *Curtin University, Australia*
Nabila Jawadim *Amiens School of Managementm France*
Sharmila Jayasingam, *Universiti Malaya, Malaysia*
Michel Kalika, *Ecole de Management Strasbourg, France*
Heather King, *Texas, USA*
Sharman Lichtenstein, *Deakin University, Australia*
Darin R. Molnar, *Oregon, USA*
Niki Panteli, *University of Bath, UK*
David Pauleen, *Victoria University of Wellington, New Zealand*
Craig Pearce, *Claremont Graduate University, USA*
Christian Petersen, *Hamburg, Germany*
Evangelia Siachou, *Athens University of Economics and Business, Greece*
Ada Scupola, *Roskilde University, Denmark*
Andreas Schroeder, *Peng Chau, Hong Kong*
Halbana Tarmizi, *Abu Dhabi University, UAE*
Kate Thornton, *Victoria University of Wellington, New Zealand*
Christine Wassenaar, *Claremont Graduate University, USA*
Jiinpo Wu, *Tamkang University, Taiwan*

Table of Contents

Section 1
Emergent Leadership Approaches in the Digital Environment

Detailed Table of Contents

Section 1
Emergent Leadership Approaches in the Digital Environment

Section 1 of this book consists of 5 chapters that explore the nature of leadership in the virtual environment

Chapter 1
Kate Thornton, Victoria University of Wellington, New Zealand

This chapter explores the concept of distributed leadership. The author argues that distributed leadership is ideally suited to support online interactions in group environments as all group members have opportunities to facilitate activities that enhance ready access to information and sharing of information.

Chapter 2
Christina Wassenaar, Peter F. Drucker and Masatoshi Ito Graduate School of Management, USA
Craig L. Pearce, Peter F. Drucker and Masatoshi Ito Graduate School of Management, USA
Julia E. Hoch, University of Technology, Germany
Jürgen Wegge, Ludwig-Maximilians-Universität München (LMU), Germany

The four authors provide a brief exploration of the concept of shared leadership as it pertains to organizing, leading and participating in a virtual team. They strongly suggest that allocating leadership responsibilities based on team members' expertise and needs might lead to more productive and balanced teams in a virtual workplace.

This chapter explores the nature of leadership in a knowledge management environment and suggests a transformation of leader behavior is required to manage a new generation of knowledge workers.

The chapter introduces a framework for analyzing governance arrangements of knowledge management (KM) programmes. The framework is then used to analyze the organizational structures, processes and relational mechanisms, including leadership matters, which guide the KM programme of a large European corporation.

The final chapter in this section considers the skills needed by leaders to enhance the development of communication practices, performance and change management in virtual teams. The authors also describe the distinctions between effective practices of face-to-face and virtual team interactions.

Section 2
Patterns of Leadership Behaviours

Section 2 of this book consists of 6 chapters that describe the behavioral aspects of different leadership in the digital enterprise.

This chapter introduces the role of a connector-leader in connecting overlapping online communities of practice (CoP) as well as meeting the knowledge needs of local organisations and communities. Connector-leaders spanned boundaries in the online community realm and had a strong online presence. As professional learners, they were strongly outward facing, identifying primarily as members of a distributed online CoP. As leaders, they were inward facing, focusing largely on the knowledge needs of local organisations and CoPs.

The authors extended our understanding of leadership in a virtual environment. Using a quasi-experiment approach, they found that 'trust' serves as a mediating role in the relationship between leadership effectiveness and team satisfaction and team performance.

This chapter investigates the role of e-leaders in building and maintaining collective awareness within virtual teams. It examines the behavioural style of virtual team leaders. Specifically, it describes the effects of leaders' behavioral leadership orientation on collective awareness building in virtual teams.

This chapter presents the results of a study investigating leadership and leadership styles in e-commerce adoption in small and medium size enterprises in Australia. The results show that top management and CEO' leadership have a key role in small and medium size enterprises (SMEs) in developing a vision for e-commerce adoption and that the dominant leadership style is directive with some signs of consultative.

Chapter 10

This chapter explores the role of a facilitator of communities of practice and identifies several tasks commonly performed by facilitators from different communities. Facilitation in CoP by itself is challenging as we are dealing with different types of CoP that exhibit different characteristics. Through content analysis of facilitators' postings the authors identified several tasks commonly performed by facilitators from different CoPs. Knowing how to accomplish those tasks will help CoP facilitators in assisting their communities to thrive.

Chapter 11

Petros Chamakiotis, University of Bath, UK
Niki Panteli, University of Bath, UK

The final chapter in this section discusses leadership approaches suitable for some virtual teams and also the personal values that drive ordinary team members to lead their teams.

Section 3
Implications for Training and Development

Section 3 of this book explores different training and development strategies that could be implemented to develop emerging leaders in the digital enterprise.

Chapter 12

Kate Thornton, Victoria University of Wellington, New Zealand
Pak Yoong, Victoria University of Wellington, New Zealand

The authors describe a case study in which action learning, a process that involves small groups of learners working on issues or problems they face in their every day work, was supported by the use of ICT, thus providing a 'blended' approach.

Chapter 13

Darin R. Molnar, CEO, eXcolo Research Group, USA

The author raises the issue of 'servant leadership' which is described as a willingness to lead by first serving others. The author argues that assessment instruments are needed to help leaders understand the level of perceived servant leadership characteristics among organizational members under their guidance.

Chapter 14

Annick Janson, Victoria University of Wellington, New Zealand

Here the author uses an extended actor network analysis approach to investigate how self-selected leaders in online communities spontaneously emerge in a virtual environment, using the online medium to gain legitimacy and coverage.

Section 4
Additional Selected Readings

The final section of this book includes 3 chapters containing previous research as a supplementary addition to the work for this publication.

The author describes current leadership research in project management, and its related theories. Subsequently, the personality profiles of successful project managers in different types of projects are presented.

The authors examine the communication behaviors of participants in two different case studies to determine if number, length, and content of messages are sufficient criteria to identify emergent leaders in asynchronous and synchronous environments.

The authors argue that it is important to recognize the importance of trust as generated through individuals that have trustful ties that cross central boundaries, that is, trust brokers. Based on a relational approach to trust in groups as well as empirical studies of distributed work groups, they argue that trust brokers can help to establish trust quickly and make the group operate in more robust and sustainable ways.

Foreword

The modern organization is the "digital enterprise." The pervasive nature of information and communications technologies has changed the way organizations are structured, the way they operate, and the way they are lead. It can now be argued that the most important factor in the success of the digital enterprise is leadership. Effective leadership of the digital enterprise means recognizing the potential of these technologies and taking advantage of the opportunities that they present to move the enterprise forward. This book is the first book that I am aware of that provides a comprehensive look at leadership in the digital enterprise.

In the digital enterprise almost everyone uses digital technology. From the factory floor or out in the field, to the office setting, to the executive suite, people are connected, they share knowledge, and they work closely together. This means that the nature of leadership changes and new forms and roles in coordinating work and leading people emerge. I like to think of these new forms of leadership as "digital leadership."

Digital leadership exercises leadership in the context of varying degrees of technology. This leadership directs, facilitates and coordinates digital work and knowledge processes in the organization. Digital leadership requires not only an appreciation of the potential of information and communications technologies to aid in leadership of an enterprise, but also recognition of the limitations of these technologies and how they are used in projecting leadership across the organization.

This book presents the work of many contributors from around the globe. The authors have taken a broad and diverse look at digital leadership in the modern organization. What is clear from these contributions is that this is an exciting emerging area of research and practice.

Enjoy!

Brent Gallupe
Queens University, Ontario, Canada

Brent Gallupe is Professor of Information Systems, Director of the Queen's Executive Decision Center, and Associate Dean - Faculty at the School of Business, Queen's University at Kingston, Canada. He also holds an on-going Visiting Professor appointment at the University of Auckland, New Zealand. His current research interests are in computer support for groups and teams, the management of international information systems, and knowledge management systems. His work has been published in such journals as Management Science, MIS Quarterly, Information Systems Research, Academy of Management Journal, Sloan Management Review, and Journal of Applied Psychology.

Preface

In the digital enterprise, individuals will use a variety of technologies to assist them in communicating, collaborating, and coordinating their activities across distance and time. These technologies are designed to enhance workflow automation, office conferencing and communications, information and knowledge sharing, shared calendaring, electronic meeting support, data interchange, videoconferencing, and so forth. The combination of these technologies may also lead to new and emerging applications or systems related to business processes such as e-business, knowledge management, e-learning, supply chain management, enterprise resource planning and so on.

Because of the pervasive nature of these business systems in many organisations, people who are the champions or implementers of these systems are often ordinary business users and typically have very little formal training in information technology. What they do have is business knowledge associated with the particular application, and the leadership and influence skills to shepherd the design and implementation of the system within their organisations. For example, the need to scope a new innovation, produce a business case, establish effective stakeholders' communications, lead a business-centred design team, provide relevant users support and train and create meaningful evaluation of systems usage. The new leadership roles may be formal or informal, operating outside of "the formal organization," - which means they have varying degrees of recognition by organisations.

In order to acknowledge the specialized work that these key people are doing, many organisations are inventing or re-defining such IT-related leadership roles by providing job titles such as: knowledge manager, knowledge broker, gatekeeper, online meeting facilitator, virtual team leader, network broker, Web content manager and so on.

In order to present the most comprehensive coverage of these emergent leadership roles in the digital enterprises, researchers in particular sub-fields were invited to contribute specific and relevant chapters for this book. Therefore the purpose of this book is to present a comprehensive description of these new leadership roles in digital enterprises and to explore the implications for human resources planning and training. The book is divided into three sections: (1) *Emergent Leadership Approaches in the Digital Environment*, (2) *Patterns of Leadership Behaviours* and (3) *Implications for Training and Development*.

Section one, *Emergent Leadership Approaches in the Digital Environment*, includes five chapters, two of which address the issue of 'leadership',,and the other three chapters discuss the nature of leadership in the digital enterprises. In "The nature of distributed leadership and its development in online environments," Kate Thornton (Victoria University of Wellington, New Zealand) explores the reasons for adopting the concept of *distributed leadership*. She argues that distributed leadership is ideally suited to support online interactions in group environments as all group members have opportunities to facilitate activities that enhance ready access to information and sharing of information. In chapter 2, "Shared leadership meets virtual teams: A match made in Cyberspace," Christina Wassenaar and Craig Pearce

(Claremont Graduate University, USA), Julia E. Hoch (University of Technology, Germany) and Jürgen Wegge (Ludwig-Maximilians-Universität, Germany) provide a brief exploration of the concept of shared leadership as it pertains to organizing, leading and participating in a virtual team. They strongly suggest that allocating leadership responsibilities based on team members' expertise and needs might lead to more productive and balanced teams in a virtual workplace. Chapter 3, by Sharmila Jayasingam (Universiti Malaya, Malaysia) and Mahfooz Ansari (University of Lethbridge, Canada), explores the nature of leadership in a knowledge management environment and suggests a transformation of leader behavior is required to manage a new generation of knowledge workers. In chapter 4, "Governance and leadership of knowledge management," Andreas Schroeder (City University, Hong Kong), David Pauleen (Massey University, New Zealand) and Sid Huff (Victoria University of Wellington, New Zealand) introduce a framework for analyzing governance arrangements of knowledge management (KM) programmes. The framework is then used to analyze the organizational structures, processes and relational mechanisms, including leadership matters, which guide the KM programme of a large European corporation. The final chapter in this section, chapter 5, by Traci Carte (University of Oklahoma, USA) and Heather King (Gabbard and Company, USA), considers the skills needed by leaders to enhance the development of communication practices, performance and change management in virtual teams. They also describe the distinctions between effective practices of face-to-face and virtual team interactions.

Section two, *Patterns of Leadership Behaviours*, includes seven chapters. In chapter 6, Jocelyn Cranefield and Pak Yoong (Victoria University of Wellington, New Zealand) introduce the role of a *Connector-Leader* in connecting overlapping online communities of practice as well as meeting the knowledge needs of local organisations and communities. In chapter 7, "Enhancing virtual learning team performance: A leadership perspective," Charlie Chen and Al Harris (Appalachian State University, USA) and Jimpo Wu (Tamkang University, Taiwan) extended our understanding of leadership in a virtual environment. Using a quasi-experiment approach, they found that 'trust' serves as a mediating role in the relationship between leadership effectiveness and team satisfaction and team performance. The next chapter examines the behavioural style of virtual team leaders. Specifically, Mohamed Daassi (University of Bretagne Occidentale, France), Nabila Jawadi (Center for Research in Management & Organization, France), Marc Favier (University of Grenoble, France) and Michel Kalika (Center for Research in Management & Organization, France) examine the effects of leaders' behavioral leadership orientation on collective awareness building in virtual teams. In chapter 9, "Exploring leadership in e-commerce adoption in Australian SMEs," Ada Scupola (Roskilde University, Denmark) investigates the leadership style of key players associated with e-commerce adoption in Australian SMEs and finds that the dominant style is 'directive'. Chapter 10, by Halbana Tarmizi and Gert-Jan de Vreede (University of Nebraska at Omaha, USA), explores the role of a facilitator of communities of practice and identifies several tasks commonly performed by facilitators from different COPs. The final chapter in this section, chapter 11, by Petros Chamakiotis and Niki Panteli (University of Bath, England), discusses leadership approaches suitable for some virtual teams and also the personal values that drive ordinary team members to lead their teams.

Section three of the book, *Implications for Training and Development*, includes three chapters. Chapter 12, by Kate Thornton and Pak Yoong (Victoria University of Wellington, New Zealand) is titled "The application of blended action learning to leadership development: A case study." In it the authors describe a case study in which action learning, a process that involves small groups of learners working on issues or problems they face in their every day work, was supported by the use of ICT, thus providing a 'blended' approach. Chapter 13, by Darin Molnar (Independent Consultant, USA), titled "Assessment strategies for servant leadership practice in the virtual organizations," raises the issue of 'servant leadership' which is described as a willingness to lead by first serving others. The author argues that assessment instruments are needed to help leaders understand the level of perceived servant leadership characteristics among organizational members under their guidance. Finally, chapter 14, "Online networks can support the rise of virtual leaders: An Actor-Network Theory Analysis," is contributed by Annick Janson (Victoria University of Wellington, New Zealand). Here the author uses an extended actor network analysis approach to investigate how self-selected leaders in online communities spontaneously emerge in a virtual environment, using the online medium to gain legitimacy and coverage.

Finally, section four of the book, *Additional Selected Readings*, also includes three chapters. Chapter 15, by Ralf Muller (Sweden & BI Norwegian School of Management, Norway) is titled "Leadership in technology project management." In it the author describes current leadership research in project management, and its related theories. The personality profiles of successful project managers in different types of projects are presented. Chapter 16, by Simeon Simoff (University of Technology, Sydney, Australia) and Fay Sudweeks (Murdoch University, Australia) titled "The language of leaders: Identifying emergent leaders in global virtual team," examines the communication behaviors of participants in two different case studies to determine if number, length, and content of messages are sufficient criteria to identify emergent leaders in asynchronous and synchronous environment. Finally, chapter 17, "Building trust in networked environments: Understanding the importance of trust brokers," is contributed by Tom Julsrud (Norwegian University of Science and Technology, Norway) and John Bakke (Telenor Research & Innovation, Norway). Here the authors argue that it is important to recognize the importance of trust as generated through individuals that have trustful ties that cross central boundaries, that is, trust brokers. Based on a relational approach to trust in groups as well as empirical studies of distributed work groups, they argue that trust brokers can help to establish trust quickly and make the group operate in more robust and sustainable ways.

Pak Yoong
Victoria University of Wellington, New Zealand

Acknowledgment

I would like to acknowledge the help of all involved in the collation and review process of the book, without whose support the project could not have been satisfactorily completed.

Most of the authors of chapters included in this book also served as referees for articles written by other authors. Thanks go to all those who provided constructive and comprehensive reviews.

Special thanks also go to the publishing team at IGI Global. In particular to Heather Probst, Elizabeth Ardner and Tyler Heath, who continuously prodded via e-mail for keeping the project on schedule. Their contributions throughout the whole process from inception of the initial idea to final publication have been invaluable.

In closing, we wish to thank all of the authors for their insights and excellent contributions to this book.

Pak Yoong
Victoria University of Wellington, New Zealand
January 2009

Section 1
Emergent Leadership Approaches in the Digital Environment

Chapter 1
The Nature of Distributed Leadership and its Development in Online Environments

Kate Thornton
Victoria University of Wellington, New Zealand

ABSTRACT

Distributed leadership is a practice that spreads leadership over a number of people who work cooperatively and interdependently to achieve the purpose of their group. Unlike heroic models of leadership, which rely on the capabilities of one person, distributed leadership encourages all members to contribute their knowledge and expertise. Online environments such as communities of practice, action learning groups and virtual teams are ideally suited to fostering the development of distributed leadership because they allow all group members ready access to information and also allow for the sharing of information between group members. This chapter will consider how distributed leadership can be encouraged in online environments by both positional and emergent leaders and by the use of appropriate technologies.

INTRODUCTION

Distributed leadership is a concept that encourages all members, rather than only the positional or formal leader, to be involved in leadership of a group. Much has been written about distributed leadership in the education sector and in some business organisations; however there has been less discussion about how leadership can be distributed in online environments, despite their increasing occurrence. Information and communication technologies facilitate the access to and sharing of information between people working and learning in online environments. This has in turn has flattened traditional hierarchies in these environments and created a culture in which all group members are able to contribute to leadership hence strengthening the functioning of the group.

This chapter aims to describe the notion of distributed leadership and how it differs from traditional models of leadership. The nature and distribution

DOI: 10.4018/978-1-60566-958-8.ch001

of leadership in three online environments: online communities of practice; virtual teams; and online action learning groups and distribution of leadership in these will then be discussed. This will be followed by an analysis of factors that affect the distribution of leadership in online environments. Future trends and issues in this area will also be signalled.

BACKGROUND

Traditional Leadership Models

Traditional models of leadership have focused on the role of individuals in positions of power and the ways in which these leaders influence their followers. Such models of leadership are often referred to as 'great man' theories or heroic leadership models. Two of the more common models of leadership are those of transformational and transactional leadership. Transformational leaders are seen to influence, motivate and inspire others (Proctor-Thomson & Parry, 2001). They are role models for the people they work with and have visions that they are able to clearly articulate. Transactional leaders work on the premise that they are able to reward followers and that their followers to desire those rewards (Day & Harris, 2002). This leadership involves the manipulation of people and situations and is not seen to encourage leadership in others. These two models both posit leadership as an individual phenomenon with leaders in the front and followers behind, though transformative leadership involves greater collaboration and "deep transformation or emancipation of those led" (Lambert, 2003, p.8).

These individualistic models have been challenged in recent times. Robinson (2004) has suggested that "the heroic model of leadership is a romantic and debilitating fiction" (p. 42), because it sets unreasonable expectations of formal leaders and ignores the leadership of others. Both transformational and transactional models have

been criticised by Fink (2005), who believes that they "have serious and conceptual flaws" and are "artificial and disconnected from reality" (p. 5). Day (2003) agrees, suggesting that these theories "do not adequately reflect or explain the current practice of effective leaders" (p. 188). Among the flaws present in the heroic model of leadership are that too much responsibility for the wellbeing of an organisation rests with one person and if they move on, a leadership vacuum is created (Robinson, 2004). Another disadvantage of the heroic model is that the leadership of others is hidden and may be discouraged. More recent literature and thinking has moved "'beyond' transformational leadership" (Day, 2003, p. 188). This involves a shift from a concept of leadership as something carried out by an individual to more collective concepts such as shared or distributed leadership.

Distributed Leadership

The notion of distributed leadership was first used in the field of social psychology in the early 1950s and reemerged in the early 1990s in organisation theory and then education (Gronn, 2002). A definition of distributed leadership, developed in the context of self-managing teams, refers to multiple leaders seeking and taking responsibility for different leadership functions and assuming complementary roles (Barry, 1991). This view is premised on the notion that "leadership is a collection of roles and behaviours that can be split apart, shared, rotated, and used sequentially or concomitantly" (Barry, 1991, p. 34). According to Gronn (2002), the term distributed leadership has two broad meanings. The first meaning refers to leadership being shared or dispersed across multiple leaders with no particular individuals providing more leadership than others. Gronn describes this view of distributed leadership as minimalist, as it does not involve an increase in leadership potential. The second meaning offers a more holistic perspective and suggests that distributed leadership involves interdependence and coordination. The interdependence aspect of distributed leadership is also emphasised in a case study of the development of a knowledge sharing system (Zhang & Faerman, 2007). These authors found that distributed leadership was characterised by two factors: interdependence, in that multiple leaders relied on each other; and the emergence and negotiation of leadership roles throughout the course of the project.

Spillane (2006) agrees with the idea that distributed leadership means more than shared leadership and states that it is the "collective *interactions* among leaders, followers, and their situation that are paramount" (p. 4). The interactive nature of distributed leadership is also discussed by Timperley (2005), who notes that "distributed leadership is not the same as dividing tasks and responsibilities among individuals who perform defined and separate organisational roles, but rather it comprises dynamic interactions between multiple leaders and followers" (p. 396). These comments reflect the notion of distributed leadership as a conjoint activity that produces an additional dynamic. In this second view of the concept, the whole is greater than the sum of its parts. A model of distributed leadership developed by Ancona, Malone, Orlikowski and Senge (2007) suggests that leadership should be viewed as a set of four interdependent capabilities: relating (building trusting relationships); sense-making (understanding contextual factors); visioning (developing an image of future possibilities); and inventing (moving from the vision to reality). They believe that the idea of a complete leader is a myth and that leaders need to be cultivating and coordinating the action of others in their organisations in order that everyone's leadership can be drawn upon.

Although there may be slightly differing understandings of the concept of distributed leadership; according to a literature review carried out in 2003, distributed leadership is distinguished by three key elements:

- Leadership is an emergent property of a group of individuals who interact rather than an individual phenomenon;
- The boundaries of leadership are open and fluid; and
- Different types of expertise are distributed across many rather than a few (Bennett, Wise, Woods & Harvey).

These authors believe that it is the first distinction that of distributed leadership being a product of collective group activity that is critical to its understanding. For the purposes of this chapter, distributed leadership will be defined as leadership that is distributed across group members and that is characterised by interdependence and cooperation.

Leaders and Followers in Models of Distributed Leadership

Distributed leadership blurs the distinctions between leaders and followers and opens up the possibility of all members of an organisation exerting influence and demonstrating leadership behaviour at various times (Harris, 2003). Although some writers such as Spillane (2006) still refer to both leaders and followers when discussing distributed leadership, others such as Gronn (2002) do not make this distinction. According to Harris, "the categorisation of leaders and followers becomes redundant as leadership is distributed throughout the organisation" (p. 76).

Distributed models of leadership do not mean that there is no place for formal or positional leadership roles. A study of twelve high impact nonprofit organisations found that a key to distributed leadership was the positional leaders who operated at the hub of a network rather than from a hierarchical position (Grant & Crutchfield, 2008). The positional leaders in this study developed leadership in others by sharing information, ideas and resources. Other roles of formal leaders that will empower others in the organisation to become involved in leadership activities are role modelling, facilitating and coaching. It has been suggested that the person in a formal leadership position has a major role in managing the organisational dynamics and provides the 'psychological glue' for the organisation (James, Mann & Creasy, 2007). According to Harris (2004, p. 14), "the job of those in formal leadership positions is primarily to hold the pieces of the organisation together in a productive relationship" and to ensure the maximization of organisation's human capacity. This coordination role is sometimes compared to that of an orchestra conductor whose job it is to ensure that the orchestra members' actions are synchronised and that skills of the musicians are heard to their best advantage.

Advantages and Disadvantages of Distributed Leadership

Distributed leadership has a number of advantages over traditional models of leadership. This include that a leadership vacuum is not created when positional leaders leave an organisation and that all members of a group have to the opportunity to contribute their strengths and skills. As Harris has suggested, distributed leadership "concentrates on engaging expertise wherever it exists in the organisation rather than seeking this only through formal position or role" (2004, p. 13). This has the effect of maximizing the capacity of people within organisations. According to Hargreaves and Fink (2003), collective intelligence is preferable to individual intelligence:

In highly complex, knowledge-based organisations, everyone's intelligence is needed to help the organisation to flex, respond, regroup and retool in the face of unpredictable and sometimes overwhelming demands. Locking intelligence up in the individual leader creates inflexibility and increases the likelihood of mistakes and errors. (p. 443)

Distributed leadership does have its disadvantages however. Timperley cautions against distributing leadership in all situations, intimating that, in some cases, the result may be "a greater distribution of incompetence" (2004, p. 417). In Barry's (1991) study of self-managing teams, distributed leadership worked only in teams where members realised the potential for different kinds of leadership to coexist. Harris (2004) suggests that traditional hierarchical structures can be a barrier to the adoption of distributed leadership as those in formal positions can resist involving and sharing information with others. There is also the challenge of deciding how to distribute leadership and who makes the decision about the distribution. Other obstacles to the adoption of models of distributed leadership include the belief that one person holds the key to the success of the organisation, and the tendency to equate leadership with position rather than function (Southworth, 2005).

This discussion has established the benefits that distributed leadership has for organisations and groups. Although there is a growing body of literature on distributed leadership, particularly in the education sector, there is little written material about how leadership can be distributed in online environments despite the trend towards their increased use in a variety of organisations. Information and communication technologies facilitate the access to and sharing of information between people working and learning in online environments and hence create an environment ideally suited to supporting distributed leadership. There appears to be considerable potential for the development of distributed leadership models in online environments despite the lack of literature and the following section of the chapter will explore how this can be fostered.

DISTRIBUTED LEADERSHIP IN ONLINE ENVIRONMENTS

Many groups that traditionally met face-to-face are now relying fully or partially on ICT to communicate and interact. Examples of these online environments include: communities of practice; virtual teams; and online action learning groups. These three groups all have different functions and ways of operating, though there are similarities between the ways in which people interact and the technologies used in these environments. Although some of these groups traditionally have formal leaders or facilitators, online interactions and technologies have the potential to encourage leadership in all group members. For this distribution of leadership to occur, participants in these groups must be empowered and encouraged to contribute to the leadership of the group. This section of the chapter will briefly introduce each of these online environments before considering how distributed leadership is enacted and encouraged in each. The formation, composition, leadership roles and technologies used by these groups will then be compared and contrasted.

Communities of Practice

Although traditionally communities of practice meet face-to-face, many are increasingly relying on ICT to enable members to communicate and share their practice. Some communities have no face-to-face contact and are known as virtual communities, whereas others rely on a combination of face-to-face meetings and online technologies and are known as blended communities of practice. "one of the keys to a successful virtual COP (community of practice) is an occasional, non-virtual, face-to-face meeting" (p. 2993). According to Cordoba and Robson (2006, p. 562) "technology mediated interaction does not substitute for physical interaction, and efforts should be made to develop continuous and regular encounters". These authors suggest that ICT should be blended with face-to-face encounters to provide a balance that fits with how the community functions.

Not all the literature considers trust building in virtual communities of practice to be problematic. Raja et al. (2006) suggest that trust can be built and maintained in both virtual and co-located environments if the members are willing to work together and there is good communication and strong leadership. Some aspects of o

A variety of technologies are used to support online communities of practice including email, telephone, asynchronous discussion forums, synchronous web-based chat forums, and audio and video-conferencing. Several writers have emphasised the importance of technology supporting rather than leading the development of communities of practice (Chua, 2006; Coakes & Clarke, 2006).

Although facilitators provide leadership through their coordinating role, leadership should be distributed throughout the community of practice with all members taking on different leadership roles at various times. Different forms of leadership distributed across communities of practice can include: boundary leadership shown by those who link the community to other communities; interpersonal leadership shown by those who nurture relationships; day-to-day leadership shown by people who organise activities; inspirational leadership provided by recognised experts; and cutting edge leadership shown by those who think outside the square (Wenger, 1998). This sharing of leadership roles can be seen as a form of distributed leadership and has the advantage of ensuring the expertise and skills of all community members is used.

Virtual Teams

A virtual team has been defined as "a collection of individuals who are geographically and/or organizationally or otherwise dispersed and who collaborate via communication and information technologies in order to accomplish a specific goal" (Zigurs, 2003, p. 340). Some virtual teams interact on an ongoing basis and others may be assembled on a short-term basis to complete particular tasks. Virtual teams can be dispersed across distance, organisations, culture and/or time. The more dimensions the team is distributed across, the more virtual it is seen to be (Zigurs). A number of advantages of virtual teams have been identified including the ability to access highly skilled individuals regardless of location, and a greater flexibility and responsiveness as team members do not have to gather in the same location and can respond at differing times (Bell & Kozlowski, 2002; Powell, Piccolo & Ives, 2004).

Technologies used in virtual teams are similar to those used in communities of practice and action learning groups and include email, videoconferencing and various other technologies such as wikis, chat and online forums. It has been suggested that the most suitable technologies depend on the complexity of the team task (Bell & Kozlowski, 2002). Less complex tasks require less collaboration and communication between team members so more basic technologies such as email will suffice. More complex tasks require greater interdependence and therefore synchronous technologies such as video conferencing and groupware allow for more in depth communication. Zigurs (2003) distinguishes between three types of tools for supporting virtual teams: communication support; information processing and process structuring. She describes communication support tools, examples of which are email, discussion boards and chats, as those which facilitate the exchange of ideas and information. The purpose of information processing tools is to evaluate information and model specific problems and process structuring tools are those that "define and/or enforce the process by which teams interact" (p. 345). Of these three types of tools, Zigurs sees process structuring as the most essential to virtual team success as they contribute most to group process.

Although virtual teams most often operate without any face-to-face contact, it has been suggested that some physical meetings are advantageous to the development of trust and the building of relationships (Powell et al., 2004; Zigurs, 2003). Such face-to-face meetings have also been found to make subsequent electronic meetings more effective. If this is not possible then strategies need to be employed that mirror some of the face-to-face interactions that exist in co-located teams or that convey social presence. Leaders who introduced web collaboration tools such virtual chat and a team web page were more highly rated by team members who used only email for team communication in a small scale study of leadership in virtual teams (Kayworth & Leidner, 2002). The building of relationships is not solely the function of positional leaders. A study of emergent leadership in virtual teams (Yoo & Alavi, 2004) found that all group members contributed to providing socio-emotional support for the team.

Leadership in Virtual Teams

Although a number of authors have written on the subject of leadership and virtual teams, most have focused solely on the role of the formal leader. Factors contributing to effective leadership in virtual teams have been identified as the capability to clarify roles, to mentor, to communicate effectively and to show support, concern and harmony (Kayworth & Leidner, 2002). These authors suggest that communications processing and social facilitation roles are more crucial in virtual than in traditional teams. The importance of building relationships is also supported by Avolio and Kahai (2003) who also suggest that leaders of virtual teams must communicate their intent clearly and use technology to reach out to team members. The need for leaders of virtual teams to employ different strategies from those used with traditional teams has been emphasised (Powell et al., 2004). One of the leadership strategies these authors suggest is becoming more flexible and being willing to share leadership with others at times. The importance of leaders of virtual teams learning how to use media to positively influence the team culture and move the team forward has also been emphasised (Zigurs, 2003).

This focus on positional leadership exists despite the acknowledgement that rapid advances in ICT mean that both leaders and followers are likely to have similar access to information (Avolio & Kahai, 2003). These authors do concede that this greater access to information means that leadership may have to move to "lower levels in organizations" (p. 328) and that "team members of a virtual team may move between being a leader and a follower" (p. 329). Another reason for a more flattened hierarchy in a virtual team is that a team member's level of expertise or status or may be hidden in a virtual team environment (Kayworth & Leidner, 2002). One writer who does conceive of leadership in virtual teams in a more collective way is Zigurs (2003) who believes that technology can encourage equal participation from all team members. She also supports the idea of distributed leadership suggesting that "individuals can share and rotate leadership roles" and that leadership can become "a collective effort distributed within the team" (p. 342). Distributed leadership in virtual teams means that different team members will take on different roles at different stages in the life of the team. These leadership roles may include task roles such as ideas generator and evaluator and team building roles such as motivator and mediator (Zigurs).

Action Learning

Action learning is a process involving people working in small groups, usually of six to eight members, to solve real problems using a questioning and reflective learning process (Marquardt, 2004). Group members may be working on a collective problem or may bring their individual issues to the group. Characteristics of action learning groups include that all members have the capacity to take action on the issue they are dealing with

and that all are committed to their own learning and that of other group members. Action learning groups met regularly, usually face-to-face, but in some cases online to share what they are working on and to question each other with the aim of identifying future actions.

Online action learning is a relatively new approach about which there is little published research. Most authors advocate for blended approaches to action learning, similar to blended communities of practice discussed above, where group members meet face-to-face as well as interacting online. The technologies used in online action learning are similar to those used in online communities of practice. A number of authors (Burns, 2001; Gray, 1999; Powell, 2001; Roche & Vernon, 2003) have described the use of various technologies to support or in some cases replace traditional face-to-face action learning set meetings. These ICTs include videoconferencing, audioconferencing, email, and online forums or bulletin boards. The majority of the action learning programmes appear to combine face-to-face meetings and online communications (Gray, 1999; Powell, 2001; Roche & Vernon, 2003). Burns (2001), who had previously been involved in face-to-face action learning, reports on a virtual action learning (VAL) set, run for British Telecom staff that used audio-conferencing. Although the set members who were based in different part of the country did not meet face-to-face during this programme, all knew each other already. Burns concluded that VAL is not as successful as face-to-face set meetings. He believes more rather than less interpersonal skills, particularly listening skills, are needed in audio-conferencing than in face-to-face meetings.

The importance of face-to-face contact between set members particularly at the beginning stages of an action learning process is acknowledged by Powell (2001) and Roche and Vernon (2003). Powell describes a study involving the use of videoconferencing to remotely support a number of existing action learning sets. He suggests that the startup stage of a set, which he describes as a nurturing process, is not conducive to remote meetings. Roche and Vernon describe an action learning project, supported by electronic technology including videoconferencing, conference calls, email networks, and bulletin boards, used to develop a virtual learning community of Australian rural and remote health services managers. The conclusions from this study are that although the online technologies were useful in reducing isolation, face-to-face interaction was also important to develop a sense of community.

Bird (2006) has explored the use of asynchronous online computer mediated conferencing (CMC) to facilitate action learning. His literature review examines the nature of action learning and how it fits within a social constructivist paradigm. He emphasises the importance of social interaction within learning communities and suggests that:

For an action learning set to function online a situation needs to be created in which facilitated, shared reflection and the social construction of knowledge can proceed in a text format. The virtual medium must allow the opposite questioning, discussion, and emotional support that leads to new thoughts, ideas and wider perspectives being shared by the set in a communal way. In short, a socially constructed knowledge must be created through the key ingredient of language (p. 4).

Online action learning sets operate differently from other online groups such as online communities of practice because of their smaller group size and more formal nature. For this reason, it is important that the virtual medium used in online action learning allows for the discussion, questioning and shared support that occurs in face-to-face action learning sets (Bird 2006).

Leadership in Action Learning Groups

Action learning is an empowering process as it encourages group members to reflect on their practice, a necessary prerequisite for identifying meaningful change. Marquardt (2004) suggests that action learning is particularly effective in developing leadership as it encourages the development of a number of important leadership competencies such as emotional intelligence and the ability to reflect, question and problem solve. He believes action learning differs from other leadership training in that the leaders are learning in context and solving real problems and that leaders (participants) rather than teachers (facilitators) are seen as the source of knowledge. Morris (1997) believes that action learning meets the requirements for effective leadership development through the support and challenge provided in action learning sets. He sees action learning encouraging the development of leaders who are questioning of their practices and who are encouraging of leadership in others. Conger and Toegel (2003), discussing the value of action learning in leadership development, suggest that learning is more useful because the learning experience is more grounded in specific and relevant issues.

Heron's work on modes of facilitation is useful in reflecting on how online action learning groups can move from more hierarchical leadership structures to distributed leadership. Heron (1999) describes three modes of facilitation: the hierarchical mode; the cooperative mode; and the autonomous mode. In the hierarchical mode, the learning process is directed by the facilitator, in the cooperative mode it is shared between the facilitator and participants, and in the autonomous mode, the participants take control of the learning process. According to McGill and Brockbank (2004) it is appropriate for the facilitator to adopt the hierarchical mode in the early stages of an

Table 1. Comparing different online environments

	Online Communities of Practice	**Virtual Teams**	**Online Action Learning Groups**
Purpose	To interact and exchange knowledge about practice within a shared domain of interest.	To work remotely towards meeting team goals and completing work tasks.	To learn through a process of sharing problems, reflecting and being questioned in order to identify future actions.
Formation	Often arise spontaneously though may be formally established.	Are established in work places.	Established in work places or as part of professional learning opportunities.
Composition	Size, structure and composition vary considerably.	Size varies but generally not larger than 15 members.	Groups are comprised of between 6 and 8 members.
Leadership roles	A variety of leadership roles identified including interpersonal and inspirational.	May have a formal leader or may be self-managing.	The facilitator usually takes a leadership role though the process encourages leadership development.
Technologies used	Email, discussion forums, chat, audio and videoconferencing, blogs, wikis.	Email, discussion forums, chat, audio and videoconferencing, blogs, wikis, electronic meeting technologies.	Email, discussion forums, chat, audio and videoconferencing.

action learning group when the participants are learning about the action learning process. In a study of online action learning (Thornton & Yoong, 2008), the facilitator moved between the hierarchical and cooperative modes. The design of the website and the facilitation of the face-to-face action learning group meetings were examples of the facilitator acting in the hierarchical mode, however, over time there was movement towards the cooperative mode with participants recognising the shift in leadership practice towards more distributed leadership over time. Examples of the facilitator sharing leadership with group members in this study include their instigation of a range of forum discussions and their questioning role in the online action learning forums.

DEVELOPING DISTRIBUTED LEADERSHIP IN ONLINE COMMUNITIES

Distributed leadership has the advantage over traditional models of leadership in that the capacity of all group members is maximised and their expertise engaged. Advances in ICT have meant that members of online communities such as communities of practice, online action learning

groups and virtual teams all have similar access to information and all have the potential to contribute to the leadership of their communities. As Zigurs (2003) has suggested, "communication technology can be an equalizer and provide the opportunity for participation of every member of the team" (p. 339). Two factors appear to be crucial to the development of distributed leadership in these online environments: leadership actions in the early stages of the community, group or team; and the use of technologies appropriate to the community, group or team (cf. Table 1).

Leadership is needed in the initial stages of a community, group or team in order to move the group forward and allow distributed leadership to emerge. Avolio and Kahai (2003) have suggested that the early stages of leadership will predict later trust, performance and satisfaction levels. This leadership may come from a positional leader or may emerge from out of the group if there is no positional leader. A number of differing leadership roles has been recognised. Barry (1991) in his study of distributed leadership in self-managing teams identified four complementary groups of leadership roles and behaviours: envisioning; organising; spanning and social. Envisioning leadership involves strategic thinking and the generation of ideas; organising leadership has a focus on structure, details, and deadlines; spanning leadership roles include networking and accessing resources; and social leadership involves paying attention to the personal dynamics of the team. In Barry's study, teams with members who collectively took on these roles were more successful than teams in which one or more of the four types were missing. Although these roles were identified in face-to-face teams, they appear applicable to online environments.

In some groups, it is the formal leader who initially takes on some or all of the roles identified by Barry (1991) and then stands back as distributed leadership emerges. In other groups, these responsibilities may be shared by group members from the outset. Positional leadership roles are not always acknowledged by virtual team members. A study of emergent and assigned leaders in virtual groups found that other group members did not necessarily recognise the leadership role of the assigned leader (Wickham & Walther, 2007). In this research, group members were perceived as showing leadership if they communicated frequently and encouraged others. Encouraging emergent leadership in others has been recognised as one of the key challenges of leaders of electronic teams (Cascio & Shurygailo, 2002). It may be that the leadership actions that encourage others to become involved in leadership may be more appropriately termed facilitating or coaching. Heron's (1999) model of facilitation referred to earlier is useful way of looking at how the formal leader or facilitator may move over time from the hierarchical mode of more directive leadership to more cooperative or autonomous model of distributed leadership.

Although both task roles such as envisioning and organising; and team building roles such as spanning and social are both essential to the effective functioning of teams, it is the team building roles that are particularly important in encouraging distributed leadership. Paying attention to social

aspects of the group's functioning and building trust is seen to be vital in the initial stages of an online group. The most effective leaders in Kayworth and Leidner's study into effective virtual team leadership were those that mentored team members and also built "healthy social climates for team members to interact with one another" (2002, p. 27). According to Avolio and Kahai (2003) successful leaders in electronic environments should focus on building relationships and trust. Frequent communication is seen to be more important in online as compared to face-to-face environments and according to Zigurs, "virtual teams need to spend more time on relational development than traditional teams do" (2003, p. 347).

Some technologies are more conducive to encouraging distributed leadership than others. Technologies that allow visual cues and more accurately mirror face-to-face interactions are more likely to increase the level of trust within the group and encourage participants to become involved in leadership activities. The use of specific tools in particular situations is recommended by Hambley, O'Neill and Kline (2007), who suggest text-based media aren't appropriate for managing conflict situations. There is a danger however of attempting to replicate face-to-face situations in online environments, as Zigurs (2003) warns, "seeking to duplicate the physical world leaves out a whole range of entirely new forms and structure of virtual interaction" (p. 344-5). The technology used in an online environment needs to be matched with the function and size of the community, group or team. Collaborative technologies that work with small groups or teams such as chats or Skype are less appropriate for use with larger teams or online communities of practice. These groups are likely to function more effectively with tools such as online whiteboards and wikis which allow for input from a greater number of people.

EMERGING ISSUES AND FUTURE TRENDS

This review of the nature of distributed leadership and its applicability to online environments has highlighted the desirability of involving all group members in leadership activities. Those in formal leadership positions in online environments may wish to consider how they can encourage their colleagues to become involved in leadership activities and hence engage their expertise and maximise their capacity. Leadership in a virtual environment requires different approaches from leadership in co-located groups and although the importance of preparing positional leaders and group members for these different environments has been emphasised (Cascio & Shurygailo, 2003; Hambley, O'Neill & Kline, 2007; Zigurs, 2003), there needs to be further research on how leadership contributions from all can be maximised.

An emerging trend that can be identified with respect to the development of distributed leadership in online environments relates to the development and use of new technologies and the preparation for leadership roles. The development and increased availability of technologies such as video walls, integrated handheld devices and various software innovations will change the way communication happens in online communities, groups and teams. More vivid and interactive technologies have the potential to enrich the activity of such groups. It has also been predicted that some technologies have the potential for taking over some of the leadership functions in virtual teams (Zigurs, 2003), hence changing the way leadership is enacted in online environments.

CONCLUSION

The availability of information and the equality of access make online environments ideally suited to the distribution of leadership. These conditions alone will not result in distributed leadership, as there are a number of contributing factors including the leadership behaviours of group members and the use of appropriate technologies. Formal leaders have an important role in developing trust and encouraging all group members to become involved in leadership. Where there are no formal leaders, others with the group must take on these roles which include facilitating social interactions and clarifying roles and purpose. Appropriate technologies that match the purpose, structure and size of the community, team or group must also be used. Technologies that encourage group members to get to know each other, to communicate effectively and to contribute their strengths and skills will encourage distributed leadership.

REFERENCES

Ancona, D., Malone, T., Orlikowski, W., & Senge, P. (2007). In praise of the incomplete leader. *Harvard Business Review*, *2007*(February), 92–100.

Avolio, B., & Kahai, S. (2003). Adding the "e" to e-leadership: How it may impact your leadership. *Organizational Dynamics*, *31*(4), 325–338. doi:10.1016/S0090-2616(02)00133-X

Barry, D. (1991). Managing the bossless team: Lessons in distributed leadership. *Organizational Dynamics*, *20*, 31–47. doi:10.1016/0090-2616(91)90081-J

Bell, B., & Kozlowski, S. (2002). A typology of virtual teams: Implications for effective leadership. *Group & Organization Management*, *27*(1), 14–49. doi:10.1177/1059601102027001003

Bennett, N., Wise, C., Woods, P., & Harvey, J. (2003). *Distributed Leadership*. Nottingham, UK: National College for School Leadership.

Bird, L. (2006). *Action learning sets: The case for running them online*. Retrieved May 5, 2006, from http://www.coventry.ac.uk/iped/papers/downloads/workbasedlearningwksp4jan2006/LenBirdActionLearningSetsOnline.doc

Bradshaw, P., Powell, S., & Terrell, I. (2004). Building a community of practice: Technological and social implications for a distributed team. In P. Hildreth & C. Kimble (Eds.), *Knowledge networks: Innovation through communities of practice* (pp. 184-201). Hershey, PA: Idea Group Publishing.

Burns, P. (2001). Report on a virtual action learning set. *Action Learning News, 20*(2), 2–7.

Cascio, W., & Shurygailo, S. (2003). E-leadership and virtual teams. *Organizational Dynamics, 31*(4), 362–376. doi:10.1016/S0090-2616(02)00130-4

Chua, A. (2006). The role of technology in supporting communities of practice. In E. Coakes (Ed.), *Encyclopedia of communities of practice in information and knowledge management* (pp. 447-452). Hershey, PA: Idea Group Reference.

Coakes, E., & Clarke, S. (2006). The concept of communities of practice. In E. Coakes (Ed.), *Encyclopedia of communities of practice in information and knowledge management* (pp. 92-96). Hershey, PA: Idea Group Reference.

Conger, J., & Toegel, G. (2003). Action learning and multirater feedback: Pathways to leadership development. In S. Murphy & R. Riggio (Eds.), *The future of leadership development* (pp. 133-151). Mahwah, NJ: Lawrence Erlbaum Associates.

Cordoba, J., & Robson, W. (2006). Understanding communities of practice to support collaborative research. In E. Coakes (Ed.), *Encyclopedia of communities of practice in information and knowledge management* (pp. 558-564). Hershey, PA: Idea Group Reference.

Day, C. (2003). What successful leadership in schools looks like: Implications for policy and practice. In B. Davies & J. West-Burnham (Eds.), *Handbook of educational leadership* (pp. 87-204). London: Pearson Education.

Day, C., & Harris, A. (2002). Teacher leadership, reflective practice, and school improvement. In K. Leithwood & P. Hallinger (Eds.), *Second international handbook of educational leadership and administration* (pp. 957-978). Dordrecht, The Netherlands: Kluwer Academic Publishers.

Fink, D. (2005). Developing leaders for their future not our past. In M. Coles & G. Southworth (Eds.), *Developing leadership: Creating the schools of tomorrow* (pp. 1-20). Maidenhead, UK: Open University Press.

Friesen, S., & Clifford, P. (2003). *Working across different spaces to create communities of practice in teacher professional development.* Paper presented at the mICTE 2003 Multimedia, Information and Communication Technologies Conference, Badajoz, Spain.

Grant, H., & Crutchfield, L. (2008). The hub of leadership: Lessons from the social sector. *Leader to Leader, 48*, 45–52. doi:10.1002/ltl.280

Gray, D. (1999). *Work-based learning, action learning and the virtual paradigm.* Retrieved May 5, 2006, from http://www.leeds.ac.uk/educol/documents/00001260.htm

Gronn, P. (2002). Distributed leadership. In K. Leithwood & P. Hallinger (Eds.), *Second international handbook of educational leadership and administration* (pp. 653-696). Dordrecht, The Netherlands: Kluwer Academic Publishers.

Hambley, L., O'Neill, T., & Kline, T. (2007). Virtual team leadership: Perspectives from the field. *International Journal of e-Collaboration, 3*(1), 40–64.

Hargreaves, A., & Fink, D. (2003). Sustaining leadership. In B. Davies & J. West-Burnham (Eds.), *Handbook of educational leadership and management* (pp. 435-450). London: Pearson Education.

Harris, A. (2003). Teacher leadership: A new orthodoxy. In B. Davies & J. West-Burnham (Eds.), *Handbook of educational leadership and management,* (pp. 44-50). London: Pearson Longman.

Harris, A. (2004). Distributed leadership and school improvement. *Educational Management Administration & Leadership, 32*(1), 11–24. doi:10.1177/1741143204039297

Heron, J. (1999). *The complete facilitator's handbook.* London: Kogan Page.

James, K., Mann, J., & Creasy, J. (2007). Leaders as lead learners. *Management Learning, 38*(1), 79–94. doi:10.1177/1350507607073026

Johnson, C. (2001). A survey of current research on online communities of practice. *The Internet and Higher Education, 4,* 45–60. doi:10.1016/S1096-7516(01)00047-1

Kayworth, T., & Leidner, D. (2002). Leadership effectiveness in global virtual teams. *Journal of Management Information Systems, 18*(3), 7–40.

Kimble, C., & Hildreth, P. (2005). Virtual communities of practice. In M. Khosrow-Pour (Ed.), *Encyclopedia of information science and technology* (pp. 2991-2995). Hershey, PA: Idea Group Reference.

Kling, R., & Courtright, C. (2003). Group behavior and learning in electronic forums: A sociotechnical approach. *The Information Society, 19,* 221–235. doi:10.1080/01972240309465

Lambert, L. (2003). Shifting conceptions of leadership: Towards a redefinition of leadership for the 21st century. In B. Davies & J. West-Burnham (Eds.), *Handbook of educational leadership and management.* London: Pearson Longman.

Marquardt, M. (2004). *Optimizing the power of action learning.* Mountain View, CA: Davies-Black.

McGill, I., & Brockbank, A. (2004). *The action learning handbook.* London: RoutledgeFalmer.

Morris, J. (1997). Minding our ps and qs. In M. Pedler (Ed.), *Action learning in practice* (3rd ed., pp. 49-59). Aldershot, UK: Gower.

Powell, A., Piccolo, G., & Ives, B. (2004). Virtual teams: A review of current literature and directions for future research. *The Data Base for Advances in Information Systems, 35*(1), 6–36.

Powell, J. (2001). *Using learning styles and action learning, over the Internet, to drive learning for innovation in small and medium enterprises - a case study from construction* [Electronic Version]. Retrieved May 15, 2006, from http://www.portlandpress.com/pp/books/online/vu/pdf/vu_ch8.pdf

Proctor-Thomson, S., & Parry, K. (2001). What the best leaders look like. In K. Parry (Ed.), *Leadership in the antipodes: Findings, implication and a leadership profile* (pp. 166-191). Wellington, New Zealand: Institute of Policy Studies and the Centre for the Study of Leadership, Victoria University of Wellington.

Raja, J., Huq, A., & Rosenberg, D. (2006). The role of trust in virtual and co-located communities of practice. In E. Coakes (Ed.), *Encyclopedia of communities of practice in information and knowledge management* (pp. 453-458). Hershey, PA: Idea Group Reference.

Robinson, V. (2004). New understandings of educational leadership. *set 2004, 3,* 39-43.

Roche, V., & Vernon, M. (2003). *Developing a virtual learning community of managers in rural and remote health services.* Retrieved May 5, 2006, from http://www.abc.net.au/rural/ruralhealth2003/stories/s799695.htm

Sainte-Onge, H., & Wallace, D. (2003). *Leveraging communities of practice for strategic advantage.* Boston: Heineman-Butterworth.

Schlager, M., & Fusco, J. (2003). Teacher professional development, technology and communities of practice: Are we putting the cart before the horse? *The Information Society, 19*, 203–220. doi:10.1080/01972240309464

Sharratt, M., & Usoro, A. (2003). Understanding knowledge-sharing in online communities of practice [Electronic Version] [from http://www.ejkm.com]. *Electronic Journal of Knowledge Management, 1*, 187–196. Retrieved June 16, 2006.

Southworth, G. (2005). Overview and conclusions. In M. Coles & G. Southworth (Eds.), *Developing leadership: Creating the schools of tomorrow* (pp. 158-173). Maidenhead, UK: Open University Press.

Spillane, J. (2006). *Distributed leadership.* San Francisco: Jossey-Bass.

Tarmazi, H., de Vreede, G., & Zigurs, I. (2007). Leadership challenges in communities of practice: Supporting facilitators via design and technology. *International Journal of e-Collaboration, 3*(1), 18–39.

Thornton, K., & Yoong, P. (2008). *The application of online action learning to leadership development: A case study.* Paper presented at 9th European Conference on Knowledge Management, Southampton, Great Britain.

Timperley, H. (2005). Distributed leadership: Developing theory from practice. *Journal of Curriculum Studies, 37*(4), 395–420. doi:10.1080/00220270500038545

Wagner, C., & Bolloju, N. (2005). Supporting knowledge management in organizations with conversational technologies: Discussion forums, Weblogs and Wikis. *Journal of Database Management, 16*(2), 1–8.

Wenger, E. (1998). *Communities of practice: Learning, meaning and identity.* Cambridge, UK: Cambridge University Press.

Wenger, E. (2006). *Communities of practice: A brief introduction.* Retrieved August 30, 2006, from http://www.ewenger.com/theory/index.htm

Wenger, E., McDermott, R., & Snyder, W. (2002). *Cultivating communities of practice.* Boston: Harvard Business School Press.

Wickham, K., & Walther, J. (2007). Perceived behaviour of emergent and assigned leaders in virtual groups. *International Journal of e-Collaboration, 3*(1), 1–17.

Yoo, Y., & Alavi, M. (2004). Emergent leadership in virtual teams: What do emergent leaders do? *Information and Organization, 14*(1), 27–58. doi:10.1016/j.infoandorg.2003.11.001

Zhang, J., & Faerman, S. (2007). Distributed leadership in the development of a knowledge sharing system. *European Journal of Information Systems, 16*, 479–493. doi:10.1057/palgrave.ejis.3000694

Zigurs, I. (2003). Leadership in virtual teams: Oxymoron or opportunity? *Organizational Dynamics, 31*(4), 339–351. doi:10.1016/S0090-2616(02)00132-8

Chapter 2
Shared Leadership Meets Virtual Teams
A Match Made in Cyberspace

Christina Wassenaar
Peter F. Drucker and Masatoshi Ito Graduate School of Management, USA

Craig L. Pearce
Peter F. Drucker and Masatoshi Ito Graduate School of Management, USA

Julia E. Hoch
University of Technology, Germany

Jürgen Wegge
Ludwig-Maximilians-Universität München (LMU), Germany

ABSTRACT

Virtual teams are generally widely dispersed by geography, and also often by culture, language and time. They are usually comprised of highly skilled professionals and are brought together in order to achieve strategic organizational goals or to work on complex projects. They do not normally meet face-to-face but, rather, build and maintain relationships using various types of communication and information sharing technologies. With the continued increase in virtual teams a new leadership model becomes critical since traditional hierarchical models might not be able to facilitate the results that the organization needs to compete in a globalized economy. The authors suggest that shared leadership (e.g., Pearce & Conger, 2003), the dynamic allocation of leadership responsibility based on the expertise of the team member and the needs of the team or project, might be the solution to more effectively creating productive, balanced teams in a virtual workplace. This chapter is a brief exploration of the shared leadership literature as it pertains to organizing, leading and participating on a virtual team.

INTRODUCTION

Drucker (1993) predicted that advances in information systems would allow information to flow more freely between more people. He believed that these changes would alter the way that managers and subordinates relate to each other in organizations. Senge (2000) observed that both the dynamic and

DOI: 10.4018/978-1-60566-958-8.ch002

inter-reliant nature of the economy would ensure the impossibility of top management being able to figure out everything on their own. Rather he stated that organizations must now seek out solutions that incorporate thinking and problem-solving at all organizational levels.

Building on these earlier ideas, is the dawn of the age of the digital enterprise. Many leading authorities believe that organizations will be increasingly rely on virtual teams to tackle their most pressing business issues (Rosen, Furst & Blackburn, 2007; Gibson & Cohen, 2003; Zacarro & Bader, 2003). Virtual teams are located over wide geographic areas, who trade or share information using technology to create new knowledge. How are these teams led? According to Pearce and colleagues (e.g., Pearce, 2008; Pearce & Conger, 2003; Pearce, Manz & Sims, in press) the most successful teams are lead via shared leadership processes, which entail the dynamic exchange of leadership roles, as the needs of the organization dictate. In a society in which knowledge work is more and more the currency of competition, allowing those who have the requisite knowledge, and the skill to share that knowledge, to lead is an increasingly important organizational imperative (Pearce, 2008).

When thinking about teams in a global economy it is ever more important to develop a shared vision yet it might even be more challenging to do so in the face of economic or environmental uncertainty— particularly since the world-wide financial meltdown of 2008. Constraints due to cultural boundaries or customs, national interests, political or resource based conflict, social norms or even technological changes or pressures also pose considerable challenges (Davis & Bryant, 2003; Saunders, Van Slyke & Vogel, 2004). In an increasingly complex business environment the importance of shared leadership as a means to aid knowledge creation will become progressively more important (Nonaka & Takeuchi, 1995; Nonaka et al., 2001).

THE EVOLUTION OF VIRTUAL TEAMS

What is a virtual team? Virtual teams are often organized as project or development teams. Lipnack and Stamps (1997) describe a virtual teams are guided by a common purpose or vision and that the members have interdependent tasks, just as face-to-face teams. They involve a group of individuals, often from multiple functions who come together temporarily for reasons such as assignments, process improvement or product innovation and/or creation.

Virtual teams are comprised of individuals working together while located in multiple, geographically discrete locations (Fulk & De Sanctis, 1995; Maznevski and Chudoba, 2000). They rely on technology to achieve member participation and to coordinate individual effort in productive knowledge work. These teams rarely meet face-to-face; rather, they work together on complicated, extended projects aided by technology-mediated communication (Townsend, De Marie, & Hendrickson, 1998). Often, the team members involved might change or shift as the requirements of the project evolve. While virtual teams generally allow team members to be more nimble and to cooperate with each other, the question of the role of the traditional vertical leader model must still be taken into consideration (Pearce, Yoo & Alavi, 2004; Shin & McClomb, 1998).

It is only in recent years that teams can truly be described as virtual. A virtual team can and will use both traditional communication channels and web-based solutions to exchange information, converse, stay in contact and collaborate with team members who might be many time zones removed. Leading these teams poses a considerable challenge for organizations (Kirkman, Rosen, Gibson, Tesluk & McPherson, 2002); they must manage people who are culturally diverse, from many different functional areas, and who cannot be limited by the traditional boundaries of geography or custom. As Rajiv Dutta, former CEO of Skype and PayPal stated in a recent interview, "The nature of work is changing, and knowledge is the driver. If you want to get the best and the brightest, you have to be open to finding talent everywhere." In this new and still evolving model leaders who are able to clearly define team responsibilities, display empathy and navigate through complex and diverse behaviors are most able to effectively lead a virtual team (Kayworth & Leidner, 2002; Malhotra, Majchrzak & Rosen, 2007).

Why do virtual teams exist? The shift to virtual teams is a result of both external and internal organizational, economic, and globalization pressures and an ever more broad assortment of communication choices that allow for seamless interactions between widely dispersed team members (Malhotra, et al., 2007). The external pressures are an effect of the changing global environment that necessitates reducing cost and developing efficiencies in order to stay competitive. As Rajiv Dutta points out very simply, "Knowledge work is very expensive." In this setting, workforces need to remain flexible, have a wide understanding of both the marketplace and internal structure, and be quick to respond. Each of these requirements can be met, at least in part, by an increased use and understanding of virtual teams.

As organizations and their operations become progressively more global in their scope, it is quickly becoming impossible to imagine a project that occurs in just one location with just one individual working on it. Miles, Snow, Mathews and Miles (1997) believe the organizations of the future will be networked organizations that support multiple teams in an almost web-like structure. For example, the design for a theme park project in Dubai might engage people locally for dealing with governmental issues, as well as senior designers in southern California and a host of engineers in India. The people on the design and build team might meet just once before the actual construction begins but in no way would this team ever think of isolating themselves from each other, or not communicating what each of them is doing, challenges, milestones met or other issues. It simply wouldn't work.

Business operations are dependent on multiple sources of talent, resources and time to achieve complicated outcomes. Teams that are dispersed have slowly been growing in frequency; especially as access to transportation and communication methods have improved. We are now seeing the latest iteration in these teams due to the facility of communication methods and shifts in bases of manufacturing away from primary markets. Having said that, as these teams become almost ubiquitous, the necessity of increasing our understanding of the challenges in creating and maintaining trust in these teams also must evolve (Jarvenpaa, Knoll & Leidner, 1998).

Internal pressures are increasingly caused by the geographic spread of employees, changes in technology, cultural overlaps in single locations, and the evolving needs of employees. Scholars have increasingly noted that people want to find meaning, and not just a paycheck, at work (Lawler & Finegold, 2000; Mohrman, Cohen & Mohrman, 1995; Pfeffer & Veiga, 1999). Rajiv Dutta echoed this point: "employees want to feel that they are not just collecting a paycheck; they need to feel as if they are part of a goal. They are hoping that the work they do and time they spend at work results in something that means more than a wage; they want to feel that they are part of something bigger." The shift into virtual teams and the knowledge work that occurs in the teams is one of the ways that this can be achieved.

What can virtual teams do? Virtual teams can be powerful tools that can leverage the best of what a diverse group of people can offer to solve complex problems. Many of these teams are created to work with a time limit or a project. Because there is an inherent component needing to complete whatever it is that the team has come together to do in the first place it allows a more simple concept of achievement to be established from the onset. Moreover, virtual teams can literally work around the clock, with work shifting times zones to follow the sun. According to Mowshowitz (1997), virtual teams are a key way by which organizations can become and remain more competitive.

LEADING VIRTUAL TEAMS

Mankin, Cohen and Bikson (1996), as well as Cordery, Soo, Kirkman, Rosen and Mathieu (in press), make a case that in virtual teams, the role, quality, and type of leadership can alter significantly: They observe that in teams that are mediated by technology, the role of leader can be shared by multiple team members, based on the needs and expertise that the project or team requires at a particular point in time. O'Hara-Devereaux and Johansen (1994:7) believe that facilitation skills, which they define as "the art of helping people navigate the processes that lead to agreed upon objectives in a way that encourages universal participation and productivity" are critical for successfully leading virtual or dispersed teams. Pauleen and Yoong (2001a, 2001b) stress that the ability to facilitate and lead a virtual team stems from the relationships that form between the team leader and members, as well as the relationships between the members themselves. They believe that these relationships can begin to address both the issues that are seen and those that are more subtle and arise due to differences in culture, interpretation and functions. These last differences might not always be spoken or immediately evident but O'Hara-Devereaux and Johansen (1994) suggest that good leaders need to be able to navigate and preemptively address these types of issues.

Are traditional leadership models still the correct approach for the virtual teams? When moving from a traditional team to a virtual team, which leadership approaches are still valid and which ones should be rethought? For example, the traditional team model has a team leader who guides and directs the majority of activities

of the team members—vertical leadership. In a virtual team it becomes difficult for the vertical leader to influence the team in the same way (Cordery, et. al., in press). In this scenario a new model, shared leadership, provides a way for these far-flung team members to contribute to knowledge creation and the leadership process, thus creating a new structure of influence that is based more on performance and contribution than a traditional team model. Recent studies have found that shared leadership can and does exist in many organizations—organizations like the military services, healthcare, manufacturing and research and development (Pearce & Conger, 2003), as well as in virtual teams (Pearce, Yoo & Alavi, 2004).

Vertical leadership. The role of a vertical leader in a virtual team is that of a facilitator or as one who empowers the team (Manz & Sims, 2001). They operate as the locus of control; the person who is the chief cheerleader for innovation and/or creativity, organizing tasks, and matching up skills and resources to best meet the needs of the project and team (Pearce, 2004). While they are often the center point of authority they must navigate the line between being the ultimate authority and giving away or empowering specific responsibilities to others so that all can achieve their goal.

Empowering leadership by the team leader in virtual teams can be a greater challenge, than in the 'traditional' team that operates in face-to-face settings. Although empowering leadership may be more difficult to engage in virtual teams it is perhaps even more important than in traditional teams (Cordery, et. al., in press; Wegge, Bipp & Kleinbeck, 2007). Since virtual teams often consist of highly skilled members and experts, the leader may sometimes not possess all the necessary skills and competencies (Gibson & Cohen, 2003; Pearce, et. al., 2004). Leadership in virtual teams in general is more difficult to perform, since it needs more time, effort, proactivity and self-initiative. The lack of face-to-face interaction makes it more difficult for the team leader to get information about team processes, manage the team dynamics, ensure communication flow and build cohesion and cooperation between the team members (Pauleen, 2003).

Pearce and Sims (2002), in a study of change management teams, found that teams that had a higher level of shared leadership also were more productive or high performing than those who were more weighted toward vertical leadership. Thus, the team leader must balance their ability to exercise power or control with the opposite extreme of leadership abdication in order to create the most optimal environment for knowledge creation. This requires the leader to cede authority at a level that might initially be uncomfortable but as Yeatts and Hyten (1998) point out, withdrawal of team member engagement, frustration, and renunciation of decision-making responsibility are common results of the team leaders inability to 'let-go'.

It is also important to note the leader's role in skills and resources allocation. The leader is generally the first person to scope the project or process and, at least initially, has the most clear idea of the desired outcome (Cox, Pearce & Perry, 2003). Their responsibility then becomes to match the correct people to the tasks that need to be accomplished, but even prior to that match-making, the leader must form the team carefully and with a specific outcome in mind (Pearce, 2004). There might not be as much initial opportunity for shared leadership with few team members but the decisions made early on will directly impact the possibility of shared leadership as the team grows.

Bosch, a large German conglomerate, purposefully implements virtual teams to tap its geographically dispersed talent pool. Here is how one team member described their leadership and team dynamics:

"In an international distribution team, instead of having team leaders delegating the work to us, we had weekly telephone conferences and biannual

meetings for three days, where we discussed and decided the topics together. The task distribution was done by the employees themselves, so I could do it for my task. Of course task distribution was also influenced by the different sites of the company, which sometimes limited the number of alternatives. In general, we were way more motivated than under the more conservative work forms. However, for this kind work it is necessary to know each other, considering individual strengths and weaknesses. Here, the biannual meetings were very important. Also the new team members could more easily be integrated in the teams in this context."

Of course virtual teams also have some special challenges. For example, one virtual team leader at Bosch explained it this way:

"If I delegate power and decision authority to the team, a power vacuum and disorientation might result. Oftentimes the local team leaders, or line managers, take away the additional "degrees of freedom" and this resource is lost for the virtual team. Therefore when I establish participative and team leadership I have to make sure that the "power" I let go is truly forwarded to the team members and is not taken away by other authorities and by the line managers.

With these comment in mind, we now move our discussion to the concept of shared leadership.

Shared leadership. Shared leadership in teams and organizations entails widely sharing power and influence. In a virtual team, it involves engaging all members of the team in the leadership of their team, where the individual members are empowered to steer and persuade other members in order to get the most out of the team as a whole (Pearce & Conger, 2003, Pearce, 2004). Put another way, shared leadership is a continuous, synchronous process of influence creation that occurs within a team that is demonstrated by both the vertical leader and team members. This also allows the creation of shared goals and deliverables and communication patterns and/or norms that need to be understood by each team member (Hoch, 2007). In a workplace that is increasingly geographically and culturally dispersed—the virtual work environment—a shared leadership model can assist in knowledge creation by allowing information to flow more freely between team members in a more timely and clear basis (Bligh, Pearce & Kohles, 2006).

Another key factor in virtual teams, as in all teams, is the development of trust between members of the team. Trust describes an expectation of team members whether or not their efforts will be reciprocated and not exploited by the other team members (Zak, Kurzban, & Matzner, 2005). Trust in virtual teams is particularly important, since low levels of trust are not only detrimental to the team task, but also are more easily exploited under conditions of high anonymity. One virtual team member at Bosch put it best when they said: "Trust is a key element to success: Trust of the team leader in *his/her* employees and trust of the employees in *their* team leaders".

To trust someone means to place oneself in a position of risk, where one relies on the other person to honor his or her contributions. Higher levels of trust, particularly in virtual teams, are a strong predictor for information sharing and increased team performance (Gibson & Cohen, 2003). Cognitive trust describes the expectation that others will be reliable and dependable, and affective trust is based on relational ties and reciprocation of care and concern. Further, one might distinguish integrity- and ability-related trust, i.e., the expectation to treat others fair (trust in integrity), but also bring the necessary skills and abilities to the team (trust in ability).

Pearce, et al. (2004) conducted a longitudinal study of virtual teams and examined the leadership patterns in those teams. They found shared leadership to be a better predictor, than vertical leadership, of several team outcomes. Specifically, they found shared leadership to be

a better predictor of team potency, social integration, problem solving quality and perceived effectiveness, than the leadership of the team leader. Similarly, Pearce and Sims (2002) found shared leadership to be a better predictor of change management team effectiveness than the leadership of the team leader. Ensley, Hmieleski and Pearce (2006), in a more recent study, found parallel effects in top management teams. They found that shared leadership among top management team members, after controlling for CEO leader behavior, was a significant predictor of firm performance. More recently still, Hoch (2007) found shared leadership to be important ingredient in product development teams. Together these results indicate an important role for shared leadership in virtual teams.

HOW CAN SHARED LEADERSHIP BE IMPLEMENTED IN VIRTUAL TEAMS?

Clearly, the role of the team leader is critical when creating and putting into practice a shared leadership environment but as Pearce (2004) points out, on par with the vertical leader, there are significant organizational influences that must be recognized in the development of shared leadership. There are at least four broad organizational systems that can be useful to facilitate shared leadership: (1) training and development systems; (2) technology systems; (3) compensation systems; and (4) cultural systems.

Training and Development Systems. In most organizations it is not common for knowledge workers to be trained further than the basics of how to get around in the company or how to use the new software systems, as they are rolled-out. While many employers have the best of intentions and say so with great vigor, a recent study in the USA discovered that many employees are given less than 24 hours of training per year (see Pearce, 2004).

There have been many scholars who have theorized about the best or most effective ways to train leaders how to lead virtual teams (e.g., Gibson & Cohen, 2003; Rosen, Furst, & Blackburn, 2006). Most claim that face-to-face meetings are critical in developing the relationships that will facilitate communication once the team is virtual. Other ideas are focused on the importance of communication by encouraging the team to create mission statements or shared goals. Further, it is generally considered beneficial for the team leader to understand and be comfortable in the various communication mediums that are available so they can set the example and mentor team members in using technology to communicate and share information.

Marks, Zaccaro, and Mathieu (2000) found that team interaction training and leader briefings positively influenced both team communication and performance by aiding the formation of team roles that encouraged the knowledge transfer critical in a virtual team. For untrained leaders, the idea of migrating to a shared leadership environment is difficult to contemplate. The idea of releasing their hard won control is, to them, almost heresy, and so even to consider the possibility of success these leaders should be gently coached, developed and guided into a deeper and clearer understanding of their critical role in a shared leadership environment (Marks, et. al., 2000; Pearce, 2004). Consider how much more unsettling it is to a traditional vertical leader, used to being the one in charge, to think of shared leadership in a virtual environment.

Technology Systems. As we have previously noted, virtual teams exist in unstable, flexible, and non-routine organizational surroundings. This environment typically results from a wide geographic distribution of team members and also new technology implementation. They are strongly focused in the areas of information management and knowledge-based work. In order to allow the team the greatest chance of success, any organization contemplating the use of virtual teams should implement adequate communication and information technology in order to enable information to flow freely, as well as provide extensive training in the used of such technology.

The *types* of media chosen are important in assisting the team members to interact and share knowledge with one another. There are some media that are synchronous, such as chat or video conferencing that can be used for direct, pseudo face-to-face communication (Wegge. 2006). Then there are asynchronous media, such as email, or voice and text messaging which are particularly useful when working across different time zones. Each of these communication methods can be a powerful tool for team efficacy if used correctly and with an understanding of its impact. It is important that team members not only know *how* to use the media but also *when* and *why*. The role of the team leader becomes critical in helping the team to understand and adapt to the norms for effective technology usage (Cordery, et al., in press).

Certain technologies can be used and applied by the team to compensate for lack of structure. It is important to create a shared knowledge or message, i.e., to make sure that all the team members have the same understanding about the team processes, the team task, and team roles and deliverables. Using technology to effectively bring the team together regardless of space and time enables the team to function more akin to a traditional co-located team.

Compensation Systems. In most organizations there are both obvious and underlying reward systems for employee behavior to which employees respond in order to receive compensation they feel is deserved for their work. Regrettably, most organizational reward systems are designed to encourage behavior that doesn't always align with the organizational values or goals (Kerr, 1975).

It often becomes evident during a transition to a team-based, shared leadership system that the reward structure does not encourage behavior that results in knowledge creation or a focus on the overall outcome of the team. For example, merit pay is almost always based on individual performance and doesn't recognize contribution to, or collaboration of, the team. Clearly, it will be critical to the overall success of a team system to also reward components of the team's outcome as a group. To wit, O'Bannon and Pearce (1999), in a quasi-experimental field study, found that employees who received team-based pay had higher pay satisfaction, and rated their fellow employees higher on teamwork, than those who did not receive team based pay, even when their total compensation was lower.

Compensating people solely as members of a team in order to create an extraordinary group of people practicing shared leadership, and creating knowledge, is, nonetheless, impractical. There are many other nuances or considerations that need to be understood when implementing a team-based model and even more when incorporating shared leadership into that team. For example, some members of the team might simply decide to coast along if they are not individually 'incentivized' for their effort. Others might under-perform if they believe their career path, promotions, or performance appraisals are adversely affected by shared leadership (Pearce, 2004). Another layer of complexity is added when the team is geographically dispersed and it is not possible to visually judge contribution to the team. In these cases, it becomes critical for technology to aid communication of individual and team activities and achievements in order to build a community of knowledge workers.

Cultural Systems. Culture is a foundational element of an organization but it is also one of the components that is most difficult to define. It exerts massive influence on the behavior of individuals within organizations (Schneider, 1990) and, oftentimes, the challenge of understanding it enough to implement a change such as moving from vertical leadership as a norm to a model of shared leadership can be daunting (Conger, Spreitzer & Lawler, 1999; Pearce & Osmond,

1996). Additionally, in a global environment it is not just the culture within an organization that governs how individuals behave but also the cultures of the countries that are represented on the team. While the United States is a culture that encourages individualism, other nations are far more likely to expect a collectively organized group as a normal model (Pearce & Osmond, 1999; Pearce, 2008).

So how is shared leadership created, supported and maintained in an organization that is comprised of people who come from different places, are motivated by different outcomes, and who all work in an organizational culture that might not have been founded on an ideal of team-based activity? One of the key factors in the development of a culture that allows shared leadership is trust (Bligh, et. al., 2006). With trust there is a belief that the work of the team and of each of the contributors in that team will be valued and recognized. Avolio (1999, pp. 138) writes, "we are being hit by re-engineering tidal wave, and that this is a house-cleaning that prepares organizations for the future. An essential ingredient in this seems to be a culture that is adaptive and prone to re-creation." It follows then, that trust, a shared understanding of vision and a foundation for how interactions take place can be a start to building a shared leadership culture.

The role of senior management and the direct vertical leader should never be discounted in the development of an environment conducive to shared leadership. These senior managers are role models who can serve as examples of how the process of shared leadership can work. They can communicate its value to the organization while still empowering those around them to participate in the decisions made by asking the most important question in leadership—"What do you think?" (Pearce, 2004).

Finally, employee selection is critical. As Michael Crooke, former CEO of Patagonia, states "My most important job as the CEO is selecting the right people for the right jobs. Then, and only then, can shared leadership take hold." When finding and hiring people, organizations can make a point of bringing in people who have a predisposition to empower, to value the team-based decision making process and who are able to thrive in a shared leadership environment.

SUGGESTIONS FOR FUTURE RESEARCH

There are many directions that might be taken to further explore the implications of shared leadership and its role or value in virtual teams. For example, research could examine the role of alternative technologies in facilitating shared leadership. Naturally, this is an ever-evolving area for research, as technology continues to develop. On the other hand, the role of cultural diversity and culture creation for virtual teams seems and important area for exploration. Of course, experimental research could prove particularly valuable, as specific mechanisms could be isolated and examined. Having said that, field research in this area, although difficult to obtain, is also important. Research, for example, that explores the antecedents, mediating and moderating variables, and outcomes of shared leadership in virtual teams will be particularly valuable additions to the field. These are just a few possible directions for further research in this area (see Conger & Pearce, 2003 for a more comprehensive treatment).

CONCLUSION

Shared leadership, by its very nature, appears to be ideally suited to the geographically distributed model of a virtual team. The concept of sharing the leadership role with the various team members based on the project needs, expertise and situation simply makes sense, especially in a team that, by its design should lead each other at various moments based on the timing or sequence of the project.

Our discussion clearly reveals that shared leadership has its place when thinking about virtual teams, their formation, their leadership and their efficacy. We highlight some of the key questions about virtual teams; specifically what they are, why they exist and what can they do. We then provide a short summary of how leadership in virtual teams differs greatly from those of traditional teams. As virtual teams continue to become more important, the necessity of understanding their dynamics has, concomitantly, become more important. As such, pressures such as culture, language, trust, compensation, training and relationship creation and maintenance will increasingly come to the fore.

The creation of a virtual team that integrates shared leadership as its core should happen at the team inception and the role of the vertical leader should not be discounted since that role is essential to empower the rest of the team in its endeavors. We would argue that the vertical leader might view him or herself as a champion or enabler, an architect of the team, and as the person who moves identified obstacles out of the way so the team can get their work done more effectively. By combining vertical and shared leadership in virtual teams we are beginning to see a glimpse of an emerging model of leadership for the digital enterprise.

REFERENCES

Avolio, B. (1999). *Full leadership development: Building the vital forces in organizations*. Thousand Oaks, CA: Sage.

Bligh, M., Pearce, C. L., & Kohles, J. (2006). The importance of self and shared leadership in team based knowledge work: Toward a meso-level model of leadership dynamics. *Journal of Managerial Psychology, 21*, 296–318. doi:10.1108/02683940610663105

Conger, J. A., & Pearce, C. L. (2003). A landscape of opportunities: Future research on shared leadership. In C. L. Pearce & J. A. Conger (Eds.), *Shared leadership: Reframing the hows and whys of leadership* (pp. 285-303). Thousand Oaks, CA: Sage.

Conger, J. A., Spreitzer, G., & Lawler, E. E. (Eds.). (1999). *The leader's change handbook.* San Francisco: Jossey-Bass.

Cordery, J., Soo, C., Kirkman, B., Rosen, B., & Mathieu, J. (in press). Leading parallel global virtual teams: Lessons from Alcoa. *Organizational Dynamics.*

Cox, A. (2005). What are communities of practice? A comparative review of four seminal works. *Journal of Information Science, 31,* 527–540. doi:10.1177/0165551505057016

Cox, J. F., Pearce, C. L., & Perry, M. L. (2003). Toward a model of shared leadership and distributed influence in the innovation process. In C. L. Pearce & J. A. Conger (Eds.), *Shared leadership: Reframing the hows and whys of leadership* (pp. 48-76). Thousand Oaks, CA: Sage.

Davis, D. D. (2004). The tao of leadership in virtual teams. *Organizational Dynamics, 33,* 47–62. doi:10.1016/j.orgdyn.2003.11.004

Davis, D. D., & Bryant, J. L. (2003). Influence at a distance: Leadership in global virtual teams. In W. H. Mobley & P. W. Dorfman (Eds.), *Advances in global leadership* (Vol. 3, pp. 303-340). Oxford, UK: Elsevier.

Drucker, P. F. (1993). *Post-capitalist society.* New York: Harper Business.

Ensley, M. D., Hmieleski, K. M., & Pearce, C. L. (2006). The importance of vertical and shared leadership within new venture top management teams: Implications for the performance of start-ups. *The Leadership Quarterly, 17,* 217–231. doi:10.1016/j.leaqua.2006.02.002

Evaristo, R. (2003). The management of distributed projects across cultures. *Journal of Global Information Management, 11,* 58–70.

Fulk, J., & De Sanctis, G. (1995). Electronic communication and changing organizational forms. *Organization Science, 6,* 337–349. doi:10.1287/orsc.6.4.337

Gibson, C., & Cohen, S. (Eds.). (2003). *Virtual teams that work: Creating conditions for virtual team effectiveness.* San Francisco: Jossey-Bass.

Goodbody, J. (2005). Critical success factors for global virtual teams. *Strategic Communication Management, 9,* 18–21.

Hoch, J. E. (2007). *Shared and vertical leadership in product development teams.* Paper presented at the International Workshop on Teamwork (IWOT), Copenhagen, Denmark.

Jarvenpaa, S. L., Knoll, K., & Leidner, D. E. (1998). Communication and trust in global virtual teams. *Journal of Computer-Mediated Communication, 3*(4).

Kayworth, T. R., & Leidner, D. E. (2002). Leadership effectiveness in global virtual teams. *Journal of Management Information Systems, 18,* 7–40.

Kerr, S. (1975). On the folly of rewarding a while hoping for b. *Academy of Management Review, 18,* 769–783. doi:10.2307/255378

Kimble, C., Hildreth, P., & Wright, P. (2001). Communities of practice: Going global. In K. P. Mehdi (Ed.), *Knowledge management and business model innovation* (pp. 220-234). Hershey, PA: Idea Group Publishing.

Kirkman, B. L., Rosen, B., Gibson, C. B., Tesluk, P. E., & McPherson, S. O. (2002). Five challenges to virtual team success: Lessons from Sabre, Inc. *The Academy of Management Executive, 16,* 67–79.

Lawler, E. E. III, & Finegold, D. (2000). Individualizing the organization: Past, present, and future. *Organizational Dynamics, 29*, 1–15. doi:10.1016/S0090-2616(00)00009-7

Lipnack, J., & Stamps, J. (1997). *Virtual teams—reaching across space, time, and organizations with technology.* New York: John Wiley & Sons.

Majchrzak, A., Malhotra, A., Stamps, J., & Lipnack, J. (2004). Can absence make a team grow stronger? *Harvard Business Review, 82*, 131–137.

Malhotra, A., & Majchrzak, A. (2005). Virtual workspace technologies. *Sloan Management Review, 46*, 11–14.

Malhotra, A., Majchrzak, A., & Rosen, B. (2007). Leading virtual teams. *The Academy of Management Perspectives, 21*, 60–69.

Mankin, D., Cohen, S. G., & Bikson, T. K. (1996). *Teams and technology.* Boston: Harvard Business School Press.

Manz, C. C., & Sims, H. P., Jr. (2001). *The new superleadership.* San Francisco: Berrett-Koehler.

Marks, M. A., Zaccaro, S. J., & Mathieu, J. E. (2000). Performance implications of leader briefings and team-interaction training for team adaptation to novel environments. *The Journal of Applied Psychology, 85*, 971–986. doi:10.1037/0021-9010.85.6.971

Maznevski, M. L., & Chudoba, K. M. (2000). Bridging space over time: Global virtual team dynamics and effectiveness. *Organization Science, 11*, 473–492. doi:10.1287/orsc.11.5.473.15200

Miles, R. E., Snow, C. C., Mathews, J. A., & Miles, G. (1997). Organizing in the knowledge age: Anticipating the cellular form. *The Academy of Management Executive, 11*, 7–24.

Mohrman, S. A., Cohen, S. G., & Mohrman, A. M., Jr. (1995). *Designing team-based organizations: New forms for knowledge work.* San Francisco: Jossey-Bass.

Mowshowitz, A. (1997). Virtual organization. *Communications of the ACM, 40*, 30–37. doi:10.1145/260750.260759

Nonaka, I., & Takeuchi, H. (1995). *The knowledge-creating company.* New York: Oxford University Press.

Nonaka, I., Toyama, R., & Konno, N. (2001). SECI, Ba and leadership: A unified model of dynamic knowledge creation. In I. Nonaka & D. J. Teece (Eds.), *Managing industrial knowledge: Creation, transfer, and utilization* (pp. 13-43). Thousand Oaks, CA: Sage.

O'Bannon, D. P., & Pearce, C. L. (1999). A quasi-experiment of gain sharing in service organizations: Implications for organizational citizenship behavior and pay satisfaction. *Journal of Managerial Issues, 11*, 363–378.

O'Hara-Devereaux, M., & Johansen, R. (1994). *Global work: Bridging distance, culture and time.* San Francisco: Jossey-Bass.

Pauleen, D. J. (2003). Leadership in a global virtual team: An action learning approach. *Leadership and Organization Development Journal, 24*, 153–162. doi:10.1108/01437730310469570

Pauleen, D. J., & Yoong, P. (2001a). Facilitating virtual team relationships via Internet and conventional communication channels. *Internet Research, 11*, 190–202. doi:10.1108/10662240110396450

Pauleen, D. J., & Yoong, P. (2001b). Relationship building and the use of ICT in boundary crossing virtual teams: A facilitator's perspective. *Journal of Information Technology, 16*, 205–220. doi:10.1080/02683960110100391

Pearce, C. L. (2004). The future of leadership: Combining vertical and shared leadership to transform knowledge work. *The Academy of Management Executive, 18*, 47–59.

Pearce, C. L. (2008). Follow the leaders. *Wall Street Journal*, pp. B8, 12.

Pearce, C. L., & Conger, J. A. (Eds.). (2003). *Shared leadership: Reframing the hows and whys of leadership.* Thousand Oaks, CA: Sage.

Pearce, C. L., & Osmond, C. P. (1996). Metaphors for change: The ALPs model of change management. *Organizational Dynamics, 24*, 23–35. doi:10.1016/S0090-2616(96)90003-0

Pearce, C. L., & Osmond, C. P. (1999). From workplace attitudes and values to a global pattern of nations: An application of latent class modeling. *Journal of Management, 25*, 759–778. doi:10.1177/014920639902500507

Pearce, C. L., & Sims, H. P. Jr. (2002). Vertical versus shared leadership as predictors of the effectiveness of change management teams: An examination of aversive, directive, transactional, transformational, and empowering leader behaviors. *Group Dynamics, 6*, 172–197. doi:10.1037/1089-2699.6.2.172

Pfeffer, J., & Veiga, J. F. (1999). Putting people first for organizational success. *The Academy of Management Executive, 13*, 37–48.

Raven, A. (2003). Team or community of practice: Aligning tasks, structures, and technologies. In C. B. Gibson & S. G. Cohen (Eds.), *Virtual teams that work: Creating conditions for virtual team effectiveness* (pp. 292-306). San Francisco: Jossey Bass.

Rosen, B., Furst, S., & Blackburn, R. (2006). Training for virtual teams: An investigation of current practices and future needs. *Human Resource Management Journal, 45*, 229–247. doi:10.1002/hrm.20106

Rosen, B., Furst, S., & Blackburn, R. (2007). Overcoming barriers to knowledge sharing in virtual teams. *Organizational Dynamics, 36*, 259–273. doi:10.1016/j.orgdyn.2007.04.007

Saunders, C., Van Slyke, C., & Vogel, D. R. (2004). My time or yours? Managing time visions in global virtual teams. *The Academy of Management Executive, 18*, 19–31.

Schneider, B. (1990). *Organizational climate and culture.* San Francisco: Jossey-Bass.

Senge, P. (2000). Classic work: The leader's new work: Building learning organizations. In D. Morey, M. Maybury, & B. Thuraisingham (Eds.), *Knowledge management: Classics and contemporary works.* Cambridge, MA: The MIT Press.

Shin, J., & McClomb, G. E. (1998). Top executive leadership and organizational innovation: An empirical investigation of nonprofit human service organizations (HSOs). *Administration in Social Work, 22*, 1–21. doi:10.1300/J147v22n03_01

Townsend, A. M., De Marie, S. M., & Hendrickson, A. R. (1998). Virtual teams: Technology and the workplace of the future. *The Academy of Management Executive, 12*, 17–29.

Wegge, J. (2006). Communication via videoconference: Emotional and cognitive consequences of affective personality dispositions, seeing one's own picture, and disturbing events. *Human-Computer Interaction, 21*, 273–318. doi:10.1207/s15327051hci2103_1

Wegge, J., Bipp, T., & Kleinbeck, U. (2007). Goal setting via videoconferencing. *European Journal of Work and Organizational Psychology, 16*, 169–194. doi:10.1080/13594320601125567

Wenger, E., McDermott, R. A., & Snyder, W. (2002). *Cultivating communities of practice: A guide to managing knowledge.* Boston: Harvard Business School Press.

Yeatts, D. E., & Hyten, C. (1998). *High-performing self-managed work teams: A comparison of theory and practice*. Thousand Oaks, CA: Sage.

Zaccaro, S. J., & Bader, P. (2003). E-leadership and the challenge of leading e-teams: Minimizing bad and maximizing the good. *Organizational Dynamics, 31*, 377–387. doi:10.1016/S0090-2616(02)00129-8

Zak, P., Kurzban, R., & Matzner, W. T. (2005). Oxytocin is associated with human trustworthiness. *Hormones and Behavior, 48*, 522–527. doi:10.1016/j.yhbeh.2005.07.009

Chapter 3

Leading in a Knowledge Era
A New Dawn for Knowledge Leaders

Sharmila Jayasingam
Universiti Malaya, Malaysia

Mahfooz A. Ansari
University of Lethbridge, Canada

ABSTRACT

Knowledge management (KM) has been found to be a critical success factor for organizational performance. However, most organizations are found to be purely focused on the technological perspectives of KM initiatives at the expense of people perspective. They fail to realize that the success of any KM system relies upon the acceptance and motivation of knowledge worker (k-worker), the primary player in any KM initiatives. Here, knowledge leaders have a crucial role to play in influencing and encouraging k-workers to adopt KM practices. However, a transformation of leader behavior is required to manage this new generation of workers. This chapter thus highlights the power-influence approach to leadership behavior in promoting and instilling KM practices among k-workers.

INTRODUCTION

Leadership is one complex phenomenon that is evolving and has been addressed from diverse perspectives. A review of the current literature (Pearce, Sims, Cox, Ball, Schnell, Smith, & Trevino, 2003; Yukl, 2006) indicates that there are a myriad of leadership models that have been constructed to define leadership behavior. Leaders have been elucidated in terms of character, mannerism, influence and persuasion, relationship patterns, role relationships, and as administrative figures. In short, leadership is defined as influence processes that affect the action of followers (Ansari, 1990; Yukl, 2006).

Recently, there is a strong call for transformation of leader behavior. The underlying essence of this call for transformation is that the various models and taxonomies on effective leader behavior that have been developed over time may no longer be directly applicable in this knowledge era. With the advent of a new generation of workers--k-workers who are clearly different from other workers--there

DOI: 10.4018/978-1-60566-958-8.ch003

is a significant change in leader-subordinate relationships (MacNeil, 2003; Viitala, 2004) with a noticeable shift of power from leaders to k-workers (McCrimmon, 1995). In fact, Gapp (2002) reported that leadership and management style has undergone a major revolution under the system of profound knowledge. In essence, k-workers require eccentric people management practices (Amar, 2001; Hislop, 2003; Ribiere & Sitar, 2003).

Although it is apparent that leadership permeates as the foundation for KM system success, there is very little research to support the relationship between leadership behavior and knowledge management (Politis, 2001). The present chapter aims at bridging this gap in the literature by advocating the use of power-influence approach to leadership in a knowledge-based context. Given a relative paucity of research in the KM area, our discussion builds upon a narrative review (rather than meta-analytic review) of the literature to develop a framework based on the power and influence taxonomy (Ansari, 1990; French & Raven, 1959; Raven, 1962).

We have divided the discussion into four major sections. First, we discuss the failure of KM initiatives and the key role of the leaders in ensuring the acceptance and eventually the improved performance of these initiatives. Second, we set the stage for further discussion on the issue of the transforming workforce and the emergence of a new generation of workers referred to as "k-workers." The discussion on the transforming workforce is an eye opener to the need for the transformed leadership behavior which would be based on the interpersonal influence and social power model. Third, we advocate the effectiveness of leadership behavior that we believe should be employed to successfully influence k-workers to embrace KM practices. Fourth, we suggest directions for future research, followed by a conclusion.

THE BACKGROUND

The Underlying Essence of KM Initiative Success

Knowledge management (KM) can be defined as the organized process of creating, capturing, storing, disseminating, and using knowledge within and between organizations to maintain competitive advantage (Darroch, 2003; Davenport & Prusak, 2000; Nonaka, 1994). It requires the transformation of personal knowledge into corporate knowledge that can be shared and applied throughout the organization (Skyrme, 1997).

Over time, KM has evolved as a strategic process that has a clear link to organizational performance. Most organizations are seeking benefits of KM in order to build on their competitive advantage such as capturing and sharing best practices, effectively managing customer relationships, and delivering competitive intelligence (Ming Yu, 2002; Syed-Ikhsan & Rowland, 2004). A survey by Reuters (2001) revealed that 90 percent of the companies which deploy KM solutions benefit from better decision making whereas 81 percent say they noticed increased productivity (as cited in Malhotra, 2001). Some companies such as the BP Amoco, Xerox, and Dearborn experience great levels of cost savings by leveraging knowledge it had (Ambrosio, 2000; Lam & Chua, 2005). In essence, KM initiative has a forceful influence on maximizing organizational performance (Axelsen, 2002; Karlenzing & Patrick, 2002; Talisayon, 2002). Bearing this in mind, most organizations are trying to outdo one another in implementing the best KM systems to evade being left out and to harvest the promised benefits (Lam & Chua, 2005).

However, despite the focus on implementing KM enabling technologies and systems, countless KM initiatives fail to realize what they set out to do (De Long & Fahey, 2000; Smith, Blackman, & Good, 2003). Disturbingly, KM experts divulged that KM failure rates are estimated to be between 50 percent and 70 percent (Ambrosio, 2000). In addition, about 84 percent of KM projects implemented had no notable result on the organizations, which indicates the failure of these projects (Lucier, 2003).

The major cause for the letdown would be the failure of organizations to comprehend that the success of the KM system does not solely rely on technology or a web of networks, but even more so on the k-workers' acceptance and commitment towards the KM system (Ambrosio, 2000; Lam & Chua, 2005; Malhotra, 2002). The fundamental nature of KM involves the attainment of organizational aspirations through strategy-driven motivation and facilitation of k-workers to develop, improve and employ their ability to deduce data and information using their experience, skills, culture, character, personality, and feelings (Beijerse, 1999). Although undeniably, information technology plays a key role in establishing KM systems, human capitals are the ones who create, share, and use the knowledge to contribute towards organizational effectiveness (Asllani & Luthans, 2003; Malhotra, 2002).

Therefore, simply boasting of a technologically advanced KM system and providing access to it will not initiate changes in behavior or lead to greater understanding (Smith et al., 2003). Instead, knowledge organizations need to focus on influencing and motivating k-workers to be committed and involved in their KM initiatives. Organizations must realize that unlike technology, human capital--the source of internal competency--cannot be copied by competitors. Thus it serves as a critical ingredient in sustaining the competitive advantage of any organization (Smith & Rupp, 2002).

However, influencing k-workers to adopt KM practices is easier said than done. The difficulty in motivating employees poses as the major stumbling block for many KM initiative implementations (Davenport, 1999; Fedor, Ghosh, Caldwell, Maurer, & Singhal, 2003; Lam & Chua, 2005).

Hence, changing the k-workers' attitude and behavior to be more supportive of KM system implementation requires the practice of excellent leadership skills (Chong, 2006a, 2006b; Gapp, 2002; Ribiere & Sitar, 2003). Forceful interactions should exist between leadership and KM to encourage k-workers to adopt KM supportive behaviors (Politis, 2001).

Then again, one would assume that the earlier models of effective leadership behavior may be applicable to the present situation. However, these traditional models have been challenged in recent times. Gapp (2002) highlighted that it is necessary for knowledge leaders to change their style to match the major upheaval of the system of intense knowledge. The need for transformed leaders arises because of the changing nature of workforce. At present, the workforce is evolving to become more knowledge based. In fact, knowledge has become a new buzz word that is taking over organizations like a tidal wave. This interesting development has paved the path for the adjustment in leader-subordinate relationships (MacNeil, 2003; Viitala, 2004). Leader power is being transferred to k-workers (McCrimmon, 1995). In short, knowledge leaders must be prepared to lead k-workers using unconventional people management practices (Amar, 2001; Ribiere & Sitar, 2003) to encourage them to be active participants of any KM initiatives.

Understanding the Transforming Workforce: The Reason for Transformed leadership

Numerous researchers have attempted to clearly define k-workers. The term "k-worker" was first coined by Peter Drucker about 50 years ago in his book *Landmarks of Tomorrow.* Drucker classified k-workers as people who rely on brains over brawn in carrying out their job. Based on his definition, Drucker (1959) quoted an extensive array of k-workers ranging from scientists to hamburger flippers. However, not many people went by this classification of a k-worker. Instead, most early researches on k-worker were exclusively focused on workers from the field of information technology. Subsequently, this classification scheme was considered to be too narrow and limited. As time went by, researchers broadened their horizon and allowed the term "k-worker" to include other workers involved in knowledge work such as lawyers, medical practitioners, business experts, and so on. Withey (2003) classified k-workers into three broad categories to help facilitate the process of understanding who k-workers actually are. The three categories were as follows: *High* (e.g., professors, scientists, researchers), *moderate* (e.g., managers, coordinators), and *low* (e.g., clerical workers, administrative officers).

Put simply, k-workers are "participants in the knowledge economy" (Spira, 2005) with the fundamental aspiration to achieve organization goal (Scott, 2005). A comprehensive yet simple definition of a k-worker would be as follows: K-workers are individuals who are highly educated and possess specialized knowledge and skills that are utilized for knowledge creation and complex problem solving that improves organizational performances through value creation (Davenport, 1999; Kelley, Blackman, & Hurst, 2007; Ware & Grantham, 2007). Essentially, their work strongly relies upon "their dependence on technical knowledge and prior expertise, their ability to manage their own schedules and process, dealing with different people to perform their work, and being in an environment with a relatively flat hierarchy and coordination among personnel that are not physically collocated" (Scott, 2005, p. 270).

This new generation of workers as often referred to as "gold-collar" workers with the underlying notion that these workers are essentially different from other workers (Amar, 2001; Kelley et al., 2007; Ribiere & Sitar, 2003). K-workers are highly knowledgeable and thus confidently exercise self-control and self-learning (Awad & Ghaziri, 2004). They equip themselves with enhanced knowledge and expertise to build their

personal career development and not for corporate advancement (Bogdanowicz & Bailey, 2002; Kelley et al., 2007). They are also willing to take risks and expect to learn from their mistakes.

In line with k-workers' wider skills, expertise and work responsibilities, they have an increasing need for autonomy and empowerment (Gapp, 2002; MacNeil, 2003). In addition, these workers need autonomy to successfully deal with their daily work that consists of ambiguous, unstructured, unpredictable, multidisciplinary, non-routine, and complex tasks (Scott, 2005). Therefore, they do not enjoy working under close supervision or direct control (Kubo & Saka, 2002). In fact, with most valuable knowledge locked within the mind of k-workers, they tend to exercise their power to decide what they want to contribute to the organization and how they want to contribute (Hislop, 2003; Lang, 2001; Syed-Ikhsan & Rowland, 2004).

K-workers have also been found to be widely connected with people and divisions both within and outside their own division. Besides relying on networks as prescribed by the hierarchy, they also tend to source for resources outside this formal network to get their job done (Scott, 2005).

Unlike their predecessors, k-workers are extremely mobile and are constantly looking for greener pastures to move on to (Bogdanowicz & Bailey, 2002; Ware & Grantham, 2007). They generally have the penchant to switch jobs often. This propensity to leave causes k-workers to take their individual knowledge with them in their search for self-advancement and this evidently exposes organizations to the risk of losing crucial knowledge—the underlying ingredient of competitive intelligence (Bogdanowicz & Bailey, 2002).

In a nutshell, k-workers "have substantially different expectations of their employers than ordinary workers" (Kelley et al., 2007, p. 208). The workforce is transforming and being different, k-workers require idiosyncratic people management practices. As leadership has often been quoted as an important element in managing k-workers (Gapp, 2002; MacNeil, 2003; Viitala, 2004; Politis, 2001, 2002, 2005), this prominent change in the workforce naturally calls for a transformation in leader behavior. We next turn our attention to discussing in depth the leader behavior that is deemed suitable in influencing and motivating k-workers.

THE KNOWLEDGE LEADER

Linking Knowledge Leader's Roles to the Influence Process: The Need for Certain Types of Power to be Perceived as Effective

People are the fundamental contributor to the social system of KM initiatives (Ribiere & Sitar, 2003; Alvesson, 2004). Past research (e.g., Crawford, 2005; Jayasingam et al., 2008; Politis, 2005) has highlighted that motivating and influencing the human capital to significantly contribute and be part of the KM initiatives requires effective leadership behavior. Despite that, there is very little pragmatic research conducted to identify the specific leadership behavior that can promote KM supportive behavior and subsequently KM initiative success.

Nevertheless, an analysis of the roles outlined by several researchers (e.g., Dfouni, 2002) for knowledge leaders clearly supports the notion that the ability to influence important players particularly the top management and k-workers to work towards a concept or idea is a crucial leadership skill that is needed in the knowledge network. The need for certain type of social power is highlighted by the fact that KM initiatives thrive through the active involvement of the human capital (Dfouni, 2002). Essentially, leaders are in a position to use their personal influence to motivate k-workers to do better and bring about innovation (Amar, 2001; Politis, 2005).

The significance of certain types of social power can be highlighted by assessing distinctive roles of a knowledge leader. Firstly, knowledge leaders are expected to convince senior management about the benefits and potential of KM initiatives (Dfouni, 2002). Chong (2006a, 2006b) stressed that the most important critical success factor for any KM initiative is top management leadership and commitment towards KM. He stated that only the top management has the ability to move all other critical success factors to support and initiate KM implementation success.

Once top management support has been established, knowledge leaders also need to obtain support from the staff (Dfouni, 2002). In order to successfully convince them and create shared awareness, knowledge leaders are also expected to develop well thought out strategies for the KM initiatives (Dfouni, 2002). The strategies would include getting staff to learn and create knowledge (Vitaala, 2004), voluntarily share their knowledge (Dfouni, 2002; Ribiere & Sitar, 2003), and finally, apply that knowledge. The successful execution of the knowledge strategies stated above requires the leader to enlist the support of the staff to carry out these practices.

For case in point, the facilitation of knowledge creation requires the leader to provide intellectual stimulation and expert guidance to encourage employees to seek new knowledge (Politis, 2001; Ribiere & Sitar, 2003; Vitaala, 2004). Leader may also need to network with sources of knowledge both inside and outside the organization to obtain access to usually unattainable expertise to bring in new ideas that would contribute towards knowledge creation and application (Sarin & McDermott, 2003; Fedor et al., 2003). To further encourage and influence employees to continuously derive new knowledge, attractive rewards must also be provided by the leader (Crawford, 2005).

On the other hand, getting people to share their distinctive knowledge is particularly challenging as employees tend to perceive a loss of power if they share their unique knowledge (Gray, 2001). Handling this behavior of knowledge hoarding requires the leader to be a role model and culti-vate trust among their staff so that they become more open to the idea of sharing knowledge (Chen, 2004; Ribiere & Sitar, 2003). In addition, rewarding knowledge sharing behaviors would also lend a helping hand to knowledge leaders to induce knowledge sharing among employees (Chen, 2004, Crawford, 2005).

In essence, being able to convince and mar-shal the support of the important participants is necessary for the successful implementation of any KM initiatives. Therefore, knowledge leaders must be able to influence and convince the top management and k-workers, who in turn would contribute to the dynamic process of knowledge creation, sharing, and application. The next sec-tion intends to provide a broad picture on ideal social power knowledge leaders should adopt or shun in order to reach out to k-workers.

The Proposed Framework

Although a number of power typologies or frameworks exist, perhaps the most influential and frequently used and cited is that of French and Raven's (1959) bases of power. A power base is the source of influence in a social relationship (Ansari, 1990). Power is defined as the ability to influence or "influence potential" (French & Raven, 1959), whereas influence is the demonstrated use of power or power in action (Ansari, 1990). Initially, French and Raven's power taxonomy distinguished among five bases of power that could contribute to the agent's overall ability to influence a target. These bases of power were reward, coercive, le-gitimate, referent, and expert. Subsequently, two more bases of power—information (Raven, 1965) and connection (Ansari, 1990; Hersey, Blanchard, & Natemeyer, 1979)--were incorporated into the French and Raven (1959) taxonomy. The general definitions of the bases of power are specified be-low to fit the case of knowledge leaders (Aguinis, Ansari, Jayasingam, & Aafaqi, 2008; French & Raven, 1959; Raven, 1965).

- *Reward power* is based on the perceiver's assessment that the knowledge leader has the ability to offers reward to them for do-ing something he or she wants.
- *Coercive power* is based on the perceiver's assessment that the knowledge leader has the ability to inflict various organizational punishments.
- *Legitimate power* is based on the perceiv-er's assessment that the agent has the right to prescribe and control others by virtue of his or her organizational position.
- *Referent power* is based on the perceiver's assessment that the knowledge leader is worthy of emulating based on a sense of identification.
- *Expert power* is based on the perceiver's assessment that the knowledge leader pos-sesses special knowledge, experience, or judgment that others do not possess themselves.
- *Information power* is based on perceiver's assessment that the knowledge leader has the ability to control the availability and accuracy of information. [1]
- *Connection power* is based on the perceiv-er's assessment that the knowledge leader is well connected with other powerful individuals.

Numerous researches have been conducted to determine the relationships between bases of power and important outcomes such as satisfac-tion, productivity, and compliance, among others. Bases of power such as expert, referent power, connection, and information power consistently had positive relationships with various criterion variables. For example, soft power bases such as expert and referent power were considered more effective (Erchul, Raven, & Ray, 2001). Ansari (1990) found connection power to affect most of the influence tactics, regardless of whether it was upward influence or downward influence. In fact, it was found that the possession of adequate

Figure 1. A proposed framework for leadership behavior for knowledge leaders

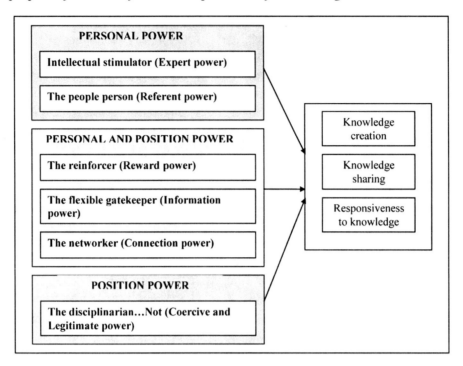

expert, referent, connection and information power clearly distinguished successful entrepreneurs from unsuccessful ones (Aguinis et al., 2008; Jayasingam, 2001). On the other hand, coercive power was negatively related to criterion variables such as commitment, satisfaction and entrepreneurial success (e.g., Hinkin & Schriesheim, 1989; Elangovan & Jia, 2000; Jayasingam, 2001).

The effect of reward and legitimate power has been found to be inconsistent. Some studies on reward power have reported positive impact on certain criterion outcomes such as quality of relationship (Aguinis, Nesler, Quigley, Lee, & Tedeschi, 1996), efficiency rating (Ivancevich & Donnely, 1970), and entrepreneur success (Aguinis et al., 2008; Jayasingam, 2001), whereas others have highlighted the negative effect on variables such as satisfaction with the leader (Bachman, Smith, & Slesinger, 1966). Legitimate power demonstrated weaker, yet significant, positive relationships in some situations such as helping relationships (Burke & Wilcox, 1971) and

compliance (Rahim, 1989). On the other hand, the use of legitimate power was found to evoke negative feelings such as dissatisfaction with the leader (Bachman, et al., 1966) and employee stress (Elangovan & Jia, 2000).

Evidently, the power framework has been useful for managers in general and entrepreneurs in particular. Given that, we are expecting KM specialists to also use these bases of power. As established earlier (in the "*Linking knowledge leader's roles to the influence process*" section), it is evident that knowledge leaders need to be actively involved in influencing people to ensure the successful implementation of KM initiatives. Therefore, using these bases of social power as the foundation, a framework is developed (see Figure 1) specifically for the knowledge leader.

The framework above clearly delineates six leadership aspects considered as important for knowledge leaders to practice to be able to influence k-workers to adopt KM practices. These six leadership dimensions were developed with refer-

Table 1. Description of the leadership dimension

Leadership dimensions	Description
Intellectual stimulator	The use of leader's expert power to stimulate intellectual activities such as knowledge creation among their staff
People person	The use of the leader's personality and warmth (referent power) that is expected to draw respect from their staff and subsequently influence them
Reinforcer	Leader's use of reward power to influence k-workers
Disciplinarian...Not	The reduced use of legitimate and coercive power in influencing k-workers
Flexible gatekeeper	The leader is expected to exercise relaxed control over information access and facilitate the dissemination of information to employees (reduced information power)
Networker	The leader should network with important others (connection power) to source for new knowledge

ence to the seven power bases discussed earlier. Theoretically, these seven bases of power can be grouped into two distinct categories—personal power and position power (Etzioni, 1961). These two concepts of power have been found to be relatively independent and each includes several distinct but partially overlapping components (Ansari, 1990; Yukl & Falbe, 1991). Position power refers to the potential influence derived from the opportunities inherent in an individual's position in the organization (Yukl, 2006; therefore, legitimate and coercive power that originate from the leaders' position are clustered together as position power. In contrast, personal power is derived from the attributes of the agent and the agent-target relationship (Yukl, 2006). Thus, expert and referent power which are derived from a leader's own training, experience and personal qualities are grouped as personal power (Ansari, 1990; Yukl, 2006). Finally, reward, information, and connection power can originate from overlapping sources—a leader's position as well as the leader's personal qualities. Therefore, these powers were grouped together.

These leadership dimensions have been reviewed to suit the needs of the knowledge network. A brief description of these dimensions is presented in Table 1.

A detailed discussion about each of these dimensions follows. As mentioned earlier, the discussion builds upon narrative reviews (rather than meta-analytic reviews) of the literature since not many studies were available on this subject in the KM area.

The Intellectual Stimulator

Researchers have long advocated that effective leaders should possess specialized knowledge and be experts in their relevant field in order to guide subordinates (Aguinis et al., 2008; Hinkin & Schriesheim, 1989; Yukl, 2006). At present, with k-workers known to be experts themselves, do we still need leaders with expertise to function as a coach or guide for them? The answer seems to be in the affirmative. In essence, although k-workers strongly embrace the "I did it on my own" concept that advocates solving all problems on their own (Amar, 2002) using their wider skills, expertise, and work responsibilities (Amar, 2001; Janz & Prasarnphanich, 2003; MacNeil, 2003), they still seek expert guidance indirectly from their respective leaders to solve their problems, without even realizing it (Amar, 2002).

Knowledge leaders need to grasp the fact that power derived from the possession of specific knowledge and not hierarchical position, facilitates influencing k-workers (MacNeil, 2003). Leaders who encouraged intellectual stimulation were found to have a positive effect on knowledge acquisition (Politis, 2001, 2002), knowledge sharing (Chen, 2004), and overall KM practices

(Crawford, 2005). This was further substantiated by findings which reported a positive relationship between leader's expert power and knowledge acquisition (Politis, 2005, Jayasingam et al., 2008), knowledge sharing, and knowledge utilization (Jayasingam et al., 2008).

Hence, influencing k-workers with specialized expertise requires leaders to lead through intellectual power, conviction, persuasion, and interactive dialog (Ribiere & Sitar, 2003). Leaders with expertise can embrace the role of knowledge coaches or experts to help novices learn how to create and utilize knowledge through guided experience (MacNeil, 2003; Amar, 2002). They can promote and support behavioral skills and traits of k-workers indispensable for knowledge acquisition (Politis, 2005). Besides guiding, leaders with expertise can also inspire k-workers to develop new ideas or stimulate their creative streak (O'regan & Ghobadian, 2004; Jong & Hartog, 2007). In short, leaders should be able to tell k-workers what they do not already know and stimulate a healthy debate that leads to the development and application of new knowledge.

The People Person

Unlike the "Intellectual Stimulator," the concept of "People Person" refers to the leaders who are relationship oriented, likeable, respected, and perceived as worthy of emulating. Effective leadership has been associated with individuals who strongly display the people person qualities (e.g., Bachman et al., 1966; Hinkin & Schriesheim, 1989; Yukl, 2006). Interestingly, knowledge based organizations have given this relationship a fascinating twist.

We advocate a "people person" leader when encouraging knowledge sharing among k-workers. In a knowledge network, leaders are expected to adopt personal mentoring and internal consulting (McCrimmon, 1995) and help build a culture of trust by demonstrating concerns, keeping promises, morality fairness, openness, honesty, discretion, consistency, integrity and delivering expected results (Ribiere & Sitar, 2003). These dispositional elements encourage trust building and social interaction and are therefore essential for knowledge sharing (Connelly & Kelloway, 2003). Individualized consideration dimension was found to positively influence knowledge sharing (Chen, 2004) in particular, and KM processes, in general (Crawford, 2005). Consequently, a leader who displays personal qualities that supports knowledge sharing will become a role model for k-workers to emulate.

However, in other scenarios such as when promoting knowledge acquisition and utilization, we believe that knowledge leaders should not rely on the display of these characteristics. Known to be independent, k-workers determine what knowledge they want to contribute and how they aim to apply it (Amar, 2001; Politis, 2005). They trust their own proficiency and do not reckon their leader to be correct based on the leader's personal appeal and relationship-oriented behavior (Politis, 2005). In fact, Politis (2001, 2002, 2005) and Jayasingam et al., (2008) found being considerate to workers and subsequently being likeable to be negatively related to knowledge acquisition.

Basically, k-workers are matured and independent enough that they no longer perceive the need for a leader to be supportive and nurturing. Instead, they want their leaders to "walk the talk." They expect their leaders to be great role models who display values such as honesty and integrity. However, the leader's personal magnetism stops at meriting respect, admiration, and identification among k-workers. Being likeable and respected may not take a knowledge leader far when it comes to getting k-workers to do things in accordance with the leader's desire. K-workers avoid doing things because they like someone. They have their own mind and strongly rely upon their own judgment.

The Reinforcer

The "Reinforcer" is different from the "Intellectual Stimulator" and the "People Person," as they do not rely on personal attributes such as expertise or personality. Instead, the use of rewards to influence people is the dominant characteristic of this leadership dimension. The form of reward varies from tangible or monetary rewards (e.g., pay, bonus) and non-tangible or non-monetary rewards (e.g., assignment of challenging task, promotions, social recognition, praise, and award). The use of any form of rewards has been claimed to be a powerful tool to reinforce behaviors needed for performance. However, there seem to be two schools of thought when analyzing the effect of reward power. Although some studies have found leaders who use reward power to have a *positive impact* on certain criterion outcomes such as quality of relationship (Aguinis, Nesler, Quigley, Lee, & Tedeschi, 1996), efficiency rating (Ivancevich & Donnely, 1970), and entrepreneur success (Aguinis et al., 2008), most studies have found *no significant relationship* with any outcomes (e.g., Elangovan & Jia, 2000; Rahim, 1989; Schriesheim, Hinkin, & Podsakoff, 1991;) or *negative effects* on various indicators of leader effectiveness (e.g., Ansari, Aafaqi, & Oh, 2008; Elangovan & Jia, 2000; Schriesheim, et al., 1991).

The same scenario seems to exist in the current knowledge-based environment. Several studies reported that reward power was negatively related or unrelated with leader effectiveness. These findings were supported in a knowledge-based environment when Politis (2002, 2005) stated that leaders who provide rewards if k-workers perform in accordance, disable rather than enable knowledge acquisition. Typically, k-workers view reward administration to motivate them as manipulative and too simplistic (Amar, 2002).

On the other hand, a good number of studies on reward power or contingent reward have reported reward as a powerful motivator in influencing k-workers' behavior and commitment (Crawford, 2005; Jayasingam et al., 2008; Kubo & Saka, 2002). The need for reward was also evident in Smith and Rupp's (2002) research that reported reinforcers such as management's concern for work-life balance, followed by career acknowledgment, professional accomplishment, remuneration, customer relations, prospects of career progression, career and intellectual challenges, workforce benefits, coworker relationships and personal growth were found to be important incentives in a knowledge-based organization to foster employee commitment. It should, however, be noted that k-workers typically indulge in KM practices for their own interest rather than for the betterment of the organization (Gal, 2004) and are extremely mobile, dangling a carrot in front of them would definitely serve as a motivating factor.

One important point to bear in mind when assigning rewards is that the link between reward and performance must be equitable. A clear link between k-workers' contribution and the reward system strongly motivates them to embrace change and display considerable involvement in KM practices (Smith & Rupp, 2003). However, it is crucial to note that when assigning reward in relation to performance the "new pay goes beyond rewarding the traditional measures of performance, and places emphasis on other measures, such as customer service, leadership, employee satisfaction, cycle time, quality, teams, skills, and competencies" (Smith & Rupp, 2002, p. 254).

Evidently, leaders need to reform their culture and reward system so that employees are encouraged to generate, implement innovative ideas (Jong & Hartog, 2007), and share their knowledge with others (Lin & Tseng, 2005; Un & Cazurra, 2004). Provided that knowledge leaders do not manipulate the use of reward in influencing k-workers, and reward k-workers fairly based on their contribution to the knowledge base of the organization, we believe reward is a powerful motivator. Leaders can resort to reward mechanisms such as assignment of interesting tasks to their k-workers or even offer personal recognition (O'Regan & Ghobadian, 2004). Leaders need to also ensure job prospects are challenging and the pay scheme is competitive enough to retain their valuable k-workers.

The Disciplinarian…..Not

The "Disciplinarian" refers to a greater reliance on the leader's formal position to influence employees. Traditionally, leaders believed they needed to exercise some form of control using their position power to create compliance (Bachman et al., 1966; Burke & Wilcox, 1971; Ivancevich & Donnely, 1970). With the passage of time, this perception was proven wrong in most cases. For example, leaders who used punishment to control their subordinates caused negative effects on levels of satisfaction and commitment (Hinkin & Schriesheim, 1989; Elangovan & Jia, 2000). In fact, leaders who used position power caused people to perceive them as ineffective (Aguinis et al., 2008; Erchul, Raven, & Ray, 2001, Yukl, 2006). In simple words, although the use of authority to gain compliance seems to be an easy way out, the reliance on position power to force subordinates to comply with the leader's request were deemed ineffective in the long run.

The effect of this power erosion is felt even more in the knowledge era. At present, the power relationship between managers and k-workers has arguably evolved and caused the attrition of formal authority in the knowledge-based environment (Amar, 2002; McCrimmon, 1995). As such, acts of controlling and reprimanding workers with the use of formal power and status is considered a barrier to KM practices such as knowledge acquisition (Politis, 2005), knowledge transfer (Riege, 2007), and knowledge application (Jong & Hartog, 2007).

The complete disregard towards the use of authority by leaders stem from k-worker's need for greater autonomy and power in the workplace. This can be attributed to their wider skills, expertise,

and work responsibilities (Amar, 2001; Janz & Prasarnphanich, 2003; MacNeil, 2003). Therefore, they do not enjoy working under close supervision or direct control (Kubo & Saka, 2002). Any attempt to manage, control, or codify organizational knowledge is likely to produce internal conflict (Hislop, 2003). In a nutshell, k-workers mock at influence attempts based solely on position power (McCrimmon, 1995).

Fundamentally, a knowledge-based organization functions best as a symbiosis and leaders are expected to avoid drawing their power from their formal position (Amar, 2002). Thus, managers can no longer depend on the traditional command and control mechanism to influence k-workers (MacNeil, 2003). A reprimand or punishment will not only obliterate k-workers' initiatives to create, share or apply knowledge, but also dampen future attempts by others (Amar, 2002). In order to promote idea generation and implementation, leaders are expected to delegate and adopt consultative measures instead of practicing excessive monitoring (Jong & Hartog, 2007).

The Flexible Gatekeeper

Besides relying on their personal and position power, leaders also tend to use their control over access of information to influence. This behavior is best described as a "Gatekeeper". They hold the key to the source of information and they hold the power of controlling the availability and accuracy of information—in other words, "information power" (Raven, 1965, 1992). Losing control over this "goldmine" reflects loss of information power (Gray, 2001, Kelly, 2007). Thus, leaders tend to avoid providing uncontrolled access to sources of information in order to maintain their indispensability (Gray, 2001). However, knowledge leaders may also be worried about the issue of knowledge protection. Bearing that in mind, they may want to govern the access to valuable information and ensure that this crucial information does not fall into the wrong hands.

Knowledge leaders may have good intentions in mind when controlling the access to valuable information. However, the tight control of information may be detrimental to the success of KM practices in the long run. With the proliferation of information, leaders would be buried in them and would eventually find it difficult to filter ceaseless flow of information. This would possibly cause a loss of relevant information needed by k-workers, as leaders would not be able to pay full attention to the limitless information available. Moreover, depriving k-workers of crucial information may affect the worker's ability to function effectively in generating ideas, sharing their information, and subsequently applying appropriate knowledge.

Instead of functioning as a "Gatekeeper", knowledge leaders should cultivate a scholarly network and foster network, and sharing of information needed for the development of expert intelligence (Smith & Rupp, 2002). K-workers need information about the needs, development, and tribulations within their business environment to process and create valuable knowledge (Beijerse, 1999; Beveren, 2002). Stimulating the dissemination of information among subordinates enhances idea generation (Jong & Hartog, 2007). Hence, if leaders control access to crucial information, they may be depriving their workers from necessary information needed to support knowledge creation.

Additionally, when leaders are perceived to control and hoard information, they would pave the path for k-workers to follow. K-workers would imitate this behavior portrayed by their leaders and knowledge sharing practices would be stifled. Leaders need to model the proper behavior to cultivate knowledge supporting culture within the organization (Ribiere & Sitar, 2003).

Furthermore, access to information provides k-workers a frame of reference of what knowledge should be applied and how to apply. K-workers need to keep up with the happenings in their business environment to ensure the knowledge they apply in their strategies are up-to-date and in-line with the current business conditions. When information availability is controlled, knowledge utilization could meet a dead end.

In summary, although maintaining control over who has access to important information is necessary, knowledge leaders should maintain some flexibility and allow k-workers to have easy access to information they specifically need. This would allow the k-workers themselves to source and filter all relevant information related to their area of interest. Instead of operating as a strict gatekeeper to information sources, they could employ mechanisms to facilitate easy yet protected knowledge access such as the use of passwords to allow authorized access. This brings about the leadership dimension "Flexible Gatekeeper" as an ideal behavior to be practiced by knowledge leaders in order to be perceived as effective.

The Networker

Connection with important others is the distinguishing feature of the "Networker" when compared to the other leadership aspects discussed earlier. Asllani and Luthans (2003) suggested that successful knowledge managers need to pay relatively more attention to networking and communication activities. Knowledge leaders who established connections both inside and outside the organization often have access to unattainable information and expertise which, in return, equips them with integrity and authenticity (Fedor et al., 2003; Sarin & McDermott, 2003). This facilitates knowledge creation within the organization as the leader would bring in new ideas and concept to further stimulate intellectual activities. Moreover, a leader's display of effort to source for knowledge from important others and share it with k-workers, displays a positive model of knowledge sharing to be emulated. To boot, leaders who establish and maintain connection with important people may bring in new knowledge to stimulate thinking and subsequently lead towards knowledge application. As a result, it is good for senior executives to network outside the organization and pull together groups with likely synergies (McCrimmon, 1995) to bring in new ideas and concepts needed for knowledge generation and application.

In a nutshell….

An overall observation of the above discussion seems to suggest that knowledge leaders can no longer go by rules of traditional leadership practices. Traditionally, leaders focused on the organization, and subsequently set out to mould their workers to display behavior that leans towards the achievement of organizational objectives. Now, with workers who are extremely independent, motivated, and autonomous, leaders should set out to serve their workers. The underlying belief is that when subordinates are catered for, they would naturally perform their best that results in improved organizational performance (Stone, Russell, & Patterson, 2004). As well, knowledge leaders need to seek and fulfill the needs of k-workers—feed their curiosity, stimulate their intellect, acknowledge their achievement, and supply them with all resource (e.g., networks, information). Providing k-workers with what they need will help them flourish.

WHAT NEXT ….

Knowledge leaders need to modify their approach when managing k-workers. However, there are many more unturned rocks that could provide interesting findings in future research. We have a few major concerns that we have not addressed here but strongly believe has a significant impact on the domain of this topic. First, our recommendations and suggestions are based on the generalized conception of a k-worker. It is possible that k-workers may be different among themselves on the basis of tenure, skill level, personality, relationship with leader, and so on. For example, with reference to Withey's (2003) classification of

high-moderate-low k-workers, it is possible that *high* k-workers may require different leadership behavior in comparison to *low* k-worker. Future research could determine whether knowledge leaders need to vary their style from one k-worker to another.

Second, we have not incorporated the cultural context when dealing with k-workers. There have been indications of cultural effects on the preferred leadership behavior among k-worker. For example, although hierarchy and position have been strongly advocated to be detrimental to KM practices, some researchers (e.g., Forstenlechner & Lettice, 2007; Jayasingam et al., 2008) have found that in different regional context, authority and power is needed to encourage knowledge sharing practices. Forstenlechner and Lettice (2007) also found regional differences in terms of preference for reward. It is important for future researchers to explore this grey area and identify whether cultural differences might influence the preference for behavior displayed by knowledge leaders.

CONCLUSION

Undeniably, KM has become the catchphrase for establishing competitive advantage. As much as we would like to believe that technological systems are the success factor for any KM initiative, we have been proven wrong over the years. With the technological systems as the foundation, any KM initiative needs human capital to ensure its success.

The human capital in the knowledge age is currently undergoing a metamorphosis. Commonly referred to as k-workers, this fresh breed of employees are pushing forth the need for organizational change. One area that is facing the pressure to evolve is the role of knowledge leaders. As leading k-workers require idiosyncratic practices, knowledge leaders should be prepared to embrace their new role with zest. Failure to cater to the expectations and preferences of this new generation of workers would definitely be detrimental in the long run.

We believe knowledge leaders to no longer hold their reigns too tightly. They should learn to exercise flexibility when leading k-workers. K-workers do not want to be suffocated with a leader always hovering over them with the pretext of keeping a watchful eye. After all, k-workers are confident, independent, and autonomous individuals. Instead, knowledge leaders should embrace the role as a facilitator or a knowledge coach that guides and serves their workers when deemed necessary. They should acknowledge valuable contribution and stimulate KM practices indirectly by being a good role model.

REFERENCES

Aguinis, H., Ansari, M. A., Jayasingam, S., & Aafaqi, R. (2008). Perceived entrepreneurial success and social power. *Management Research, 6*, 121–137. doi:10.2753/JMR1536-5433060204

Aguinis, H., Nesler, M. S., Quigley, B. M., Lee, S., & Tedeschi, J. T. (1996). Power bases of faculty supervisors and educational outcomes for graduate students. *The Journal of Higher Education, 67*, 267–297. doi:10.2307/2943845

Amar, A. D. (2001). Motivating knowledge workers to innovate: A model integrating motivation dynamics and antecedents. *European Journal of Innovation Management, 4*, 126–132. doi:10.1108/14601060110399289

Amar, A. D. (2002). *Managing knowledge workers: Unleashing innovation and productivity.* Westport, CT: Quorum books.

Ambrosio, J. (2000). *Knowledge management mistakes.* Retrieved November 23, 2005, from http:/ www. computerworld.com/industrytopics/ energy/story/ 0, 10801,46693,00.html

Ansari, M. A. (1990). *Managing people at work: Leadership styles and influence strategies.* Newbury Park, CA: Sage.

Ansari, M. A., Aafaqi, R., & Oh, S. H. (2008). *Social power and leader-member exchange: The impact of power distance orientation in the Malaysian business context.* Unpublished manuscript, University of Lethbridge, Canada.

Asllani, A., & Luthans, F. (2003). What knowledge managers really do: An empirical and comparative analysis. *Journal of Knowledge Management, 7*, 53–66. doi:10.1108/13673270310485622

Awad, E. M., & Ghaziri, H. M. (2004). *Knowledge management.* Upper Saddle River, NJ: Prentice Hall.

Axelson, M. (2002). Smartwear. *Australian CPA, 72*(4), 62–64.

Bachman, J. G., Smith, C. G., & Slesinger, J. A. (1966). Control, performance and satisfaction: An analysis of structural and individual effects. *Journal of Personality and Social Psychology, 4*, 127–136. doi:10.1037/h0023615

Beijerse, R. P. (1999). Questions in knowledge management: Defining and conceptualizing a phenomenon. *Journal of Knowledge Management, 3*(2), 94–109. doi:10.1108/13673279910275512

Beveren, J. V. (2002). The model of knowledge acquisition that refocuses knowledge management. *Journal of Knowledge Management, 6*(1), 18–22. doi:10.1108/13673270210417655

Bogdanowicz, M. S., & Bailey, E. K. (2002). The value of knowledge and the value of the new knowledge worker: Generation X in the new economy. *Journal of European Industrial Training, 26*, 125–129. doi:10.1108/03090590210422003

Burke, R. J., & Wilcox, D. S. (1971). Bases of supervisory power and subordinate job satisfactions. *Canadian Journal of Behavioural Science, 3*, 183–193. doi:10.1037/h0082260

Chen, L. (2004). *An examination of relationship among leadership behavior, knowledge sharing, and organizational marketing effectiveness in professional service firms that have been engaged in strategic alliances.* Unpublished doctoral dissertation, Nova Southeastern University (Proquest Digital Dissertation Abstract, 3125998, 303).

Chong, S. C. (2006a). KM implementation and its influence on performance: An empirical evidence from Malaysian multimedia super corridor (MSC) companies. *Journal of Information and Knowledge Management, 5*(1), 21–37. doi:10.1142/S0219649206001293

Chong, S. C. (2006b). KM critical success factors: A comparison of perceived importance vs implementation in Malaysian ICT companies. *The Learning Organization, 13*(3), 230–256. doi:10.1108/09696470610661108

Connelly, C. E., & Kelloway, E. K. (2003). Predictors of employee's perception of knowledge sharing cultures. *Leadership and Organization Development Journal, 24*(5), 294–301. doi:10.1108/01437730310485815

Crawford, C. B. (2005). Effects of transformational leadership and organizational position on knowledge management. *Journal of Knowledge Management, 9*(6), 6–16. doi:10.1108/13673270510629927

Darroch, J. (2003). Developing a measure of knowledge management behaviors and practices. *Journal of Knowledge Management, 7,* 41–54. doi:10.1108/13673270310505377

Davenport, T. H. (1999). *Human capital: What it is and why people invest it.* San Francisco, CA: Jossey-Bass.

Davenport, T. H., & Prusak, L. (2000). *Working knowledge.* Cambridge, MA: Harvard Business School Press.

De Long, D. W., & Fahey, L. (2000). Diagnosing cultural barriers to knowledge management. *The Academy of Management Executive, 14*(4), 113–129.

Dfouni, M. (2002). *Knowledge leaders' critical issues: An international Delphi studies.* Unpublished master's thesis, Concordia University, Montreal, Canada (Proquest Digital Dissertation Abstract, MQ77669, 211).

Drucker, P. F. (1959). *Landmarks of tomorrow.* New York: Harper.

Elangovan, A. R., & Jia, L. X. (2000). Effects of perceived power of supervisor on subordinate work attitudes. *Leadership and Organization Development Journal, 21,* 319–328. doi:10.1108/01437730010343095

Erchul, W. P., Raven, B. H., & Ray, A. G. (2001). School psychologists' perceptions of social power bases in teacher consultation. *Journal of Educational & Psychological Consultation, 12,* 1–23. doi:10.1207/S1532768XJEPC1201_01

Fedor, D. B., Ghosh, S., Caldwell, S. D., Maurer, T. J., & Singhal, V. R. (2003). The effects of knowledge management on team members' rating of project success and impact. *Decision Sciences, 34,* 513–539. doi:10.1111/j.1540-5414.2003.02395.x

Forstenlechner, I., & Lettice, F. (2007). Cultural difference in motivating global knowledge workers. *Equal Opportunities International, 26*(8), 823–833. doi:10.1108/02610150710836154

Gal, Y. (2004). The reward effect: A case study of failing to manage knowledge. *Journal of Knowledge Management, 8*(2), 73–83. doi:10.1108/13673270410529127

Gapp, R. (2002). The influence the system of profound knowledge has on the development of leadership and management within an organization. *Managerial Auditing Journal, 17*(6), 338–342. doi:10.1108/02686900210434131

Gray, P. H. (2001). The impact of knowledge repositories on power and control in the workplace. *Information Technology & People, 14*(4), 368–384. doi:10.1108/09593840110411167

Hinkin, T. R., & Schriesheim, C. A. (1989). Development and application of new scales to measure the French and Raven (1959) bases of social power. *The Journal of Applied Psychology, 74*, 561–567. doi:10.1037/0021-9010.74.4.561

Hislop, D. (2003). Linking human resource management and knowledge management via commitment. *Employee Relations, 25*(2), 182–202. doi:10.1108/01425450310456479

Ivancevich, J. M., & Donnely, J. H. (1970). Leader influence and performance. *Personnel Psychology, 23*, 539–549. doi:10.1111/j.1744-6570.1970.tb01371.x

Janz, B. D., & Prasarnphanich, P. (2003). Understanding the antecedents of effective knowledge management: The importance of knowledge-centered culture. *Decision Sciences, 34*(2), 351–384. doi:10.1111/1540-5915.02328

Jayasingam, S. (2001). *Entrepreneurial success, gender, and bases of power.* Unpublished master's thesis, Penang, University Science Malaysia.

Jayasingam, S., Jantan, M., & Ansari, M. A. (2008). Influencing knowledge workers: The power of top management. In *Proceedings of the Knowledge Management International Conference 2008 (KMICE '08)*, Langkawi, Malaysia.

Jong, J. P. J., & Hartog, D. N. D. (2007). How leaders influence employee's innovative behavior. *European Journal of Innovation Management, 10*(1), 41–64. doi:10.1108/14601060710720546

Karlinzing, W., & Patrick, J. (2002). Tap into the power of knowledge collaboration. *Customer Interaction Solutions, 20*(11), 22–26.

Kelley, L. L., Blackman, D. A., & Hurst, J. P. (2007). An exploration of the relationship between learning organizations and the retention of knowledge workers. *The Learning Organization, 14*(3), 204–221. doi:10.1108/09696470710739390

Kelly, C. (2007). Managing the relationship between knowledge and power in organizations. *Aslib Proceedings: New Information Perspectives, 59*(2), 125–138.

Kubo, I., & Saka, A. (2002). An inquiry into the motivations of knowledge workers in the Japanese financial industry. *Journal of Knowledge Management, 6*(3), 262–271. doi:10.1108/13673270210434368

Lam, W., & Chua, A. (2005). The mismanagement of knowledge management. *Aslib Proceedings: New Information Perspective, 57*(5), 424–433.

Lang, J. C. (2001). Managerial concerns in knowledge management. *Journal of Knowledge Management, 5*(1), 43–57. doi:10.1108/13673270110384392

Lin, C., & Tseng, S. (2005). The implementation gaps for the knowledge management systems. *Industrial Management & Data Systems, 105*(2), 208–222. doi:10.1108/02635570510583334

Lucier, C. (2003). When knowledge adds up to nothing: Why knowledge management fails and what you can do about it. *Development and Learning in Organizations, 17*(1), 32–35. doi:10.1108/14777280310795739

Macneil, C. M. (2003). Line managers: Facilitators of knowledge sharing in teams. *Employee Relations, 25*(3), 294–307. doi:10.1108/01425450310475874

Malhotra, Y. (2001). *It is time to cultivate growth.* Retrieved May 5, 2008, from http://www.brint.net/members/01060524/britishtelecom.pdf

Malhotra, Y. (2002). Why knowledge management systems fail? Enablers and constraints of knowledge management in human enterprises. In C. W. Holsapple (Ed.), *Handbook on knowledge management 1: Knowledge matters* (pp. 577-599). Heidelberg, Germany: Springer-Verlag.

McCrimmon, M. (1995). Bottom-up leadership. *Executive Development*, *8*(5), 6–12. doi:10.1108/09533239510093215

Ming Yu, C. (2002). Socializing knowledge management: The influence of the opinion leader. *Journal of Knowledge Management Practice, 3*, 76–83.

Nonaka, I. (1994). A dynamic theory of organizational knowledge creation. *Organization Science, 5*, 14–38. doi:10.1287/orsc.5.1.14

O'Regan, N., & Ghobadian, A. (2004). Testing the homogeneity of SMEs: The impact of size on managerial and organizational processes. *European Business Review, 16*(1), 64–79. doi:10.1108/09555340410512411

Pearce, C. L., Sims, H. P., Cox, J. F., Ball, G., Schnell, E., Smith, K. A., & Trevino, L. (2003). Transactors, transformers and beyond: A multimethod development of theoretical typology of leadership. *Journal of Management Development, 22*, 273–307. doi:10.1108/02621710310467587

Politis, J. D. (2001). The relationship of various leadership styles to knowledge management. *Leadership and Organization Development Journal, 22*(8), 354–364. doi:10.1108/01437730110410071

Politis, J. D. (2002). Transformational and transactional leadership enabling (disabling) knowledge acquisition of self-managed teams: The consequences for performance. *Leadership and Organization Development Journal, 23*(4), 186–197. doi:10.1108/01437730210429052

Politis, J. D. (2005). The influence of managerial power and credibility on knowledge acquisition attributest. *Leadership and Organization Development Journal, 26*(3), 197–214. doi:10.1108/01437730510591752

Rahim, M. A. (1989). Relationships of leader power to compliance and satisfaction with supervision: Evidence from a national sample of managers. *Journal of Management, 15*, 545–556. doi:10.1177/014920638901500404

Raven, B. H. (1965). Social influence and power. In I. D. Steiner & M. Fishbein (Eds.), *Current studies in social psychology* (pp. 371-382). New York: Holt, Rinehart, Winston.

Raven, B. H. (1992). A power/interaction model of interpersonal influence: French and Raven thirty years later. *Journal of Social Behavior and Personality, 7*, 217–244.

Ribiere, V. M., & Sitar, A. S. (2003). Critical role of leadership in nurturing a knowledge-supporting culture. *Knowledge Management Research and Practice, 1*, 39–48. doi:10.1057/palgrave.kmrp.8500004

Riege, A. (2007). Actions to overcome knowledge transfer barriers in MNCs. *Journal of Knowledge Management, 11*(1), 48–67. doi:10.1108/13673270710728231

Sarin, S., & McDermott, C. (2003). The effect of team leader characteristics on learning, knowledge application and performance of cross functional new product development teams. *Decision Sciences, 34*(4), 707–740. doi:10.1111/j.1540-5414.2003.02350.x

Schriesheim, C. A., Hinkin, T. R., & Podsakoff, P. M. (1991). Can ipsative and single-item measures produce erroneous results in field studies of French and Raven's (1959) five bases of power? An empirical investigation. *The Journal of Applied Psychology, 76*, 106–114. doi:10.1037/0021-9010.76.1.106

Scott, P. B. (2005). Knowledge workers: Social, task, and semantic network analysis. *Corporate Communications: An International Journal, 10*(3), 257–277. doi:10.1108/13563280510614519

Skyrme, D. (1997). *Knowledge management: Making sense of an oxymoron.* Retrieved July 5, 2005, from http://www.skyrme.com/insights/22km.htm

Smith, G., Blackman, D., & Good, B. (2003). Knowledge sharing and organizational learning: The impact of social architecture at ordnance survey. *Journal of Information and Knowledge Management Practice, 4.* Retrieved December 20, 2004, from http://www.tlainc.com/articl50.htm

Smith, G., & Rupp, W. T. (2002). Communication and loyalty among knowledge workers: A resource of the firm theory view. *Journal of Knowledge, 6*(3), 250–261. doi:10.1108/13673270210434359

Smith, G., & Rupp, W. T. (2003). Knowledge workers: Exploring the link among performance rating, pay, and motivational aspects. *Journal of Knowledge, 7*(1), 107–124. doi:10.1108/13673270310463662

Spira, J. B. (2005). *In praise of knowledge workers.* Retrieved April 23, 2008, from http://www.kmworld.com/Articles/ReadArticle.aspx?ArticleID=9605

Stone, A. G., Russell, R. F., & Paterson, K. (2004). Transformational versus servant leadership: A difference in leader focus. *Leadership and Organization Development Journal, 25*(4), 349–361. doi:10.1108/01437730410538671

Syed-Ikhsan, S. O. S., & Rowland, F. (2004). Benchmarking knowledge management in a public organization in Malaysia. *Benchmarking: An International Journal, 11*(3), 238–266. doi:10.1108/14635770410538745

Talisayon, D. (2002). Knowledge and people. *Business World,* p. 1.

Un, C. A., & Cuervo-Cazurra, A. (2004). Strategies for knowledge creation in firms. *British Journal of Management, 15,* 27–41. doi:10.1111/j.1467-8551.2004.00404.x

Viitala, R. (2004). Towards knowledge leadership. *Leadership and Organization Development Journal, 25*(6), 528–544. doi:10.1108/01437730410556761

Ware, J. P., & Grantham, C. E. (2007). Knowledge work and knowledge workers. Retrieved April 24, 2008, from http://www.thefutureofwork.net/assets/Knowledge_Work_and_ Knowledge_Workers.pdf

Withey, M. J. (2003). Development of scale to measure knowledge work. *International Journal of Knowledge, Culture, and Change Management, 3.* Retrieved April 24, 2007, from http://www.management.journal.com

Yukl, G. (2006). *Leadership in organizations.* Upper Saddle River, NJ: Prentice Hall.

Yukl, G. A., & Falbe, C. (1991). Importance of different power sources in downward and lateral relations. *The Journal of Applied Psychology, 76,* 416–423. doi:10.1037/0021-9010.76.3.416

ENDNOTE

[1]	Expert power and information power are related but distinct constructs. Expert power refers to the knowledge leader's personal knowledge and skills, whereas information power refers to the knowledge leader's ability to secure accurate information (Aguinis et al., 2008).

Chapter 4
Governance and Leadership of Knowledge Management

Andreas Schroeder
Victoria University of Wellington, New Zealand

David Pauleen
Victoria University of Wellington, New Zealand

Sid Huff
Victoria University of Wellington, New Zealand

ABSTRACT

This chapter introduces a framework for analyzing governance arrangements of KM programs. The framework is used to analyze the organizational structures, processes and relational mechanisms, including leadership matters, which guide the KM program of a large European corporation. The analysis focuses on the issues KM leaders and staff encounter in defining their KM position in the organization as well as issues regarding their collaboration with each other. The results of the study highlight the impact that various factors exert on the development of the KM governance configuration and the role of the KM leader. The chapter concludes with recommendations detailing important governance and leadership aspects which contribute to the establishment of KM in the organization.

INTRODUCTION

The importance of knowledge as a core strategic resource for organizations has been widely recognized (Davenport & Prusak, 1998; Nonaka, 1994). While organizations have traditionally focused on resources such as labor, land and capital, knowledge as a critical resource has increasingly received the attention of organizations and their decision makers. Drucker (1993) states that "we

are entering the knowledge society in which the basic economic resource is knowledge and where knowledge workers will play a central role" (p. 7). Knowledge is driving innovation and organizations are competing with knowledge and knowledge intensive products in this emerging knowledge based economy. Drucker, together with a range of other management researchers (e.g. Liebeskind, 1996) concludes that knowledge is the most important asset that a firm possesses.

DOI: 10.4018/978-1-60566-958-8.ch004

This recognition of knowledge as an important basis for organizational success has encouraged firms to focus on appropriate ways for its management. Knowledge management (KM) has emerged as a field which focuses on the management of diverse knowledge resources and knowledge processes in an organizational context. The KM field focuses on tools and concepts from established disciplines which address various knowledge processes (Raub & Rüling, 2001). KM seeks to strategically integrate these diverse elements to support knowledge creation and knowledge sharing in organizations. Stimulated by the well-publicized benefits of KM, many organizations have started to actively engage in KM activities. Recent data shows, for example, that 24 percent of Fortune 500 companies have created the role of Chief Knowledge Officer (CKO), and 80 percent have formalized their KM activities through the development of a KM strategy (Holden, 2004).

Though a large number of organizations have adopted KM programs, a considerable number of these programs do not provide the expected benefits to the organizations. Fluss (2002) observes that KM programs and individual initiatives have a high rate of failure, and Chua and Lam (2005) even state that: "KM projects attract an alarmingly high level of risk" (pg. 15). While the importance of managing knowledge and the potential of the KM field are widely recognized, organizations often struggle to establish and maintain successful KM programs. Research has identified a range of factors which contribute to the failure of KM programs. Among the main reasons for these failures are a lack of business integration and alignment, a lack of clear strategic objectives, unclear distribution of authority and user involvement as well as a lack of top management and leadership support (Chua & Lam, 2005; Riege, 2005; Storey & Barnett, 2000). Often, KM programs do not meet the requirements of the business and fail to attract attention and support from senior management. While KM programs focus on integrating and coordinating tools and initiatives across the

organization, often the decision making authority for these efforts has not been clarified.

In related disciplines, a lack of business integration and unclear allocation of responsibilities are considered symptoms of inappropriate governance arrangements (A. E. Brown & Grant, 2005). Governance arrangements describe the structures, processes and mechanisms through which responsibilities are allocated and strategic decisions are made. In the IT domain, sophisticated governance arrangements are attributed to improved business-IT alignment and the creation of significantly higher returns on IT investment (Weill, 2004). It has been shown that a focus on IT governance has significantly improved IT performance in organizations (Van Grembergen, 2004). Despite the value of governance research in related disciplines, little research has been conducted which focuses on governance in a KM context. Very few studies focus on the governance of KM programs and investigate the diversity of arrangements which guide the development of KM programs. This chapter addresses this lack of governance research which has been identified as a critical gap in the knowledge management literature.

The following sections identify the core aspects of knowledge management and describe the governance concept. A KM governance framework is then introduced which outlines the diversity of governance configurations which have emerged in organizational KM programs of organizations. Next, a case organization is introduced and its KM governance configuration is analyzed and discussed. The chapter concludes by highlighting some of the important governance related considerations, including the role of leadership, when establishing a KM program.

KM AND ITS GOVERNANCE

KM has emerged as a field which focuses on the management of the diverse knowledge resources and knowledge processes in an organizational context. One of the most prominent definitions of KM is provided by Wiig (2000) who defines KM as "the systematic, explicit, and deliberate building, renewal, and application of knowledge to maximize an enterprise's knowledge-related effectiveness and returns from its knowledge assets" (p.6). Hence, KM integrates a series of explicit organizational initiatives such as the implementation of electronic repositories or the establishment of communities of practice among staff members to systematically address and support the different knowledge processes in the organization.

Organizations have established different approaches to do KM. Hansen et al (1999) have identified two distinct KM approaches: the codification approach and the personalization approach. A codification approach describes a KM program which emphasizes the externalization, dissemination and storage of knowledge. Organizations which adopt this approach focus on the creation of knowledge assets and on making these knowledge assets available for reuse throughout the organization. This KM approach is also termed a people-to-document approach since it is characterized by a reliance on information technology through which codified knowledge assets can be stored, indexed and made available throughout the organization (Desouza, Jayaramam, & Evaristo, 2002). The goal of this approach is to connect people with reusable codified knowledge through the use of IT tools. A personalization approach, on the other hand, describes a KM program which focuses on linking people together to encourage the sharing of tacit knowledge and the creation of new knowledge through interactive discourse (Hansen et al., 1999). The personalization approach, which is also termed a people-to-people approach, is characterized by moderate IT investments and a focus on initiatives such as the development of communities of practices to encourage the exchange of knowledge between staff (Binney, 2001). Technical tools are mostly used for communication purposes, and employees are explicitly rewarded for mentoring and direct knowledge sharing activities.

The cross-disciplinary nature of KM is one of the reasons why the approaches taken to do KM by different organizations are so diverse. In order to support various knowledge processes, KM borrows from a wide range of organizational disciplines, including Information Systems, Human Resources and Quality Management (Nordin, Pauleen, & Gorman, 2009fc; Raub & Rüling, 2001). This interdisciplinary character of KM poses practical implementation challenges for organizations. Among the main concerns are questions such as: where does KM fit into the organizational structure, and how should the initiatives be controlled and guided in order to create the expected benefits for the organization? A governance perspective helps to address these questions.

In the IT domain governance is generally defined as "the distribution of … decision-making rights, and responsibilities among enterprise stakeholders, and the procedures and mechanisms for making and monitoring strategic decisions" (Peterson, 2004, p.8). It is a thoroughly studied phenomenon in the IT domain and since the IT discipline constitutes one of the major contributing disciplines of the KM domain (Kim, Yu, & Lee, 2003; Nordin et al., 2009fc) it is used here to conceptualize the governance phenomenon in a KM context.

IT based research generally focuses on three perspectives to conceptualize the governance phenomenon: the formal governance structures, the formal governance processes and the informal relational mechanisms which play a role in guiding and directing the IT program (Peterson, 2004). The majority of these IT based studies focus on the investigation of formal IT governance arrangements, in particular on the centralization or decentralization of the IT governance structures (Sambamurthy & Zmud, 1999). Governance processes have been a focus of a range of maturity models which distinguish between different levels of formalization for strategy development and

Table 1. KM governance framework (adapted from Schroeder et al, 2007)

Structural aspects	Specific variations of the structural aspects of KM governance
Distribution of KM authority	Centralised, Federal, Decentralised
Reporting point of KM	Support function, Business function
Form of KM organization	Standing organization, Hybrid organization, Community based organization
KM governance groups	Internal director group, Focus group, Customer group, No governance group
Process aspects	**Specific variations of the procedural aspects of KM governance**
KM strategy development	Formal process, Informal process, No strategy
Planning and decision making	Internally focused, Externally focused
Reporting and monitoring	Advanced reporting, Basic reporting, No reporting
Funding	Fixed budget, Project based budget, No budget
Relational aspects	**Specific variations of the relational aspects of KM governance**
KM: Top management	Personal network KM leader, KM sponsor
KM: Business	Physical co-location, Account management structure, Staff transfer schemes, Frequent operational interaction, Personal network of the KM leader
KM: Support function	Physical co-location, Liaison roles, Staff transfer, Communities of practice, Personal network of the KM leader, Integration of the KM leader in other initiatives

decision making arrangements (Luftman, 2003). The relational mechanisms have received less attention in IT governance research even though it has been recognized that these informal discussions and alliances play a significant role in the formulation of the organizational IT direction (C. V. Brown, 1999).

The KM Governance Framework

Elsewhere, we have defined KM governance as *the structures, processes and relational mechanisms established to steer, coordinate and control explicit and deliberate knowledge management initiatives in an organization* (Schroeder, Pauleen, & Huff, 2007). In order to establish a systematic way of analyzing governance configurations in the KM domain, we have devised a KM governance framework (table 1). Based on established governance theory from related domains this KM governance framework focuses on the structures, processes and relational mechanisms, which contribute to the control and guiding of the KM program in organizations.

The KM governance structure defines the formal roles and positions through which KM programs are developed and guided in organizations. The framework considers four structural aspects to characterize the KM governance structure of an organization: 1) the 'distribution of KM authority' characterizes the division of KM decision making rights in the organization and distinguishes between centralized, decentralized and federal structures; 2) the 'reporting point of KM' focuses on the location of KM in the organization and differentiates between KM functions which are associated with support functions or operational business functions; 3) the 'form of the KM group,' describes the way in which the KM responsibilities are institutionalized in the case organization as either full-time KM functions or community based part time KM roles; 4) the fourth and final structural aspect refers to the establishment and form of 'KM governance committees'.

In addition to these four structural aspects, four process aspects describe the formal mechanisms and procedures through which the KM programs are guided: 1) the 'KM strategy development' focuses on the existence of an explicit strategy for the KM program and the level of formality used for its development; 2) 'KM planning & decision making' describes the activities through which individual KM initiatives are selected and prioritized and includes the extent to which non-KM staff are involved in these processes; 3) 'reporting & monitoring' identifies the mechanisms through which the KM organization gives account to its respective reporting points characterized by its level of sophistication; 4) 'KM funding & budget allocation' describes the arrangements through which resources for KM projects and services are acquired focusing on the source of the funds as well as the mechanisms through which these funds are obtained.

The third aspect of the KM governance framework focuses on the relational KM governance mechanisms. Relational governance includes mechanisms outside the formal structures and processes, especially the KM leadership, which contribute to the development of the KM program and its integration with the rest of the organization. Three levels of strategic relationships are considered: 1) 'relational mechanisms between KM and top management' focuses on the informal ways through which senior management guides the development of the KM program. Mechanisms which contribute to this informal governance include personal relationships between the KM leader(s) and senior management as well as the KM sponsor at the top of the organization. 2) 'relational mechanisms between KM and the business' comprises the informal arrangements through which representatives from the business side of the organizations contribute to guiding the development of the KM program. Among the mechanisms which are considered, are physical co-location, account management structure and staff transfer schemes among others. Finally, 3) 'relational mechanisms between KM and support functions' include the arrangements through which representatives from the other support functions contribute to guiding and developing of the KM program. Mechanisms

which are considered include collocation of KM staff and personal network of the KM leader.

This KM governance framework accounts for the diversity of mechanisms which help to control and guide the development of the KM program in an organization. It serves as the basis for the systematic analysis and categorization of the KM governance configurations of the case organization subsequently described in this chapter.

THE ORGANIZATION

The case organization is a large European provider of technology services. The core business of the organization focuses on the provision of a wide range of traditional as well as new and innovative technology services to private and corporate customers. The organization is very diverse with some parts focusing on providing reliable and efficient services, while other parts are focused on developing innovative new products and services for its customers. In the last years the organization has acquired a number of subsidiaries within Europe and internationally.

Together with its subsidiaries the organization includes more than 80,000 staff and has a turnover of more than US$30 billion. The organization has a divisional structure with three major business groups each focusing on the provision of a particular range of technology services. The three business groups, are headed by a corporate headquarters which focuses on the overall strategy and the integration of the different services. The business groups have developed into fairly self-contained entities with their own headquarters and support functions. In the last decade the relationship between corporate headquarters and the individual business groups has repeatedly been reconfigured, shifting between forms of centralization and decentralization. These reconfigurations created a number of substantial organizational restructurings over the last several years.

The culture of the organization is described

Figure 1. Timeline of KM programs

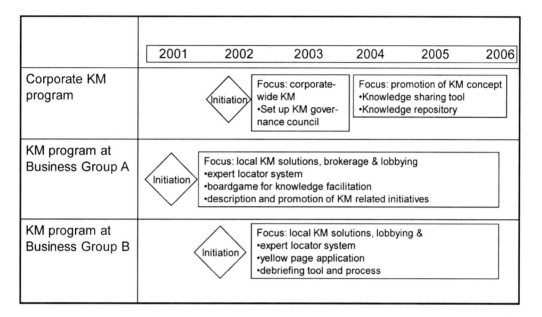

as extremely diverse. This diversity is attributed to the variety of services provided and each business unit's independence. Some parts of the organization are described as having start-up characteristics with largely team-based working environments, while other parts are portrayed as highly hierarchical bureaucracies with a strong emphasis on line management. As a whole, the organization is described as highly political with complex relationships and frequent power struggles among stakeholders. A reported lack of trust amongst the different divisions is linked to overlaps in service portfolios and competition between the business groups.

KM programs at the case organization were launched between 2001 and 2002 at two levels of the organization: at corporate headquarters as well as in two of the three business groups (see Figure 1).

KM at Corporate Headquarters

The KM program at corporate headquarters was officially launched in 2002 by the senior man-

agement board. It was the initial objective to develop an organization-wide KM program. An organization-wide KM governance framework would identify roles, specify decision making mechanisms, and synchronize and direct KM activities throughout the organization. The development and implementation of generic KM tools and KM related infrastructure was also part of the initial KM concept. The CIO championed the KM program as an opportunity to officially assign KM responsibility to somebody other than the IT department. The situation was described by a corporate KM staff member:

"The CIO was happy that KM was properly allocated in the organization and that they [the IT department] were not the only ones responsible for the related tools and practices."

The five staff of the KM function were mostly recruited internally. The KM staff had a wide variety of organizational and technical backgrounds. The KM leader of the group was an experienced manager with a background in quality management and a considerable history in the organization. The KM function was allocated to the internal consulting group, alongside other functions, such as business process, e-business and project management.

One of the first tasks of the corporate KM program was the establishment of a KM governance council to bring together stakeholders of KM related activities and interested decision makers throughout the organization. The objective of the governance council was to identify a common goal among stakeholders and achieve consensus regarding the organization-wide KM program. However, the KM governance council ran into difficulties due to incompatible KM perspectives and was abandoned within the first year. Since no collaboration could be established and no support from the business groups could be obtained, the objective of the corporate KM program was subsequently changed. Instead of aiming for an organization-wide approach, the corporate KM program turned to providing KM consulting services. The new focus was to provide support and expertise for individual projects in different parts of the organization, in order to ultimately promote the KM concept to the wider organization.

Through the consulting based KM approach, the corporate KM function became involved in a number of projects throughout the organization. Among these projects was the development of a knowledge sharing tool for a widely distributed working team and a knowledge repository to consolidate the administration of a range of complex contracts as well as a large knowledge repository for the entire in-house consulting function. These particular projects were not only selected to help individual parts of the business, but also to create a portfolio of reference KM projects to further promote the KM concept in the organization, and to increase awareness and understanding of potential KM activities.

KM at Business Group A

The KM program at Business Group A was initiated in 2001 by the HR director of the business group. It was part of a wider restructuring of the HR department. The initial objective for the KM program was to develop capacity for KM and to integrate KM aspects into other organizational initiatives. The KM program was not set up to address an immediate or particular issue in the organization.

The KM group consisted of five staff who were mostly appointed from within the HR department and who predominantly came from a non-technical background. The KM function was led by a dual leadership team: an administrative manager and a subject matter manager. The administrative manager had been in the organization for more than 10 years where he has held different management positions within the HR department. The subject matter manager had been a KM consultant who previously held contracts as a staff trainer in other parts of the organization.

The KM function formed part of the HR department which is a headquarters support function of the business group. The KM function was positioned alongside functions such as change management and the organizational culture group. The KM leader reported to the HR director through another management level. In addition to this reporting relationship, a wider group of delegates was established to assist the development of the KM program. During an initial review of KM related activities within the business group, the KM function identified a number of staff and stakeholders who were interested in the potential of KM tools and practices. This group of around 25 staff and stakeholders were brought together on a regular basis. They acted as a sounding board for the KM program and reviewed and discussed the planned initiatives. Members of the group also forwarded interesting project opportunities to the KM function. However, no explicit KM strategy was established to define the goals and overall objectives of the KM program. The subject matter manager reported: *"The only comment from above was, that the general direction is correct".*

The KM program at Business Group A was mainly focused on the provision of localized KM solutions. The provision of localized KM solutions referred to projects such as the development of an expert locator systems or the development of a board game to help facilitate knowledge sharing among call centre staff. All KM projects were conceptualized as pilot projects and an emphasis was put on developing a solution which could easily be adopted by other parts of the business group. The KM function also focused on identifying good KM practices in the organization which were publicized on the intranet in order to encourage wider adoption of these KM practices in the business group. The KM program was solely focused on addressing issues within its host business group and did not integrate with other parts of the organization.

KM at Business Group B

As with Business Group A, the KM program at Business Group B was initiated as part of a restructuring of the HR department in 2002. The KM function was formed as part of an intellectual capital group, which also included change management and performance management functions. Due to budget cuts, only the KM and change management functions were established.

The KM function consisted of two staff, the KM leader and one assistant. The KM leader had been with the wider organization for a number of years, and had a background in intranet development and web design. Due to the financial difficulties which the organization had experienced in the previous years, the KM function had only a small operational budget. The lack of funds prevented the KM function from growing to the initially intended size.

The KM leader reported to the manager of the intellectual capital group and had two reporting

levels between him and the senior management board. It was pointed out by the KM leader that his superiors had little interest and understanding of the objectives of the KM program and that he also received little top management support for its development. Similar to the other business group, the KM leader had also sought to establish a KM advisory board which would review the KM program and contribute to its individual initiatives. However, the development of this group proved to be difficult due to the large international distribution of the business group. No operating group of KM representatives was established.

Like the other business group, the KM program at Business Group B focused on establishing localized projects in the form of pilot projects which could subsequently be replicated in other parts of the organization. Among these pilot projects were the conceptualization of a business intelligence search engine and the development of an expert locator application. In addition to these projects, the KM leader was also integrated into a range of other projects to provide KM related advice. The KM program at Business Group B was limited to its particular business group and did not integrate with other parts of the organization.

THE KM GOVERNANCE CONFIGURATION OF THE ORGANIZATION

In this section the KM governance configuration of the case organization is systematically analyzed. The analysis is based on the KM governance framework discussed earlier and focuses on the structures, processes and relational mechanisms (see table 2).

KM Governance Structure

The KM governance structure of the organization is identified by a diversity of formal roles and positions. Overall, the distribution of the KM

Table 2. KM governance categorization of the case organization

Structural aspects	Specific variations of the structural aspects of KM governance
Distribution of KM authority	Federal KM
Reporting point of KM	Headquarter support function (HR & inhouse consulting)
Form of KM organization	Standing KM function
KM governance groups	Focus group (Business Group A) No governance group (Corporate Group, Business Group B)

governance authority can be characterized as having a federal structure. A corporate KM function was established with the goal to coordinate the different KM projects in the organization. In addition KM functions in two of the three business groups were established, which only focused on the KM programs and projects of their respective business unit. Interestingly, all of the three KM groups were allocated with support functions as the corporate KM function is part of the in-house consulting group while both divisional KM functions are part of the HR department. The KM groups were established as standing functions while the entire KM staff of the organization was full-time allocated to the KM program. Furthermore, formal governance groups were established to assist the development of the KM program, but only for one of the KM functions: while the KM group at Business Group A had established a KM governance committee, both the corporate KM group and the KM group at Business Group B tried to establish a governance group but failed.

Following the established governance literature, the distribution of authority can be considered to be the most prominent characteristic of an organizational governance structure (C. Brown, 1997). In the IT domain, federal governance structures are often highlighted for their potential to provide the organizational initiative with a central focus while also providing opportunities for local variations to cater for particular needs of the individual business groups (Sambamurthy & Zmud, 1999). Unfortunately, no such benefits were reported for the case organization, which may be due to the

fact that the federal structure was the result of an unsuccessful attempt to centralize the KM program. At the time the corporate KM function was charged with the task of integrating the distributed KM program, the entire organization started to further decentralize giving the KM functions in the business group the necessary political power to resist the centralization attempts, as reported by the corporate KM leader:

"The individual business division obtained such power that they did not allow headquarters to dominate their programs. [...] During this time there were a lot of central projects which did not get buy-in."

Similar scenarios in which a change in organizational power impacted the development of governance structures, were reported in the IT governance literature by Brown and Magill (1994). Hence, the KM based observation here confirms with findings from the IT domain, which have identified that governance structures generally tend to mirror organizational structures (A. E. Brown & Grant, 2005; C. Brown & Magill, 1994; Ein-Dor & Segev, 1982; Sambamurthy & Zmud, 1999; Tavakolian, 1989). Arrangements which run counter to this principle face resistance.

KM Governance Processes

Governance processes identify the formal mechanisms and procedures through which organizational initiatives are guided in their development.

The case organization exhibits only a small number of formal governance structures. None of the KM groups developed a formalized strategy for the direction of their overall KM program, and decisions about the actual KM projects were mostly done internally with little outside stakeholder involvement. The reporting and monitoring was limited to simple standard reporting processes focusing on project progress reports and justification of the resource consumption. With regards to the funding & budget allocation process, differences between the three KM functions can be identified. The corporate KM group and the KM group at Business Group A obtained an ongoing budget from which the operational costs and most projects were funded. Hence, it can be described as General KM budget. The KM group at Business Group B did not have access to such a budget for KM projects and services and required the beneficiaries of the KM projects to provide direct funding.

The formalization level of governance processes is a critical question in most governance research, and maturity models have been established which clearly identify and rank the sophistication of the governance configurations. The IT Governance Institute (2003) provides a particularly prominent model which conceptualizes governance maturity along five levels: informal, adhoc, repeatable, defined and managed. By applying this maturity model to the KM governance situations of the case organization, an overall low level of governance sophistication can be observed. Considering that for the entire organization no KM strategy was established and no external stakeholders were involved in the decision making the level of the overall governance maturity can only be considered as 'adhoc': the development of the program was largely based on the initiative of the KM function itself.

To observe such a low sophistication of the governance processes in such a large organization is a surprise. Organizational research has identified that large organizations in general tend to develop more formalized governance processes (Miller, 1987). Research in the IT domain has also identified that large organizations have more formalized planning practices (Doll & Torkzadeh, 1987). However, differences between KM and IT also seem to impact the sophistication of the formal governance processes employed. Since KM programs require considerably less investment than IT programs, a lower formalization level may be appropriate for governing the KM program. Another explanation for the lower sophistication of governance processes is the lower level of urgency for KM programs and their individual initiatives. A considerable number of IT systems in organizations are mission critical while most KM tools and initiatives do not have such an immediate impact on the organization. The low sophistication level of the KM governance processes encountered here is likely to be a combination of these factors.

KM Governance Relational Mechanisms

Relational KM governance mechanisms focus on the informal (or less formal) structures and processes which guide the development of a KM program. In the case organization it was observed that the informal relationships between both KM and the top management as well as KM and the business side were limited. The interactions between all three KM functions and the business side or top management were only based on formal interactions. Informal relationships were only identified between the KM functions and the other support functions as all three KM functions in the organization have reported strong relational ties and frequent interactions with other support functions

In particular, representatives of the KM functions identified the lack of informal relationships between KM and the business as a considerable disadvantage, and they reported difficulties identifying potential users of their projects in the business. This lack of informal relationships can partially be explained by the particular project based KM approach the case organization had adopted. In all three cases the interaction between business and KM function was focused around individual projects. The corporate KM function was either directly approached by the business to help with a particular problem or the wider in-house consulting group handed over a business request to the corporate KM function. However, no regular interaction between corporate KM and the business took place beyond the project level. The interaction of both business group level KM functions was also limited to individual projects that were mostly pro-actively identified by the KM leaders. Hence, no ongoing collaboration was established which would have created an understanding of the requirements businesses had, and the projects and services the KM program could offer. This situation had led to cases in which KM tools were developed that did not address explicit requests from the business and significant efforts had to be made by the KM function to launch and pilot them.

While the interactions with the business side were fairly limited, all three KM functions were in ongoing communication with other support functions. The corporate KM function frequently collaborated with other parts of the in-house consulting group, where they were integrated into projects, or projects were passed on to them through this network. The KM function at Business Group A collaborated with other HR support functions, and the KM leader sat on a number of steering committees. The KM leader at Business Group B reported that he extensively collaborated with the change management group, which shared the same reporting point as the KM function. All of the participants described these interactions as very important means for project collaboration and project acquisition. However, it remained an ongoing challenge to also engage the parts of the organization which did not share the same reporting point in the overall governance structure.

THE QUESTIONS UNDERLYING KM GOVERNANCE

KM governance describes the mechanisms which control and guide the organizational KM program. Control and guidance include formal governance structures and processes, as well as informal relational mechanism. However, these different governance aspects are not necessarily independent from each other. By considering the relationship and dependencies of these KM governance mechanisms, a number of questions emerge:

- Where should KM be located in the organization?
- Should KM governance be formalized?
- What is the role of the KM leader?

Each of these questions is briefly addressed below.

Where should KM be Located in the Organization?

The analysis has shown that all three KM functions were associated with support functions which were related to the headquarters of the respective business parts of the organization. The literature has identified that KM functions are either allocated to business functions or support functions such as HR or IT (Maier, 2002). It could be assumed that the association with a particular function also determines the development of the KM program, for example, an association with an HR function leads to the establishment of an people-oriented KM program while an association with the IT function leads to the development of a technical oriented KM program. Surprisingly, this was not the case in this organization as the KM approaches were well balanced between technical and organizational elements.

However, what can be observed is that the allocation has impacted the development of relationships between the KM functions and the wider organization. It can be seen that all three KM functions established ongoing relationships with other support functions, which can be explained by their close association in the organizational structure. As KM is an interdisciplinary management program, individual initiatives need to be well integrated with the other support functions. Hence an allocation with the other support functions has the potential to create value for the entire KM program. But at the same time an association with the business function would create value as it is likely to facilitate a close relationship and integration between KM and the business. Hence, both positions have their benefits and drawbacks as KM programs can derive distinct benefits from their particular associations. Care needs to be taken to establish the appropriate mechanisms and instruments to complement the existing governance structures.

What is particularly interesting in this case is that due to the allocation with support functions, the KM functions had not only failed to develop important relationships with the business but had also threatened the reputation of the whole KM program. Members of the KM groups had pointed out that the functions to which the KM leaders reported had weak reputations in the organization, which in turn impacted the development of the KM programs. The KM leader of Business Group A explained that the association with the HR department had an impact on the acceptance of the KM program in the organization. The HR department in this organization was perceived as having a focus on compliance issues instead of being strategic and innovative:

"Our HR department is not very well regarded in the organization [...] it is seen as something that only calculates your remaining days of annual leave."

Such an impact on the reputation of the KM program through its association with an HR func-

tion has also been reported by other researchers (Oltra, 2005). However, the corporate KM function faced a similar challenge due to its position at corporate headquarters. The KM leader explained that corporate headquarters is often described as trying to dominate and interfere with business group initiatives. In addition he noted:

"A lot of projects driven from headquarters departments have failed, and therefore few people are enthusiastic about them."

Being affiliated with corporate headquarters had created difficulties in promoting the KM program and engaging the wider organization. Considering these observations it seems advisable to not only consider the placement of the KM function with regard to the opportunities for integration of the KM program, but also with regard to the reputation of the associated functions.

It is shown in this case that the position of the KM function matters. While it did not matter with regards to the nature of the KM approach, it did matter with regards to the relationships and the reputation of the KM program. Both of these aspects are very important. While no generic recommendation can be derived from this, it clearly shows that care must be taken to position the KM function strategically, as the position might either create opportunities or barriers for the development of the KM program.

Should KM Governance be Formalized?

A review of the KM governance processes indicated a very low level of formalization. No formal KM strategy was established and the reporting processes were also limited. In the IT governance domain the level of formalization is considered very important. The level of formalization is considered a sign of IT governance sophistication, and widely accepted maturity models argue that it should be the objective of an organization to formalize the IT governance processes (Van Grembergen, 2004).

At this point, however, it is not clear if such a formalization of the governance processes is also necessary for the development of KM programs. Formalized control processes are expensive, and as KM tools and applications often do not have the value or urgency of IT, it is difficult to justify such highly formalized control processes. While explicit KM strategies and sophisticated reporting processes might improve the strategic alignment of the KM program and the transparency of the actual KM initiatives, it might also create unnecessary overhead which is not necessarily important for all organizations. However, one KM governance process which seemed to be critical for the development of the KM program is the way individual KM initiatives are prioritized. As the KM domain provides a large number of interesting applications and possible projects, it seems very important to establish mechanisms which clearly identify those projects the organization or departments actually require. In the present case, tools and practices were developed by the KM function without developing the case for a clear need in the organization. Hence, care should be taken that processes are in place which integrate the users into the priorization of potential projects. Such prioritization mechanisms are particularly important in instances like the present case organization, where the KM function is not part of the business and few informal relationships have been established which would provide avenues for feedback from the business.

What is the Role of the KM Leader?

One of the most critical aspects in the whole KM governance discussion is the role of the KM leader. Related research has shown that KM leaders can build relationships to the top of the organization, bridge the gap to the business and even create a close liaison with other support functions (Schroeder & Pauleen, 2007). However, in the present case none of the KM leaders managed to build relationships to the top of the organization or to the business. While this can be attributed to the location of the KM function in the organization, it can also be related to the personal background of the KM leaders in the organization. Even though all three KM leaders had worked in the organization beforehand, they had all been part of support functions, and none of them had actual experience in the business. Such a background clearly made it difficult for the KM leaders to establish relationships with the business.

The background of successful leaders has also been investigated in the IT domain, and it has been determined that it is advantageous to nominate a CIO with a business background (Stephens, Ledbetter, Mitra, & Ford, 1992). CIO's need to bridge IT and business, and having experience in both domains clearly facilitates the understanding of the subject domain, as well as creating the necessary relationships in the organization. Identifying the optimal background of a KM leader is even more difficult since KM initiatives often do not only require an understanding of business and IT, but also an understanding of HR, quality management and records management. While it is already difficult to find a good CIO, it is even more difficult to find a KM leader who had exposure in all these areas. The fact that KM leaders require a unique skill set, has also been reported by Awazu & Desouza (2004) and it can be safely assumed that most KM leaders do not have such a rare and diverse background. Considering that a single person is unlikely to have developed expertise in such an array of disciplines, the focus of recruiting a KM leader should be on his or her ability to create relationships and integrate the various areas of expertise in the organization.

Due to their association with support functions all three KM functions were detached from the operational business. Furthermore, the respective KM leaders also had their background in the support functions, which made it even more difficult to establish the necessary relationships between KM and the business. Other organizations have made a conscious decision to recruit respected business professionals from within the organization, and it was shown that such a move had been very beneficial for creating the necessary buy-in for the KM program (Schroeder et al., 2007). Clearly, the KM leader plays a critical role in the establishment of the KM program by complementing the existing governance structures and processes and mitigating its deficiencies. While the governance structures and processes may help certain aspects of the KM program, it is the KM leader with his or her background and the ability to create relationships, who allows for the emergence of informal governance as viable mechanisms for control and guidance of the KM program.

CONCLUSION

Research into the governance of KM is still relatively new. A large number of organizations have established dedicated KM programs but little is known about the structures and processes which have been put in place to direct and organize KM. For KM to play an effective role in an organization and to obtain the expected benefits, it requires an appropriate position in the organizational structure and embeddedness in the organizational processes. Important questions to ask are: where should KM be located in the organization?; which level of the hierarchy should KM report to?; through which processes and structures should the KM function obtain its direction?; and who should lead the KM program?

The present case study has introduced the KM governance configuration of a large divisionalised organization. Three independent KM functions had been set up independently at different levels. It has been shown that all three KM functions faced considerable difficulties in developing their KM program due to a lack of top-level support and

difficulties in establishing relationships with the business. This case helps to illustrate the concept of KM governance, and draws attention to the complexity of issues around it. The governance framework which was developed as part of this research has the potential to assist KM leaders in reviewing the governance arrangements of their respective KM program. The framework constitutes a tool which can be used to describe the current KM governance situation and to communicate the governance configurations which the organisations need to establish.

Further research should continue to examine the issues outlined above, so as to develop a theory that better explains the developments of organizational KM and illustrates how success and failure of KM are influenced by the governance configuration adopted. Ultimately, the research goal should be to provide further theoretical support for practitioners who seek to implement, modify or assess their KM program supported by an appropriate KM governance configuration.

REFERENCES

Awazu, Y., & Desouza, K. C. (2004). The knowledge chiefs: CKOs, CLOs and CPOs. *European Management Journal, 22*(3), 339–344. doi:10.1016/j.emj.2004.04.009

Binney, D. (2001). The knowledge management spectrum - understanding the KM landscape. *Journal of Knowledge Management, 5*(1), 33–42. doi:10.1108/13673270110384383

Brown, A. E., & Grant, G. G. (2005). Framing the frameworks: A review of IT governance research. *Communications of the AIS, 15*, 696–712.

Brown, C. (1997). Examining the emergence of hybrid IS governance solutions: Evidence from a single case site. *Information Systems Research, 8*(1), 69–94. doi:10.1287/isre.8.1.69

Brown, C., & Magill, S. L. (1994). Alignment of the IS functions with the enterprise: Toward a model of antecedents. *MIS Quarterly, 18*(4), 371–403. doi:10.2307/249521

Brown, C. V. (1999). Horizontal mechanisms under differing IS organization contexts. *MIS Quarterly, 23*(3), 421–454. doi:10.2307/249470

Chua, A., & Lam, W. (2005). Why KM projects fail: A multi-case analysis. *Journal of Knowledge Management, 9*(3), 6–17. doi:10.1108/13673270510602737

Davenport, T. H., & Prusak, L. (1998). *Working knowledge: How organizations manage what they know.* Boston, MA: Harvard Business School Press.

Desouza, K. C., Jayaramam, A., & Evaristo, R. (2002). *Knowledge management in non-collocated environments: A look at centralized vs. distributed design approaches.* Paper presented at the HICSS.

Doll, W. J., & Torkzadeh, G. (1987). The relationship of MIS steering committee to size of firm and formalization of MIS planning. *Communications of the ACM, 30*(11), 972–978. doi:10.1145/32206.32213

Drucker, P. (1993). *Post-capitalist society.* Oxford, UK: Butterworth Heinemann.

Ein-Dor, P., & Segev, E. (1982). Organizational context and MIS structure: Some empirical evidence. *MIS Quarterly, 6*(3), 55–69. doi:10.2307/248656

Fluss, D. (2002). Why knowledge management is a "dirty" word. *Customer Interface, 15*(2), 40–41.

Hansen, M. T., Nohria, N., & Tierney, T. (1999). What's your strategy for managing knowledge? *Harvard Business Review, 77*(March-April), 106–116.

Holden, N. J. (2004). *National culture and diversity of knowledge-sharing styles.* Paper presented at the KMAP 2004, Taipei, Taiwan.

IT Governance Institute. (2003). *Board briefing on IT governance.* Retrieved May 3, 2007, from http://www.itgi.org

Kim, Y.-G., Yu, S.-H., & Lee, J.-H. (2003). Knowledge strategy planning: Methodology and case. *Expert Systems with Applications, 24*(3), 295–307. doi:10.1016/S0957-4174(02)00158-6

Liebeskind, J. P. (1996). Knowledge, strategy, and the theory of the firm. *Strategic Management Journal, 17*(Winter special issue), 93-107.

Luftman, J. (2003). Assessing IT/business alignment. *Information Systems Management, 20*(4), 9–15. doi:10.1201/1078/43647.20.4.20030901/77287.2

Maier, R. (2002). *Knowledge management systems: Information and communication technologies for knowledge management.* Berlin, Germany: Springer Verlag.

Miller, D. (1987). The genesis of configuration. *Academy of Management Review, 12*(4), 686–701. doi:10.2307/258073

Nonaka, I. (1994). A dynamic theory of organizational knowledge creation. *Organization Science, 5*(1), 14–37. doi:10.1287/orsc.5.1.14

Nordin, M., Pauleen, D., & Gorman, G. (2009). fc). Investigating KM antecedents: KM in the criminal justice system. *Journal of Knowledge Management, 13*(2). doi:10.1108/13673270910942664

Oltra, V. (2005). Knowledge management effectiveness factors: The role of HRM. *Journal of Knowledge Management, 9*(4), 70–86. doi:10.1108/13673270510610341

Peterson, R. R. (2004). Crafting information technology governance. *Information Systems Management, 21*(4), 7–21. doi:10.1201/1078/44705.21.4.20040901/84183.2

Raub, S., & Rüling, C.-C. (2001). The knowledge management tussle - speech communities and rhetorical strategies in the development of knowledge management. *Journal of Information Technology, 16*(2), 113–130. doi:10.1080/02683960110054807

Riege, A. (2005). Three dozen knowledge sharing barriers managers must consider. *Journal of Knowledge Management, 9*(3), 18–35. doi:10.1108/13673270510602746

Sambamurthy, V., & Zmud, R. W. (1999). Arrangements for information technology governance: A theory of multiple contingencies. *MIS Quarterly, 23*(2), 261–290. doi:10.2307/249754

Schroeder, A., & Pauleen, D. (2007). KM governance: Investigating the case of a knowledge intensive research organisation. *Journal of Enterprise Information Management, 20*(4), 414–431. doi:10.1108/17410390710772696

Schroeder, A., Pauleen, D., & Huff, S. (2007). *Towards a framework for understanding KM governance*. Paper presented at the ICIS.

Stephens, C. S., Ledbetter, W. N., Mitra, A., & Ford, F. N. (1992). Executive or functional manager? The nature of the CIO's job. *MIS Quarterly, 16*(4), 449–467. doi:10.2307/249731

Storey, J., & Barnett, E. (2000). Knowledge management initiatives: Learning from failure. *Journal of Knowledge Management, 4*(2), 145–156. doi:10.1108/13673270010372279

Tavakolian, H. (1989). Linking the information technology structure with organizational competitive strategy: A survey. *MIS Quarterly, 13*(3), 309–318. doi:10.2307/249006

Van Grembergen, W. (2004). *Strategies for information technology governance*. Hershey, PA: Idea Group Publishing.

Weill, P. (2004). Don't just lead, govern: How top-performing firms govern IT. *MIS Quarterly Executive, 3*(1), 1–17.

Wiig, K. (2000). Knowledge management: An emerging discipline rooted in a long history. In D. Charles & D. Chauvel (Eds.), *Knowledge horizons: The present and the promise of knowledge management* (pp. 3-26). Woburn, MA: Butterworth-Heinemann.

Chapter 5
Managing in the Time of Virtualness

Traci A. Carte
University of Oklahoma, USA

Heather M. King
Gabbard & Company, USA

ABSTRACT

Virtual teams are increasingly being utilized by organizations in order to bring together far-flung expertise using collaborative technologies rather than physical relocation. While many organizations have been quick to utilize technology to enable this new virtual team structure they have been slower in recognizing the needed complementary shifts in management practices surrounding such teams. This chapter seeks to offer advice to managers in this new time of "virtualness." Interviews were conducted with a variety of individuals engaged in virtual team activities asking about communication practices, performance, change management, and leadership. The authors further probed about what technologies were in use by teams and what areas of the team processes could be improved. Finally, they asked the participants to draw distinctions between their views on effective practices of face-to-face teams and effective practices of virtual teams. From this interview data, insights are offered into social and managerial issues that drive virtual team performance.

INTRODUCTION

Virtual teams are becoming significantly more common and important in this increasingly global business environment. Organizations have recognized that in order to respond quickly to market needs, it is necessary to have teams of experts to collaborate – regardless of their locale. There are a plethora of communication and collation technologies currently available to enable a virtual team structure: E-mail, web-based knowledge repositories, group calendars, instant messaging, chat, electronic whiteboards and videoconferencing tools. Moreover, telephone, audio conferencing and fax are still commonly

DOI: 10.4018/978-1-60566-958-8.ch005

used communication technologies especially with small to medium sized organizations utilizing virtual teams.

In the past, technological barriers were seen as the greatest obstacle to virtual team success. With technology advancements and the proliferation and wide-spread availability of internet technologies, this barrier has been reduced. The most prominent barrier to virtual team success now is the extension of appropriate social and management methods to the virtual team structure. This challenge has not gone unnoticed; many have recognized that if organizations do not foresee and respond appropriately to this potential barrier, virtual teams are likely to fall short of expectations (DeSanctis and Poole, 1997; Handy, 1995; Victor and Stephens, 1994).

There is little current theory to guide research on the leadership and management of virtual teams (Bell and Kozlowski, 2002). Recent studies suggest that successful technology-mediated leadership is likely different from leadership in face-to-face teams. For instance, successful virtual leaders are likely to coach (O' Connell, et al, 2002) or facilitate (Cascio, 1999) rather than direct team members' behavior because virtual teams rarely meet face-to-face (Kirkman, et al, 2004), and more "hands on" styles of management are untenable in this distributed setting. Some previous research has focused on the link between communication behaviors of leaders and team outcomes (c.f., Klaus and Bass, 1981). This focus may be particularly salient for studies of virtual teams. While leadership in the more traditional face-to-face context may emerge using a variety of mechanisms, in the virtual context it likely relies largely on the communication effectiveness of the leader. Barge and Hirokawa (1989) propose "communication competency" as an alternative conceptualization of leadership.

Within a virtual context, communication competency is often closely related to technology competency. Managers in the new virtual age must master an assortment of communication and collaboration technologies to facilitate effective communication. There is little research to support this effort. Various theories of "fit" suggest that effective technology use can be facilitated by a fit between the task characteristics and the capabilities of the technology (Zigurs and Buckland, 1998) or the media (Menneke, et al., 2000). However the technology employed has to do more than "fit" the task, it also has to fit team norms, organizational expectations, and user preferences. In addition to facilitating downward communication (i.e., from leader to member) technology must also facilitate horizontal communication (i.e., from member to member). Unfortunately, even when the available technology fits the task, virtual teams can often experience difficulty building rapport. Studies have shown that this rapport is so difficult to build across virtual team members because communication is less efficient and often it is difficult for team members to remain aware of other team member's presence (McGrath and Hollingshead, 1994; Olson and Olson, 2003).

The purpose of this chapter is to explore a number of factors within a manager's control that can lead to different performance outcomes for virtual teams. We interviewed team leaders as well as team members to describe communication practices, evaluation processes, and leadership effectiveness exhibited in their field-based teams. The interview data suggest managers who understand how to use technology to effectively communicate are more likely to facilitate positive team processes and outcomes. Synthesizing the interview data with contemporary academic research we offer guidance to managers about technology best practices.

BACKGROUND

Effective virtual teams require competency in computer-mediated communication. Collaborative technologies can have a positive impact on group behavior and group efficacy resulting in an increase in information exchange between group members. Previous studies have drawn a connection between information exchange and improved team productivity (Brown et al 2004, Burke and Chidambaram, 1999; Mennecke and Valacich, 1998). The theory of task/technology fit (TTF) argues that the efficacy of a group's use of collaborative technologies can be facilitated by a fit between the task characteristics and the capabilities of the collaborative technology (Zigurs and Buckland, 1998). Task-Media Fit (TMF) suggests that lean media such as e-mail or group support systems provide improved outcomes only for simple, idea generating tasks (Mennecke and Valacich, 1998). While understanding how technology features and task characteristics might be well matched, we seek to understand how technology use might benefit teams from a more holistic approach.

As McGrath (1991) observes, groups engage in multiple, interdependent functions on multiple, concurrent projects. Further, within any given activity a group may alternatively or simultaneously focus on task accomplishment and/or the social needs of the team resulting in more complex temporal behavior patterns. Some past researchers have labeled activities focused on anything other than task accomplishment as "process losses" (Steiner, 1972); however, these so called process losses are potentially the group focusing on improved interaction or satisfaction which is likely not dysfunctional at all. For example, teams engaging in a complex project, involving multiple interdependent tasks need to complete current tasks as well as develop relationally in preparation for future tasks; perhaps even allowing for short term performance declines in order to achieve improved outcomes over the long term (McGrath, 1991). As such, the recommendations made by previous technology fit theories may be incomplete in that they focus on the productivity outcome ignoring potentially complex paths and groups' with multiple outcome focuses (i.e., short term productivity and long term relational devel-

opment)(McGrath, 1991; Menneke et al, 2000). Extending this previous research to the managerial perspective suggests two potential prescriptions: clearly establishing performance goals, and effective management of non-routine change.

Performance goals. A fundamental task engaged in by managers is the articulation and assignment of performance goals. Clearly established performance goals incent desired behaviors, and it has been found that without these teams tend to spend excessive time on lower priority activities and have difficulty adjusting to changes in the team's membership (Hacker and Lang, 2000). While it is important that teams with on-going charters be given time to alternatively engage in both task-oriented as well as relationship-oriented behaviors, teams without a clear understanding of their assigned tasks are clearly doomed to be less effective. Further, virtual teams are often described as having some barriers to effective communications among their membership as well as with their leadership due to the relative leanness of communication technologies (compared to face-to-face communication). This suggests a greater communication burden rests on managers of virtual teams. The effective communication of performance goals is potentially more difficult and paradoxically more important. In a recent study of virtual teams, researchers found managers that provide more detail on what tasks need to be completed and that created clear division of tasks between team members tended to have higher performing teams (Kayworth and Leidner, 2001/2002). It is important to note that effective communication in the context of virtual teams must include an effective strategy for using technology to communicate with the team as well as a strategy for enabling inter-team communication. When technologies are utilized effectively to communicate goals, virtual team members focus their efforts on higher priority tasks, are better able to collaborate on project work and ultimately deliver the results management expects on a more consistent basis.

Table 1. Data sources

Nature	Number
Individual interviews	12 (approximately 45 minutes each)
Group interviews(included team leader and members)	3 (approximately 1 hour each)
Total individuals interviews	37 (8 leaders, 29 members)
Number of different teams involved	8 (1 internationally dispersed, 4 nationally dispersed, 3 dispersed within a single US state)
Number of different organizations involved	5

Managing change. Studies have found that when non-routine change occurs, objectives and goals may become less clear, resource requirements may change or become unknown, and it may be difficult to create shared perceptions of goals or to maintain commitment (Badham et al, 1997). This clearly has an adverse effect on virtual team performance and it is important that management involve teams in organizational change through technologically mediated communication and training. Often a manager's ability to facilitate needed change is enhanced or deterred by the level of trust placed in him/her by subordinates. While trust may be difficult to develop and maintain in a virtual context, it is an important mediating link between leadership and performance in general (Podsakoff, et. al., 1990; Jung and Avolio, 2000) and its development is believed critical for virtual teams because direct supervision is not possible (Avolio, Kahai, and Dodge, 2000). Such performance-enhancing trust must be bi-directional. Effective virtual managers must have trust in their team to carry out needed tasks even in the face of non-routine changes, and the team must trust the manager to provide clear, accurate communication about the nature of such changes. Such trust is facilitated by effective use of communication technologies.

In the remainder of this chapter we provide a description of our study method, sources and nature of data, a summary of the interview data collected, and managerial recommendations resulting from our findings. Ultimately we hope

this chapter provides deeper understanding for managers about when and how to use various technologies to effectively communicate with virtual teams in to enhance trust, build rapport, and meet team performance goals.

STUDY METHOD

Interviews were conducted with a variety of individuals engaged in virtual team activities. Participants varied from the virtual team managers – who themselves were moderate or absolute in their own degree of virtuality – to virtual team members who could be classified as absolute virtual team members. The interview participants varied in their virtual function; some were members of self-managing service teams, others were members of departmental and functional teams and finally, some were members of cross-functional management or product development teams. The size of the organizations with which these individuals were employed varied from medium (between 300 and 1,000 employees) to large (over 1,000 employees). Table 1 provides a summary of the sources of data used in this chapter.

The participants were asked about their team's communication practices, performance, change management and leadership. They were also probed about what technologies were in use by their team and what areas of their teams processes could be improved and how. Finally, they were asked to draw distinctions between their views on effective practices of face-to-face teams and effective practices of virtual teams. Our questions (provided in Appendix A) were intended to elicit responses that could help us develop an understanding of the work practices surrounding effective management of virtual teams.

Through these interviews it was determined that the issue that most concerned leadership with regard to virtual teams was managing performance from afar while the issue that concerned virtual team members most was feeling connected to the organization through times of change. The following is a discussion of the issues for leadership in managing performance and change for their virtual teams as well as practical methods for managing both.

ORGANIZATIONS AND THE HIGH PERFORMING VIRTUAL TEAM

Ultimately whether or not a team is deemed successful can be summed up in the question: "Did the team produce the intended results within the specified timeline?" With this question in mind, managers must recognize that while traditional teams operate in the same space and time, or synchronously their virtual team counterparts often communicate asynchronously requiring time and space coordination efforts on which traditional (or face-to-face) teams typically spend much less effort (Montoya-Weiss, et al., 2001). This extra coordination effort can result in virtual teams facing greater difficulty than their face-to-face counterparts in managing the project which includes keeping pace with a schedule and ensuring that project goals are viable. Studies related to virtual teams and performance have found that appropriate measurement systems can provide some advantages in allocating and tracking work resulting in increased performance across the team. But what should a leader do if performance metrics are in place and the virtual team's performance

continues to return less than desired results? For leaders managing virtual teams and for members of virtual teams, there is an added dimension of complexity when allocating and tracking work. Evidenced by our interview data, it is critical that managers consider the mode of communication used to communicate this information to and between team members.

The Link between Technology, Communication and Performance

Interviews of the team members involved in this study revealed that the technology medium chosen for virtual teams contributes substantially to performance. Of the team members interviewed, all were aware of specific performance expectations from leadership and their individual contribution to the overall product. Despite the ability of all team members to recite performance and role expectations, the actual level of performance achievement varied greatly. This turns the focus to, not *what* was communicated, but *how* was it communicated.

Of the interviewees, various modes of communication were utilized to collaborate among team members and between members and team managers – some as simple as phone and email and others that frequently used web-based applications and similar technology-mediated communication tools. During the interviews, participants were asked to rank how effective they perceived their communication to be among team members and between members and leaders. From this question, it was clear that those teams utilizing more sophisticated modes of communication believed their communication was significantly more effective. Participants were also asked to assess their team's performance. Analysis of this self-reported information revealed a strong positive relationship between technology level and percentage of performance goals attained. These results suggest that as the features available in the technology utilized by virtual teams increased, the perception of communication efficiency increased and both had a strong impact on overall team performance (or at least on perceptions of performance). Explanations for this may be that more sophisticated communication mediums allow team members to collaborate with more ease – meaning that they coordinate their tasks more efficiently, assess progress and needs more quickly, and share knowledge more openly.

Further support for these findings can be found in several studies which stated that communication medium can have a positive impact on collective group behavior and group efficacy; this results in an increase in communication effectiveness in the form of information exchange between group members and previous studies have drawn a connection between these factors and improved team productivity (Brown et al 2004, Burke and Chidambaram, 1999; Mennecke and Valacich, 1998).

Also, the interviewees that were virtual team managers in organizations using more advanced technology to mediate communication, stated more often than other team managers that they felt they knew their team well and were better able to identify problems before escalation and anticipate resource needs of the team before the needs became obstacles to performance. According to managers interviewed, their primary function was to monitor virtual team progress, act as a resource to the team, and communicate expectations. Advanced technology created an improved foundation for communication not only among virtual team members but between team members and team managers as well. While high performing team members did not credit team leadership for their team's higher performance, nearly all lower performing team members reported a lack of communication and/or poor relations between themselves and their manager.

MANAGING ORGANIZATIONAL CHANGE AND VIRTUAL TEAMS

Lack of involvement in organizational change and ineffective virtual team preparation for change were the most prevalent themes among team members interviewed. Dealing with change is a challenge for face-to-face teams in most organizations however, virtual team members consistently stated in interviews that they felt out of touch with the home office, that they were the last to know about change, and that they were given less information and/or training for changes. With increasing competition and new technologies requiring organizations to continuously look for ways to gain competitive advantages, change is ironically becoming the constant state. In order to capitalize on opportunities as they arise, companies must be flexible enough to meet the challenge while having systems in place to provide direction. The purpose of change management is to effectively and strategically manage change to maximize business results. Managing change allows organizations to put processes and systems in place that help change move more smoothly through the organization, and managing change should benefit employees by keeping them involved and informed throughout the change process. Even with the recent focus on managing change in many organizations, managers still struggle with consistently extending these practices to their virtual teams.

Innate flexibility, adaptability and quick responsiveness to change are considered traditional advantages of a virtual organization (Grabowski and Roberts, 1999). However, organizations often fail to leverage communication and training appropriately to enable virtual teams to react and actively participate in organizational change. Our interviews suggest team members felt alienated from the organization and, when changes involved team systems or processes, they often felt alienated from other team members as well. During times of change, it is exceedingly important to consider the special needs of the virtual team. When non-routine change occurs, objectives and goals may become less clear, resource requirements may change or become unknown, and it may be difficult to create shared perceptions of goals or to maintain commitment (Badham et al, 1997). It is necessary during change for leadership to communicate to virtual team members regarding performance expectation and roles at a higher frequency than times of regular operations.

Communication Effectiveness and Change

A risk of virtual teams is that they may feel removed from the organization's goals and from each other – because accountability can be lax in the virtual environment, this group of stakeholder may feel that they have less at stake in terms of the organization's success than the manager in the office facing the issues everyday. The most effective method for gaining commitment to change is involving affected employees in the decision making. Managers of virtual teams were asked how they involved their team members in changes. Many admitted that due to the fast-pace with which they were expected to implement change, it is rare that they have the time to illicit the opinions or ideas of team members. Typically, the manager would discuss the change with the virtual team member whom they interacted with most frequently (not always the team leader). Team members interviewed confirmed this through their comments that communications about change typically came to them through the trickle-down effect – meaning someone in the group was informed and then eventually this information made it to the rest of the team. Both managers and team members agreed that this often led to misinformation.

Interviewees were asked to rank their organization's change effectiveness (as it related to virtual team involvement) and this information

was analyzed against the perceived communication effectiveness of the organization. The ratings given by interviewees supported the idea that communication effectiveness plays a significant role in how team members perceive change processes. Individuals that believed their communication was less effective also tended to believe that change processes were not as effective within their organization. These same individuals commented that they were often the last to know when something happened within the organization and were often given very little if any information or instructions with regard to the change. Conversely, individuals who believed their communication to be more effective stated that they were often told about changes prior to implementation and, for changes that affecting the virtual teams directly, team members were asked for input on the potential benefits, costs and implementation methods for the changes.

Interestingly though, when the data collected on technology level was analyzed against perceived change effectiveness in order to ascertain whether a relationship existed between the two, it was found that the relationship was U-shaped (see Figure 1). For organizations engaged in less sophisticated technology use, change effectiveness was generally rated as poor by team members. A significant increase in perceived change effectiveness was seen for organizations in the moderate technology range. However, a slight decrease in perceived change effectiveness was found for organizations utilizing a high level of technology. This may simply be a matter of organizations using technology for many things – but not to improve communications about upcoming changes. Alternatively, this may suggest that when team leaders and other organizational leadership engage in communication which over-promises on the planned changes, virtual team members were particularly sensitive to it because the technology-mediated communications they receive significantly shape their understanding of the organization and its actions. Further, sophisticated communication

Figure 1. Relationship between technology and perceived change effectiveness

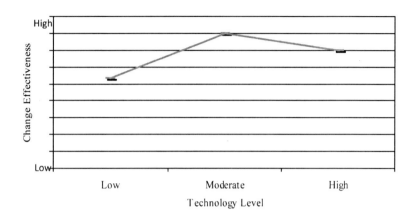

and collaborative technologies provide a sort of organizational memory about promises made, as such it is relatively easy for a virtual team member to recall what was promised and compare it to what was delivered.

Training for Change

Whenever a change occurs in the organization, it is necessary to determine if employees and teams have the knowledge, skills and abilities (KSA) to operate effectively after the change. If not, then training must be delivered to provide these KSA's. Of the individuals interviewed, various methods of training delivery were used including face-to-face training, distribution of literature such as electronic or paper manuals or other information packets, and web-based instruction. Web-based instruction is a growing method for training delivery among virtual teams and face-to-face teams (Goldstein and Ford, 2002). Of the interviews conducted for this study, a small percentage of the interviewees reported receiving web-based instruction. Of those team members and managers who did utilize web-based instruction, they felt that the training process varied little between virtual teams and their face-to-face counterparts. These team members also felt that typically, their training was adequate. Overall, the satisfaction

level for the interviewees who had received either face-to-face training or web-based instruction was judged, based on commentary, to be higher than that of interviewees who had received literature or no training.

SOLUTIONS AND RECOMMENDATIONS

The key points described in this chapter are summarized graphically in Figure 2. Our interview data suggests that how technology is used certainly has an impact on virtual teams. This is not surprising given that most, if not all, virtual team communication and collaboration occurs via technology. Further, our interview data suggests leadership and strong change management practices are keys to virtual team success. But, these too seem to depend on effective use of technology. However, what might be the specific collaborative features needed?

Recent work suggests that collaborative technologies include two bundles of capabilities. The first of these, labeled reductive capabilities, are features or functionality of collaborative technologies whose use results in communication patterns which are less personal, more participative, and slower among virtual teams compared

Figure 2. Key findings

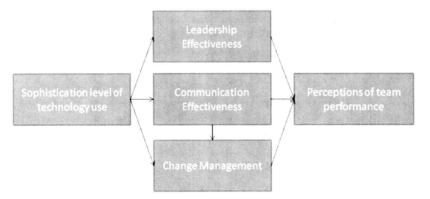

to the communication patterns of face-to-face teams. The second, labeled additive capabilities are features of the technology that endow a group with enhanced communication and collaboration capabilities typically not available to face-to-face groups (Carte and Chidambaram, 2004). Further, it has been argued that reductive capabilities may be helpful early in a group's life and/or when the group is focused on relational development. Conversely, additive capabilities may be of more value later in the group's life and/or when task accomplishment takes high priority. These capabilities along with examples are provide in Table 2.

While this previous research suggests what capabilities are needed (i.e., both additive and reductive capabilities – perhaps at different points in a group's life), there is still a need to select which specific collaborative technologies to make available to a team. Leaders should work with team members to find the most effective communication medium for team members and leaders. Previous work suggests that teams, when faced with a number of technology alternatives, tend to select the technologies that the majority of members already know how to use (Becker, et al., 2005). This suggests that using technology currently available and in use by the team, but perhaps using more features, may be a strategy for virtual team leaders in improving virtual team communication and performance. Alternatively,

when team leaders or other organizational management have a clear preference for a technology with which the team is unfamiliar training for the whole team is important – rather than limiting training to a few "specialists." Further, given our findings which link technology perceptions with perceptions about communication effectiveness, performance and change management, we would recommend routinely surveying teams about their perceptions of the available collaborative technologies to ensure their needs are met

Once an effective communication medium is in place, it is important that leadership communicate clear roles and responsibilities to team members. Outdated job descriptions or loose guidelines around expected project outcomes are not adequate to ensure the team understands how they are expected to utilize each other to reach the desired end. Using a web-based project planning tool with clear resource assignments, timelines and anticipated duration of activity was typically favored by the development and special project teams interviewed. According to those teams, using this or similar tools left nothing up to interpretation and created accountability for the individuals and the team. Managers of virtual teams also stated that utilizing a web-based technology to communicate expectation and timelines served the dual role of allowing managers to check progress on tasks (which

Table 2. Capabilities of collaborative technologies

Capabilities and description	Collaborative Technologies				
	Email	*Groupware (e.g., Lotus Notes)*	*Group Support Systems (e.g., GroupSystems)*	*Desktop Conferencing (e.g., NetMeeting)*	*Chat Rooms*
Reductive Capabilities					
Visual Anonymity Reduces salience of surface-level diversity •Lowers evaluation apprehension • Forces members to articulate their ideas in writing	High	High	High	Low (with Audio) None (with Video)	High
Equality of Participation • Provides a level playing field and allows minority opinions to be voiced • Removes constraints of turn-taking	Moderate	Moderate	High	Low	High
Synchronous Interaction •Slows down interactions •Reduces ability to coordinate •Enables members to think about issues before responding	No	No (in most cases)	Yes (in most cases)	Yes	Yes
Additive Capabilities					
Coordination Support •Enables group to keep track of people, projects and priorities •Helps coordinate complex multi-person projects	No	Yes	Yes (in some cases)	Yes	No
Electronic Trail •Enables easy retrieval of communications •Provides audit trail and helps in clarification of issues	Yes	Yes	Yes	Yes	No
Enhanced Capabilities	Image & File Transmission	Document Storage & Retrieval	Decision Support Features	Audio- & Video- Conferencing	Instant one-on-one Messaging

members updated frequently) without the appearance of micro-managing.

Having improved communication will improve the rapport between team members – contributing to the team's overall ability to cope with change. Additionally, leadership should seek to involve virtual team members in shaping change which means eliciting their feedback and ideas prior to implementation when possible. Further, prior to implementation leadership should conduct a training needs assessment for virtual team members affected by change and if at all feasible, provide training in the form of web-based or face-to-face

training. Based on the interviews conducted and prior studies completed, it is clear that the small investment required to take these steps should bring a greater return in the form of team productivity.

CONCLUSION

One facet to the challenge of managing a virtual team is the question of how to produce effective virtual teams. This study supports prior assertions that the use of more advanced technology and, thereby more effective communication, plays a significant role in inter-team dynamics and further shows that this relates to higher performing teams. Further, virtual team managers in this study stated that the level of technology present is a significant factor in their ability to perceive the team's resource needs and to gage the team's progress toward performance goals. While high performing teams did not cite their manager's contribution to goal achievement, lower performing teams did comment on the lack of managerial support they received.

This study also focused on the managerial issue of how organizational change can be more effectively implemented with virtual teams. Information gathered through interviews suggests that technology has a positive relationship with perceived change effectiveness to a point but that overall communication effectiveness – of which technology is only a part of the whole – has a more significant role. Interviewees believing that their organizations were more change effective also cited, beyond technology, that their organizations elicited their opinions on changes directly affecting them and communicated the change to them prior to implementation. Ultimately, what this means is that it is not enough for organizations to provide virtual teams with advanced technology, they must also incorporate virtual team members into the early stages of the change process. This will require a shift in thinking and process for most leaders but as virtual teams become even more prevalent in organizations, it is likely that this will become a natural component to how things get done.

REFERENCES

Avolio, B. J., Kahai, S., & Dodge, G. E. (2000). E-leadership: Implications for theory, research, and practice. *The Leadership Quarterly*, *11*(4), 615–668. doi:10.1016/S1048-9843(00)00062-X

Badham, R., Couchman, P., & McLoughlin, I. P. (1997). *Implementing vulnerable socio-technical change projects. Innovation, organizational change and technology*. London: ITB Press.

Barge, J. K., & Hirokawa, R. Y. (1989). Toward a communication competency model of group leadership. *Small Group Behavior*, *20*(2), 167–189. doi:10.1177/104649648902000203

Bass, B. M. (1990). *Bass and Stodgill's handbook of leadership*. New York: Free Press.

Becker, A., Carte, T., & Chidambaram, L. (2006). Shared realms of consideration in virtual teams: Some field-based experiences. In *Proceedings of the Americas Conference on Information Systems*, Acapulco, Mexico.

Bell, B. S., & Kozlowski, S. W. J. (2002). A typology of virtual teams: Implications for effective leadership. *Group & Organization Management*, *27*(1), 14–49. doi:10.1177/1059601102027001003

Brown, H. G., Poole, M. S., & Rodgers, T. L. (2004). Interpersonal traits, comlementarity and trust in virtual collaboration. *Journal of Management Information Systems*, *20*(4), 115–137.

Burke, K., & Chidambaram, L. (1999). How much bandwidth is enough? A longitudinal examination of media characteristics and group outcomes. *MIS Quarterly*, *23*(4), 557–580. doi:10.2307/249489

Carte, T. A., & Chidambaram, L. (2004). A capabilities-based theory of technology deployment in diverse teams: Leapfrogging the pitfalls of diversity and leveraging its potential with collaborative technology. *Journal of the AIS*, *5*(11-12), 448–471.

Cascio, W. F. (1999). Virtual workplaces: Implications for organizational behavior. In C. L. Cooper & D. M. Rousseau (Eds.), *Trends in organizational behavior: The virtual organization*. Chichester, England: Wiley.

DeSanctis, G., & Poole, M. S. (1997). Transitions in teamwork in new organizational forms. In B. Markovsky (Ed.), *Advances in group processes* (Vol. 14, pp. 157-176). Greenwich, CT: JAI Press.

Gerber, B. (1995, Apr)... *Training. Minneapolis*, *32*(Iss. 4), 36.

Goldstein, I. L., & Ford, J. K. (2002). *Training in organizations: Needs assessment, development and evaluation* (4ᵗʰ ed.). Florence, KY: Wadsworth Publishing.

Grabowski, M., & Roberts, K. H. (1999). Risk mitigation in virtual organizations. *Organization Science, 10*(6), 704–721. doi:10.1287/orsc.10.6.704

Hacker, M., & Lang, J. D. (2000). Designing a performance measurement system for a high technology virtual engineering team. *International Journal of Agile Management Systems, 2*(3), 225–232. doi:10.1108/14654650010356130

Handy, C. (1995). Trust and the virtual organization. *Harvard Business Review, 73*(3), 40–50.

Jung, D. I., & Avolio, B. J. (2000). Opening the black box: An experimental investigation of the mediating effects of trust and value congruence on transformation and transactional leadership. *Journal of Organizational Behavior, 21*(8), 949–964. doi:10.1002/1099-1379(200012)21:8<949::AID-JOB64>3.0.CO;2-F

Kayworth, T., & Leidner, D. (2001/2002). Leadership effectiveness in global virtual teams. *Journal of Management Information Systems, 18*(3), 7–40.

Klauss, R., & Bass, B. M. (1981). *Impact of communication*. New York: Academic Press.

McGrath, J. E. (1991). Time, interaction, and performance (TIP): A theory of groups. *Small Group Research, 22*(2), 147–174. doi:10.1177/1046496491222001

McGrath, J. E., & Hollingshead, A. B. (1994). *Groups interacting with technology: Systems, ideas, evidence and an agenda*. Newbury Park, CA: Sage.

Mennecke, B., Valacich, J., & Wheeler, B. (2000). The effects of media and task on user performance: A test of the task-media fit hypothesis. *Group Decision and Negotiation, 9*, 507–529. doi:10.1023/A:1008770106779

Mennecke, B. E., & Valacich, J. S. (1998). Information is what you make of it: The influence of group history and computer support on information sharing, decision quality, and member perceptions. *Journal of Management Information Systems, 15*(2), 173–178.

Montoya-Weiss, M., Massey, A., & Song, M. (2001). Getting it together: Temporal coordination and conflict management in global virtual teams. *Academy of Management Journal, 44*(6), 1251–1262. doi:10.2307/3069399

O'Connell, M. S., Doverspike, D., & Cober, A. B. (2002). Leadership and semiautonomous work team performance: A field study. *Group & Organization Management, 27*(1), 50–65. doi:10.1177/1059601102027001004

Olson, G. M., & Olson, J. S. (2003). Human-computer interaction: Psychological aspects of human use of computing. *Annual Review of Psychology, 54*, 491–516. doi:10.1146/annurev.psych.54.101601.145044

Podsakoff, P., MacKenzie, S., Moorman, R., & Fetter, R. (1990). Transformational leader behaviors and their effects on follows' trust in leader, satisfaction, and organizational citizenship behaviors. *The Leadership Quarterly, 1*, 107–142. doi:10.1016/1048-9843(90)90009-7

Steiner, I. D. (1972). *Group process and productivity*. New York: Academic.

Victor, B., & Stephens, C. (1994). The dark side of the new organizational forms: An editorial essay. *Organization Science*, *5*(4), 479–482. doi:10.1287/orsc.5.4.479

Zigurs, I., & Buckland, B. (1998). A theory of task/technology fit and group support systems effectiveness. *MIS Quarterly*, *22*(3), 313–334. doi:10.2307/249668

APPENDIX A

Interview Questionnaire

1. At what organization are you employed?
2. What is your position at the organization?(specifically, management or team member)
3. How many members of the team are virtual members?
4. What is the purpose of the team?
5. Are the team member's dispersed internationally, nationally, or locally?
6. What is the primary means of communication for the team?
7. What is the frequency of communication between team members?
8. How effective is this communication method?

Scale of 1 -10, where 10 is extremely effective and 1 is not effective at all

9. Please explain the rating of communication effectiveness.
10. If the current method is not effective, what might be more effective?
11. Does this team have performance goals or metrics?
12. What are these performance goals or metrics?
13. How are they measured?
14. Are these performance goals or metrics linked to pay?
15. Are the performance metrics for this team different than those for the f2f teams?
16. How effective are these performance metrics for the virtual team? Scale of 1 to 10
17. Please explain the rating of performance metric effectiveness.
18. If these metrics are not effective, what might be more effective?
19. When change occurs in the organization, how is the virtual team informed?
20. Do you feel the virtual team is more or less accepting of changes in the organization?
21. If training is required for a change, how does the virtual team receive training?
22. How does the change process (communication and training) vary between the f2f teams and the virtual team?
23. Overall, how effective is the change management procedure between the organization and the virtual team?Scale of 1 to 10
24. If the change management process is ineffective, what might be more effective?
25. If you are a virtual team manager, what are some of the special issues you have to manage to with the team?
26. If you manage both virtual teams and f2f teams, how is your management style different with the two?
27. Do you spend more or less time managing a virtual team as opposed to a f2f team?
28. Please explain why the time is different between the two (if it is)

Section 2
Patterns of Leadership Behaviours

Chapter 6

Knowledge Brokers in Overlapping Online Communities of Practice
The Role of the Connector–Leader

Jocelyn Cranefield
Victoria University of Wellington, New Zealand

Pak Yoong
Victoria University of Wellington, New Zealand

ABSTRACT

This chapter argues that leaders need to better understand the roles played by informal knowledge brokers in connecting overlapping online communities of practice (CoPs). It illustrates how distributed individuals playing a key knowledge broker role – the Connector-leader – helped to drive transformative professional change. The research context was a professional development programme for New Zealand schools that promoted a new, student-centric teaching approach. The research project explored how online CoPs facilitate professional knowledge transfer, focusing on how new knowledge is embedded in interpretive frameworks and practices. Connector-leaders spanned boundaries in the online community realm and had a strong online presence. As professional learners, they were strongly outward facing, identifying primarily as members of a distributed online CoP. As leaders, they were inward facing, focusing largely on the knowledge needs of local organisations and CoPs. This study extends previous research into the boundary spanner and knowledge broker, introduces new ideas about the nature of boundaries in CoPs, and promotes a system-level view of knowledge flows, emphasising the importance of both visible and invisible dimensions of online knowledge brokering.

1.0 INTRODUCTION

When it comes to fostering innovation in a way that drives change, certain types of individuals have been found to play more significant roles than others. A key role is played by those people who introduce new knowledge in such a way that it becomes accessible to their peers and organisations, by translating, adapting, or converting it to work within the new organisational or community context. These

DOI: 10.4018/978-1-60566-958-8.ch006

people typically operate across the boundaries of organisations and/or communities, performing informal, but highly skilled and complex roles. They are known as *knowledge brokers* (Brown and Duguid, 1998; Davenport and Prusak, 1998; Harragon and Sutton, 1997; Wenger, 1998). In the twenty-first century, three significant trends can be seen as bringing the role of the *knowledge broker* into the spotlight, making it critical for managers to recognise and leverage the value of knowledge brokers.

The first of these trends is that the acquisition, cultivation and exploitation of knowledge is becoming increasingly valued, with flexible and relevant knowledge being viewed as a necessary foundation for innovation, agility, and success. This was once considered as primarily an organisational-level issue (Earl and Scott, 1998; Nonaka, 1998; Van Buren, 1999), but recognition of the strategic value of knowledge is also occurring at the level of nations; for example, as governments redesign their education systems to support the goals of economic transformation, innovation and sustainability. For example, in New Zealand (the setting for our research) the focus of education has been described as "…shifting from the transfer of specific knowledge to an emphasis on developing the skills to use and create new knowledge" (NZ Ministry of Education, 2008, p.5).

The second significant trend is that the internet, coupled with new web-based technologies and increasing bandwidth, is providing unprecedented opportunities for communicating beyond the former boundaries of the institution, enterprise and community. As a result, many organisations are placing an increased emphasis on the use of online communities of practice, designed to better connect people, share knowledge and create economies (Dubé, Bourhis et al., 2006).

The third trend of significance concerns the recent evolution of online communities of practice (online CoPs). Workers once typically belonged to exclusive, offline CoPs that spanned the boundaries of organisations (Lave and Wenger, 1991).

More recently, so-called knowledge workers often belonged to closed, facilitated, platform-centric online CoPs. Today's professionals, however, exist in a more open and complex online CoP system. They are more likely than ever to belong to multiple, overlapping CoPs, comprising both formal and informal, as well as online and offline dimensions. Today's online CoP environment has been described by Castro (2004; 2006) as an *online CoP ecology;* a space comprising diverse, largely open overlapping communication spaces, within which individuals use a variety of online tools and resources. For example, the same individuals who contribute to online forums may be participating in less formal online settings, using blogs, wikis and other Web 2.0 technologies.

In combination, these three trends can be seen as creating a new context for the *knowledge broker:* It is one in which the number of inter-community boundaries has multiplied and in which the ease with which individuals can traverse such boundaries is relatively high. At the same time, the level of organisational control over the online CoP environments within which their workers participate can be seen as diminished through the more open nature of the environment, and the increasingly distributed nature of content. This makes the role of the knowledge broker both more critical and more complex than ever before. In such an environment, it is important for leaders to understand the role of *knowledge brokers*, the nature of the work they perform, and how to manage and support them.

This chapter aims to partially address a lack of research in this area. It reports on a research project that investigated how knowledge was embedded in the context of online CoPs. The chapter begins with a review of literature concerning the significance of knowledge transfer, how it can be supported by IT, and the nature of the *knowledge broker* role. It then outlines the context and motivation for the study and summarises the research method. This is followed by an in-depth discussion of how one key broker role (the *Connector-Leader*) facilitated the transfer of knowledge, and a consideration of the implications for leaders.

1.1 How Can IT Support Knowledge Transfer?

The theme of knowledge transfer underscores our focus on knowledge brokerage. As has been outlined above, this theme is significant because economic versatility and success is seen as being tied up with the ability of organisations, communities and nations to import, transfer and leverage new knowledge, using it to help them to purposefully adapt in the face of changing conditions.

In the late twentieth century, aiming to expedite knowledge transfer, larger organisations began to implement so-called knowledge management (KM) systems; costly systems designed to capture and store corporate knowledge for internal transfer and reuse. These systems have not, unfortunately, lived up to their early apparent promise (Wagner and Bolloju, 2005), and it has been argued that the real value and potential of IT for supporting knowledge transfer is not yet well understood (Albino, Garavelli et al., 2004).

At least a partial explanation for the limited success of KM systems must lie in the fact that these systems do not take into account the critical influence of roles and relationships in the knowledge transfer process. Studies show that managers glean significantly more information from personal sources than impersonal ones (Cross, Parker et al., 2001), and research in the traditions of knowledge management, the community of practice, social networking, and innovation diffusion demonstrates that relationship-based, person-to-person communication is a key to successful organisational knowledge transfer (Brown and Duguid, 2000; Cross, Parker et al., 2001; Lave and Wenger, 1991; Nonaka and Takaeuchi, 1995; Orlikowski, 2002; Rogers, 2003; Sanchez, 2005). This body of research gives weight to Wagner and Bolloju's (2005) contention that inexpensive, modular technologies, such as discussion forums, weblogs (blogs) and wikis; also known as *social* or *collaborative technologies*, may be well-suited for supporting knowledge management by online communities.

Our research provides further support for this view. It outlines how a key knowledge brokerage role, that of the *Connector-Leader*, facilitated the successful use of social online technologies for knowledge transfer in the context of (a group of interconnected) online communities. Before outlining the research context and method, we briefly review the literature about key brokerage roles and online communities of practice.

1.2 Knowledge Broker Roles

People who connect different communities, groups, or networks, through their membership of, or association with, two or more such groups are known as *boundary spanners* (Allen, 1977; Cross and Prusak, 2002; Tushman, 1977). These people may also be valuable *knowledge brokers*, transferring knowledge across the boundaries they bridge by identifying needs and opportunities, promoting new ideas, and facilitating their uptake by recombining and adapting them to fit the recipient context (Brown and Duguid, 1998; Davenport and Prusak, 1998; Harragon and Sutton, 1997; Wenger, 1998). With today's growing emphasis on the strategic importance of knowledge transfer these people can play a unique and valuable role for organisations.

Being a *knowledge broker* is a complex, multi-dimensional role. Brokers need a mixture of judgement, communication and relationship management skills, including *gatekeeping* (monitoring information, identifying that which has a good potential 'fit', and filtering out that which is unsuitable) (Allen, 1967; Ancona and Caldwell, 1992; Cranefield and Yoong, 2007a; Katz and Tushman, 1981), *translating* and *interpreting* (converting knowledge to fit the recipients' context) (Cranefield and Yoong, 2007b; Holden and Von Kortzfleisch, 2004; Pawlowski and Robey,

2004; Wenger, 1998), and the ability to co-ordinate and align different perspectives (Wenger, 1998). For effective brokering, skills of persuasion and advocacy are also likely to be of value (Cranefield and Yoong, 2007a).

Despite the complexity of their work, and the range of expertise required, *knowledge brokers* typically perform non- or semi-official roles that are accorded low institutional recognition (Tushman, 1977; Wenger,McDermott et al., 2002). In addition, organisations with silo-based structures are poorly equipped to support people who operate across boundaries, finding it difficult to recognise and measure the value of such roles. Knowledge brokers themselves may experience feelings of inadequacy, arising from what Wenger (1998) describes as a sense of "uprootedness" that comes from being "neither in nor out" (p.110). In combination, these factors paint a picture of valuable workers operating within a situation of vulnerability, making it imperative for managers to better understand the value they provide and how to support them. In order to understand these important roles, we also need to explore the changing nature of 'boundaries' associated with communities of practice.

1.3 CoPs and the Changing Nature of Boundaries

A Community of Practice (CoP) is a group of people who interact on a regular basis and are united by a shared interest area or profession, and by the value they place on shared learning in that area (Wenger, 1998A; Wenger et al., 2002). Its members share *"a concern, a set of problems, or a passion about a topic, and...deepen their expertise in this area by interacting on an ongoing basis"* (2002, p.4). According to Wenger (ibid), a CoP is distinguished by (1) a sense of *joint enterprise* around a topic of interest, (2) ongoing relationships of *mutual engagement* that bind individuals, and (3) a *shared repertoire* of communal resources that members have developed, including artefacts, assumptions, language, and understandings.

Professional knowledge has traditionally been transferred via CoPs that span organisational, or intra-organisational boundaries, based around the *situated learning* that occurs through repeated face-to-face interactions (Lave and Wenger, 1991; Wenger, 1998). In the late twentieth century, CoPs gained a new dimension, as large enterprises and organisations began to introduce online CoPs. While online CoPs rely largely on ICT to connect their members, members may also meet face to face (Dubé et al., 2006; Lai et al., 2005). Online CoPs use a combination of traditional communication media (such as phone, teleconference and fax), and sophisticated technological tools (such as e-mail, videoconference, newsgroup, forum, chat, on-line meeting space, shared database, website, and intranet) to establish a shared virtual collaborative space.

The advent of online CoPs can be seen as changing traditional CoPs by (a) diminishing the need for members to be co-located, eroding old CoP boundaries and extending their reach, and (b) extending CoP members' learning opportunities to include non-situated, online interactions. Despite many studies undertaken in online communities, there is, as yet, no good understanding of how this non-situated dimension of learning, or knowledge transfer, occurs.

The recent ubiquity of low-cost online collaboration tools can be seen as further transforming CoPs. Early online communities were typically formal, facilitated groups, bounded by a shared virtual discussion space. Today, however, non-bounded, informal online CoPs also exist, within the dense areas of blogging networks (Efimova and Hendrick, 2005). In these unfacilitated communities, discussions are distributed amongst the blogs of members, who employ various technological practices (such as RSS feeds and social bookmarking) to follow the community's conversation. Castro (2006) outlines how in today's environment of multiple, open online communication channels, many overlapping CoPs simultaneously exist, with individuals often participating in more than one community. The decreasing cost of collaboration and information exchange has created an environment where community members communicate more frequently than before: *"Now we can see more frequent interactions, hundreds of times more activity than in primitive communities"* (ibid, p.5). In relationship to our themes of knowledge transfer and brokerage, the increasing complexity of the online community environment can be seen as creating many new boundaries within the online realm, thus increasing opportunities – and the need – for boundary crossing and brokerage.

We now briefly review the current state of knowledge concerning the nature of roles in CoPs, with a focus on *knowledge broker* roles.

1.4 Knowledge Broker Roles in CoPs

The roles played by CoP members have been variously categorised in the literature. Roles may be formal or informal; appointed or emergent, and they may evolve according to the stage of development that the community has reached (Fontaine, 2001; Wenger et al., 2002; Saint-Onge and Wallace, 2003). In a 2001 study of CoPs in 18 firms, Fontaine (2001) identified four kinds of roles: knowledge domain or practice roles, leadership roles, community support roles and knowledge intermediary (or broker) roles. The knowledge intermediary roles included facilitators, content co-ordinators and journalists. Studies of online CoPs typically focus on the role of a facilitator or moderator (e.g. Johnson, 2001). However, there is little understanding of how knowledge brokerage occurs in the absence of a facilitator; for example in the more complex, open, and unfacilitated online CoP environments such as those identified by Castro and Efimova. This can be seen as an emerging and important area of research given the high uptake of collaborative Web 2.0 technologies. In addition, there is also a lack of research that considers how knowledge brokerage occurs

between online and offline CoPs, or between the online and offline dimensions of CoPs.

2.0 RESEARCH CONTEXT

Our study was an exploratory case research project that investigated the embedding of professional knowledge in the context of online communities of practice (CoPs). It aimed to identify how online CoPs facilitate the transfer of professional knowledge and, in particular, to explore the process through which new knowledge is *embedded* (contextualised and integrated into interpretive frameworks and work practices). The project also set out to identify the technologies, roles, and other factors that contribute to the embedding process.

The context for our research was a three-year professional development programme that aimed to integrate ICT into school teaching while building effective practice. It relied on a combination of online community activity and face-to-face workshops to transfer knowledge within, and between, clusters of schools. The knowledge at the heart of this programme was about how to integrate ICT into teaching practice in a way that supported a new, strongly student-centred teaching approach. For many programme participants, this amounted to paradigm shift. It challenged the teacher's very role, their relationship with students, and their definition of effective practice. The programme was underpinned by a government strategy to embed effective teaching practices more thoroughly at system level, leveraging existing ICT and community infrastructure.

We define *embedded knowledge* as knowledge that is highly customised, context-specific, or sticky (Szulanski, 2000), and that is strongly integrated with other contextual knowledge. The process of *embedding* knowledge could be seen as 'the whole point' of knowledge transfer: Unless new knowledge is embedded, it will be unevenly dispersed and/or applied in limited ways, leading to isolated, temporary benefits. It is necessary to embed new professional knowledge in individuals and organisations in order to keep practice current, to reflect changing governmental, environmental, and societal concerns, to respond to new understandings, and in the process of doing this, align the new approach at an organisational level. The process of embedding knowledge has also been seen as a way of facilitating convergence in the interpretive frameworks of employees (Sanchez, 2005). Despite its importance, the knowledge embedding process is poorly understood. There is neither clarity about what the process constitutes, nor understanding of how it can be facilitated. Our research set out to help address this gap and to contribute to the gaps in the online CoP research literature as outlined above.

3.0 METHOD

Our interpretive study used qualitative case research methods. We initially conducted semi-structured interviews with 41 members of four 'blended' communities of practice (online CoPs whose members also met face-to-face; for example at workshops). Participants were selected from fifteen schools involved in four school clusters based in regional and provincial New Zealand centres, spanning a total distance of 900 km. They were lead teachers (school-based change agents), non-lead teachers, school leaders (principals and deputy principals) and cluster facilitators. Interviews were also conducted with a national programme facilitator and the project leader.

Two data gathering rounds were undertaken, with interview questions being refined as preliminary themes began to emerge. In the course of data gathering that it emerged that certain key individuals belonged to an additional informal community. This was a nationally distributed, virtual and facilitator-less online 'blogging' community, focused on ICT and change. In order to better understand the role of this community, four

further members of this community, from different clusters of schools, were interviewed. Additional key data included online community records such as Skype transcripts, blog content, and Delicious and Twitter records.

We coded the data using text analysis (Cresswell 2003) via NViVo software. A large set of emergent and envivo codes was gradually reduced, and bridging and theoretical codes were created as key categories, relationships and trends emerged. Preliminary results were validated at a participant workshop. Our findings concerning a key knowledge brokerage role, the *Connector-leader*, are outlined below. These were a subset of a larger set of findings, which is reported on elsewhere.

3.1 The Connector-Leader

Amongst those interviewed was a core group of eight people whom we described as *Connector-leaders*. These people were well-respected individuals who belonged to a distributed, unofficial and informal online community of movers and shakers, and whose opinions teachers in the local, school cluster-based communities followed. *Connector-leaders* were influential identities who bridged boundaries within the online community realm, connecting people at a global and national level, while exhibiting theoretical and/or practical leadership. They were *outward facing* with respect to their organisations and when managing their own learning needs, and they had a strong online presence. However, when it came to their leadership activities, they took on a more *inward facing* role with respect to their organisation and official local community. Both aspects of the *Connector-leader* role are described below and summarised in figure 1, together with information about the two overlapping online CoPs to which they belonged.

Figure 1. The Connector-leader Role: outward & inward facing aspects and brokering practices

Aspect of Role	Outward facing (Learner)	Inward Facing (Leader)
Nature of community	Distributed, unofficial online CoP	Locally-based, official school cluster CoPs
	Members: leaders with experience, enthusiasm and shared beliefs (thinkers & doers)	Members: teachers with a strong practical focus
Level and nature of online activity	High activity (visible & invisible); multiple tools (blogs, IM, Twitter, RSS, Delicious etc)	Lower activity; preference for invisible tools (IM, email)
Nature of communication with CoP members	RSS feeds, social bookmarking, culture of 24x7 communication (push and pull)	Blog publishing; proactive delivery to followers in response to response to perceived needs (push) and requests (pull)
Brokering practices	**Matching theory & practice** **Being sounding boards** **Seeking and providing assistance** (24x7 community mentality)	**Filtering and focusing knowledge** (Screening, prioritising, reducing) **Reinforcing and contextualising knowledge** (adapting to fit local needs) **Helping and feeding followers** (Just-in-time practical support)

3.1.1 Outward Facing Learner Role

Connector-Leaders (CLs) were outward facing in their identity as professional learners. In other words, they had a particularly strong allegiance with their online community, seeing it as essential to their development. (*"I'm using my community to better my own teaching practice"*). There was a sense that these people saw themselves as having outgrown their local organisation and community, and genuinely needed the stimulation and support of others who were like-minded about technology and its role in facilitating more student-centred teaching practice:

"... (I'm) on the periphery of the cluster.... I've also joined an on-line group of friends around the world, who are interested in the same sort of thing...I feel somewhat I have outgrown this cluster... I'm still in that community... but I've got people I look to and ask for things who aren't geographically close."

"(When I had a problem) my blogging community was the one that made me feel better. It wasn't my colleagues in the classroom next door, because they couldn't offer me any advice, because that wasn't how their classroom operated, and there really isn't anyone at school whose class operates like mine... There isn't anyone who's as passionate about the technology in the classroom as I am."

CLs engaged in a high level of online activity in their outward-facing role, typically being connected and available online for well over 12 hours a day. They used a wide range of online communication tools to keep in touch, including blogs, RSS feeds, Twitter, IM tools, email, and (in a few cases) Second Life. These people shared a common belief about, and enthusiasm for, the potential of ICT for enhancing learning, when employed in a student-centric way by teachers. When posting content on their blogs and on online forums, they selected themes that were consonant with this belief.

The online communications of CLs, which were centred around, and most visible on blogs, had a range of individual approaches. Some CLs were primarily *doers* in orientation. They took a largely pragmatic focus, outlining practical ways of teaching with technology, addressing problems and telling success stories. Other CLs were more *thinkers* in orientation: They positioned themselves as local thought leaders, taking a more analytical and critical perspective, and narrating on trends and ideas in relationship to their local context. This *thinker-doer* duality amongst the community of CLs was leveraged by individual CLs as they recognised the strengths of others, building powerful, reciprocal relationships. Such relationships helped them to better connect practice with theory and vice-versa:

"(He's) the thinker, and I'm the doer, and I think that that's probably why... our relationship works so well, because he really examines why we're doing things, and really looks at the pedagogy... he really looks at the foundation, whereas I don't know why I do it, I just do it because it feels right. We're good sounding boards for one another... He's made me stop and think about, 'What are the reasons behind doing this? Why is this a good thing to do?, What's the motivation behind doing it? Is it really good teaching practice to be doing this? Is this really going to help the students learn?'... He grounds me, because I get quite carried away."

Over time, the CLs' blogs accumulated value, as the amount and range of their content increased. A CL's status was further elevated if their blog attracted feedback from revered international educators:

"It grows and grows and grows, until you're putting a comment on really posh people's blogs. And they're putting comments on yours!"

Interactions with international thought leaders from outside their community were a considerable motivator. These not only increased the individual's sense of recognition, but also raised

their game, forcing them to think and operate at a higher level than before.

CLs also provided a voluntary just-in-time support service for each other and their followers. This helped to bind the community and sustain a spirit of reciprocity. It was made possible by a culture of staying online for long periods and a 24x7 community support mentality:

"It doesn't matter what time it is, you can ask a question, you can ask for some feedback... say you've got a technical problem, you can put that out there... and your community will always come back."

Instant messaging (IM) and Twitter were the tools of choice for seeking and providing assistance. Competence with technology was essential for the successful delivery of student-centred ICT-based learning, so assisting with technical issues was important. CLs also sought help from each other in finding quotes for their blog postings, sought feedback on emerging ideas, and requested input into communal resources, such as voice-threads. Drawing together complementary perspectives in these ways served to mutually reinforce a core set of beliefs and promote perseverance.

Online activity amongst CLs was not always visible on blogs, often being undertaken via IM, Twitter, or e-mail. A novel method of mutual support was the use of Twitter to provide a real-time back-channel commentary on keynote speakers at an annual conference, when CLs had a rare opportunity to meet face-to-face. This allowed CLs to benchmark and synthesise their thinking, to 'piggyback' on each other's responses to the speaker, and to establish a common interpretive framework. This real-time form of knowledge brokering helped to deepen the level of thinking.

"After I... begun to have more contact with people within the conference via twitters it changed the dimension of the conference. It changed from be-

Figure 2. Overlapping online CoPs and the Connector-leader (knowledge broker) community

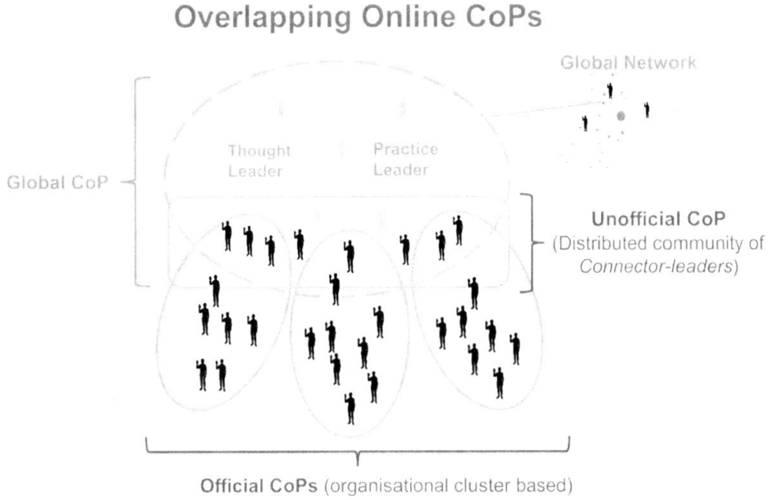

ing...thoughts between the speaker and myself to the possibility of having other people's opinions i.e. the (keynote speaker's) presentation and the twitters and examples that were given in rebuttal or agreement with her presentation. It meant that I was questioning and thinking during the keynote to a higher dimension than if I was just sitting there listening to HER."

As *knowledge brokers*, the CLs can be seen as bridging two important online boundaries: (a) the inner boundary between their own distributed national leadership community and the (one or more) locally-based online communities of school clusters which they worked with and (b) the exterior boundary between their online leadership community and a larger international online community of experts; educators with similar beliefs about technology. Together, the CLs can be seen as forming a bridging online community, or middle layer, between their local online communities and an international community. This, in turn, was part of a global network of edubloggers (see figure 2).

3.1.2 Inward Facing Leadership Role

While being outward facing as learners, CLs played important *inward facing* roles as knowledge leaders. They facilitated the uptake of new knowledge at a local cluster and school level, through a range of ongoing knowledge brokering activities. These practices, and the ways in which CLs communicated with the official online CoPs, are summarised below, with examples.

Filtering and Focusing
CLs used specific foci to frame their online engagement. These changed over time, and included learning models, ways of using a particular technology, and 'seasonal' community themes, such as Prensky's metaphor of teacher as *digital immigrant* (Prensky, 2005-6). These changing foci ensured that content fitted the emerging student centred paradigm, suited local contexts, and provided interesting, relevant and accessible frameworks for their readers. CLs applied these foci to scan, screen and filter the large quantity of international blog content which was being produced daily, seeking material that was a good fit for local community needs.

"It's just getting an understanding of the way other people think, and seeing that there's bits and parts- maybe large parts, maybe small parts- of what they're saying that fit with what I'm thinking, and what I believe."

There were two stages of filtering. The first, rough stage was done by using RSS feeds that alerted them to new content based on tagged keywords, and by subscribing to the blogs of selected thought leaders who themselves had acted as filterers:

"There's about five people... I'll subscribe to the RSS feed in my Bloglines, and so I see everything that they stick on their Del.icio.us...I've picked up some real gems...it's getting other people to do the work for you... I use other people as a filter."

This rough filtering was followed by a closer, manual appraisal of content quality:

"Making (teaching) BETTER is a focus for me ... Not just different but better. That is a filter for me in evaluating the worth of ideas or innovations".

The whole filtering process was described by one CL as being a daily process, somewhat like conducting triage. Filtering material from their peers also allowed them to rapidly benchmark and validate their own thinking prior to making a posting.

"I think what the on-line community manages to do is get the information you want a heck of a lot quicker, and from a variety of places, so you can validate it. And see if this stream of thinking is... in other people's papers."

Reinforcing and Contextualising

CLs worked hard to ensure that their blog content was strongly relevant to those in their local communities, aiming to attract and retain readership and give ideas more sticking power. As well as referencing the quality third party material they had filtered out, they reinforced it by extending the themes, adding new contextual commentary, and/or remixing the ideas of others in new ways. Putting a new spin on a familiar theme, or packaging it differently, was a valued way of localising knowledge, generating novelty, and underlining and enriching key themes.

"Whilst I may put a bit of a different spin on things, and adapt it for the New Zealand way of life, basically I'm taking somebody else's ideas... I'm adapting ideas. I've got a few ideas of my own, but because I'm learning, I don't want to reinvent the wheel... Hence my philosophy about whatever I know, I'm quite happy to share, and pass it on."

"I've been exploring the Reggio Emilia philosophy for the last wee while...and I think most of it fits really well with an inquiry learning type focus. And (I'm) just trying to find ways – over-arching theories, I suppose, that package up the thinking, give it a structure...(In) some of (my postings)...I've taken this bit from one person, this bit from someone else, and packaged it up differently."

Further reinforcing and contextualising practices that helped to embed the new professional knowledge included tagging content to fit emerging *folksonomies* (for discovery by users of social bookmarking).

" I put it into my Delicious, and I mark it for Allan, or for Susan, so they can link through to it that way.

Provocative blog posts that "stirred things up" also helped to reinforce themes, forcing people to engage more deeply with key ideas:

"I think it's actually quite helpful to have people who markedly disagree. That makes people justify what they're saying... And that means that people can actually engage with the ideas a bit harder, too, rather than just taking it all as read."

Helping and Feeding of Followers

CLs were also strongly aware of the needs of their local community members. They helped them to find solutions to their problems (via their unofficial 24X7 online help service), introduced them to others with similar interests, and actively delivered relevant content to selected individuals as urls, via e-mail and skype. We termed this more active form of brokerage the *feeding* of followers.

Over time, by reinforcing a recurring set of related themes in the ways outlined above, the CLs helped to embed them within their own community, and amongst their followers.

"New conversations are always happening, but then we're sometimes going back to the old conversation and putting a new spin on it."

The CL's dual role, as an outward facing professional learner and an inward facing leader – enabled them to provide a variety of benefits as *knowledge brokers*. Through their online communications as mutual learners they gained understandings which they could pass on to local teachers; and through their roles enacting change at the local school or cluster level, CLs acquired relevant, original stories to feature on their blogs. This enhanced their credibility, and the value and novelty of their blogs. Examples of real classroom practice showing the value of ICT provided global leaders with material that exemplified the ideas they espoused. As one CL pointed out, it would be risky to operate as an international thought leader without having access to evidence that verified your point of view:

"It makes them think about the process that's going on. It makes them reflect on what is actually working. Because there must be a huge amount of pressure (for them)... when you share something, you can be really enthusiastic about it, but (if) it's actually not worked that well, and so you would have to be really careful if you were way up there... because others will follow in your footsteps."

4.0 IMPLICATIONS AND CONCLUSION

As with any case study that uses interpretive methods, our results cannot be easily applied to other contexts. However, the discovery of the *Connector-Leader* role – *knowledge brokers* who connected overlapping CoPs and who were simultaneously outward and inward facing with respect to the organisation – can be seen as a significant finding in this study. It illustrates the fact that multiple boundaries can and do exist in today's complex online CoP environment, and underlines the importance, complexity, and potential specialisation involved in today's knowledge brokerage roles. While it may not be easy for organisational leaders to identify online *knowledge brokers*, failure to do so, and to recognise the value of such roles, may inhibit endeavours to manage organisational knowledge and change.

The study also demonstrates the usefulness of taking a system level view to identify knowledge transfer processes and knowledge-related roles in the context of the changing organisation; i.e. the need to recognise the interplay of the formal and informal, and the online and offline dimensions, of CoPs. If leaders do not adopt a system level view, they risk only seeing part of the picture of how knowledge is transferred: In our study, a few participants in positions of leadership portrayed the CLs as being enthusiastic but socially-deprived eccentrics – people whose long hours of extramural online activity had little relevance to the so-called "ordinary teacher". The true value of CLs was difficult to recognise owing to the fact that most communication between CLs and the people who followed them was effectively invisible. It was usually undertaken via email, IM, and/or face-to-face discussion. The existence of a group of followers in schools who had a low online visibility but strong face-to-face communication skills was critical to the subsequent uptake, use and adaptation of the new professional knowledge.

This study also underlines the need for managers to recognise the potentially high value of non-official and invisible online communications. In our study, IM technologies played a key role in the success of knowledge brokering. Owing to the invisibility of this kind of online communication it may be difficult for managers to identify the nature of knowledge brokers' work and its benefits. It may, however be possible to build trusted relationships with individuals who are active online, in order to identify the key brokers to support. This should not be seen in an way as a recommendation for any kind of monitoring or screening of online activity, which we found relied strongly on brokers' ability to counterpoint private and public, and visible and invisible, online communications.

Perhaps the biggest challenge for managers that arises from this study is the fact that although the knowledge brokers (CLs) were creating considerable value for their local CoPs, they were strongly *outward facing* in their orientation as professional learners. Employees with a strong external focus can be easily seen to be non-aligned with organisational goals, or non-focused on work priorities. This is of concern because, owing to the CLs' strong online reputations, with blogs effectively creating personal brands), it was easy for them to secure new employment. (In the course of the project, two CLs who reported being under-appreciated by their managers did indeed change their place of work.) These factors suggest the need for managers to consider personalised career development for those in critical knowledge broker roles, and to foster the mentoring of new brokers, with an eye to succession planning. The CLs in our study had grown into their roles over time, moving gradually towards the confident, regular use of visible online communication technologies. It therefore seems likely that the best people for identifying (and mentoring) tomorrow's knowledge brokers are the incumbents; those with the best visibility to online brokers-in-waiting.

The final implication of this study is that even knowledge brokers who are external to an organisation – in the case of this study, a distributed online community of knowledge brokers – may be of immense value to that organisation. In other words, there can be considerable potential value in an external community of knowledge brokers, provided that there is someone with appropriate skills connecting the organisation to that group, acting as a local knowledge broker, bridge or intermediary. This means that if an individual broker leaves an organisation, this person is very likely to nonetheless continue to provide value – albeit at an arms-length – provided that their brokering role is backfilled by someone with suitable brokering skills. In other words, if a key individual leaves, it is not necessary to build a new community, but it is vital to recognise where the community of knowledge brokers exists, and to successfully repair the bridge to this community.

Our research also suggests that there is a need for future research that considers the nature of knowledge brokerage in today's complex online communities; in particular, field studies which investigate how managers might best support such roles. Action research may be an appropriate method for such studies, allowing immediate application of findings. Although challenges exist in gaining visibility to the full extent of broker activity in the context of overlapping online communities, such activities are nonetheless important to study, given the complexity of today's CoPs and the different kinds of communication technologies that they employ.

REFERENCES

Albino, V., Garavelli, A., & Gorgoglione, M. (2004). Organization and technology in knowledge transfer. *Benchmarking: An International Journal, 11*(6), 584–600. doi:10.1108/14635770410566492

Allen, T. (1967). Communications in the research and development laboratory. *Technology Review, 70*, 31–37.

Allen, T. (1977). *Managing the flow of technology: Technology transfer and the dissemination of technological information within the r&d organization.* Cambridge, MA: MIT Press.

Ancona, D., & Caldwell, D. (1992). Bridging the boundary: External activity and performance in organizational teams. *Administrative Science Quarterly, 37*(4), 634–665. doi:10.2307/2393475

Brown, J., & Duguid, P. (1998). Organizing knowledge. *California Management Review, 40*(3), 90–111.

Brown, J. S., & Duguid, P. (2000). *The social life of information.* Boston: Harvard University Press.

Castro, M. (2004). *The community of practice ecosystem: On competition, cooperation, differentiation, and the role of blogs* [Electronic Version 0.9]. Retrieved July 5, 2004, from http://www.knowledgeboard.com/lib/1567

Castro, M. (2006). *Revisiting communities of practice: From fisherman guilds to the global village.* Paper presented at the 3rd European Knowledge Management Network Summer School, Madrid, Spain. Retrieved February 29, 2008, from http://www.knowledgeboard.com/item/2713

Cranefield, J., & Yoong, P. (2007). Inter-organisational knowledge transfer: The role of the gatekeeper. *International Journal of Knowledge and Learning, 3*(1), 121–138. doi:10.1504/IJKL.2007.012604

Cranefield, J., & Yoong, P. (2007). The role of the translator/ interpreter in knowledge transfer environments. *Journal of Knowledge and Process Management, 14*(2), 95–103. doi:10.1002/kpm.271

Cross, R., Parker, A., Prusak, L., & Borgatti, S. P. (2001). Knowing what we know: Supporting knowledge creation and sharing in social networks. *Organizational Dynamics, 30*(2), 100–120. doi:10.1016/S0090-2616(01)00046-8

Cross, R., & Prusak, L. (2002). The people who make organizations go - or stop. *Harvard Business Review, 80*(6), 104–112.

Davenport, T., & Prusak, L. (1998). *Working knowledge: How organizations manage what they know.* Boston: Harvard Business School Press.

Dubé, L., Bourhis, A., & Jacob, R. (2006). Towards a typology of virtual communities of practice. *Interdisciplinary Journal of Information, Knowledge, and Management, 1*, 69–93.

Earl, M., & Scott, I. (1998). *What on Earth is a CKO?* London: London Business School Press.

Efimova, L., & Hendrick, S. (2005). *In search for a virtual settlement: An exploration of Weblog community boundaries.* Updated version of a paper presented at the Communities and Technologies Conference 2005. Retrieved September 3, 2008, from https://doc.telin.nl/dsweb/Get/Document-46041/weblog_community_boundaries.pdf

Fontaine, M. (2001). Keeping communities of practice afloat: Understanding and fostering roles in communities. *Knowledge Management Review, 4*(4), 16–21.

Harragon, A., & Sutton, R. (1997). Technology brokering and innovation in a product development firm. *Administrative Science Quarterly, 42*, 716–749. doi:10.2307/2393655

Holden, N., & Von Kortzfleisch, H. (2004). Why cross-cultural knowledge transfer is a form of translation in more ways than you think. *Knowledge and Process Management, 11*(2), 127–137. doi:10.1002/kpm.198

Johnson, C. (2001). A survey of current research on online communities of practice. *The Internet and Higher Education*, (1): 45–60. doi:10.1016/S1096-7516(01)00047-1

Katz, R., & Tushman, M. (1981). An investigation into the managerial roles and career paths of gatekeepers and project supervisors in a major r&d facility. *R & D Management, 11*, 103–110. doi:10.1111/j.1467-9310.1981.tb00458.x

Lave, J., & Wenger, E. (1991). *Situated learning: Legitimate peripheral participation*. Cambridge, UK: Cambridge University Press.

Ministry of Education. (2008). *Statement of intent, 2008-2013*. Wellington, New Zealand: Ministry of Education.

Nonaka, I. (1998). The knowledge-creating company. In *Harvard Business Review on Knowledge Management*. Boston: Harvard Business School Publishing.

Nonaka, I., & Takaeuchi, N. (1995). *The knowledge creating company: How Japanese companies create the dynamics of innovation*. New York: Oxford University Press.

Orlikowski, W. J. (2002). Knowing in practice: Enacting a collective capability in distributed organizing. *Organization Science, 13*(3), 249–274. doi:10.1287/orsc.13.3.249.2776

Pawlowski, S., & Robey, D. (2004). Bridging user organizations: Knowledge brokering and the work of information technology professionals. *MIS Quarterly, 28*(4), 645–672.

Prensky, M. (2005-6). Listen to the natives. *Educational Leadership, 63*(4), 8–13.

Rogers, E. (2003). *The diffusion of innovations* (5th ed.). New York: The Free Press.

Saint-Onge, H., & Wallace, D. (2003). *Leveraging communities of practice for strategic advantage*. Boston, MA: Butterworth-Heinemann.

Sanchez, R. (2005). Knowledge management and organizational learning: Fundamental concepts for theory and practice [Electronic Version]. *Working Paper Series, Lund University, Institute of Economic Research*. Retrieved September 3, 2007, from http://econpapers.repec.org/paper/hhblufewp/2005_5F003.htm

Szulanski, G. (2000). The process of knowledge transfer: A diachronic analysis of stickiness. *Organizational Behavior and Human Decision Processes, 82*(1), 9–27. doi:10.1006/obhd.2000.2884

Tushman, M. L. (1977). Special boundary roles in the innovation process. *Administrative Science Quarterly, 22*(4), 587–605. doi:10.2307/2392402

Van Buren, M. (1999). A yardstick for knowledge management. *Training and Development Journal, 53*(5), 71–78.

Wagner, C., & Bolloju, N. (2005). Supporting knowledge management in organizations with controversial technologies: Discussion forums, Weblogs, and Wikis. *Journal of Database Management, 16*(2), 1–8.

Wenger, E. (1998). *Communities of practice. Learning, meaning and identity*. Oxford, UK: Cambridge University Press.

Wenger, E., McDermott, R., & Snyder, W. (2002). *Cultivating communities of practice*. Boston: Harvard Business School Press.

Chapter 7
Enhancing Virtual Learning Team Performance
A Leadership Perspective

Charlie C. Chen
Appalachian State University, USA

Albert L. Harris
Appalachian State University, USA

Jiinpo Wu
Tamkang University, Taiwan

ABSTRACT

Debate abounds over whether a virtual team is an effective substitute for traditional face-to-face team and can sustain itself. Drawing upon literature on leadership, trust, computer-mediated communication, and teams, the authors propose a theoretical model of online learning team effectiveness. A quasi-experiment was conducted to empirically test the impact of team trust, propensity to trust, leadership effectiveness, and communication frequency on the effectiveness of virtual learning teams and team satisfaction and performance. The results support the majority of the authors' hypotheses. Trust serves as a mediating role in the relationship between leadership effectiveness and team satisfaction and team performance. Practical implications and future trends are discussed at the end of the chapter.

INTRODUCTION

Virtual teams operate across spatial and time difference via electronic means (McShane & Von Glinow, 2000). They are formed according to tasks, membership and roles (Duarte & Snyder, 1999). Virtual teams exist in many forms to achieve ad hoc and operational purposes. For instance, virtual teams are formed to help an organization recover from disasters. Cisco utilizes virtual teams to facilitate the coordination and communication process within the company and with business partners. Some companies form virtual teams to increase productivity and creativity. Open source software development heavily relies on virtual teams to advance. Call centers are another form of a virtual team to provide customer and technical support services. Virtual teams are prevalent within and outside many

DOI: 10.4018/978-1-60566-958-8.ch007

organizations, and in the open source community. The virtual form has many advantages over co-located teams (where team members are physically located together). These include; the flexibility of team coordination and reorganization, reduction of travel budget, frequency of communication, and fast responses to customers' needs (Suchan & Hayzak, 2001).

Virtual teams formed to perform e-learning activities have a definite set of tasks, such as discussing a business case or completing a case report, to complete within a predetermined length of time. An instructor plans, designs, executes and completes a course. The instructor is responsible for the learning effectiveness of students throughout the course. The instructor performs these responsibilities as a typical project manager; the instructor can approve or disapprove the project outcomes delivered by the virtual learning team. Team members can alternate roles as either a project manager or a team member. Despite the difficulty of establishing social goals (e.g. trust) and aggregating the disparate interest of virtual team members, virtual teams designed for a learning purpose often have clearly stated educational goals, such as a deadline for assignments, course materials to study, and exams to take. The clarity of purpose and the participatory processes are two of the best predictors of a virtual team's success (Lipnack and Stamps, 1997). As such, it is plausible that it is easier to establish a virtual community in the higher education environment than in the business context.

In this chapter, we will present an initial investigation into how a leader's effectiveness can influence the effectiveness of a virtual learning team. In addition, the relationships between trust, trust propensity, and communication frequency are examined and their impacts on virtual learning team effectiveness are assessed.

BACKGROUND

A virtual team is made of a group of people working independently and interdependently to achieve a common goal (Jarvenpaa and Leidner, 1999; Lipnack & Stamps, 2000). A virtual learning team could be composed of instructor, students, guest speakers, and assistants, all working together to improve the learning effectiveness for students, and teaching effectiveness for instructors.

Learning Effectiveness of Virtual Teams

Virtual learning teams need to address the desired pedagogical goals (Leidner & Jarvenpaa, 1995). Effective learning models include the traditional classroom, constructivism, and collaborationism (Leidner & Fuller, 1997). The focus of traditional classroom learning is the dispersion of information, rather than information processing. Its primary weakness is the lack of an active learning process (Kolb, Rubin, & McIntyre, 1984). Experiential exercises are effective approaches in improving communication skills, building self-confidence and motivating knowledge-sharing among team members in the traditional classroom (Gove, Clark, & Boyd, 1999). Constructivism focuses on the knowledge construction process and is an inductive approach to improve the knowledge transfer effectiveness of a learner. Collaborationism differs from the other two learning models in that it exposes students to diversified ideas and provides a more realistic learning context (Leidner & Fuller, 1997; Leidner & Jarvenpaa, 1995). Potential benefits are the improvement of shared understanding, communication and listening skills, and participation.

Collaborative knowledge creation and sharing activities have been evident in a wide range of forms, such as the vertical organizational integration in a supply chain to reduce uncertainty and

92

improve transactional efficiency (Williamson, 1975), professional virtual communities, and online learning communities. In the online learning community, collaborative learning is an active learning approach to advance one's knowledge and to solve class problems in a collaborative fashion (Alavi, 1994).

Team-based learning in a cooperative mode is more effective than learning in an individual or a competitive manner to improve a student's (1) higher-level reasoning skills, (2) new ideas and procedural innovation, (3) critical thinking skills, (4) creative responses (Leidner & Jarvenpaa, 1995), and (5) motivation to learn (Leidner, & Fuller, 1997). The instructor is a coach who facilitates the learning process. Students need to actively engage themselves in the team-based learning process to succeed in collaborative learning, discovery learning and high order reasoning (Charan, 1976).

However, it is more challenging to have effective collaborative learning in a virtual space than in a physical space. Interpersonal relationships in a virtual team are more fragile because of a lower degree of internal communications and cohesiveness and the absence of contextual factors such as social cues and social presence. Based on group formation and process theory, interpersonal contexts are a prerequisite to the formation of virtual teams (Connerley & Mael, 2001). A lack of social context may result in doubt, distrust and suspicion among team members, which inhibits the operation of the virtual team. The fast fluidity of team formation can also potentially weaken the cohesiveness of virtual team (Dineen & Noe, 2003).

The satisfaction or dissatisfaction of team members in a virtual learning team is attributed to intrinsic and external factors (Chyung, & Vachon, 2005). Motivation-hygiene theory (Herzberg, 1968) asserts that job satisfaction is more related to intrinsic factors (recognition, achievement, and responsibility), whereas job dissatisfaction is more closely related to external factors (e.g. salary and work conditions). Many studies of e-

learning also validate this proposition. Intrinsic factors, such as a higher computer self-efficacy of learners (Lee, Vogel & Limayem, 2002), a high degree of engagement into online activities (Richardson, Long & Woodley, 2003), and a strong sense of community (Rovai, 2002), can help improve satisfaction of e-learners. On the contrary, external factors, such as poor course design and instruction quality (Young, 1999) and difficulty using e-learning systems (Berner & Adams, 2004), can result in attrition from and complaints about e-learning activities. Improving external factors, such as the social presence factor of e-learning systems (adding video feature to the audio-based lecturing) (Berner & Adams, 2004), and the usability of e-learning systems (Johnson, et al., 2004), does not significantly improve the satisfaction level of e-learners. This leads to speculation that improving the internal management process of an online learning community via leadership is a potentially effective approach to improving satisfaction levels of members. It is a challenge to ensure that team members participate and support the online learning activities, given that they are affected by uncontrollable extraneous factors that are not directly related to learning tasks (Duarte & Snyder, 1999) throughout the course. Team governance is an issue that has been underestimated. In particular, we hypothesize that the lack of effective leadership is one key inhibitor of virtual team success. Without this important factor, accomplishing the predetermined learning goals in a virtual team may be difficult.

Leadership Effectiveness

Leadership effectiveness is defined as the effective utilization of limited resource to achieve objectives (Avolio & Kahai, 2003). Existing literature has investigated leadership effectiveness from various perspectives and dimensions (see Table 1). There are three established theories in leadership effectiveness: trait theory, contingency theory and behavioral complexity theory. Trait theory

Table 1. A review of leadership effectiveness dimensions

Researchers	Dimensions of Leadership Effectiveness
Reddin (1970)	Objectives achievement.
House (1971)	Motives of subordinates, job satisfaction and popularity of a leader
Vroom & Yetton (1973)	Decision quality and popularity of a leader
Fiedler (1967)	Objective measurement of; that is, levels of objective being achieved. For instance: productivity and job performance.
Dansereau, Graen & Haga (1973)	Job performance, satisfaction and turnover rate
O'Reilly & Roberts (1974)	Performance, satisfaction and organizational commitment
Hersey & Blanchard (1982)	Matching leadership styles with the degree of sophistication of subordinates
Hunt & Osborn (1982)	Actual job performance and satisfaction levels related to results
Hoy & Miskel (1987)	Reputation of a leader, accomplishment of organizational objectives, satisfaction of team members
Yukl (2002)	The degree of objective accomplishment by the leader's team or organization. Attitudes of subordinates toward their leader. Perceived performance for the contribution of a leader to his team viewed by outsiders (third party) or subordinates

assumes that a leader is "born, not made." An organization is more likely to succeed when led by individuals with leadership traits. The complexity of internal and external environments has rendered this viewpoint less valid in virtual teams, where the missing social/context cues caused by technological incapability can potentially undermine strong leadership traits, such as charisma and social status (Dubrovsky, Kiesler & Sethna, 1991).

Contingency theory emphasizes the degree of fitness between leadership roles and the external environment. Leadership roles can be classified into task-centered vs. relationship-centered leaderships based on the least preferred co-worker instrument (Fiedler, 1967). Task-centered leaders emphasize task accomplishments and achievements of subordinates, while relationship-centered leaders emphasize interpersonal relationships among coworkers and their emotional needs. This bipolar view oversimplifies the behavioral complexity of leadership roles and may overlook innumerable social contingencies in the virtual environment, such as the use of anonymity to sidestep conflict interests and avoid the blame of making false messages. Behavioral complexity theories assume that a leader needs to function in multiple

roles to succeed in a rapidly changing environment (Hooijberg, 1996). These theories further identify the number of behavioral repertoires an effective leader needs in order to succeed in a complex environment. Paradox and contradiction are common phenomena in a complex environment. A leader needs to have the ability to deal with them by playing competing or contradictory roles, if necessary, to move the entire team toward the accomplishment of team goals. Under this view, the contingencies of leadership in the virtual team can be analyzed more appropriately. We focus our attention on this theory and its connections to leadership effectiveness in the virtual environment.

The relevance of these variables varies with the research objectives and could have very different results in different situations. Measures of leadership effectiveness also need to incorporate multiple dimensions. A review of leadership literature reveals that there are at least four approaches to measure leadership effectiveness: (1) objective versus perceptual measures, (2) acceptance versus rejection of the leader, (3) individual versus group performance measures, and (4) productivity versus satisfaction. The focus of this chapter is to understand the learning performance and satisfaction of virtual learning teams. Therefore, we will combine the group performance with satisfaction as the measures of the effectiveness of virtual learning teams.

IMPROVING VIRTUAL LEARNING EFFECTIVENESS WHEN USING TEAMS

To enhance virtual learning effectiveness, one or more of the variables for successful virtual learning teams must be improved. Team effectiveness is about whether a team can successfully achieve its predefined goals. Two major measures for the success of team performance include performance and attitudinal indicators. A performance indicator is concerned with the percentage of goals being achieved, while an attitudinal indicator is concerned with team relationships (Gladstein, 1984; Lurey & Raisinghani, 2001). The former indicator can be further measured subjectively (Lurey & Raisinghani, 2001; McDonough, Kahn & Barczak, 2001) or objectively (Gladstein, 1984) to see if the project goals (scheduling, scope, budget, quality) stated at the beginning of a project have been achieved. The latter indicator can be assessed by satisfaction measurements of cooperation, team effectiveness, team members' job performance (Gladstein, 1984), results (Warkentin, Sayeed, & Hightower, 1997) and the decision making process (Paul, et al., 2004). Literature on leadership and team effectiveness indicates that leadership effectiveness can help predict team effectiveness in both performance and satisfaction levels (Neuman & Wright, 1999; Ozaralli, 2003).

Improving a Team Member's Propensity to Trust Other Members

No trust, no team. Team members need to have a strong belief – trust – at the outset of the team formation in order to accelerate the social exchange

process. Social goods are intangible and hard to measure (Kelley & Thibaut, 1978). Reciprocation among individuals is a typical social exchange activity based on the beliefs of exchange partners (Gefen & Ridings, 2002; Blau, 1964).

An individual's trust orientation or propensity to trust is a stable personality trait; that is, the willingness to trust others (Mayer, Davis, & Schoorman, 1995). This orientation can directly or indirectly affect the degree of one's trust (Jarvenpaa & Leidner, 1999; Jarvenpaa, Knoll, & Leidner, 1998). Team members' actual contributions to the team project are fundamental to the success of a virtual team project. A stronger orientation or propensity to trust can lead to actual trust. It is important to incorporate the trust factor into the design of a virtual team (Neuman & Wright, 1999).

Improving Leadership Effectiveness

A leader is essential in executing and monitoring a project and dealing with roadblocks (Duarte & Snyder, 1999). In the field of organizational dynamics, leadership is one of the critical success factors for team cooperation (Avolio & Kahai, 2003; Hart & Mcleod, 2003; Jarvenpaa & Leidner, 1999; Jarvenpaa, Knoll, & Leidner, 1998; Kayworth & Leidner, 2002; Zigurs, 2003). Virtual teams differ from face-to-face (F2F) teams primarily in that a team leader heavily depends on information technologies to lead and communicate with team members, as well as to disseminate and transfer information. Information technology as a primary communication channel can potentially both increase or undermine the capability of a leader to exercise his/her leadership in the virtual team (Avolio & Kahai, 2003).

A leader is a "relationship mediator." An effective leadership strategy is to build relationships among team members and encourage understanding and caring for one another. This strategy can help improve the overall degree of trust (Pauleen, 2003). Positive leadership can help build trust quickly and continuously maintain trust relationships (Jarvenpaa & Leidner, 1999; Jarvenpaa, Knoll, & Leidner, 1998).

Improving the Impact of Communication Frequency

A team needs to proactively engage in an effective communication process to build trust, such as providing relevant information and timely feedback (Jarvenpaa & Leidner, 1999). Communication is one of the most important tasks for the success of a team project. The Project Management Institute asserts that a project manager spends about 98% of his/her time on verbal and nonverbal communications. Trust is one of the direct outputs of communication (Suchan & Havzak, 2001).

We believe that critical success factors for a virtual team are not much different from a traditional team. Teams in both forms need a clear purpose (Huszczo, 1996), measurable goals, smaller team size of 3-12 people (Lipnack & Stamps, 1997), establishment of team norms or operating guidelines (Scholtes, 1988), effective communication and decision making skills and processes (Aranda, Aranda, & Conlon, 1989), and team interactions (Kimball, 1999). Virtual teams primarily differ from F2F teams in their heavy reliance on information communication and technology (ICT) media as a link among people and for communications (Lipnack & Stamps, 1997). Four dimensions determine the degree of digitalization for a virtual team: geography, time, organization and culture (Zigurs, 2003). The higher one of these four dimensions, the higher degree a virtual team needs to rely on the support of ICT. ICT links can be either synchronous or asynchronous tools to perform interpersonal communications, collaboration and coordination (O'Hara-Devereaux & Johansen, 1994). Synchronous ICT tools vary with the dimensions of social presence and information richness, and can be classified as text-, audio- and video-conferencing systems. Asynchronous ICT tools include e-mail, discussion forms, bulletin

boards, workflow, scheduling and other project management applications. Regardless of the communication channels, the more frequently virtual learning team members communicate with one another, the more likely they are to exchange information and learn from one another, and as a result, team members can increase their learning effectiveness. Figure 1 summarizes the above discussion into four critical factors leading to the effectiveness of virtual learning teams.

Improving Team Trust

Trust is an important factor for the success of a virtual team. As important as the team goals, trust is the emotional link that connects members of a virtual team (Lipnack & Stamps, 1997). Despite this, it is easier to engender mistrust in the virtual team because of dissimilar backgrounds of team members and the lack of social contexts. Many studies (Jarvenpaa & Leidner, 1999; Jarvenpaa, Knoll, & Leidner, 1998) have found evidence supporting their argument on the importance trust among team members has on the success of a virtual team. Trust is an efficient mechanism to improve communication efficiency and team cohesiveness.

A seminal study about the critical success factor of virtual teams at IBM, Sun Microsystems and Motorola found that trust is the prerequisite to the success of virtual teams (Lipnack & Stamps, 1997). The physical distance among team members (O'Hara-Devereaux & Johansen, 1994) and the necessity of building trust at the outset of virtual team formation further substantiate the importance of trust issues in virtual teams. For virtual teams to succeed, a higher level of trust needs to be established at the beginning and ending periods of a project (Jarvenpaa & Leidner, 1999). In the early stages of project implementation, trust can be improved by (1) active social exchanges, (2) communications conveying enthusiasm, (3) the ability to cope with technical and task uncertainty, and (4) initiative among members (Lewis

Figure 1. Four critical factors to the success of virtual learning teams

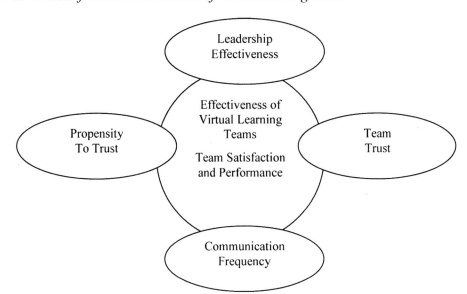

& Weigert, 1985). Trust can be improved in the latter stage by having (1) equitable, regular and predictable communication, (2) substantive and timely response, (3) strong leadership, and (4) message transitions from procedural to task focus. Trust is a multidimensional construct comprised of cognitive (competence) and affective (emotional connections) elements (Lewis & Weigert, 1985). Affective elements of trust are more important than cognitive elements in a fragile environment like virtual teams (Meyerson, Weick & Kramer, 1996). Virtual teams must quickly form trust (Meyerson, Weick & Kramer, 1996). Relative importance of the cognitive versus affective aspects of trust is contingent upon the type of social relationship, situation, and system (Lewis & Weigert, 1985). A virtual learning team that nurtures trust throughout the team operation process will naturally lead to higher team effectiveness than virtual teams that do not nurture trust throughout the process.

METHODOLOGY

In order to scientifically examine the importance of these four factors – team trust, communication

frequency, propensity to trust, and leadership effectiveness – in relation to the effectiveness of virtual learning teams, we formed 45 virtual learning teams out of 178 subjects with an average of 4 members within each team. These virtual teams elected a team leader on day one and engaged in a six-week virtual learning process without seeing each other. All virtual teams needed to study business cases available at http//digitalenterprise. org/cases/index.html. Cases posted on the website included America Online, Classmates, Ofoto, and Dell Computer, Inc., just to name a few. The instructor randomly assigned a case to each virtual team and had specific questions for the assigned virtual teams to address. Team members evaluated the effectiveness of their leader, and in turn the leader evaluated the contribution of team members to the team project. The mutual evaluation process was designed to motivate the team towards accomplishing team goals. To facilitate the communication process among team members, five communication channels were made available to them: messenger, E-mail, online synchronous meeting room, online asynchronous meeting room, and MSN discussion groups. An MSN discussion group is a many-to-many communication medium that allows the transfer of image, video and files.

Measurement and Analysis

The measure of leadership effectiveness was adapted from another leadership study (Kayworth & Leidner, 2002). Team members assessed their virtual team leader's (1) performance, (2) managerial success, and (3) overall managerial effectiveness. Team trust was assessed using Jarvenpaa & Leidner's (1999) measurement. A member's propensity to trust was measured using another instrument from Jarvenpaa & Leidner's (1999) study. Communication frequency was calculated by (1) adding the number of posted messages and articles and dividing by the number of team members to obtain the frequency of asynchronous communication among team members; and (2) adding the number of participants who joined the MSN discussions and dividing by the number of team members. This study did not control and collect information about the use of e-mails.

Team effectiveness was measured by team learning performance and satisfaction of team members. To measure learning performance, the instructor and his teaching assistant assessed the quality of the team reports for a final grade. The grades were determined based on the rigor, creativity, and formatting of the reports. The final grade was in three ranking orders: high (above 85 points), middle (84-75 points) and low (below 74 points). Team satisfaction was based on the assessment of subjects' emotions and future prospects for their virtual team with an instrument from Tjosvod's (1988) group and organization study. All items of these instruments were on a five-point Likert scale.

After data were collected in the end of six-week long of virtual learning process, we adopted the statistical method Partial Least Square (PLS) (Stevens, 1996) to examine if any causal relationships existed among the five factors studied, and how strong the relationships were. We found that an

individual's propensity to trust others will directly influence the actual trust. Cultural backgrounds, experiences, and personality traits can influence an individual's inclination, disposition or propensity to trust others (Mayer, Davis, & Schoorman, 1995). The instructor randomly grouped members into a virtual learning team without matching their cultural backgrounds or personality traits. Without having the shared social context, our evidence shows that an individual is very likely to rely on his/her propensity to trust others at the beginning of a virtual learning team formation. Leadership effectiveness is another influential factor for trust building among team members. However, when team members do not know one another and are not physically located together, the higher communication frequency does not help close trust propensity within the group.

Results

The collected data shows that no relationship was found between communication frequency and trust. This finding is contradictory to the importance of repeated interactions for the development of trust in the F2F context (Lewis & Weigert, 1985). Trust is another form of psychological contract that is created through the expectations of reciprocal obligations among teammates (Rousseau, 2001). Communication frequency alone may not be sufficient for the formation of the trusting behavior in the virtual learning context. It may be more important to examine the quality of each discussion, the duration, and the intensity of each discussion, rather than the quantity (communication frequency). This argument is particularly germane to virtual learning teams, because team members are more likely to engage in continuous and frequent interaction to avoid reneging and incongruence-based incidents before the project deadline (Huszczo, 1996; Piccoli & Ives, 2003). As such, a virtual learning team tends to create a higher level of trust among team members in the latter stage of team activities. This has demonstrated the incapability of communication frequency to create high levels of trust throughout the team formation process.

Trust and both dimensions of team effectiveness (team learning performance and satisfaction of team members) were positively correlated, indicating the important role of team trust in virtual learning group performance and team member attitude. Previous research on group performance and satisfaction in a face-to-face setting has proven the critical role of trust in team success and healthy team dynamics (Mayer, Davis, & Schoorman, 1995). Our study confirms and extends those findings to virtual learning teams. As expected, leadership effectiveness has a strong impact on team effectiveness. A closer examination shows that leadership effectiveness has a stronger impact on team satisfaction than on team performance. Conflicts and disagreements among team members are often shown in the latter stage of virtual learning activities. A leader in the virtual learning team is more likely to focus on coordinating team members to harmonize internal and external relationships, as well as mitigate their conflicts and crisis for most of time. A virtual learning team leader can wait until the latter stage of the team project to shift to task-oriented leadership. The dyadic dynamics of leadership roles are unique features to the virtual learning team and need to be fully considered during the formation process.

Unexpectedly, communication frequency is related to team performance but not to satisfaction. It is possible that in the context of online learning tasks, group communication and coordination is essential to obtaining good performance (i.e., grade), but not necessarily higher satisfaction. Groups interacting via computer-mediated communication may experience more conflict and disagreement. Because fewer social and context cues can be efficiently communicated through mediated communication, it is more difficult to resolve any conflicts and disagreements. Hence, the relationship between the frequencies of me-

diated communication and team satisfaction is unclear and worth further investigation.

Limitations

There are some noteworthy limitations that imply interesting and fruitful further research. First, team performance and dynamics may be highly task-dependent. In this study, only a few tasks were used to evaluate team performance. The results of study may not be generalized to other types of tasks. In addition, our results may not be duplicated when other online learning software is used. There are many course management systems available in the market today, and even more being developed. Different e-learning software may provide different levels of support for communication and collaboration. To summarize, further investigation with other tasks and e-learning software is necessary to develop more robust and generalizable findings.

Second, because of the cross-sectional design of this study, no causation can be determined. The significant paths between constructs can only be interpreted as a correlation, and the causal inferences are solely based on theoretical arguments. Further studies employing longitudinal or controlled experimental design may provide even more convincing evidence of the critical roles of leadership effectiveness, trust, and communication frequency. Finally, team performance was evaluated by a single instructor. We recognize the need to replicate our study using multiple instructors to eliminate the possibility of bias or inaccuracy in the evaluation process.

PRACTICAL IMPLICATIONS AND FUTURE TRENDS

Online learning is becoming an important educational tool. However, the factors that may influence the success of a virtual learning team have not been studied extensively. Whether the factors that impact the effectiveness of traditional face-to-face teams will also play critical roles in online learning has yet to be determined. Our study has several contributions to the research literature and provides some practical implications and future trends to virtual learning team effectiveness.

First, our experiment confirms that leadership effectiveness plays the same important role in online learning as in face-to-face learning. Even though online team leaders cannot lead the team in a traditional face-to-face manner, their importance in coordinating group effort and promoting team trust is still a stronger predictor of team effectiveness. Escriba-Moreno, Canet-Giner and Moreno-Luzon's (2008) study shows that formalization can enforce coordination inside and among virtual teams, and participative leadership style can promote team trust. Effective coordination is also indispensible to the improvement of satisfaction of team members. Piccoli, Powell and Ives' (2004) study shows that self-directed virtual teams report higher individual satisfaction with the team and project than behavioral control teams. Our findings corroborate with each other and emphasize the importance of assigning effective leaders to virtual learning teams to improve team performance. When managing virtual learning teams, an instructor can purposely assign students who demonstrate the ability to coordinate and involve members into learning activities as virtual learning team leaders. This design is an effective solution to greatly improve learning performance of virtual learning teams.

Second, we found that communication quantity is not sufficient to improve virtual team performance and satisfaction. Though communication frequency is linked to performance, to improve satisfaction, other ways to measure communication quality instead of quantity need to be adopted in the future to investigate the role of communication in virtual team effectiveness. In comparison, the success of open source software (OSS) development relies heavily on the ability of motivating developers to continuously provide constructive

inputs and deliver projects. Communication quality has been proven to be one important variable to increase OSS team performance (Stewart, 2006). Stewart's findings about the positive impact of communication quality on the performance of virtual learning teams are further confirmed by our results. Diversity is an important asset to global virtual teams. Yet, ineffective control of miscommunication and conflicts can result in dysfunctional virtual teams (Humes and Reilly, 2007). When forming virtual learning teams, it is important to monitor the communication quality in addition to promoting the importance of participation based on the communication frequency.

Finally, the significant direct and mediating roles of trust in virtual team effectiveness were tested in this study. Although trust is widely agreed upon as a critical predictor of face-to-face team efficiency, its role in the virtual learning team has not yet been explored extensively. Our research represents one of the first to study trust in an online-learning team. The absence of physical contacts and long distance compromises trust (Monalisa, et al., 2008). This study suggests trust among team members can be improved via three measures: (1) propensity to trust, (2) leadership effectiveness, and (3) communication quality.

Managers and educational professionals who would like to improve the efficiency of virtual teams can gain some insight from our theoretical framework. To improve team performance, practitioners can consider assigning effective team leaders, encouraging quality communication, and promoting interpersonal trust among team members. They can also provide training and workshops to improve the leadership effectiveness of assigned or elected team leaders.

CONCLUSION

An effective virtual learning team needs to address both a team's learning performance and individual team members' satisfaction levels.

Leadership effectiveness, trust, and communication frequency can potentially have a direct impact on the effectiveness of a virtual learning team. This study proposes a comprehensive framework to investigate the relationship among these factors. A PLS structural equation model was used to test the collected data and analyze the hypothesized relationships. We found that trust is an influential factor in improving the effectiveness of a virtual team. To cultivate the trust of team members, it is important to assess their propensity to trust. We explored the mediating effect of trust and confirmed its critical impact on team effectiveness. We also found that communication frequency does not have a direct relationship with trust and team satisfaction. However, communication can significantly improve team performance. Leadership effectiveness has a direct influence on the improvement of trust and team effectiveness.

This study integrates the theories of leaderships and virtual teams into the e-learning context. Like other forms of virtual teams, a virtual learning team relies heavily on the support of information communication systems and is susceptible to the use of such systems. It is often argued that communication frequency is one indicator of the successful use of e-learning systems to improve team effectiveness. This study disputes the argument that this indicator is not an effective one to predict team effectiveness. Other factors in virtual team communication, such as the degree of interactiveness, social presence, and the quality of communication need further investigation.

REFERENCES

Alavi, M. (1994). Computer-mediated collaborative learning: An empirical evaluation. *MIS Quarterly, 18*(2), 159–174. doi:10.2307/249763

Aranda, E. K., Aranda, L., & Conlon, K. (1998). *Teams: Structure, process, culture, and politics.* Upper Saddle River, NJ: Prentice Hall.

Avolio, B., & Kahai, S. (2003). Adding the "e" to e-leadership: How it may impact your leadership. *Organizational Dynamics, 31*(4), 325–338. doi:10.1016/S0090-2616(02)00133-X

Berner, E. S., & Adams, B. (2004). Added value of video compared to audio lectures for distance learning. *International Journal of Medical Informatics, 73*(2), 189–193. doi:10.1016/j.ijmedinf.2003.12.001

Blau, P. M. (1964). *Exchange and power in social life.* New York: John Wiley & Sons.

Charan, R. (1976). Classroom techniques in teaching by the case method. *Academy of Management Review,* (3): 116–123. doi:10.2307/257280

Chyung, S. Y., & Vachon, M. (2005). An investigation of the profiles of satisfying and dissatisfying factors in e-learning. *Performance Improvement Quality, 18*(2), 97–103.

Connerley, M. L., & Mael, F. A. (2001). The importance and invasiveness of student team selection criteria. *Journal of Management Education, 25,* 471–494. doi:10.1177/105256290102500502

Dansereau, F., Cashman, J., & Graen, G. B. (1973). Instrumentality theory and equity theory as complementary approaches in predicting the relationship of leadership and turnover among managers. *Organizational Behavior and Human Performance, 10,* 184–200. doi:10.1016/0030-5073(73)90012-3

Dineen, B. R., & Noe, R. A. (2003). The impact of team fluidity and its implications for human resource management research and practice. *Research in Personal and Human Resource Management, 22,* 1–38. doi:10.1016/S0742-7301(03)22001-6

Duarte, D. L., & Snyder, N. T. (1999). *Mastering virtual teams: Strategies, tools, and techniques that succeed.* San Francisco: Jossey-Bass Publishers.

Dubrovsky, V., Kiesler, S., & Sethna, B. (1991). The equalization phenomenon: Status effects in computer-mediated and face-to-face decision making groups. *Human-Computer Interaction, 6*(2), 119–146. doi:10.1207/s15327051hci0602_2

Escriba-Moreno, M. A., Canet-Giner, M. T., & Moreno-Luzon, M. (2008). TQM and teamwork effectiveness: The intermediate role of organizational design. *The Quality Management Journal, 15*(3), 41–59.

Fiedler, F. E. (1967). *A theory of leadership effectiveness*. New York: McGraw-Hill.

Fornell, C., & Larcker, D. F. (1981). Evaluating structural equation models with unobservable variables and measurement error. *JMR, Journal of Marketing Research, 18*(1), 39–50. doi:10.2307/3151312

Gefen, D., & Ridings, C. (2002). Implementation team responsiveness and user evaluation of customer relationship management: A quasi-experimental design study of social exchange theory. *Journal of Management Information Systems, 19*(1), 47–69.

Gladstein, D. L. (1984). Groups in context: A model of task group effectiveness. *Administrative Science Quarterly, 29*(4), 499–517. doi:10.2307/2392936

Gove, S., Clark, M. A., & Boyd, B. (1999). *Moving metaphors: Recipes for teaching management via experiential exercises*. Paper presented at the Academy of Management Annual Meeting.

Hart, R. K., & Mcleod, P. L. (2003). Rethinking team building in geographically dispersed teams: One message at a time. *Organizational Dynamics, 31*(4), 352–361. doi:10.1016/S0090-2616(02)00131-6

Hersey, P., & Blanchard, K. (1982). *Management of organizational behaviour* (4th ed.). Englewood Cliffs, NJ: Prentice-Hall.

Herzberg, F. (1968). One more time: How do you motivate employees? *Harvard Business Review, 46*(1), 53–63.

Hooijberg, R. (1996). A Multi-Directional approach toward leadership: An extension of the concept of behavioral complexity. *Human Relations, 49*(7), 917–946. doi:10.1177/001872679604900703

House, R. J. (1971). A path-goal theory of leader effectiveness. *Administrative Science Quarterly, 16*, 321–339. doi:10.2307/2391905

Hoy, W. K., & Miskel, C. G. (1987). *Educational administration: Theory, research, and practice* (3rd ed.). New York: Random House.

Humes, M., & Reilly, A. H. (2007). Managing intercultural teams: The eorganization exercise. *Journal of Management Education, 32*(1), 118. doi:10.1177/1052562906294988

Hunt, J. G., & Osborn, R. N. (1982). Toward a macro-oriented model of leadership: An odyssey. In J. G. Hunt, U. Sekaran, & C. A. Schriesheim (Eds.), *Leadership: Beyond establishment views* (pp. 196-221). Carbondale, IL: Southern Illinois University Press.

Huszczo, G. E. (1996). *Tools for team excellence*. Palo Alto, CA: Davies-Black.

Jarvenpaa, S. L., Knoll, K., & Leidner, D. E. (1998). Is anybody out there? Antecedents of trust in global virtual teams. *Journal of Management Information Systems, 14*(4), 29–64.

Jarvenpaa, S. L., & Leidner, D. E. (1999). Communication and trust in global virtual teams. *Organization Science, 10*(6), 791–815. doi:10.1287/orsc.10.6.791

Johnson, T. R., Zhang, J., Tang, Z., Johnson, C., & Turley, J. (2004). Assessing informatics students' satisfaction with a Web-based courseware system. *International Journal of Medical Informatics, 73*(2), 181–187. doi:10.1016/j.ijmedinf.2003.12.006

Kayworth, T. R., & Leidner, D. E. (2002). Leadership effectiveness in global virtual teams. *Journal of Management Information Systems, 18*(3), 7–40.

Kelley, H. H., & Thibaut, J. (1978). *Interpersonal relations: A theory of interdependence.* New York: Wiley.

Kimball, L. (1999). Facilitating what you can't see: How to run a cyberspace team. *Technology for Learning, 1/3.*

Kolb, D. A., Rubin, I. M., & McIntyre, J. M. (1984). *Organizational psychology: Readings on human behavior in organizations.* Englewood Cliffs, NJ: Prentice-Hall.

Lee, F., Vogel, D., & Limayem, M. (2002). Virtual community informatics: What we know and what we need to know. In *Proceedings of the 35th Hawaii International Conference on System Sciences.* Hawaii: IEEE.

Leidner, D. E., & Fuller, M. (1997). Improving student learning of conceptual information: GSS supported collaborative learning vs. individual constructive learning. *Decision Support Systems, 20,* 149–163. doi:10.1016/S0167-9236(97)00004-3

Leidner, D. E., & Jarvenpaa, S. L. (1995). The use of information technology to enhance management school education: A theoretical view. *MIS Quarterly, 19*(3), 265–291. doi:10.2307/249596

Lewis, J. D., & Weigert, A. (1985). Trust as a social reality. Social forces. *Social Forces, 63*(4), 967–985. doi:10.2307/2578601

Lipnack, J., & Stamps, J. (1997). *Virtual teams: Reaching across space, time and organization with technology.* New York: John Wiley & Sons, Inc.

Lurey, J. S., & Raisinghani, M. S. (2001). An empirical study of best practices in virtual teams. *Information & Management, 38*(8), 523–544. doi:10.1016/S0378-7206(01)00074-X

Mayer, R. C., Davis, J. H., & Schoorman, F. D. (1995). An integrative model of organizational trust. *Academy of Management Review, 20*(3), 709–734. doi:10.2307/258792

McDonough, E. F., Kahn, K. B., & Barczak, G. (2001). An investigation of the use of global, virtual, and collocated new product development teams. *Journal of Product Innovation Management, 18*(2), 110–120. doi:10.1016/S0737-6782(00)00073-4

McShane, S. L., & Von Glinow, M. A. (2000). *Organizational behavior.* Boston: Irwin McGraw-Hill.

Meyerson, D., Weick, K. E., & Kramer, R. M. (1996). Swift trust and temporary groups. In R.M. Kramer (Ed.), *Trust in organizations: Frontiers of theory and research* (pp. 166-195). Thousand Oaks, CA: Sage Publications, Inc.

Monalisa, M., Daim, T., Mirani, F., & Dash, P. (2008). Managing global design teams. *Research Technology Management, 51*(4), 48–59.

Neuman, G. A., & Wright, J. (1999). Team effectiveness: Beyond skills and cognitive ability. *The Journal of Applied Psychology, 84*(3), 376–389. doi:10.1037/0021-9010.84.3.376

O'Hara-Devereaux, M., & Johansen, R. (1994). *Global work: Bridging distance, culture, and time.* San Francisco, CA: Jossey-Bass.

O'Reilly, C. A., & Roberts, K. H. (1974). Information filtration in organizations: Three experiments. *Organizational Behavior and Human Performance, 11,* 253–265. doi:10.1016/0030-5073(74)90018-X

Ozaralli, N. (2003). Effects of transformational leadership on empowerment and team effectiveness. *Leadership and Organization Development Journal, 24*(6), 335–344. doi:10.1108/01437730310494301

Paul, S., Seetharaman, P., Samarah, I., & Mykytyn, P. P. (2004). Impact of heterogeneity and collaborative conflict management style on the performance of synchronous global virtual teams. *Information & Management, 41*(3), 303–321. doi:10.1016/S0378-7206(03)00076-4

Pauleen, D. (2003). Leadership in a global virtual team: An action learning approach. *Leadership and Organization Development Journal, 24*(3), 153–162. doi:10.1108/01437730310469570

Piccoli, G., & Ives, B. (2003). Trust and the unintended effects of behavior control in virtual team. *MIS Quarterly, 27*(3), 365–396.

Piccoli, G., Powell, A., & Ives, B. (2004). Virtual teams: Team control structure, work processes, and team effectiveness. *Information Technology & People, 17*(4), 359–379. doi:10.1108/09593840410570258

Reddin, W. J. (1970). *Managerial effectiveness.* New York: McGraw Hill.

Richardson, J., Long, G., & Woodley, A. (2003). Academic engagement and perceptions of quality in distance education. *Open Learning, 18*(3), 223–244. doi:10.1080/0268051032000131008

Rousseau, D. M. (2001). Schema, promise and mutuality: The building blocks of the psychological contract. *Journal of Occupational and Organizational Psychology, 74*(4), 511–542. doi:10.1348/096317901167505

Rovai, A. P. (2002). Sense of community, perceived cognitive learning, and persistence in asynchronous learning networks. *The Internet and Higher Education, 5*(4), 319–332. doi:10.1016/S1096-7516(02)00130-6

Scholtes, P. R. (1988). *The team handbook: How to use teams to improve quality.* Madison, WI: Jointer Associates Inc.

Stevens, J. (1996). *Applied multivariate statistics for the social sciences.* NJ: Mahwah: Lawrence Erlbaum Publishers.

Stewart, K. J. (2006). The impact of ideology on effectiveness in open source software development teams. *MIS Quarterly, 30*(2), 291–314.

Suchan, J., & Hayzak, G. (2001). The communication characteristics of virtual teams: A case study. *IEEE Transactions on Professional Communication, 44*(3), 174–186. doi:10.1109/47.946463

Tjosvold, D. (1988). Cooperation and competitive interdependence. *Group Organizational Studies, 13*, 274–289. doi:10.1177/105960118801300303

Vroom, V. H., & Yetton, P. W. (1973). *Leadership and decision making.* Pittsburgh, PA: University of Pittsburgh Press.

Warkentin, M. E., Sayeed, L., & Hightower, R. (1997). Virtual teams versus face-to-face teams: An exploratory study of a Web-based conference system. *Decision Sciences, 28*(4), 975–996. doi:10.1111/j.1540-5915.1997.tb01338.x

Williamson, O. E. (1975). *Market and hierarchies: Analysis and antitrust implications.* New York: Free Press.

Young, J. R. (1999). Course for instructors helps keep students. *The Chronicle of Higher Education, 46*(11), A59.

Yukl, G. (1975). Toward a behavioural theory of leadership. In Houghton, et al. (Eds.), *The management of organizations and individuals.* London: Ward Lock Educational.

Zigurs, I. (2003). Leadership in virtual teams: Oxymoron or opportunity. *Organizational Dynamics, 31*(4), 339–351. doi:10.1016/S0090-2616(02)00132-8

Chapter 8
Building Collective Awareness in Virtual Teams:
The Effect of Leadership Behavioral Style

Mohamed Daassi
University of Bretagne Occidentale, France

Nabila Jawadi
CREPA, Center for Research in Management & Organization, France

Marc Favier
University of Grenoble, France

Michel Kalika
*Ecole de Management Strasbourg, Université Robert Schuman, CREPA Center for Research in
Management & Organization, France*

ABSTRACT

This chapter investigates the role of e-leaders in building and maintaining collective awareness within virtual teams. The authors examine the effects of behavioral leadership orientation on collective awareness building. The study explores the bi-dimensional structure of both collective awareness and leader behavior orientation. According to this conceptualization, activity-awareness is linked to task-oriented behaviors of e-leaders. Activities related to goal clarification, coordination and work monitoring are expected to provide more visibility regarding team members' actions and their contribution to work completion. At the same time, social awareness is developed through the e-leaders' relation-oriented behaviors. The development of aspects related to interpersonal relationships such as trust, cohesion, and conflict management reduce uncertainty regarding the behavior of team members. Interviews conducted with 12 members of two virtual teams confirm the authors' theoretical development and emphasize information management as a key managerial practice for e-leaders to build collective awareness.

DOI: 10.4018/978-1-60566-958-8.ch008

INTRODUCTION

Virtual teamwork, enabled by advances in information and communication technologies, seems to have become a prerequisite in the network economy. Virtual teams are composed of *"geographically and/or organizationally dispersed co-workers that are assembled using a combination of telecommunications and information technologies to accomplish an organizational task"* (Townsend *et al.*, 1998, p. 18).

Virtual teams provide new opportunities for organizations as they allow them to reduce business costs, bridge time and space distances, and bring together experts regardless of their locations (Kayworth and Leidner, 2001-2002). Despite these advantages, virtual teams face greater challenges than their traditional counterparts, as they are made up of disparate members who must rely on information and communication technologies (ICT) instead of direct face-to-face communication. One major challenge for virtual teams is to build shared understanding that helps team members to face the uncertainty and ambiguity of the virtual context. These mechanisms are hindered by the use of Information and Communication Technologies (ICT) to communicate and coordinate work rather than face-to-face contact and direct interactions (Hinds & Weisband, 2003).

In this regard, the development of collective awareness within the team is considered as an effective means to establish visibility and clarity regarding the actions and behavior of team members. It helps them to reduce the uncertainty of virtual relationships and to establish a collaborative work environment.

On the other hand, many studies have underlined the importance of e-leaders in fostering cohesiveness, developing and maintaining trust (Jarvenpaa *et al.*, 1998; Kanawattanachaï and Yoo, 2002), and enhancing performance (Hardin *et al.*, 2006; Lurey and Raisinghani, 2001). Less is known about how e-leaders contribute to building and maintaining collective awareness

in virtual teams (Weisband, 2002) as well as the mechanisms that help them to do so. Indeed, as a recent topic in virtual team literature, research on collective awareness has tended to focus on defining the concept within the virtual context and identifying its changing facets. Little attention has been paid to its effects and relations with other organizational mechanisms such as trust, cooperation or leadership.

The aim of this chapter is to identify the contributions made by the leaders to collective awareness building in virtual teams. We attempt to develop an integrative framework based on the current literature on both collective awareness and leadership within virtual teams in order to define a body of relevant managerial actions. We illustrate our developments with the results of two case studies that we conducted to analyze factors influencing collective awareness management in virtual teams (Daassi, 2006). The case studies are based on interviews with twelve members of two virtual teams. The interviewees were asked about their perceptions regarding the need for e-leaders and their contribution to collective awareness development.

This chapter is organized as follows. In the first section, we present an overview of collective awareness. We set out the definition and dimensions of the concepts and the reasons behind the need for collective awareness. The second section discusses the theories and taxonomies related to e-leadership as well as the different perspectives adopted to analyze it. This section also demonstrates the relevance of a behavioral approach in studying leadership and collective awareness building in virtual teams. The third section attempts to establish the links between the two concepts and explores what actions and behaviors allow e-leaders to manage collective awareness. Our analysis is illustrated with verbatim extracted from the interviews. Finally, the conclusion sum-up our results, present our theoretical and managerial contribution and point to some of the limitations and possible extensions of our work.

COLLECTIVE AWARENESS

While collective awareness has been widely studied in traditional face-to-face teams, it constitutes a new topic in virtual team literature. The interest generated by this concept is heightened by its importance with respect to the problems of uncertainty and ambiguity in virtual work situations. Before analyzing the role of collective awareness in the way virtual teams function, we need to explain which facets are covered by the concept and its dimensions.

Definition and Dimensions

Collective awareness in virtual teams has been defined in various ways.[1] Here, we subscribe to Daassi and Favier's definition of collective awareness as "*a common and shared vision of a whole team's context which allows members to coordinate implicitly their activities and behaviors through communication*" (Daassi and Favier, 2005, p.2). Contrary to the other definitions in the Human-Computer Interaction field, which rely on what is called 'awareness mechanisms' (Dourish and Bellotti, 1992), the definition adopted acknowledges the *human* role in collective awareness building.

Collective awareness is referred to more broadly as a shared mental model of the team, designating a collective understanding or mental representation of knowledge that is shared by team members (Klimoski and Mohammed, 1994). According to Mathieu *et al.* (2000), these organized knowledge structures allow individuals to interact with their environment, thus building mutual knowledge of information and awareness that the others possess.

As a consequence of the multitude of definitions, groupware systems have addressed several types of awareness. However, many of the types of awareness presented cover the same requirements and can be linked together. In this study, we implement a typology developed by Prinz (1999), which distinguishes two types of awareness:

On the one hand, *Activity awareness* denotes knowledge about the project-related activities of other team members. This involves, for example, being informed about what the other members are doing at a given moment. Activity awareness implies information-related awareness that focuses on the activities performed to achieve a specific shared task.

On the other hand, *Social awareness* refers to knowledge about the team members, and in particular, their social situation. Social awareness includes information about the presence and activities of people in a shared environment. What do they do outside their work context? Are the other members attentive? What is their emotional state level of interest?

This taxonomy is broadly in line with the findings of Bales (1950) Interaction Processes Analysis, where he distinguishes task-oriented from socio-emotional processes. The bi-dimensional structure of collective awareness was also validated by Daassi and Favier (2007) through the creation of a measurement scale.

The Need for Collective Awareness

Collocated team members have the advantage of being constantly aware simply via their social abilities such as nonverbal cues, face-to-face communication or direct control. Feedback about what others are doing is consequently immediate and can be accomplished passively (Weisband, 2002). However, in virtual teams there is no such opportunity. Cramton (2001) identified five factors that inhibit mutual knowledge creation in a dispersed collaboration context. Factors include failure to communicate and retain contextual information, unevenly distributed information, difficulty in communicating and understanding the silence of information, differences in speed of access to information and problems interpreting the meaning of silence.

Virtual team members face enormous uncertainty due to the lack of visibility concerning the activities and behaviors of others, and delayed feedback. They are less able to make inferences about other members' knowledge, and thus less able to anticipate others' actions (Cramton, 2002; Rooij *et al.,* 2007). Virtual team members need to reduce their uncertainty about each other by exchanging information to raise awareness of others, their tasks and the team's progress.

In a face-to-face context, team members can rely on voice levels, smiles and raised eyebrows to determine whether they are being understood (Wilson, 2003). However, the digital environment does not offer these nonverbal cues - which, in turn, can increase uncertainty about others' activities and behaviors, and the feeling of isolation. Effectively, computer-mediated communication environments are characterized by limitation in time and space for accessing information and a lack of visibility regarding the work being carried out by the group. Thus, it is difficult to convey or discern successful comprehension, current focus of attention or concomitant attitudes and affect (Carroll *et al,* 2003). In such a context, team members may need to actively monitor the others' activities to remain informed about their joint work (Gambetta, 1988).

To reduce uncertainty, 'awareness information' that answers the "who, when, why, where and what" questions regarding collective actions are basic requirements, thereby enabling co-workers to coordinate more effectively.

Why Build Awareness?

Collective awareness plays an important role in determining the success or failure of virtual teams (Cramton, 2001; Weisband, 2002). We argue that collective awareness is a prerequisite for effective tasks and behavioral coordination in virtual teams.

Adequate human behavior requires awareness of the overall situation of the actors, resources and knowledge involved. Thus, building and maintaining awareness among team members is a crucial factor in facilitating coordination and enhancing teamwork performance. As Schlichter *et al* (1997) suggest, awareness is important to keep team members up-to-date with important events, thereby contributing to their ability to make conscious decisions. Furthermore, collective awareness reduces the effort needed to coordinate tasks and resources by providing a context in which to interpret utterances, and to anticipate and predict others' actions and behaviors (Gutwin *et al,* 1996). According to Hinds and Weisband (2003, p. 22), *"when behavior is predictable, more assumptions can be made about what is being done and what needs to be done so that work can move forward without constant monitoring and consultation."*

Collective awareness allows 'virtual' co-workers to adjust their own activity in order to build synergy of skills and efforts. The emergence of a common vision within a virtual team should support cooperative approaches and behavior as well as the mutualisation of knowledge and collective practices. According to Cramton (2001), mutual knowledge increases the likelihood of comprehension because it allows speakers *"to formulate their contributions with an awareness of what their addressee does and does not know"* (Krauss and Fussell, 1990, p. 112).

For all these reasons, building and maintaining collective awareness in virtual teams is an important process that requires the involvement of all the actors and, above all, of the team leader. In their managerial activities, e-leaders accomplish actions, establish rules and adopt behaviors that influence collective awareness. What e-leaders do is related to members' behaviors as well as work activities and aims at providing more visibility about their actions and their contribution to the work in hand. These ideas will be developed in the following section.

LEADERSHIP IN VIRTUAL TEAMS

E-leadership is becoming a largely studied topic in virtual teams' literature. Several studies have attempted to identify the contribution of e-leaders to team management and performance (Hoyt et Blascovich, 2003 ; Kayworth et Leidner, 2001-2002). They have explored the activities and behaviors that allow e-leaders to establish coordination mechanisms, relationship building and conflict resolution. Leadership theories developed for face-to-face contexts are used to analyze these questions and to test their validity in the virtual context.

In this paragraph, we will try to formulate an appropriate definition of e-leadership and identify its main characteristics. We will then justify the adoption of the behavioral perspective in order to understand the contribution of e-leaders to the development of collective awareness.

Definition and Characteristics

Despite the interest e-leadership, no clear definition has as yet been developed. Avolio *et al.,* (2001) define e-leadership as "*a social influence process mediated by AIT (advanced information technologies) to produce a change in attitudes, feelings, thinking, behavior, and/or performance with individuals, groups and/or organizations. E-leadership can occur at any hierarchical level in an organization and can involve one-to-one and one-to-many interactions within and across large units and organizations. It may be associated with one individual or shared by several individuals as its locus changes over time*" (p. 617). According to this definition, the only difference between leadership and e-leadership is that the former occurs in a face-to-face context while the latter is mediated through ICT.

We think that this understanding of e-leadership may lead to confusion and exclude important characteristics of the concept. Indeed, research output on leadership in a digital context has

indicated deep differences that distinguish this form of management from traditional face-to-face leadership.

According to Kayworth and Leidner (2001-2002), e-leaders face new challenges that arise from the team members' dispersion and their reliance on ICT to achieve their work. These challenges arise from cultural differences, the distortion of social mechanisms (such as trust building and communication), technological problems and the achievement of work activities. "*Given these challenges with communication, technology, logistic and culture, we argue that virtual team environment may be more complex than their traditional counterpart*" (Kayworth and Leidner, 2001-2002: p. 10).

In this regard, e-leaders have to develop specific virtual skills to help them effectively manage virtual context parameters. Cascio and Shurygailo (2003) identify these skills as virtual communication, virtual collaboration and virtual socialization. They consist of establishing clear rules for exchanging social and work information exchange and of, for professional behaviors and the electronic coordination mechanisms that facilitate task accomplishment. These new e-leadership functions are based on effective technology management, which may be the most important challenge of e-leaders. Technology selected to communicate and to coordinate work has to take into account the nature of the team members tasks and communications needs. The information value of electronic tools related to their richness should contribute to work effectiveness by providing relevant information about work activities and other team members (Kirkman and Mathieu, 2005).

In addition, e-leaders have to pay particular attention to individual skills regarding the use of and the learning of technology. Problems of technophobia (Kayworth and Leidner, 2001-2002) or computer self-inefficacy (Townsend *et al.,* 1998) may inhibit technology use by members and consequently negatively impact on team performance. To resolve this problem, e-leaders may consider technology training sessions before the team members begin the work.

In addition to the new facets of e-leadership, research in the field has also explored other issues concerning emergent leadership, e-leadership effectiveness, the roles and functions of e-leaders, etc. This stream of research is based on the theoretical background developed for face-to-face leadership. One of the purposes was to test the relevance of these theories in studying e-leadership. The results show that certain theories can help us to understand and analyze e-leadership and provide a new means of studying this organizational mechanism (Avolio *et* al., 2001; Kayworth and Leidner, 2001-2002, Yoo and Alavi, 2002).

E-Leadership and Theory

In a recent literature review on leadership in virtual teams, Misiolek (2005) concludes that different approaches have been adopted to examine e-leadership. All these approaches are inspired from organizational leadership in face-to-face contexts. They can be classified into one of the following paradigms: trait, behavioral, or contingency theories. All of these theories can help us identify factors that contribute to leadership effectiveness. Misiolek (2005) also noted that new perspectives such as shared leadership have emerged in the study of e-leadership such as shared leadership.

According to trait theories, effective leaders are those who have personal innate characteristics that distinguish them from other people in the organization and legitimize their position as leaders. These traits may derive from physical appearance, attitudes, human relations, etc. This stream of research was designed to find a universal model of leadership characteristics that contribute to their effectiveness. However, it failed to define such a set of characteristics as leaders' traits differ from one person to another and it is impossible to identify all of the characteristics involved. In addition, leadership effectiveness depends on other factors such as the leaders' behavior and contingency factors (House and Adita, 1997).

For the behavioral perspective, the focal question is: which set of observable behaviors generates leadership effectiveness? Researches in this field have developed diatomic behavioral models such as transformational versus transactional leadership, theory X versus theory Y, etc. (Yoo and Alavi, 2004). These models are based on the identification of leaders' activities that can be classified into two main categories:

- **Task-oriented activities** deal with goal clarification, activity planning, coordination, direction, task repartition, etc.
- **Relationship oriented activities** relate to socio-emotional support, mentoring, facilitation, conflict resolution, etc.

While this perspective has been widely adopted in studies of organizational leadership, it has failed to establish a clear link between leaders' behaviors and their effectiveness in all organizational situations.

Contingency theories have been developed to find responses to this issue. Their objective is to determine situational factors that influence leadership effectiveness (Friedler, 1967; Hersey and Blanchard, 1982). According to contingency approaches, leadership effectiveness depends on contextual factors in addition to the roles and activities of leaders. These factors may relate to the nature of the task accomplished, hierarchical links, power distribution, organizational rules, etc.

The contingency perspective provides a wide and relevant approach to the study of leadership as it integrates leaders' characteristics, their behavior and roles, and situational factors to examine their effectiveness. However, it cannot take all organizational situations into account or analyze their effects on leadership performance.

All of these theories have been tested in the context of virtual teams. The results have pointed to the advantages of the behavioral perspective in studying e-leadership. They also highlight new perspectives of e-leadership such as behavioral complexity (Kayworth and Leider, 2001-2002) and shared leadership (Misiolek, 2005).

In their study of leadership effectiveness, Kayworth and Leidner (2001-2002) found that effective leaders play an important role in both work and relationship management. They are effectively perceived as mentors, facilitators, coordinators, planners, etc. These results support the behavioral perspective with its task-oriented and relationship-oriented dimensions.

Yoo and Alavi (2002) tested trait, behavioral and contingency theories in a study of emergent leadership in virtual teams. Their results also support behavioral theory. They found that emergent leaders send more task-oriented and relationship-oriented messages than other members. Sudweeks and Simoff (2005) also examined emergent leadership and its relationship with communication behavior. They used number, length and nature of messages exchanged to identify emergent leaders. Their findings suggest that emergent leaders are more active than other members and send more task-oriented messages.

Hoyt and Blascovich (2003) analyzed the effects of leadership style on virtual team performance. They compared transactional and transformational leadership and found that transformational leadership is associated with higher levels of qualitative performance (satisfaction, cohesiveness, trust) and that transactional leadership is associated with higher levels of quantitative performance (output quality, efficiency).

All these results lend support to the behavioral perspective and show its relevance in the study of e-leadership. We have therefore adopted it in our theoretical and empirical work to analyze the contributions made by e-leaders to collective awareness management. More specifically, we try to show which task-oriented and relationship-oriented mechanisms e-leaders use to establish collective awareness in their teams.

LEADING VIRTUALLY: IMPLICATIONS FOR COLLECTIVE AWARENESS

Although, the contribution of e-leaders is an important factor in collective awareness development, interest in this issue is relatively limited. We noted that only Weisband (2002) has examined the relationship between team awareness and leadership in virtual teams. She analyzed two activities: initiating structure as a task-oriented activity and consideration as a relationship-oriented activity. The study results suggest that early structure initiation is positively associated with collective awareness, which in turn leads to higher performance. The author also noted that regular and frequent communication contributes to high awareness and performance.

To fill this gap in the literature, we have analyzed the activities and behaviors that allow e-leaders to manage collective awareness in their teams.

We base our arguments on perceptions collected from interviews conducted with members from two virtual teams. The first team is composed of engineers and managers working in a high-tech international firm. This team will be called HighT. The second team is composed of researchers working on a research project for a French organization. This team will be called Research. In the first team, members usually work together on different projects so, they have acquired some knowledge about each other and their respective work routines. However, in the second team, the members are working together for the first time and only for the length of the project. They have never worked together in the past and do not expect to work together again in the future (Meyerson *et al.*, 1996).

Six interviews were conducted with each team and all were recorded and transcribed to facilitate content analysis. Our results highlight the importance of e-leaders in collective awareness building and the activities they execute for this purpose. These activities are related to work and relationship development.

AWARENESS BUILDING

Collective awareness problems in virtual teams derive from uncertainty and lack of visibility of the members' actions and behaviors. Factors that may contribute to this uncertainty are generated by the lack of knowledge between members, their physical separation and their high interdependence. Collective awareness mainly relies on information exchange. It is thus up to the leader to create and then reinforce a climate of shared collective awareness. Team leaders have to develop appropriate strategies for collective awareness building. They have to manage information in order to enhance the members' mutual knowledge of one another and to make their actions and behaviors more visible.

More specifically, the leader must promote interaction between team members. With interaction, team members accumulate knowledge about their teammates' behaviors, work styles, schedules and habits, in short, they develop "awareness information." Frequent interaction and immediate feedback are required conditions for sharing information and for being a useful team member (Weisband, 2002). The duration of the collaboration and the frequency of intra-team contacts lead to the development of a reciprocal sense of connection between the team members. This allows virtual team members to feel good together and to develop a sense of sharing.

The leaders' role in establishing collective awareness was highlighted by several of the interviewees. One member of Research team noted:

"In projects where people do not know each other, collective awareness in the team will rely heavily on the leader's attitude. The leader may either be open to others and facilitate communication, or will discourage exchange and interaction between

team members. In this case, members will not communicate as easily as in the first case. We can say that according the case, collective awareness will be more or less important."

Leaders should pay attention to which information is exchanged since this is the foundation for the creation of collective awareness. To fit the precepts of behavioral theory, this information may be classified into task-oriented and relationship-oriented activities that respectively influence activities and social awareness.

Task-Oriented Activities

To reduce uncertainty about work, e-leaders' activities involve clarifying objectives, planning, coordination and monitoring (Kayworth and Leidner, 2001-2002; Yukl et al., 2002). Goal clarification is the first step in collective work organization. It is based on communicating performance objectives (quantitative and qualitative), role repartition and expectations, and resource distribution.

Goal clarification contributes to initiating team structure, which has been identified as a key performance factor in several leadership studies (Locke and Lutham, 1990). Goal clarification must be accompanied by plans and schedules that specify *"what to do, how to do it, who will do it, and when it will be done"* (Yukl et al., 2002: p. 18). These activities imply the team members' participation in determining plans and deadlines according to their competencies and the time needed to accomplish the work. Planning is an important activity for team effectiveness. It helps evaluate the contribution of each member and whether he/she has respected the performance objectives, and it gives more clarity and visibility to individual actions within the team.

In this regard, one member of the HighT team noted that: *"The climate of collective awareness consists in clearly defining objectives, competencies, all the members' tasks, when he/she has to intervene and why. This must be done by the team leader."*

The leader of this team also added: "Virtual context work must be visible for all the team members: we must be able to say this is done or this has to be done, and who has done it or who will do it. We have to manage this virtual aspect and translate it into actions. We have to indicate the direction to follow, write up the results and transform them into actions."

The role of the coordinator is to establish rules for performing the tasks and exchanging information between the team members. In this case, e-leaders identify the links between the different tasks and subsequently between the team members. They determine the level of interdependence and set up mechanisms that help manage this interdependence. In so doing, e-leaders help members to discover each other's working habits and to subsequently adapt their behavior and actions.

Coordination by e-leaders involves distributing the work between team members and allocating resources for each task. In addition, they have to establish the rules for behavior and communication that should be respected by all the team members.

Monitoring members' activities implies collecting information about work progress, individual performance, the respect of deadlines, output quality, etc. This can be monitored through observation, regular work progress reports, holding meetings or performance indicator analyses. The purpose is to detect dysfunctions in time and to resolve them quickly.

These activities require the introduction of mechanisms that ensure fast and regular feedback. These mechanisms should also foster cooperative and collaborative behavior and discourage disruptive behavior.

Relationship-Oriented Activities

Activities that contribute to the development of social awareness are trust and cohesion management, and conflict resolution.

Building trust between team members encourages them to share more information about the work in hand. It also helps develop cooperative behavior that leads to more collaboration in completing work. E-leaders contribute to building trust by encouraging exchange of information, holding regular meetings with all the members, ensuring fast and regular feedback to work queries and problems, etc. (Jarvenpaa *et al.*, 1998; Kanawattanachaï et Yoo, 2004). The e-leader needs to play a federating role in order to obtain adherence to the team objectives and to build a shared social context between team members. This shared context is based on accepted behaviors and work rules, and on a common mental model.

Cohesiveness management is based on building group identity. E-leaders need to foster the emergence of a collective identity, resulting the combination of individual identities. The group identity will be built on shared values, accepted behaviors and rules and collective adherence to team objectives. Group identity has been identified as a key cohesion factor. It contributes the team being considered as a unique entity with strong links between its component members.

Cohesiveness management also relies strongly on diversity management. One of the main characteristics of virtual teams is the diversity of the members. This diversity arises from cultural differences (members having different cultures and ethnic origins), organizational differences (members belonging to different organizations), and professional differences (members having different skills). The challenge for e-leaders is to create a source of richness from this diversity for the team. This can be achieved through early presentations of team members or training sessions on diversity management before the beginning of the project.

Figure 1. E-leadership contribution to collective awareness building

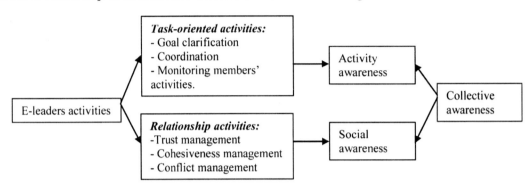

Conflict management helps e-leaders to build both trust and cohesion in their team. In the virtual context, problems may arise from a lack of information about team members and the uncertainty of their actions. E-leaders must act rapidly when problems appear in the team and choose the appropriate mode of conflict resolution. Solutions include avoidance, accommodation, collaboration, competition and compromise (Montoya-Weiss *et al.*, 2001; Shin, 2005). Montoya-Weiss (2001) demonstrate that the collaborative style is the most effective as it results in positive consequences (acceptance and adoption of proposed solutions).

To summarize our developments and results, we have drawn Figure 1, which presents the contribution of e-leadership activities to activity and social collective awareness building.

CONCLUSION AND FUTURE TRENDS

In this chapter, we explored the leader's role in creating and maintaining a collective awareness climate within virtual teams. We suggest that a leader's behavioral orientation (task and relations) influences the nature of information exchanged (task-related and relations-related), which in turn influences collective awareness (activity and social). Our contribution to the field of virtual teams is situated at both theoretical and managerial level.

On the one hand, we investigated two important concepts for the performance of virtual teams. Both collective awareness and leadership are identified as key factors in the success of virtual teams. In addition, we prepared the first essay to analyze e-leadership relations and collective awareness building. Our results show that e-leaders play an important role in maintaining collective awareness within their teams. They have to accomplish work-related and relationship-related activities designed to reduce the uncertainties associated with virtual work. The focal activity of e-leaders is information management, as information is the main source which allows team members to build shared knowledge of one another's actions and behaviors. In this regard, a member of the Research team noted that: "*Collective awareness depends heavily on information. It is really fundamental.*"

Thus, from the managerial perspective, e-leaders should pay particular attention to information gathering and distribution. They need to encourage exchange and interaction between members to share information about work and personal behavior in order to build mutual knowledge and a common social context. E-leaders also have to pay attention to technology issues related to ICT availability and their effective use by team members.

In spite of these theoretical and managerial implications, our work has some limitations that could be addressed in future extensions.

Our analyses were based on interviews with twelve virtual team members. More qualitative studies based on the content analysis of e-mails and discussions exchanged between leaders and team members would undoubtedly improve our understanding of this topic. We noted a lack of empirical studies identifying the factors that affect the relationship between collective awareness and leadership orientation in virtual teams. Alternatively, we need to examine how contextual factors, including the nature of the task, technology features, team size and culture may interact with leadership behavior to influence collective awareness within virtual teams.

Previous research found that collective awareness feeds on exchange of information which occurs across time and is shared between members depending on their level of progress in the common project (Daassi *et al.*, 2006). Resulting from the accumulation of experience, it is the duration of such exchanges that makes it possible to establish a climate of collective awareness. Future inroads that could be made along the lines of our research include looking further into the effects of leadership behavior on collective awareness over time.

In addition, it would also be interesting to explore the impact of leader gender on collective awareness given that previous studies report that women tend to focus on social-oriented activities while men focus more on task-oriented activities (Wood & Rhodes, 1992; Dennis, Kinney & Hung, 1999).

REFERENCES

Avolio, B. J., Kahaï, S. S., & Dodge, G. E. (2000). E-leadership: Implications for theory, research, and practice. *The Leadership Quarterly*, *11*(4), 615–668. doi:10.1016/S1048-9843(00)00062-X

Bales, R. (1950). *Interaction process analysis*. Cambridge, MA: Addison Wesley.

Carroll, J.-M., Neale, D.-C., Isenhour, P.-L., Rosson, M.-B., & McCrickard, S. (2003). Notification and awareness: Synchronizing task-oriented collaborative activity. *International Journal of Human-Computer Studies*, *58*, 605–632. doi:10.1016/S1071-5819(03)00024-7

Cramton, C. D. (2001). The mutual knowledge problem and its consequences for distributed collaboration. *Organization Science*, *12*(3), 346–371. doi:10.1287/orsc.12.3.346.10098

Cramton, C. D. (2002). Finding common ground in dispersed collaboration. *Organizational Dynamics*, *30*, 356–367. doi:10.1016/S0090-2616(02)00063-3

Daassi, M. (2006). *La conscience collective au sein des équipes virtuelles: Déterminants, mesure set nature dynamiques*. Unpublished doctoral dissertation, University of Grenoble, France.

Daassi, M., Daassi, C., & Favier, M. (2005). Integrating visualization techniques in groupware interfaces. In S. Dasgupta (Ed.), *encyclopedia of virtual communities and technologies*. Hershey, PA: Information Science Reference.

Daassi, M., & Favier, M. (2005). Groupware and team aware. In S. Dasgupta (Ed.), *Encyclopedia of virtual communities and technologies*. Hershey, PA: Information Science Reference.

Daassi, M., Jawadi, N., Favier, M., & Kalika, M. (2006). An empirical investigation of trust's impact on collective awareness development in virtual teams. *Int. J. Networking and Virtual Organisations*, *3*(4), 378–394. doi:10.1504/IJNVO.2006.011867

De Rooij, J., Verburg, R., Andriessen, E., & Den Hartog, D. (2007). Barriers for shared understanding in virtual teams: A leader perspective. *The Electronic Journal for Virtual Organizations and Networks*, *9*, 64–77.

Dennis, A. R., Kinney, S. T., & Hung, Y.-T. C. (1999). Gender differences in the effects of media richness. *Small Group Research, 30,* 405–437. doi:10.1177/104649649903000402

Dourish, P., & Bellotti, V. (1992). Awareness and coordination in shared workspace. In . *Proceedings of the, CSCW92,* 107–114.

Fiedler, F. E. (1967). *A theory of leadership effectiveness.* New York: McGraw-Hill.

Gambetta, D. (1988). *Trust: Making and breaking cooperative relations.* Oxford, England: Basic Blackwell.

Gutwin, C., Greenberg, S., & Roseman, M. (1996). Workspace awareness in real-time distributed groupware: Framework, widgets, and evaluation. In *Proceedings of the HCI'96 Conference on People and Computers XI, Computer-Supported Cooperative Work.*

Hersey, P., & Blanchard, K. (1982). *Management of organizational behavior: Utilizing human resources.* Englewood Cliffs, NJ: Prentice Hall.

Hinds, P. J., & Weisband, S. (2003). Knowledge sharing and shared understanding in virtual teams. In C. B. Gibson & S. G. Cohen (Eds.), *Virtual teams that work: Creating conditions for virtual team effectiveness* (pp. 21-36). San Francisco: Jossey-Bass.

House, R. J., & Aditya, R. N. (1997). The social scientific study of leadership: quo vadis. *Journal of Management, 23*(3), 409–473. doi:10.1177/014920639702300306

Hoyt, C. L., & Blascovich, J. (2003). Transformational and transactional leadership in virtual teams and physical environments. *Small Group Research, 34*(6), 678–715. doi:10.1177/1046496403257527

Jarvenpaa, S. L., Knoll, K., & Leidner, D. E. (1998). Is there any body out there? Antecedents of trust in global virtual teams. *Journal of Management Information Systems, 14*(4), 29–64.

Jawadi, N., Daassi, M., Kalika, M., & Favier, M. (2007). Virtual teams: The role of leadership in trust management. In L.-L. Brennan & V.-E. Johnson (Eds.), Computer-mediated relationships and trust: Managerial and organizational effects (pp. 34-45). Hershey, PA: Information Science Reference.

Kanawattanachaï, P., & Yoo, Y. (2002). Dynamic nature of trust in virtual teams. *Strategic Information System, 11,* 187–213. doi:10.1016/S0963-8687(02)00019-7

Kayworth, T., & Leidner, D. (2001-2002). Leadership effectiveness in global virtual teams. *Journal of Management Information Systems, 18*(3), 7–40.

Kirkman, L. B., & Mathieu, J. E. (2005). The dimensions and antecedents of team virtuality. *Journal of Management, 31*(5), 700–718. doi:10.1177/0149206305279113

Klimoski, R., & Mohammed, S. (1994). Team mental model: Constract or methaphor? *Journal of Management, 20*(2), 403–437. doi:10.1016/0149-2063(94)90021-3

Krauss, R., & Fussell, S. (1990). Mutual knowledge and communicative effectiveness. In J. Galegher, R. Kraut, & C. Egido (Eds.), *Intellectual teamwork: Social and technological foundations of cooperative work* (pp. 111-146). Hillsdale, NJ: Lawrence Erlbaum.

Locke, E. A., & Latham, G. P. (1990). *A theory of goal setting and task performance.* Englewood Cliffs, NJ: Prentice Hall.

Mathieu, J. E., Heffner, T. S., Goodwin, G. F., Sala, E., & Cannon-Bowers, J. A. (2000). The influence of shared mental models on team process and performance. *The Journal of Applied Psychology, 85*(2), 273–283. doi:10.1037/0021-9010.85.2.273

Misiolek, N. I. (2005). *Patterns of emergent leadership is ad hoc virtual teams.* Unpublished doctoral dissertation, School of Information Studies, Syracuse University.

Prinz, W. (1999). NESSIE: An awareness environment for cooperative settings. In *Proceedings of the Sixth European Conference on Computer Supported Cooperative Work* (pp. 391-410).

Sudweeks, F., & Simoff, S. J. (2005). Leading conversations: Communication behaviours of emergent leaders in virtual teams. In *Proceedings of the 38ᵗʰ Hawaii International Conference on System Science.*

Townsend, A. M., DeMarie, S. M., & Hendrickson, A. R. (1998). Virtual teams: Technology and the workplace of the future. *The Academy of Management Executive, 12*(3), 17–29.

Weisband, S. (2002). Maintaining awareness in distributed team collaboration: Implication for leadership and performance. In P. Hinds & S. Kiesler (Eds.), *Distributed work* (pp. 311-333). Cambridge, MA: MIT Press.

Wilson, S. (2003). Forming virtual teams. *Quality Progress, 36*(6), 36–41.

Wood, W., & Rhodes, N. D. (1992). Sex differences in interaction style in task groups. In C. Ridgeway (Ed.), *Gender, interaction, and inequality* (pp. 97-121). NY: Springer-Verlag.

Yoo, Y., & Alavi, M. (2004). Emergent leadership in virtual teams: What do emergent leaders do? *Information and Organization, 14*, 27–58. doi:10.1016/j.infoandorg.2003.11.001

Yukl, G., Gordon, A., & Taber, T. (2002). A hierarchical taxonomy of leadership behavior: Integrating a half century of behavior research. *Journal of Leadership & Organizational Studies, 9*(1), 15–32. doi:10.1177/107179190200900102

Zigurs, I. (2003). Leadership in virtual teams: Oxymoron or opportunity? *Organizational Dynamics, 31*(4), 339–351. doi:10.1016/S0090-2616(02)00132-8

ENDNOTE

[1] See Daassi *et al.* (2005) for complete discussion of the proposed typologies.

Chapter 9
Exploring Leadership in E-Commerce Adoption in Australian SMEs

Ada Scupola
Roskilde University, Denmark

ABSTRACT

This chapter presents the results of a study investigating leadership and leadership styles in e-commerce adoption in small and medium size enterprises in Australia. The results show that top management and CEO' leadership have a key role in small and medium size enterprises (SMEs) in developing a vision for e-commerce adoption and that the dominant leadership style is directive with some signs of consultative. Furthermore the study shows that e-commerce adoption is becoming a strategic process and in this process top management is taking into consideration both the organizational knowledge and the knowledge of external consultants.

INTRODUCTION

Technological development is impacting the business landscape by providing new ways and opportunities to conduct business. In the last decade e-commerce has especially created new possibilities to change ways of doing businesses or create new business models. In such a changing environment the role of the leader is becoming vital. "Leaders as opposed to managers are creating the visions and make the necessary plans and steps to keep their organizations competitive. In the past the role of

managers was to organize, delegate and get the job done. Nowadays companies need leaders that can establish visions and can guide the company in turbulent times (Cope and Waddell, 2001; Jago, 1982; Bower and Gilbert, 2007). This is especially true for small and medium size enterprises (SMEs) which are believed to highly benefit from e-commerce (OECD, 2002). There is much disagreement about how to classify SMEs. In this article the definition of the Australian Bureau of Statistics (ABS) is adopted according to which a small and medium size business is any business employing less than

DOI: 10.4018/978-1-60566-958-8.ch009

200 employees (www.abs.gov.au). Also different definitions of e-commerce can be found in the literature. In this study e-commerce is defined as the business activities conducted using electronic data transmissions via the WWW and the focus is on business-to-business e-commerce in opposition to business-to-consumer e-commerce.

Most of the literature on SMEs' e-commerce adoption focuses on factors that affect the adoption decisions or factors that distinguish adopters from non adopters (e.g. Jeyaraj et al., 2006; Sabherwal et al., 2006). Previous studies have also found that the decision to adopt is influenced by environmental factors such as competitive pressure or suppliers' pressure (Thong, 1999); organizational factors such as top management support or employees knowledge (Palvia and Palvia, 1999) and technological factors such as perceived benefits of the technology (e.g. Iacovou et al., 1995) . More recently, studies are focusing on the strategic impact (e.g. Drew, 2003) or the impact of the perceived strategic value of e-commerce on the adoption decision (e.g. Grandon and Pearson, 2003). However the role of leadership in e-commerce adoption has not received much attention in the literature on e-commerce and IT adoption, which is the motivation for this study. The basic research question is:" What is the role of leadership in e-commerce adoption in small and medium size enterprises and what are the predominant leadership styles?" This question is important because the major reasons for adopting e-commerce are creating or maintaining a competitive advantage, improving customer satisfaction and keeping pace with competition as a survey conducted by Cope and Waddell (2001) about the main goals for adopting e-commerce in various industries shows.

The chapter is structured as follows. The next section presents a literature review of ICT adoption frameworks in SMEs, while the following section discusses the role of leadership and presents the theoretical framework used in the paper. This is followed by a description of the research design,

the data collection process, and the companies' background. The remainder of the chapter presents the analysis, discussion of the results, implications for practice, and conclusions and limitations.

THEORETICAL BACKGROUND

Adoption of Innovation

A fundamental approach to studying the adoption of new technologies is the diffusion of innovations (Rogers, 1995). Organizational innovations can be defined as the development and implementation of products, technologies, systems or ideas that are new to the company (Rogers, 1995). Therefore e-commerce can be defined as a type of innovation for the company adopting it. Prior studies in organizational innovation and diffusion of information technology suggest a number of factors that affect adoption and diffusion of information technology and e-commerce within a company (e.g. Kurnia & Johnston, 2000; Chau & Tam, 1997; Premkumar & Ramamurthy, 1995; Grandon and Pearson, 2003). Even though the factors affecting ICT and e-commerce adoption have been grouped into different categories (see Jeyaraj et al., 2006 for a thorough literature review), many authors (e.g. Kurnia & Johnston, 2000; Scupola, 2009) show that they can be mainly categorized according to the three contexts of Tornatzky and Fleischer's (1990) model: the environmental context, the organizational context and the technological context. Similarly we use these three contexts in organizing the literature review in this chapter as shown in Table 1.

External Environmental Context

The external environment is the arena in which an organization conducts its business. Tornatsky and Fleischer (1990) distinguish three main groups of factors within this context: industry characteristics such as competition and customer supplier rela-

Table 1. Factors affecting adoption of e-commerce, EDI and IT/IS in SMEs

Context	Factors	Authors
Environmental Context	Competitiveness Competitive Pressure Customer/Supplier Pressure Government Influence Quality of access to E-commerce Related Services Trade Associations Public Administration External Pressure Environmental Characteristics	Lertwongsatien and Wongpinunwatana (2003) Scupola (2003) Iacovou et al. (1995) Palvia & Palvia (1999) Kuan and Chau (2001) Thong (1999)
Organizational Context	Size Innovation Champion Top Management Support Existence of IT Department Employees IT Knowledge Organizational Readiness Owner Related Factors Organizational Characteristics CEO Characteristics	Lertwongsatien and Wongpinunwatana (2003) Scupola (2003) Mirchandani and Motwani (2001) Iacovou et al. (1995) Palvia & Palvia (1999) Kuan and Chau (2001) Thong (1999)
Technological Context	Perceived Benefits Perceived Compatibility Perceived Barriers Perception of IS Attributes	Lertwongsatien and Wongpinunwatana (2003) Scupola (2003) Mirchandani and Motwani (2001) Iacovou et al. (1995) Thong (1999)

tionships, technology support infrastructure and government intervention. Iacovou et al. (1995) found that external pressures, divided into competitive pressure and imposition by trading partners, were determinant in SMEs' EDI adoption. Competitive pressure was also found important by Thong (1999). Similarly Kuan and Chau (2001) in a study to understand factors distinguishing EDI adopters from non adopters, found that adopters perceive a higher government pressure and a lower industry pressure then non adopters. Finally Scupola (2003) found that government role, public administration, trade associations and suppliers pressure had an important role in SMEs' e-commerce adoption within the external environment in Southern Italy.

Organizational Context

The organizational context represents the factors internal to an organization influencing an innovation adoption. These factors are a source of

structures, processes and attributes that constrain or facilitate adoption (Tornatzky and Fleischer, 1990). Many factors belonging to this context have been found important in explaining information technology innovation and e-commerce adoption. For example, Iacovou et al. (1995) identified organizational readiness, operationalized as financial and technological resources of the firm as a major factor in SMEs' EDI adoption. Palvia and Palvia (1999) conclude that owner characteristics have a greater impact on ICT satisfaction, while other factors such as training and education represent reasons for dissatisfaction.

These results are also supported by Thong (1999) that showed that the CEO characteristics have a major importance in IS adoption and by Kuan and Chau (2001). Mirchandani and Motwani (2001) include employees' IT knowledge and top management support as factors distinguishing small business e-commerce adopters from non adopters, while Scupola (2003) in addition found that the innovation champion and financial resources were also relevant factors. Finally, Lertwongsatien and Wongpinunwatana (2003) show that adopters, prospectors and laggards differ significantly on the extent of top management support and existence of the IT department.

Technological Context

The technological context represents the pool of technologies available to a firm for adoption, which can be both the technologies available on the market and the firms' current equipment. The decision to adopt a technology depends not only on what is available on the market, but also on how such technologies fit with the technologies that a firm already possesses (Tornatsky and Fleischer, 1990; Chau and Tam, 1997). Many studies have investigated the impact of the innovation characteristics on the innovation process. For example Iacovou et al. (1995) states that relative advantage (e.g. perceived benefits and barriers), compatibility (both technical and organizational) and trialability (e.g. pilot tests) are among the main attributes. This was also supported by Mirchandani and Motwani (2001) and partially by Scupola (2003). Lertwongsatien and Wongpinunwatana (2003) find that prospectors and adopters are significantly different from laggards in perceived benefits and perceived compatibility.

THE IMPORTANCE OF LEADERSHIP IN SMES' E-COMMERCE ADOPTION

As showed by the above literature review, many studies (e.g. Jeyaraj et al., 2006; Thong, 1999; Thong and Yap, 1996) have pointed out the importance of the organizational context in information technology innovation and within this context have investigated the effects of the organizational characteristics and individual characteristics. Within the organizational characteristics, previous e-commerce adoption research has often focused on the characteristics of the CEO (e.g. Sabherwal

et al., 2006). The argument goes that he/she has a major role in the business, which is especially important in SMEs where the CEO is often also the owner and is responsible for the survival of the business (Thong and Yap, 1995). Examples of characteristics investigated are CEO's IT knowledge and attitude towards IT innovations. For example Thong (1999) explored the role of CEO's IT knowledge and innovativeness in IT adoption. However CEOs in small companies are often not especially knowledgeable about information technology, which can be a major barrier to adoption (e.g. Cragg and King, 1993). Finally previous literature (e.g. Thong, 1999; Thong and Yap, 1995) pointed out that the CEO is generally the single point of authority, usually does not share information with other organization's employees and suggest that the CEO is the only one with access to the information needed to identify new opportunities, therefore management support is crucial for innovation adoption. CEO and top management, and especially their leadership, becomes even more important considering that small and medium size businesses have limited slack resources to invest in information technology and e-commerce (e.g. Iacovou et al., 1995). There are many definitions of leadership. The most common one is that "leadership is both a process and a property. The process of leadership is the use of noncoercive influence to direct and coordinate the activities of the members of an organized group towards the accomplishment of group objectives. As a property, leadership is the set of qualities or characteristics attributed to those who are perceived to successfully employ such influence" (Jugo, 1982). Leadership (Ready, 2004; Kotter, 2001; Goleman, 2004) might be especially important in establishing a vision and enforcing organizational rules and policy to facilitate e-commerce adoption in the organization (e.g. Scupola, 2008). In a seminal article, Kotter (2001) states that leadership is about coping with change, while management is about copying with complexity. An important leadership role is setting a direction, a vision for the company in specific domains, including for example e-commerce adoption. According to Kotter (2001, p. 87) "what's crucial about a vision is not its originality but how well it serves the interests of important constituencies-customers, stockholders, employees" and how it can be translated into a realistic company strategy". Another important role of leadership is aligning people in such a way that everybody in the company supports the established vision. This is very important as modern organizations are characterized more then ever by interdependence among employees and managers by their work, management systems and technology. Finally it is important that leaders are able both to motivate others and develop others' leadership skills (Kotter, 2001; Zaleznik, 2004; Ready, 2004). There are different theoretical approaches to leadership. The most important are universal vs. contingent theories of leadership and the ones focusing on leadership styles such as autocracy vs. democracy (Jugo, 1982). Here we focus on leadership styles. Research on leadership shows that leadership and leadership styles might be contingency-based and culturally embedded (e.g. Jago, 1982). Therefore, since this empirical investigation has been conducted in Australia, a model based on a study of Australian firms has been chosen here for the investigation: the Dunphy and Stace (1990) model.

The Dunphy and Stace (1990) Model of Leadership Styles and Change Management

This model provides a comprehensive method to analyze different levels and degrees of change and leadership styles. By drawing on the theory of change management by Dunphy and Stace (1990) and the study conducted by Cope and Waddell (2001) about auditing of leadership styles in e-commerce adoption, I use the following conceptualization of leadership styles and types of organizational change to investigate e-commerce leadership in this study:

1. Collaborative. This involves widespread employees' participation in important decisions about the organizations' future, and about the means of bringing about the organizational change.
2. Consultative. This style involves consultation with employees, primarily about the means of conducting the organizational change, with their possible limited involvement in setting goals of relevance to their area of expertise or responsibility.
3. Directive. This leadership style involves the use of managerial authority and direction as the main form of decision making about the organization's future, and about the means of bringing about organizational change.
4. Coercive. This style of leadership involves managers/executives or outside parties forcing or imposing change on key groups in the organization (Dunphy and Stace, 1993, p. 6).

Also Dunphy and Stace (1990) identified four types of organizational change an organization can undertake as a response to different stimuli, including the external environment. In e-commerce adoption, such stages can be described as follows:

1. "Fine Tuning". Organizational change which is an ongoing process characterized by fine tuning occurring in different departments to prepare for electronic adoption and use. Personnel is being developed and trained to suit the organizational adoption of e-commerce and some groups are formed within the organization to focus on e-commerce.
2. Incremental Adjustment. Organizational change which is characterized by incremental adjustments to the changing environment. The emphasis is here shifted from traditional business to a new way of conducting business (e-business). Such change involves distinct modifications (but not radical change) to

corporate business strategies, structures and management processes.

3. Modular transformation. Here organizational transformation is characterized by the major realignment of one or more department to embrace e-commerce. The process of radical change is focused on one of these subparts as for example introduction of significantly new process technologies affecting key departments or ways of conducting business.

4. Corporate Transformation. Organizational change which includes a radical transformation of the business strategies to include also e-commerce and many processes and procedures have been changed to accommodate e-commerce.

Even though these leadership styles and organizational transformation types were not developed originally by keeping the small ad medium size enterprises in mind, the assumption is made here that the four leadership styles mentioned above can be of use to investigate leadership in SMEs. However it is clear that parts of the four transformational stages are mainly characteristic of bigger companies. This is taken into consideration in the analysis.

RESEARCH APPROACH AND DATA COLLECTION

In order to investigate the role of leadership in e-commerce adoption in small and medium size businesses, the case study method (Yin, 2003) has been used. Yin (2003) defines a case study as "an empirical inquiry that investigates a contemporary phenomenon within its real-life context and relies on multiple sources of evidence (p. 13)". By following Yin (2003), the case study method can be used in this study to corroborate existing research, learn the state of the art of the role of leadership in SMEs' e-commerce adoption, and understand the na-

ture and complexity of such a phenomenon in a natural setting.

Data Collection and Research Design

The data collection includes face-to-face semi-structured, focused interviews, information provided on the company web sites, and other documents provided by the companies. The interviews were conducted with CEOs or managers that had a key role in the adoption and implementation of e-commerce. To increase reliability an interview protocol was used and a case study database was developed (Yin, 2003). The questions of the protocol were divided into two parts. Part one captured company background information such as the type of business, revenues, number of employees. Part two focused on gaining information about e-commerce adoption, web page sophistication, type and role of leadership in e-commerce adoption.

Triangulation has been achieved by visiting and analyzing each company web site before and after the interview and by analyzing annual reports and other material provided by the companies.

The questionnaire was pre-tested and minor revisions were made after the first interview. Each interview lasted between one and one and a half hour. All interviews were tape-recorded and transcribed. Notes were also taken during the interviews. Following Yin (2003) the data were analyzed by following the "general strategy of relying on theoretical orientation" of the case. Specific analytic techniques included putting information into different arrays, making matrixes of categories and placing evidence within such categories (Yin, 2003; Miles and Huberman, 1994).

Company Selection Process

The companies were selected on the basis of representativeness of the region industrial sectors and accessibility according to the following criteria:

1. The companies should have already implemented e-business or were planning to do so in the near future, thus being adopters or prospective adopters.

2. They should be registered companies, could be classified as SMEs according to the number of employees and should be located in the same geographical region to ensure that external factors such as government policy, availability of support services, and education of the available workforce were the same.

3. The companies could belong to different business sectors including high-tech/knowledge intensive sectors as these businesses have been shown to be more advanced in their use of Internet technologies then firms in other business sectors (Drew, 2003). Here the assumption has been made that 1) a sample of companies belonging to different business sectors would lead to more variety in the data regarding leadership in e-commerce adoption then a sample of companies belonging to the same sector; 2) companies in the high tech/knowledge intensive sectors, being ahead of others in e-commerce adoption, could provide interesting insights for prospectors and laggards (Lertwongsatien and Wongpinunwatana 2003).

A research assistant at Queensland University of Technology, who in advance had been instructed about the objective of the study and the companies' selection criteria helped in contacting and selecting the sample companies. Due to the companies' wish, the company names are kept undisclosed.

COMPANIES BACKGROUND

The age of the firms ranged from 6 to 40 years. Even though there is a wide spreading among the companies with regard to the number of employees, the spreading is very small in terms of revenues, which are between 15 and 20 million Australian dollars. One company however did not provide any financial information. The firms had a wide range of experience with e-commerce. One company (A3) offered the capability to download software components from the web site, however it was not charging for it yet. The project was still at experimental stage, but the company was planning to charge for it in the future if it was a success. A2 offered online training and online customer support on the web site. They had traded products on the web site in the past, but it turned out to be a mistake mainly due to the complexity of their products. A2 has an Intranet which proved to be quite a useful tool for knowledge management and sharing. A summary of the companies' characteristics is provided in Table 2.

Company A1 is in the business of site and facilities management. It has existed since 1964, but it had been privatized at the beginning of 2000. The company has 35 employees and yearly revenues of 15-16 millions Australian dollars. At the time of the interview, A1 had a web site from which it was possible to download company information and contained a database of tenants. However the company was investigating the possibility of implementing an advanced e-commerce platform in order to become a service provider to the tenants. The idea to adopt e-commerce came from the CEO/owner of the company.

The second company (A2) develops financial service software, and was established in 1983. It is privately owned by 4 people. The CEO owns 80 percent of the company and has been the one initiating the e-commerce project. It has an EDB department of 5 people. A2 offers online customer

Table 2. Characteristics of the companies

Firm	Business Type	Years in business	Number of employees	Leadership Style	Yearly revenues in AU$	E-commerce Platform Facilities
A1	Site and facilities Management	40	35	Directive/consultative	16-17 Millions	Presently the web site provides info and contains a database of tenants. Were planning to implement a full e-commerce platform.
A2	Financial Service Software Consultant	20	140	Directive/consultative	19-20 Millions	Web site supports online customer support, online training, and online customer relationship management. Traded online in the past.
A3	Consulting	6	3	Directive/consultative	No Data	Possibility to download trial software from the web site for free. Plans to make clients paying for it in the future.
A4	Design and Manufacturing	32	80	Directive/consultative	15 Millions	It is planning to adopt a full e-commerce platform. There was at that time disagreement within top management about what e-commerce features to support.

support to its clients as well as online training. In the past they had traded online, but they had stopped doing so, mainly due to the nature of their products which are too complicated with a lot of ways they can be configured often depending on the customer business model. It might have helped if they had taken a more gradual approach to e-commerce.

The third company (A3) is in consulting and serves SMEs, larger size companies and government departments, such as the department of education. It is possible to download some software application components from the web side for trial by the client companies, but the company does not charge for it yet. They plan to do so in the future, if it becomes a success.

The fourth company (A4) was established in 1971, and manufactures point of sale objects such as displays and illuminated signs. They designed and made the products in house. They regularly purchased office supplies from online catalogues as well as raw material and at the time of the interview had a very basic e-commerce platform.

They were planning to develop more sophisticated e-commerce in the near future, but at that time there was disagreement in the top management about what e-commerce features to support.

ANALYSIS AND RESULTS

Leadership in E-Commerce Adoption

Importance of Leadership. The first main result of this study is that leadership is important in order for companies to adopt e-commerce. As discussed in the theoretical background, an important leadership role is setting a direction, a vision for the company in specific domains. In e-commerce adoption, leadership implies that managers have the intuition that e-commerce will bring some benefits that can justify the investment, even though there is no certainty on the return on investment as showed by the following citation:

At that time (when we decided to adopt) we had some ideas about benefits, but we did not realize the extent of the benefits until when we started using it for some time (Financial Manager, A1")

Another important role of leadership is aligning people and departments in such a way that everybody in the company supports the established vision. For example in A2, this is achieved by empowering the marketing department to be responsible for the content of the web page and to advise top management about what to do as showed by the following statement:

It is mainly the marketing department (3 people) that is responsible for Home page content and development and to make suggestions to the CEO and top management.....(Manager, A2)

Another statement showing the visionary leadership in SMEs' e-commerce adoption is the following:

"We have adopted Internet ..because we wanted to say we exist and this is what we want to do, to enhance our own branding and marketing; we wanted to be out there on the web..((Financial Manager, A1).

Leadership styles. The second main result of the study is that the predominant style of leadership in SMEs' e-commerce adoption is the directive, with some indications that the leadership style is moving from directive to consultative or a combination of both. Top management consults both with company employees and external consultants. For example in A1, initially the initiative had been taken by the CEO, who had mainly showed a directive form of leadership, but lately he was changing towards a more consultative leadership style as the following citation shows:

It was the CIO (that decided to adopt e-commerce)... he had a lot of clients and then decided to

go with Internet, see ...the management decides... Only now management starts listening to suggestions from employees.. (Manager, A1)

The same was the case in A4:

..Only now management starts listening to suggestions from the EDB department..(Manager, A4)

Usually top management consult with employees about how to go to implement e-commerce in the company (e.g. what changes to be made and what features to support) only after the decision to adopt has been made. However, the employees are also involved in setting goals of relevance to their expertise area or responsibility, even though only to a limited extent (A1, A2, A3, A4) as the following citations shows:

...Employees also can make suggestions on web sites ...(Manager, A2)

In A2, there had been an employee that on her own initiative started analyzing competitors' web sites and found out that they were more user friendly than their own. Top management decided then to change their web site after her suggestion to make the web site more user-friendly and easy to use and operate. In all the four companies interviewed, top management considers e-commerce as a strategic innovation opportunity that could benefit or damage the company and as such it is carefully considered and discussed both internally to the company and with external consultants. For example in A4 the CEO and other top managers had had much discussion about future e-commerce plans, but they were disagreeing about its strategic impact and therefore about what to do.

There is big disagreement in management about what should be put in it (the web site). You are giving a lot of importance to the web page. ..(Manager, A4)

Organizational change. Regarding organizational change as a consequence of e-commerce adoption, it can be concluded that all the four organizations interviewed are mostly in a stage of "Fine Tuning". Organizational change due to e-commerce adoption is an ongoing process characterized by fine tuning occurring in different places or departments in the organization. Personnel is being developed and trained to suit the organizational adoption of e-commerce and some groups are formed within the organization to focus on e-commerce. For example, in A2 the two people in the marketing department had the responsibility of taking care of the structure and content of the web page and to advise top management about what to do or what changes to make. However some sign of "incremental adjustment" are also found. For example A2 offers online customer support to its clients as well as online training, which has changed some processes in the organization. Also A1 was investigating the possibility of implementing an advanced e-commerce platform in order to become a service provider to the tenants, which would have expanded the type of business the company was in to embrace e-business.

DISCUSSION OF FINDINGS

This study shows that the role of leadership is essential in e-commerce adoption. These results support the findings of other studies where top management support is important in e-commerce adoption (e.g. Lertwongsatien and Wongpinunwatana, 2003; Mirchandani and Motwani, 2001). However, if previous studies (e.g. Thong, 1999; Thong and Yap, 1995) show that the CEO is generally the single point of authority, usually does not share information with other organization's employees and is the only one with access to the information needed to identify new opportunities, this study shows that CEO's leadership styles are moving from a directive to a more consultative

type of leadership style by discussing e-commerce adoption with other managers, company's employees and consultants. This is in line with the results of the study conducted by Cope and Waddell (1994), where by auditing leadership styles in e-commerce in Australia they found out that by far the majority was consultative with very little collaborative and directive, but surprisingly more coercive. Top management and the CEO are interested in the employees' knowledge, whether it is about customer needs as for example in A2, IT knowledge as for example in A1 or simply needs for some e-commerce or IT applications as in A3. CEOs and top management use such knowledge as input to their decision making. These results could be explained by the complexity of e-commerce technologies and by the lack of specialized e-commerce knowledge by the CEO.

Furthermore this study shows that e-commerce adoption is based on top management vision and planned, strategic decision making. That is the adoption of e-commerce is not happening by chance as for example due to the son or a friend of the CEO/owner being acquainted with Internet as found in other studies (e.g. Poon and Swatman, 1999) or by using an ad hoc approach as showed by Marshall et al. (2000). This could be due to the complexity of implementing e-commerce.

The study finds that companies are starting making an "informal" plan or strategy for e-commerce adoption as also found by Drew (2003). The importance of a strategic approach to e-commerce adoption is supported by the experience of A2, which had to reduce the e-commerce capabilities when it realized that their products were too complicated to be configured and sold on the web. Therefore also the importance of "fit" between the technology and the business the company is in, as also pointed out by Mirchandani and Motwani (2001).

Finally this study shows that the managers/owners are recognizing the importance of the knowledge generated within the company. New theories of strategic management are emphasizing knowledge and the dynamic aspects of organizational knowledge creation as important in increasing the firms' innovation capability and competitive advantage (E.g. Nonaka, 1994). These theories argue that while new knowledge is developed by individuals, management plays a critical role in articulating and applying this knowledge (Grant, 1996).

FUTURE TRENDS: IMPLICATIONS FOR PRACTICE

The main implications for SMEs' managers and owners is that adoption of e-commerce offering more advanced features than just presentation of company's information on the web site for marketing purposes or use of e-mail, requires first of all that managers show leadership in this field. Leadership is especially important in establishing a vision and enforcing organizational rules and policy to facilitate e-commerce adoption in the organization (e.g. Scupola, 2008). Another implication for management is that it is important to value and take into consideration the employees' knowledge and suggestions both in the strategic planning phase and in the implementation phase of e-commerce, thus adopting a leadership style that has at least some traits of the consultative type. This is mainly due to the complexity of e-commerce and the fact that adopting e-commerce implies the allocation of resources and investments that are more substantial than just establishing an Internet connection or developing and maintaining a simple static web page.

CONCLUSIONS AND LIMITATIONS

This study has contributed to understand leadership and leadership styles in e-commerce adoption in small and medium size enterprises. The main findings can be summarized as follows:

top management and CEO e-commerce leadership are determinants for e-commerce adoption; the predominant e-commerce leadership style in Australian SMEs is directive moving towards consultative thus taking into consideration both the organizational knowledge and the consultants' knowledge in the decision to adopt or implement e-commerce.

Even though the study presents some interesting results, it is however not free from limitations. First of all the number of sample companies is limited and belong to different business sectors among which high tech industries/knowledge intensive industries. Therefore it might be difficult to generalize the results from this study to specific industrial sectors. Second, all the sample companies were located in a metropolitan area. Therefore it might be difficult to generalize the results to regional areas, defined as geographical areas located outside metropolitan centres and major cities. Nevertheless, this research gives some interesting insights into the role of leadership in SMEs e-commerce adoption. The results of this study can be useful to researchers, owners and practicing managers of small and medium size enterprises wishing to adopt e-commerce.

Finally, the limitations of this study can also be considered as the starting point for further research. For example, the study could be replicated in service companies or regional areas, and further research could investigate the emergence of strategies or the role of organizational knowledge in e-commerce adoption in SMEs. Also a follow up survey to a large sample of SMEs could strengthen the results of this study.

REFERENCES

Bower, J. L., & Gilbert, C. G. (2007). How managers' everyday decisions create or destroy your company's strategy. *Harvard Business Review*, *2007*(February), 72–79.

Chau, P. Y. K., & Tam, K. Y. (1997). Factors affecting the adoption of open systems: An exploratory study. *MIS Quarterly, 21*(1), 1–24. doi:10.2307/249740

Cragg, P., & King, M. (1993). Small firm computing: Motivators and inhibitors. *MIS Quarterly*, 47–59. doi:10.2307/249509

Creswell, J. W. (1998). *Qualitative inquiry and research design*. Thousand Oaks, CA: Sage Publications.

Drew, S. (2003). Strategic uses of e-commerce by SMEs in the east of England. *European Management Journal, 21*(1), 79. doi:10.1016/S0263-2373(02)00148-2

Goleman, D. (2004). What makes a leader? *Harvard Business Review*, 82–91.

Grandon, E., & Pearson, J. M. (2003). Strategic value and adoption of electronic commerce: An empirical study of Chilean small and medium businesses. *Journal of Global Information Technology Management, 6*(3).

Grant, R. M. (1996). Towards a knowledge-based theory of the firm. *Strategic Management Journal, 17*, 102–122.

Iacovou, C. L., Benbasat, I., & Dexter, A. S. (1995). Electronic data interchange and small organizations: Adoption and impact of technology. *MIS Quarterly, 19*(4), 465–485. doi:10.2307/249629

Jago, A. G. (1982). Leadership: Perspectives in theory and research. *Management Science, 28*(3), 22. doi:10.1287/mnsc.28.3.315

Jeyaraj, A., Rottman, J., & Lacity, M. J. (2006). A review of the predictors, linkages, and biases in IT innovation adoption research. *Journal of Information Technology, 21*(1), 1–23. doi:10.1057/palgrave.jit.2000056

Kotter, J. (2001). What leaders really do. *Harvard Business Review*, (December): 85–96.

Kuan, K., & Chau, P. (2001). A perception-based model of EDI adoption in small businesses using technology-organization-environment framework. *Information & Management, 38*, 507–521. doi:10.1016/S0378-7206(01)00073-8

Kurnia, S., & Johnston, R. B. (2000). The need for a processual view of inter-organizational systems adoption. *The Journal of Strategic Information Systems, 9*(4), 295–319. doi:10.1016/S0963-8687(00)00050-0

Lertwongsatien, C., & Wongpinunwatana, N. (2003). E-commerce adoption in Thailand: An empirical study of small and medium enterprises (SMEs). *Journal of Global Information Technology Management, 6*(3), 67–83.

Marshall, P., Sor, R., & McKay, J. (2000). The impacts of electronic commerce in the automobile industry: An empirical study in Western Australia. In [Berlin, Germany: Springer Verlag.]. *Proceedings of the CAiSe, 2000*, 509–521.

Mirchandani, D. A., & Motwani, J. (2001). Understanding small business electronic commerce adoption: An empirical analysis. *Journal of Computer Information Systems*, (Spring): 70–73.

Nonaka, I. (1994). A dynamic theory of organizational knowledge creation. *Organization Science, 5*(1). doi:10.1287/orsc.5.1.14

OECD. (2002). *Measuring the information economy 2002*. Retrieved August 20, 2004, from http://www.oecd.org

Palvia, P. C., & Palvia, S. C. (1999). An examination of the IT satisfaction of small-business users. *Information & Management, 35*(3), 127–137. doi:10.1016/S0378-7206(98)00086-X

Poon, S., & Swatman, P. M. C. (1999). An exploratory study of small business Internet commerce issues. *Information & Management, 35*(1), 9–18. doi:10.1016/S0378-7206(98)00079-2

Premkumar, G., & Ramamurthy, K. (1995). The role of interorganisational and organizational factors on the decision mode for adoption of interorganisational systems. *Decision Sciences, 26*(3), 303–336. doi:10.1111/j.1540-5915.1995. tb01431.x

Ready, D. (2004). Leading at the enterprise level. *MITSloan Management Review, 45*(3), 87–91.

Rogers, E. M. (1995). *Diffusion of innovations* (4th ed.). New York: The Free Press.

Sabherwal, R., Jeyaraj, A., & Chowa, C. (2006). Information system success: Individual and organizational determinants. *Management Science, 52*(12), 1849–1864. doi:10.1287/ mnsc.1060.0583

Scupola, A. (2003). The adoption of Internet commerce by SMEs in the south of Italy: An environmental, technological and organizational perspective. *Journal of Global Information Technology Management, 6*(1), 51–71.

Thong, J., & Yap, C. (1995). CEO characteristics, organizational characteristics and information technology adoption in small business. *Omega . International Journal of Management Sciences, 23*(4), 429–442.

Thong, J. Y. L. (1999). An integrated model of information systems adoption in small business. *Journal of Management Information Systems, 15*(4), 187–214.

Tornatzky, L. G., & Fleischer, M. (1990). *The processes of technological innovation.* Lanham, MD: Lexington Books.

Zaleznik, A. (2004). Managers and leaders: Are they different? *Harvard Business Review,* (January): 74–97.

Chapter 10
Patterns of Facilitation in Online Communities of Practice

Halbana Tarmizi
Abu Dhabi University, UAE

Gert-Jan de Vreede
University of Nebraska at Omaha, USA

ABSTRACT

Communities of practice have gained foothold in knowledge management initiatives. Still, there are challenges for COP to thrive and to serve its purpose. Facilitation can help COP in overcoming some of the challenges. However, facilitation in COP by itself is challenging as we are dealing with different types of COP that exhibit different characteristics. Through content analysis of facilitators' postings the authors identified several tasks commonly performed by facilitators from different COPs. Knowing how to accomplish those tasks will help COP facilitators in assisting their communities to thrive.

INTRODUCTION

Online communities have become part of our daily life in the Internet era. There are many reasons why people join online communities. Ridings and Gefen (2004) in their survey-based study on online communities listed several categories of motivation for online involvement. Those categories include: (1) exchange information: obtain and transfer information about at topic, educate about a topic or learn new things; (2) social support: obtain and give emotional support; (3) friendship: make friends; (4) recreation: look for entertainment; (5) common interest: love of the topic of the community; and (6) technical reasons: because of technical features in the community. They found that *information exchange* is the most common reason why people joining online communities, followed by looking for *friendship*.

There are various types of online communities (Stanoevska-Slabeva & Schmid, 2001): (1) discussion communities: communities that provide venue for exchanging information with reference to a defined topic; (2) task-and goal-oriented communities: communities strive to achieve a common goal by way of cooperation; (3) virtual worlds: communities

DOI: 10.4018/978-1-60566-958-8.ch010

that provide virtual settings of complex worlds; and (4) hybrid communities: communities that contain several types of communities. Another typology of online communities differentiates five types of communities from business perspectives (Hummel & Lechner, 2002). Those five types of communities are (1) gaming communities; (2) communities of interest; (3) business-to-business communities; (4) business-to-consumer communities; and (5) consumer-to-consumer communities.

As more people are relying on online interaction to satisfy their needs for information, managers have to understand and eventually accommodate these needs in their organizations. They have to take a lead in addressing and looking for the best solutions to serve their employees. One of the goals should be to provide a venue for them such as Community of Practice (COP) which could be considered to be a discussion community (Stanoevska-Slabeva & Schmid, 2001). Many view a COP as a type of community of interest (Fischer, 2001). A Community of Practice (COP) is a specific type of community that has gained popularity as part of knowledge management initiatives in organizations (Hildreth, Kimble, & Wright, 2000; Wenger & Snyder, 2000). Wenger and Snyder (2000) define a COP as a group of people who are informally bound together by shared expertise and a passion for joint enterprise. Based on this definition, a COP does not have to be within an organization. It can exist as an independent online community. The Internet lowers the barriers to form this type of communities, since finding those who shared expertise and a passion is no longer limited by space and time. Learning in COP, according to Wenger (1998), has four main characteristics: (1) it takes place in *practice*; (2) it happens as being a *member of a community*; (3) it becomes *meaningful* since it is a part of experience; and (4) it helps in developing *identity*.

COMMUNITIES OF PRACTICE AND PARTICIPATION

At the same time, a COP can suffer from lack of participation among its members. Several studies have identified challenges related to active participation in COPs, e.g., Ardichvili et al. (2003), Gray (2004), and Wasko and Faraj (2000). Therefore, member participation can not be taken for granted. It is obvious that an effort is needed to create a functioning COP.

Therefore, our chapter will focus on facilitation of online communities of practice, since this type of community has tremendous potentials for organization as well as Internet users in general and we believe that facilitation can help in overcoming some of the problem with participation. A need of facilitators in COP has been highlighted in several studies, including Johnson (2001), and Gray (2004). Facilitation can be defined as activities carried out to help groups in accomplishing their tasks or achieving their desired outcomes. Studies of facilitation in Group Support Systems (GSS) field have shown that it can benefit groups and making meetings more productive. As members of online communities of practice involve in collaborative activities, they will face challenges such as disagreements and/or conflicts that could lead to disruptive behaviors. Their discussions could become a lengthy debate that is no longer relevant and beneficial to the community. In such cases, facilitator can help communities and guide them through a better way of collaboration. Dubé, Bourhis, and Jacob (2006) identified 21 structuring characteristics that will influence challenges faced by those communities. They categorized those structuring characteristics into four categories, i.e., (1) demographics of the communities; (2) organizational context; (3) membership characteristics; and (4) technological environment. They found that different characteristics create different challenges for the communities.

Some practitioners differentiate several types of COP based on its main purposes. The three most common types of COP are (i) a helping commu- nity, (ii) a best practice community and (iii) an innovation community (APQC, 2000). A helping community serves the needs of its members to help one another in their daily tasks, activities or routines. This type of community can also be setup around people interest or hobby with the goal to help its members answering questions related to their interests or hobby. A best-practice community is focusing on capturing and shar- ing lessons learned from community members. Through this process, other members can learn and reuse those practices in accomplishing their tasks. This type of community will prevent mem- bers from doing same mistakes or reinventing the wheel. An innovation community would play a significant role in knowledge management in organization, since it will involve in stewarding body of knowledge. This type of community can become source of knowledge for entire organiza- tion in its domain.

As we are dealing with different types of COP, there is a need to understand how facilitator involves in those communities. In particular, we need to identify a general pattern of their involve- ment in COP. Understanding their involvement would help us in designing tools needed to sup- port facilitation as well as in providing training for COP facilitators.

FACILITATOR TASKS

Facilitation can be found in various types of on- line communities, especially those that involve discussions and have a large membership. Most facilitators will focus on keeping order in those communities, as well as administrative tasks. Further, Berge and Collins (2000) in their studies about online discussion communities found that most facilitators will be involved in tasks, such as archiving messages, deleting messages, or adding subscribers. We argue that facilitators in COP have a broader role than those in other online

communities. The main reason for that is that in a COP, the facilitators will be responsible to create an environment that is conducive for information exchange as well as knowledge creation, which is the main purpose of a COP.

Therefore, this work aims to further our under- standing of facilitators' tasks in communities of practice, because we view this as an important step in creating a successful COP in an organization. Moreover, this work contributes by highlighting differences of facilitating online communities, especially online communities of practice. This work identifies the most common tasks performed by online COP facilitators. Tarmizi and de Vreede (2005) developed a task taxonomy of facilitators in COP, based on processes within a COP as formulated by Gongla and Rizzuto (2001). The taxonomy was developed by taking an overview of facilitation tasks in the Group Support Sytems (GSS) field as a basis(Clawson & Bostrom, 1996), as this field has done extensive studies on facili- tation, see e.g., Niederman, Beise, and Beranek (1993), Clawson and Bostrom (1996), Romano, Nunamaker, Briggs, and Mittleman (1999) and de Vreede, Boonstra, and Niederman (2002). In their study Clawson and Bostrom (1996) identified sixteen facilitation functions in GSS. However, we considered one of those functions, i.e., demonstrate flexibility, more as behavior than as a function. For this reason, we adopted only fifteen of the sixteen items. At the same time, we considered differences between COP and GSS in term of environments as well as characteristics. A GSS session will tend to have stable participants, while a COP will have fluid membership, as members join and leave. This will expand the facilitator's tasks to help new members in communities. As a COP is always in need for new blood to thrive, facilitators could help communities by promoting their communities to potential members. Since a COP could be part of an organization, COP facilitators need to be in constant contact with the management of the organization where the community is embedded. This will ensure that management is aware about how the COPs in their organization run and at the same time COP members can be reminded about the policy and directions taken by the organization. Based on those additional needs and challenges, Tarmizi and de Vreede (2005) identified a total of 33 tasks for facilitators in COP. Table 1 shows those tasks including its definitions.

Some of those tasks are related to interaction with community members as well as other community's activities, while others are related to interaction with entities outside the community, such as other COPs or organizations. Therefore, we can divide the items into two categories: (1) Internal, those tasks that are directed toward internal functioning of the COP; and (2) External, those tasks that are related to the functioning of the COP as a whole in its environment. Furthermore, the internal category can be divided into three different types: (1) facilitator as information source for the community; (2) facilitator as inspirator to community members; and (3) facilitator as guide. The external category is also divided into three types, consisting of the facilitator as (1) an information source for the outside world; (2) a public relations manager representing the community and its members; and (3) an investigator searching for and collecting useful information for the community. For detail discussion of this, please refer to Tarmizi and de Vreede (2005).

METHOD

Posting made by facilitators offered a window to understand facilitators' involvement in a community. By analyzing the contents of their postings, we could gain some understanding and insight on what types of tasks a COP facilitator tried to accomplish through his/her postings. For this purpose, we collected a random sample of postings made by facilitators in several online COPs from different sizes and types. The variety of the communities ensured that we were not dealing with

only one type of COP. It also took into account different challenges faced by different communities as highlighted by Dubé et al. (2006). A content analysis was conducted on the collected postings using the facilitator's task taxonomy (Tarmizi & de Vreede, 2005) as categories. This method has been extensively used in communication research, especially in the mass communication field (Lombard, Snyder-Duch, & Bracken, 2002). After a short training and measuring intercoder agreement, two coders conducted the content analysis. They placed each of the postings into one of the categories independently. This method has been utilized in several studies related to computer-mediated communications, e.g., Mowrer (1996) and Walther and Tidwell (1995).

RESULT AND DISCUSSION

The goal of this work is to identify the most common tasks among those 33 facilitator tasks performed by facilitators. We found that five tasks are the most commonly performed by facilitators across communities of practice. Those tasks are (1) task of presenting information, (2) task of keeping community focus on its purposes, (3) task of promoting understanding of the tools, (4) task of helping community or community members through suggestions, and (5) task of building members' cooperative relationship. This result is achieved through content analysis of 221 postings from six different communities. Here, we will discuss each of those tasks, as we believe those tasks represent an important aspect of COP facilitation regardless of types or characteristics of each community. These will represent general pattern of facilitation in COP. Additional tasks might be needed in specific COP to address specific challenges. Understanding what tasks are important for facilitators to be performed in COP will help managers in organizations to decide how to best support these communities in their organizations. Furthermore, it should help

Table 1.

1	**Listens to members, makes sense from their expression as well as integrates information from members:** Facilitator listens to community members, tries to make sense from members expressions and integrates information from members and presents it to members.
2	**Understands technology/tools and its capability:** Facilitator familiarizes herself with the technology supporting community activities.
3	**Create comfort with and promote understanding of the tools and tool outputs:** Facilitator carefully introduces and explains tools to the community; directly addresses negative comments and inconveniences caused by tools.
4	**Presents information to community:** Facilitator gives clear and explicit instructions; uses clear and concise language in presenting ideas; makes summaries during and after the discussion; identifies the interesting contributions from the less interesting ones.
5	**Brings important information to new members:** Facilitator tells new members of community about important information regarding this community. Those information could include facilities, rules and members' rights and obligations
6	**Answering new members concern** Facilitator addresses and answers concerns of new community members
7	**Informs members regarding management concern:** Facilitator informs all community members regarding concern from management of the organization where the community is embedded.
8	**Create and maintain an open, positive, and participative environment:** Facilitator draws out individuals by asking questions; uses activities and technology to get people involved early on.
9	**Develops and asks the right questions:** Facilitator asks questions to trigger members' thinking
10	**Promote ownership and encourage group responsibility:** Facilitator helps a group take responsibility for and ownership of the discussion outcomes and results; stays out of their content; turns the floor over to the others.
11	**Encourage multiple perspectives:** Facilitator encourages looking at issues from different point of views; uses techniques, metaphors, stories, and examples to set the group to consider different frames of reference.
12	**Encourages new members to participate in community's activities:** Facilitator approaches and encourages new members to participate actively in community activities.
13	**Introduces new members to the community:** Facilitator introduces every new member to the community.
14	**Plans community meeting:** Facilitator plans the meeting ahead of time, including agenda, announcement and invitation to members.
15	**Keeps community focus on its purpose:** Facilitator clearly communicates the purpose of the community to the members up front; makes community purpose visible to the members; keeps the members focused on and moves along with the community purpose in mind.
16	**Selects, prepares and supports appropriate tools for the community:** Facilitator appropriately matches tools (both computer-based and manual) to the task(s) and need(s) of the community, selects tools that fit type of community, prepares tools (both computer-based and manual) and figures out and solves common technical difficulties.
17	**Directs and manages community meeting or discussion:** Facilitator guides community during the meeting or discussion
18	**Builds cooperative relationships with among members:** Facilitator helps develop constructive relationships with members and among members.
19	**Mediates conflicts within community:** Facilitator helps members of the community to solve conflict among them
20	**Scans the community:** Facilitator is aware of any kind of activities within her community.

continued on following page

Table 1. continued

21	**Comes up with suggestions, if it is necessary:** Facilitator is ready to make suggestion to the community
22	**Guides community to match organizational process:** Facilitator guides the community to synchronize its activities with process within the organization, so that it would be easier for the community to work with other communities or other organizational units.
23	**Communicates with other existing communities:** Facilitator involves in communication with other existing communities in the organization.
24	**Responds to any request from outside toward his community:** Facilitator is the gateway for any request toward and from the community and should respond to it appropriately.
25	**Shares experiences with potential communities:** Facilitator shares his experience in serving her community with potential communities, if they ask for it.
26	**Reports to management about the community progress:** Facilitator informs management regarding the progress of her community.
27	**Initiates contact to potential community members:** Facilitator approaches potential community members.
28	**Promotes her community to potential members:** Facilitator promotes her community to potential members in order to attract them to join the community.
29	**Implements strategy for attracting new members:** Facilitator implements the agreed strategy for attracting new members.
30	**Argues for independency of communities in front of management:** Facilitator advocates for independency of her community from any intervention from management.
31	**Mediates communication between management and community:** Facilitator helps in mediating communication between community and management.
32	**Gathers information from various sources:** Facilitator uses all available sources to get information from outside the community, which could be used, e.g. for identifying potential members, management concerns, activities in organizations.
33	**Scans the environment:** Facilitator is aware of any kind of activities outside her community.

them in knowing what resources are needed for a COP to serve its purpose and in evaluating COP facilitation in their organizations.

1. Presenting Information

Most of the time, COP members join the community to look for information or to exchange information. They will post questions or request for information from their communities. If they do not get an answer for their questions or the information they are looking for, they will feel that their communities cannot satisfy their needs. Therefore, they will be more likely to leave the current communities and move to another one. To prevent this, a COP facilitator need to be proactive in addressing the needs of the community mem-

bers. If a COP facilitator finds members' questions that have not been answered by other members, he or she needs to take steps to help those members. Several practical steps that can done by a COP facilitator include: (1) informing members where to find the answers or the information that they need; (2) directing them to previous discussions found in the community; (3) informing them about other members who are subject matter experts in a particular area.

As Gray (2004) noticed in her study, most of the postings by members are normally related to asking for information. Millen, Fontaine, and Muller (2002) found that having access to information is one of the key benefits of joining communities of practice. Therefore, presenting information plays an important role for facilitators in managing members' participation. They should encourage others who have more information about certain topics to come forward and present them to the community. One of the communities in our study exhibited a high percentage of this activity, with more than 70% of collected postings being of this type. Information presented by facilitators to community members varied in details and purpose. The information could be as simple as giving feedback addressing a member's concern or it could also be a lengthy opinion answering a question raised by a member.

To fulfill this task, a COP facilitator needs to be aware of important activities and information in his community. He needs to be proactive in seeking information and knowing about what is going on in the community as well as outside the community. Within an organization, a facilitator needs always to be in contact with management and should relay management concerns to community members. As Ardichvili et al.(2003) noted that some members were afraid in sharing information due to feeling of inferiority. To address that issue, a COP facilitator needs to encourage all members to share information and to give them a clear guidance on good information sharing practices.

2. Keeping Community Focus on its Purposes

In COP discussions can become lengthy. A lengthy discussion can lose focus as members start replying with non-related issues. For example, a discussion about how to modify your mobile phone to use for sending data could lose its focus as members start discussing subscription plans from different wireless service providers in the same thread. This discussion leads to a group of members arguing for one provider and other members arguing against it, which then leads to debating something that is no longer related to the original topic. This heated discussion will distract members from the original topic of the thread and make those who are still interested in the original topic feel disturbed.

It could even lead to potential conflicts among members. In this case, a COP facilitator needs to be aware when he or she needs to intervene and remind members about keeping the focus on the original topic. He or she can also suggest to those who are interested in a discussion about subscription plans of various wireless service providers to open a separate thread.

Therefore, guiding the community is another important aspect of COP facilitation. Our content analysis showed how facilitators were heavily involved in trying to keep a focus on each of the discussions started in their communities. A high percentage of postings made by facilitators in some of the communities were related to enforcing or urging members to keep their posts in a thread on the topic or to keep posting in a subforum relevant with the purpose of this subforum. This effort was made either in response to members' complaint or by monitoring discussions or subforum itself. They tried to keep off-topic posting to a minimum or to keep irrelevant thread out of a subforum. To achieve this goal, they used several resources, including:

- Reminding or warning
- Editing members' posts
- Putting a thread under moderation
- Banning a members from the community
- Closing a thread
- Moving a thread or topic to appropriate subforum.

For this task, facilitators need to monitor ongoing discussions closely. Ability to sense the right time to intervene is needed, as it will keep discussions on track, but not appearing as too rigid. Using humorous or anecdotal expressions could be helpful in achieving this purpose. Facilitators need to use all available tools or approaches wisely. Banning a members or closing a thread should only be used as the last resort of facilitation. Facilitators need to explain why he or she views that a discussion has gone out of track and what members need to do to bring it back on track. Facilitator can also send private message to initiate one-on-one communication with members to raise their awareness about codes and rules in the community.

By keeping community focus on its purpose, facilitators help their community and its members lowering the cost of participation. A community with high irrelevant postings or contributions could drive away its valuable members, as they perceive that the cost of participation is too high (Cosley, Frankowski, Kiesler, Terveen, & Riedl, 2005). Kahai, Sosik and Avolio (2004) argue that without any tool to help members focus, too many ideas or contributions could make it difficult to sort out good ideas or quality contributions. This difficulty in turn could reduce member satisfaction.

3. Promoting Understanding of the Tools

Members join a COP to find information or to exchange information. As members start looking for information, most of the time they will post questions and seek answers from other members. They will be disappointed when nobody responds to their request. Yet, some of those questions may actually be very common and have been previously discussed on many occasions. They could find that information easily, if they know how to use some of the tools in their communities. Answers to some of those questions are scattered throughout the community, such as in old discussion threads, in WIKI's or in COP files. In this case, a facilitator needs to make members aware on how to use the tools in their communities to find information. He or she can direct members to use search functions in COP to find discussions in old threads. COP facilitators can also promote the use of WIKI's in communities to gather important information about certain topics in one place.

Therefore, understanding tools available to a community is a key to member's participation. Therefore, members should feel comfortable with

tools and features available in their communities. Tools or features that are difficult to use will increase the cost of participation among members. This in turn will create a reason for them to leave their communities. Davis' (1989) Technology Acceptance Model indicates that perceived ease of use is one of the important factors in user acceptance of information technology. Therefore, we expect that facilitators will play important role in addressing this aspect.

The result of our content analysis indicates involvement of facilitators in most of the observed communities in promoting understanding of existing tools in their communities. This task was part of the facilitator's role as an information source. As our analysis was based on public postings, there is a possibility that this involvement occurred through one-on-one interaction too, such as through private messaging. Therefore, this task might be more widely performed than what we observed. This act of promoting understanding of a particular tool in a community occurred either as an answer to a question or as an effort to raise awareness among members about particular tool. In order to help members in understanding a particular tool, a facilitator needs to have a sufficient level of understanding about the tools used in their communities. Without this, he will have difficulty in helping members understand the communities' tools.

As technology supporting online communities is advancing, members will have more tools and features available. At the same time, facilitators need to understand those tools and features and should be able to help members in mastering them. The arrival of Web 2.0 could add more features to COPs, but also more challenges to members. Integrating WIKI, videos as well as 3D capability and social networking features to COP platform will surely increase its capability and attractiveness (Ives, 2008). With ability to promote understanding of those tools, facilitators can help members in optimizing the use of those features and move their communities forward. As Thomas, Bostrom, and Goug (2007) noted, persuasion is one of the important skills needed to convince members to use technologies.

4. Helping through Suggestions

As members cannot find answers to their questions or cannot get the information they are looking for, they will become dissatisfied with their communities. The likelihood for them to abandon their communities will then increase. They will look for other COPs, inside or outside their organizations, to satisfy their needs. To minimize this dissatisfaction, a COP facilitator needs to be proactive to members' needs. He or she needs to act as a subject matter expert to address members' questions or information needs. A COP facilitator could help those members by suggesting answers to their questions by supplying information.

Therefore, in some communities, the involvement of facilitators included helping members through suggestions that helped in solving their problems. In one of the studied communities, most of the postings from facilitators were related to suggestions. In this type of helping community (APQC, 2000), most of the activities of the facilitator exhibited advice or suggestions to solve raised problems. In this case, facilitators had to act as subject matter experts to keep the community vibrant and engaging. Without their involvement in answering members' questions, their communities would become less valuable, which could lead to members deserting the communities.

The importance of this task is especially observed in medium size COPs, where facilitators sometimes have to take responsibility as information source for members. In such case, facilitators will try answering questions asked by members, if those questions remain unanswered for a period of time. By answering those questions, facilitators hope that members can feel the benefit of their COP as information source and that they will involve actively in the communities either by asking questions, providing solutions or

sharing ideas. Ardichvili et al. (2003) noted that sometimes members, especially new members, are reluctant in sharing their ideas, as they are not sure about the significance or importance of their ideas. Therefore, encouragement from facilitators could help in overcome those feelings among members.

5. Building Members' Cooperative Relationship

As members participate in discussions, some of them could start making unnecessary remarks that would be perceived as insults or personal attacks by other members. Discussions then turn into 'name calling' or endless arguments that are no longer relevant to the original topics and useful for the community. All of these could lead to conflicts among members. Before this occurs, a COP facilitator needs to build a spirit of cooperation among members. He or she can remind members to be open-minded and to respect others' opinions. COP facilitators need to intervene in any conflict as early as possible. Through this intervention, members will go back to focus on the original discussion topics and at the same time it will prevent the environment of the community to become poisonous with conflicts.

Therefore, creating a collaborative environment within a community is a key for COP to thrive. Therefore, members should exhibit a high degree of cooperative relationship among them. This is especially important for an innovation COP, where cooperative relationship is the key for innovation. As members feel comfortable collaborating and sharing ideas with other members, they are more likely to come up with innovative ideas or creation.

Facilitators were also clearly involved in building cooperative relationship among members. They can involve in curbing uncooperative behaviors by some members. For example, facilitators can urge them to stop unnecessary actions or personal attack. In delivering this message to the members, facilitators conveyed other related messages, such as a warning to stay on topic and respecting opinions from others.

To accomplish this task, facilitators need to encourage members to respect multiple perspectives and to create and maintain an open, positive, and participative environment. All these will lead to enhance cooperative relationship among members. Furthermore, facilitators can also initiate activities that can foster cooperative relationship. Through those activities, members can see that they can trust and rely on other COP members to solve their problem.

FUTURE TRENDS

As more people and organizations will utilize COP as part of their knowledge sharing activities, facilitators will face challenges on how to achieve that goal and to deliver the full potential of communities of practice. At the same time, with the advancement in Web 2.0 and Social Networking new tools and technologies for COP will emerge. Members will face more challenges in understanding and using those technologies. They will seek more help from facilitators in mastering them. Therefore, facilitators need to understand capabilities of those technologies in order to optimizing their usefulness for their communities.

Future studies in this area should include:

1. Exploring changes in facilitation as technology for COP platform advances. Knowing how technology will have impacts on facilitation will help facilitators in preparing for their assignments. At the same time, it helps in determining what tools are needed for facilitators to accomplish their tasks in the future;

2. Looking at facilitators' involvement from members' point of view. Understanding what

COP members expected from facilitators will help in train facilitators to meet those expectations. Meeting members' expectation could help communities to thrive; and

3. Designing tools to support facilitation in COP. As we can identify tasks that are most commonly performed by facilitators, we should look for tools that could help facilitators to perform those tasks. By making those tools available to facilitators, we could be sure that COP facilitators are well equipped to face challenges in their communities.

Those studies should help in making COP a better place for sharing and advancing knowledge. At the same time, those studies will help facilitators in delivering their services to their communities and in making COP a center of knowledge management initiative in an organization.

CONCLUSION

Our chapter has highlighted several tasks that we identified from postings made by COP facilitators in several communities. Those tasks can be found across different types of COPs. Therefore, we can assume that those tasks are necessary for any COP. While we are able to capture some of the tasks performed by facilitators in COPs, there are other activities that could not be captured through content analysis of public postings. In order to capture comprehensive tasks performed by facilitators, additional methods, such as interviews are needed. However, we have captured tasks that are most commonly performed by facilitators in online communities of practice. Understanding those tasks will help managers in knowing how to support COPs and facilitators in their organizations. At the same time, it will help facilitators in preparing for their assignments.

REFERENCES

APQC. (2000). *Building and sustaining communities of practice: Final report. Research report.* Houston, TX: American Productivity and Quality Center.

Ardichvili, A., Page, V., & Wentling, T. (2003). Motivation and barriers to participation in virtual knowledge-sharing communities of practice. *Journal of Knowledge Management, 7*(1), 64–77. doi:10.1108/13673270310463626

Berge, Z. L., & Collins, M. P. (2000). Perceptions of e-moderators about their roles and functions in moderating electronic mailing lists. *Distance Education, 21*(1), 81–100. doi:10.1080/0158791000210106

Clawson, V. K., & Bostrom, R. P. (1996). Research-driven facilitation training for computer-supported environments. *Group Decision and Negotiation, 5*(1), 7–29.

Cosley, D., Frankowski, D., Kiesler, S., Terveen, L., & Riedl, J. (2005, April 2-7). *How oversight improves member-maintained communities.* Paper presented at the SIGCHI 2005 Conference on Human factors in Computing Systems, Portland, Oregon, USA.

Davis, F. D. (1989). Perceived usefulness, Perceived ease of use, and user acceptance of information technology. *MIS Quarterly, 13*(3), 319–340. doi:10.2307/249008

de Vreede, G. J., Boonstra, J., & Niederman, F. (2002). What is effective GSS facilitation? A qualitative inquiry into participants' perceptions. In *Proceedings of the 35th Annual Hawaii International Conference on System Sciences, 2002* (pp. 616-627).

Dubé, L., Bourhis, A., & Jacob, R. (2006). Towards a typology of virtual communities of practice. *Interdisciplinary Journal of Information, Knowledge, and Management, 1*, 69–93.

Fischer, G. (2001). Communities of interest: Learning through the interaction of multiple knowledge systems. In *Proceedings of the 24th Annual Information Systems Research Seminar In Scandinavia (IRIS'24), Ulvik, Norway* (pp. 1-14).

Gongla, P., & Rizzuto, C. R. (2001). Evolving communities of practice: IBM Global Services experience. *IBM Systems Journal, 40*(4), 842–862.

Gray, B. (2004). Informal learning in an online community of practice. *Journal of Distance Education, 19*(1), 20–35.

Hildreth, P. M., Kimble, C., & Wright, P. (2000). Communities of practice in the distributed international environment. *Journal of Knowledge Management, 4*(1), 27–38. doi:10.1108/13673270010315920

Hummel, J., & Lechner, U. (2002). *Social profiles of virtual communities.* Paper presented at the 35th Annual Hawaii International Conference on System Sciences, 2002.

Ives, B. (2008). *Tomoye: Bringing Web 2.0 to communities of practice.* Retrieved June 16, 2008, from http://www.theappgap.com/tomoye-bringing-web-20-to-communities-of-practice.html

Johnson, C. M. (2001). A survey of current research on online communities of practice. *The Internet and Higher Education, 4*(1), 45–60. doi:10.1016/S1096-7516(01)00047-1

Kahai, S. S., Sosik, J. J., & Avolio, B. J. (2004). Effects of participative and directive leadership in electronic groups. *Group & Organization Management, 29*(1), 67–105. doi:10.1177/1059601103252100

Lombard, M., Snyder-Duch, J., & Bracken, C. C. (2002). Content analysis in mass communication: Assessment and reporting of intercoder reliability. *Human Communication Research, 28*(4), 587–604. doi:10.1111/j.1468-2958.2002.tb00826.x

Millen, D. R., Fontaine, M. A., & Muller, M. J. (2002). Understanding the benefit and costs of communities of practice. *Communications of the ACM, 45*(4), 69–73. doi:10.1145/505248.505276

Mowrer, D. E. (1996). A content analysis of student/instructor communication via computer conferencing. *Higher Education, 32*(2), 217–241. doi:10.1007/BF00138397

Niederman, F., Beise, C. M., & Beranek, P. M. (1993). Facilitation issues in distributed group support systems. In *Proceedings of the 1993 conference on Computer personnel research* (pp. 299-312).

Ridings, C. M., & Gefen, D. (2004). Virtual community attraction: Why people hang out online. *Journal of Computer-Mediated Communication, 10*(1).

Romano, N. C. J., Nunamaker, J. F. J., Briggs, R. O., & Mittleman, D. D. (1999). Distributed GSS facilitation and participation: Field action research. In *System Sciences, 1999. HICSS-32. Proceedings of the 32nd Annual Hawaii International Conference on* (pp. 1-12).

Stanoevska-Slabeva, K., & Schmid, B. F. (2001). *A typology of online communities and community supporting platforms.* Paper presented at the 34th Annual Hawaii International Conference on System Sciences.

Tarmizi, H., & de Vreede, G. J. (2005). A facilitation task taxonomy for communities of practice. In *Proceedings of the Eleventh Americas Conference on Information Systems* (pp. 1-11).

Thomas, D. M., Bostrom, R. P., & Gouge, M. (2007). Making knowledge work in virtual teams. *Communications of the ACM, 50*(11), 85–90. doi:10.1145/1297797.1297802

Walther, J. B., & Tidwell, L. C. (1995). Nonverbal Cues in computer-mediated communication, and the effect of chronemics on relational communication. *Journal of Organizational Computing, 5*(4), 355–378.

Wasko, M. M. L., & Faraj, S. (2000). "It is what one does": Why people participate and help others in electronic communities of practice. *The Journal of Strategic Information Systems, 9*(2-3), 155–173. doi:10.1016/S0963-8687(00)00045-7

Wenger, E. C. (1998). *Communities of practice: Learning, meaning, and identity.* New York: Cambridge University Press.

Wenger, E. C., & Snyder, W. M. (2000). Communities of practice: The organizational frontier. *Harvard Business Review, 78*(1), 139–145.

Chapter 11
E–Leadership Styles for Global Virtual Teams

Petros Chamakiotis
University of Bath, UK

Niki Panteli
University of Bath, UK

ABSTRACT

With time, an increasing number of organizations deploy global virtual teams (GVTs) in an effort to respond to the demands and the competitive nature of the global business arena. Leadership, a factor that is arguably central to the successful functioning of collocated teams, is much altered in view of the virtual backdrop, and thus, management practices, when referring to GVTs' operation and effectiveness, have to be re-addressed. This chapter explores the contribution of a leader-coordinator in GVTs and – by drawing upon interviews with staff that participate in intra-organizational virtual teams of an eminent global operator – it discusses leadership approaches suitable for those teams. In addition, this chapter attempts to unveil and discuss the personal values that drive ordinary virtual actors to emergently lead their teams. Ultimately, the chapter suggests e-leadership styles which could be of foremost value to current and future virtual teams and virtual organizations.

INTRODUCTION

Global Virtual Teams (GVTs) have attracted an overwhelming attention and popularity among both academics and practitioners. GVTs are often viewed as a means to accomplish an organizational task by breaking any geographical or time constraints (Lipnack & Stamps, 1997), whilst enabling organizations to gain advantage of globally dispersed

expertise and knowledge (Bell & Kozlowski, 2002; Hargrove, 1998). The forenamed consider GVTs to be organizing units of work which stem from technological advances, respond to the need for product and service differentiation, and create horizontal organizational structures due to their far-flung nature. In spite of the numerous advantages that the virtual milieu can implicitly offer, researchers and practitioners posit an oxymoron when virtual

DOI: 10.4018/978-1-60566-958-8.ch011

team working comes into practice (Handy, 1995; Kaboli *et al.*, 2006).

Goodbody (2005), for instance, argues that less than 30% of virtual teams are led successfully, and this could be attributed to virtual actors considering themselves a substitute, rather than an evolution of face-to-face communication (Caulat, 2006). Not surprisingly, cultural diversity, lack of trust and face-to-face communication, insufficient training and time difference represent some of the novel hurdles that companies have to deal with. Therefore, while exploring GVTs' nature, potential and efficiency, one needs to question what constitutes the role of a leader is within a virtual arrangement, and what their contribution to the success of these teams could be. Though as we argue – virtual leadership, or e-leadership as we will refer to it here, has attracted a lot of attention in the literature – it still necessitates investigation.

This study questions the use of traditional leadership styles and explores new models of shared leadership, while identifying the values which may motivate virtual team members to emerge as leaders. In doing so, we discuss the gaps in the existing literature and, with the use of an empirical study, we explore different e-leadership styles that may be appropriate for GVTs. Specifically, the study commences with a definition of GVTs and a brief description of their challenges and opportunities, while thereafter we continue with a synopsis of leadership approaches and styles employed in collocated or virtual settings.

What makes this issue topical and interesting for study lies in the fact that information technology is continuously transforming organizational arrangements by adding new variables, and affecting the way people work, the tools they use, the relationships amongst themselves, and ultimately the quality of their performance. Therefore, our aim here is to bridge the lacuna between traditional and virtual leadership, and produce a number of applicable recommendations that will amplify GVTs' potency and effectiveness. Overall, this chapter discusses different emergent e-leadership styles in GVTs, which could be of foremost value to current and future virtual organizations that operate internationally and wish to improve their management styles. Finally, the implications for research and practice will be explored in the chapter.

BACKGROUND

Global Virtual Teams

Virtual teams comprise individuals who are geographically, organizationally and time dispersed, and are brought together via technological means of communication in order to accomplish a certain organizational task (Alavi & Yoo, 1997; DeSanctis & Poole, 1997; Jarvenpaa & Leidner, 1999; Townsend *et al.*, 1998). In the literature, it is unanimously acknowledged that virtual teams are different from normal teams in that they are flatter environments with high degree of physical separability – in other words they are intact workgroups – guided by a common purpose and facilitated by technologically advanced communication channels (Duarte & Snyder, 1999; Henry & Hartzler, 1998; Lipnack & Stamps, 1997). In addition, Bal *et al.* (2000) summarized some common characteristics assembled in GVTs, such as goal orientation, geographical dispersion, deployment of computer-supported networks, coordination of interrelated activities, mutual accountability in terms of the outcome, joint decision making and problem solving, and finite duration.

GVTs are anticipated to play a prominent role in the structural design of organizations in the future, as they offer several advantages to both the employer and the employee (Alavi & Yoo, 1997; Townsend *et al.*, 1998). Bell and Kozlowski (2002) argue that GVTs offer organizations the chance to access the best-qualified people from every field irrespective of geographical limitations, while providing a high degree of flexibility to the employee by enabling them to work remotely. Presently, though, researchers and practitioners have pinpointed opportunities afforded by GVTs, while several studies have emphasized implicit challenges and problems. Powell *et al.* (2004), for instance, attempted to discern what is known about GVTs from what is not known and urged researchers to investigate the proneness of certain virtual tasks to generate problems and conflicts. In what follows, we discuss, based on current literature, the key issues that are related to leading GVTs in an effort to better explore this theme.

E-LEADERSHIP: STYLES AND CHALLENGES

In the traditional organizational literature, leadership is considered to be a process whereby one member influences and controls the behaviour of the other members toward a common goal (Burns, 1978). Leadership in virtual teams refers to the ability of one person to influence the behaviour of others in a virtual, computer-mediated environment; thus e-leadership. Although e-leadership has been discussed both as a theme in and of itself, and in terms of its effect upon team processes and outcomes (Jarvenpaa *et al.*, 1998; Jarvenpaa & Leidner, 1999; Kayworth & Leidner, 2002; Malhotra,et al. 2007, Tyran *et al.*, 2003; Yoo & Alavi, 2004), little is known about its different styles.

Different leadership styles exist in the traditional leadership literature. In addition to transformational (which motivates team-members to pass from an individual to a collective level) and transactional leadership (which is based on exchange theory, namely on relationships that are seen as having two-way benefits) (Bass, 1998), attention has been paid to several other styles. For example, there are occasions when outstanding personalities steer others (people, companies and nations) to safety during a crisis (Collins, 1998), and this is known as *heroic leadership*. Likewise,

there are people who possess a magnetic presence and are known as *charismatic leaders*, while other leaders require obedience and conformity and are known as *authoritarian leaders*. Those leaders base their behaviours on their view of people being incapable of mastering their forces and lacking personal ambitions (Senge, 1990). Further, *situational leadership* is centrally dependant upon all variables that make one environment different from another, such as organizational culture (MacBeath, 1998), and *learning-centred* or *instructional leadership* is premised on the desire to learn and become better (Fidler, 1997). As opposed to the majority of leadership styles, *distributed leadership*, which can be also phrased as *dispersed*, *shared* or *collaborative*, represents a newly but an increasingly popular idea within the leadership literature (Mehra *et al.*, 2006).

In general, there is some agreement that traditional leadership styles are not suitable to emergent types of organizational arrangements, including GVTs. For example, Shamir (1999) discusses the inappropriateness of current leadership theories and practices for the newly emergent organizations. He argues that as organizations increasingly become boundaryless, flattened, flexible, project-based and team-based, the need for coordination becomes vital and this can be achieved through shared meanings and values. Therefore, as he puts it, *"the main function of organization leaders becomes that of being 'centres of gravity' in the midst of weakening frameworks, and balancing the centrifugal forces exerted by loosely coupled structures, fragmented cultures, temporary membership and technologies that increase the distance between leaders and members"* (p. 59). Snow *et al.* (1992) argued that GVTs stand in need of caretakers, or else *ad hoc* managers who will be responsible for the successful functioning of the teams, including coordination at different levels. Subsequently, Vogel *et al.* (2001) explained that such caretakers contribute to the team by supporting regular, detailed, and prompt communication, and by identifying individual role relationship and responsibilities.

According to Kerber and Buono (2004), virtual leaders should pull together their subordinates' strengths, and act against the centrifugal forces such as local priorities or time differences. Not surprisingly, they relate the e-leader to the collocated one, placing them in the absolute centre of any activity or responsibility. Virtuality prevents leaders from reaching consensus with their teams, due to the novel hurdles, such as cultural diversity, time difference, insufficient training and technophobia. In view of those problems, Lipnack & Stamps (2000) introduced the term *polycephalous* which originates from the Greek language and means *'to have multiple leaders'*. This idea relates back to *distributed leadership* which disproves any leadership styles used in the past. Advocates of this style find that emergent types of work teams which are primarily based around networks depend on the availability of multiple leaders within the team, rather than the traditional top-down approach between the leader and team members (Mehra *et al.*, 2006).

Indeed, Zigurs (2003) agreed that in GVTs the leadership role shifts from one individual to the other, as the wide breadth of leadership attributes needed while a team accomplishes its tasks is unlikely to be covered by a single person. This argument is also congener to the functional approach to leadership which focuses on individual behaviours within a group, in which all serve leadership functions towards the aimed goals (Pavitt, 2004). The functional approach is also supportive of the views that, on the one hand, leadership behaviours are performed by more than one people, and on the other hand, that different players present similar leadership behaviours at different times.

Further to different players involved, GVTs also experience the use of different computer-mediated communication channels. Thus, depending on the channels used, each leader has to deal with different degrees of *virtualness* (Staples *et al.*, 1999); with some media revealing more social cues and therefore more richness than others. Ac-

cording to the *media richness theory*, the higher the degree of richness in the channels used in virtual teams, the more synchronous and effective the communication becomes (Daft & Lengel, 1986; DeRosa *et al.*, 2004). Though this theory has been criticized for ignoring social and contextual variables (Markus, 1994; Panteli, 2002), it has significant importance in our understanding of communication patterns in GVTs and affects the relationships among virtual team members and their leaders.

Motivation is an issue that has not seen much attention within this topic. McClelland and Burnham (1976), for example, introduced the *Leadership Motive Profile* in an effort to connect a successful leader's profile with various types of motivation. On the other hand, a sense of personal growth, a sense of being worthwhile and a feeling of achievement represent some key factors that may motivate team leaders (McKee, 2004). Still, there is the fear that the achievement motivation (which entails personal success motivation), however beneficial it could be, could also have as a result that leaders concentrate more on retaining their leadership position, thus aiming at personal rather than collective success (De Hoogh *et al.*, 2005).

WHEN LEADING GVTS COMES INTO PRACTICE: THE 'ALPHA' CASE STUDY

Issues, Controversies, Problems

Following the discussion so-far, we decided to focus on a specific case study in order to respond to our research questions and provide pragmatic solutions. In this section, we present the results of our empirical study that aimed to uncover the emergence of e-leadership in GVTs. In what follows, we briefly describe the research approach adopted and present the results of the study.

Research Approach

Our empirical study is exploratory in nature, aiming to gain insight into an issue that has seen limited research and focuses on human beings and behaviours. Case studies generally represent the most appropriate research strategy for investigations at the exploratory phase (Yin, 2003). Our single case study approach involved semi-structured interviews with five individuals.

The laddering method, which *"elicits the higher level abstractions of the constructs that people use to organize their world"* (Bourne & Jenkins, 2005), is hereby employed to extract the consequences that originate from the employees' virtual activities and, by extension, the values that drive them to take control and lead their teams, with or without realizing it. Though it has been used in psychology (Wright, 1970), consumer research (Gutman, 1982), and in human resources management (Jolly *et al.*, 1988), laddering has not been extensively used in management research (Bourne & Jenkins, 2005).

Laddering represents a semi-structured interviewing technique which can be the richest single source of data (Gillham, 2000), while it involves a series of direct probes, typified by the *'Why is that important to you?'* question, with the goal of determining sets of linkages between the key perceptual elements across the range of attributes (A), consequences (C) and values (V) (Reynolds & Gutman, 1988). Attributes are the functional benefits of a product. In the case of GVTs, participation in GVTs can be seen as an initial attribute. Consequences are the benefits that flow from these attributes. They explain how they affect the individual or rather *emotional benefits*. Finally, values are the motivations underlying consequences and attributes of participating in GVTs. A simple ladder will be of the following form (Figure 1):

Figure 1. Simple ladder

The Selected Organization

In consideration of the aims and the limitations of this study, we decided to take a focus on a distinguished high-tech company in the computer and office equipment industry, a Fortune 500 company. The company, which we call Alpha for confidentiality, operates at a global level, and increasingly depends on permanent and temporary intra-organizational virtual arrangements consisting of people who work for the same company, but live in different geographical areas across the globe. According to the company's mission statement, Alpha views its employees as the most valuable assets, and encourages everyone to produce innovative ideas and take initiatives before their higher-ups tell them to do so. Further, being a prominent global operator, Alpha provides its employees with cutting-edge technologies and modern communication tools, and is committed to providing a pleasant working atmosphere, while knowledge-sharing, learning from the past, and motivation are importantly promoted through its organizational philosophy. Lastly, Alpha's senior employees base rewards on performance, they engage their staff in lifelong learning, and they develop leaders who are responsible for exemplifying the company's values and achieving the anticipated goals. Overall, Alpha's culture is reflected in its fluid hierarchical structures, the staff's continuing education, and the fact that everyone is stimulated to innovate and become a leader.

Data Collection Procedure and Analysis

The study was carried out between June and August 2007 and it drew upon interviews with several members based in the UK, some of whom have acted as emergent GVT leaders. In-depth interviews are preferably conducted in non-threatening and quite environments which help interviewees to be introspective and elaborate on their experiences (Saunders *et al.*, 2007). The personal contact with each of them also provided an overall image of their personality, as in-depth interviews afford perceptions that cannot be recorded or measured. The interviews were recorded using a digital recorder, while hand-written notes were also taken in case the recorder was damaged.

Each interviewee was asked to provide an insight into the day-to-day problems and challenges faced not only by e-leaders, but also by other staff who often participate in GVTs. Interviews lasted approximately 45 minutes each and were listened to twice in order not to miss important elements, and to remove bias.

The laddering technique helped us unveil the personal values that drive people to lead their teams. The *'why'* probe continued until no further insight was possible, and it was assumed that we had reached the level of values. After identifying performed leadership behaviours, a second set of questions – which was very important in formulating the ladders – was initiated. This phase brought forth the functional and emotional benefits, and self-expressive values the virtual actor seeks whilst leading a GVT. The last set consisted of follow-up questions in order to re-analyze the answers previously given and to cover implicit vagueness. Only three of the interviewees have

performed as emergent leaders in current and past GVTs, and consequently, only three ladders where formulated.

Lastly, a diagrammatical representation of each interview was formulated, in which all the ladders of the interviewee were combined. Besides, visual displays such as diagrams and matrixes are helpful in analyzing data and drawing conclusions (Gengler & Reynolds, 1995). Due to space limitations, the tables classify both consequences and values into certain broad categories. In these tables, we only refer to consequences and values with frequency of 2 or above, as frequency of just 1 is considered to be insignificant.

Results and Analysis

Here, we present a summary of the characteristics of the five employees who were interviewed (Table 1). All five of them are referred to as Persons A, B, C, D and E, preserving their confidentiality. There is homogeneity in terms of age, nationality and other variables, but all have different personalities, different experiences and different approaches. Subsequent to this summarizing table is the analysis of the interviewees, classified by person. Each of the five employees first describes the framework of their GVT experience, and then we critically present their views and stories about the issues that concern this study.

Person A

Person A represents an open character, and this perhaps contributes to her being a successful leader. She gives the impression of a professional who knows how to be effective and efficient in terms of the company's productivity, yet she approaches virtuality with anxiety, as *"working from different physical locations can be scary."*

The UK branch, being a Global Business Unit (GBU), plays a central role in guiding and advising, and therefore, every employee assumes leadership responsibilities somehow. Typically,

Table 1. Presentation of interviewees

	Person A	Person B	Person C	Person D	Person E
Gender	F	F	M	M	M
Nationality	British	British	British	British	British
Field	Production	Commodity Management	Development	Management	Procurement
Role	Line Operator	Procurement Specialist	Technical Specialist	Leader	Manager
Virtual Experience	7 years	9 years	10 years	More than 10 years	More than 10 years
Assigned Leader	No	Yes	No	Yes	No
Emerged Leader	Yes	Yes	No	Yes	No
Leadership Realization	No	Yes	-	Yes	-
Leader's Acceptance	Yes	Yes	Yes	Yes	No
Perceived Outcome Success	99%	80-90%	88%	99%	100% plus risks

she collaborates with the USA, and the main body of the GVTs she works in remains stable and does not exceed 10 partners. She uses teleconferencing, phone calls, net-meetings, share rooms, and she believes that *"email is **the best and the worst thing ever**; when a [email] response becomes unprofessional, I always pick up the phone."* Regarding technology expertise, she considers that *"if everyone had the skills to fully exploit what technology offers, **we would be unstoppable** and more productive."*

She has experienced cultural diversity problems such as different sense of humour, which can easily create misunderstandings. Hence, each time a problem arises, she starts an escalation as diligently as possible. Her role is to ensure that a product maintains a high standard throughout the production process and reaches its end destination on time. Her responsibilities are well-defined and she sees herself as *"... a vehicle that initiates a call for a virtual meeting, knows the right people, and has the ability **to pull everyone together**."* According to her, when a colleague's voice becomes the one most heard, then they are usually accepted as emergent leaders.

Person B

Person B promotes an image of a leader who will not hesitate to act differently and take the initiative. As manufacturing is outsourced at Alpha, Person B's task it to ensure that quality remains high. Thus, she interacts with suppliers over the phone, via email (continuously), by teleconferencing (twice a week), by videoconferencing (once a month), while she also has face-to-face meetings (quarterly). She often posits lack of agreement and coordination as symptoms of diversity. Figure 2 represents a product development process as described by Person B.

Person B is often the one to set and finalize a meeting, whilst she also assumes the pay-back analysis, and intervenes when a decision cannot be reached. She has observed situations where *"there is a gap and someone steps in and expresses their opinion. When I do this, I speak to people individually first and then **I am confident I represent everyone**."* She believes that there is always a leader, because, as she puts it, *"**there's always a checkpoint;**"* let alone that *"in China, they might say 'yes', and you think they replied*

Figure 2. An example of e-leadership: case of shared leadership

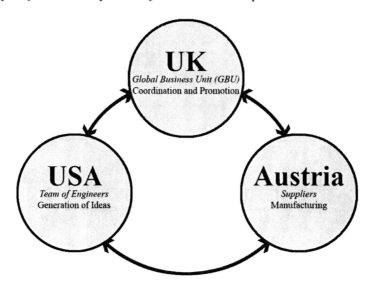

to your question, even though they mean 'yes, I'm listening.'"

As a leader, she has to *"be inclusive and pull people back from wanting to go into the details, although sometimes it's of value* **to let the conversation flow and then pull it together.*** She argues that *"people cannot put their head over the fence and see, because* **communication is not good enough***" and that GVTs require more though than traditional teams, since separation hinders relationship building. For her, an e-leader should meet the following criteria:

- One should not be blinked with the target, as they can become dictatorial
- to have the desire for efficiency
- to be learnt from and listened to
- have experience in both leading, and the scientific field
- to take value from leading and move forward
- work before the meetings
- make your team willing to engage with the tasks by affecting the dynamics
- adapting the leading style according to the circumstances

Person C

Person C, a technical specialist within a development group, works with the same virtual people for a number of years, which connotes established relationships with his virtual colleagues and guaranties high level of collaboration in the long-term. Person C appreciates Alpha's culture that allows fluid structures. Development tasks are classified into three stages: *early stage, physical development*, and *post-development support*; Person C is involved in the two latter development processes and he collaborates with five employees from the USA. He mainly uses telephone, email and file sharing, and he travels at least twice a year to the USA in order to attend face-to-face meetings, though he also does individual meetings. He generally prefers voice, but *"the technical stuff has to be written, so you end up with pictures and graphs"*. Additionally, he observes the *"absence of coming to one's office and saying: 'hey, have a look at this'; in GVTs* **you don't get the body language, only the voice language."***

When their old manager retired, a new employee took over this managerial role in order to build their team's framework only, since they *"...*

Figure 3. An example of e-leadership: case of co-leadership

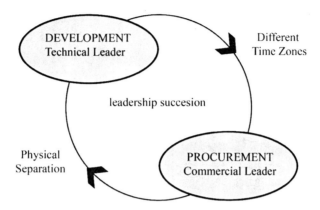

are all sufficiently experienced and self-driven to need guidance; but in virtual working *you don't always understand the situation correctly.*" Judging by his 10-year experience, he defines a set of qualities for a successful e-leader:

- combination of both technical and managerial skills
- to be reflected in the results
- excellent inter-personal relationships
- ability to re-establish lines of communication and levels of trust
- ability to pull all different strengths together

Sometimes, one leader from one area is matched by a leader in another area and therefore *co-leadership* is indicated. Separation in time also requires co-ordination between different leaders, whereby when one leader is unavailable, they hand over to the co-leader and *vice versa*, and this can be easily delineated in figure 3.

Person D

"Electronic management is wonderful if it doesn't have to work, if it's a yes or no answer; for complicated things, **you just cannot do it.**"

Person D represents an experienced leader who is simultaneously engaged in multiple virtual projects and whose job *"goes across all technologies"*. He is a centred leader who supervises projects lasting from 1 to 15 years. He believes that *"there's nothing like speaking to someone; Even if they speak a different language; the next step would be: come over to see me."* Emails are also continual, while he uses video-conferencing 3 or 4 times per week.

He is positive that *"Without a leader, the project will definitely fall"*, though many times a member of staff who is in expert automatically becomes the emergent leader. Equally important Person D views the role of all sub-leaders of a project while a project unfolds, since often *"... I might be the leader and then hand on to somebody that takes the next stage."* Moreover, he sees relationship establishment as paramount and he argues that one has to understand personally their subordinates, since *"... maybe they have a disabled mother; the leader must understand that."* The grey area in GVTs is owed to language barriers, different working practices and cultural differences.

He explains that *"... the idea of a product might be born in the USA and the actual implementation of it could be in China; the actual testing of it could be in Germany; **people perceive the same procedures differently** and this impacts cost and time."* Thus, he adjusts his leadership style according to each GVT. Further, he notes that *"... the Japanese will not make a decision, unless*

E-Leadership Styles for Global Virtual Teams

everyone agrees on that; that's a generalization, but they like to be able to agree; they don't like to say 'no' to your face; so they'll find all sorts of ways around it; but when they make a decision, they stick to it."

Person E

As opposed to Person D, Person E prefers the term *leader* over *manager*, because the former is about motivating people, whereas the latter is about telling people what to do. Person E gives the impression of a systematic manager, with his level of experience being reflected by the leisure with which he narrates events. In the projects that he is accountable for, they always hit the deadline which indicates a high degree of achievement, yet they take risks and make compromises in order for the product to punctually reach its final destination, the customer.

Person E prioritized the communication media his team uses, according to their efficiency, as follows:

- face-to-face is the best
- Beta (a pseudonym) is a wonderful full size proprietary video-conferencing system produced by Alpha. One can see a number of TV screens opposite them and then have up to 3 groups talking to each other, and there is a table that joins the screen.

"It's like you're all sitting in the same room physically; it's full size, so you see one person at each frame with high quality and no delays."

- Traditional video-conferencing, where the camera faces the table, is regarded as the next best.
- Audio conferencing
- Delta (a pseudonym) is a proprietary type of instant messaging similar to MSN, which offers security and can be used between two people while a meeting is going on.
- Email is only used to confirm what has

been agreed or to pass on information. It is not used as a debating tool, because it creates misunderstandings and people get offended.

"... people perceive sense of humour differently, and emoticons play a role; you don't see what is serious or not; a joke is really risky, **it requires a good relationship**, otherwise we don't make jokes; if it's a tricky subject and I don't make jokes in writing."

- Telephone is often better than emails for conversations

Big product programme meetings use video-conferences twice per week, while the senior management staff attend video-conferences once per week for approximately two hours. Still, emails are only used for confirmation and passing on data, or rarely for peer-to-peer debates.

From his experience, when all virtual team members feel ownership of the team's objectives, a good relationship is developed, and the chance of achieving the target is increased. They have "... *both centred and shared leadership, because as a management chain we have matrix organizational structures."* Along with shared leadership though, they also try to maintain clear accountability. Nonetheless, they often break each project down and they "... *assign different leaders for each stage."*

In Person E's view, a good e-leader needs a toolbox of skills, a combination of hard and soft skills, and he also argues that, *"behaviour is far more important, though you have to adjust to the personality of your team".* Further, an e-leader has to

- check whether the continuously changing established procedures are followed
- replay what has just been said
- emphasize the learning outcome
- build relationships remotely
- ensure messages have been received
- measure the outcome

Table 2. Hierarchical classification of consequences

Consequences	Frequency
Understanding / Learning / Contributing	3
Thrill / Desire / Interest	3
Collaboration and Sharing	2
Uncertainty / Problems	2
Everyday life and Society	2
Becoming Better / Comfortable	2

- optimize things for next time
- ask for feedback (not in the form of criticism or calibration)

Person E narrated a current story where one e-leader is not being fully accepted by the rest of his group, as the group comprises very high-level people who do not agree with the leader's practices, and thus, the project is slowing down. Similarly, he currently faces a second situation where three e-leaders are responsible for one project and *"... roles are not clear and issues start to appear."* Therefore, as he states, *"... we'll sit together in two-week time [using Beta video-conferencing] and discuss the roles; if there are personal issues, then face-to-face is always the best way; if there are constraints, we'll try voice-to-voice, but if it's not resolved, we'll approach the local manager."*

Leaders' Motivation

The elicited ladders are cited in the Appendix and the results in terms of the emergent leaders' motivation are synopsized in tables 2 and 3. The reasons why people were urged to undertake a leadership position are presented in the first table. All three of them responded to the question *"why did you feel that you had to become the leader."* One representative respond was: *"It's the desire for efficiency actually"* (Person B). Notably, Person D stated that *"there is never any certainty, you make the certainty; and it's the thrill of getting*

things done." Another prominent reason was that the company should thrive in the future and that employees should share knowledge (Person A), learn from their mistakes (Persons A and B), contribute to the commonweal and to Alpha's promotion (Person B), and improve their everyday lives (Person D).

However, it is found that it is not the above reasons *per se* that actually drive virtual actors to partially or fully lead their GVTs. The interviewees valued those reasons because they linked them to the concepts summarized in Table 3. It is therefore evident that more abstract and fundamental motives exist when adopting leadership behaviours.

The interviewees reached the values-level via a variety of different ladders, despite the time limitations. They linked this level with the knowledge they gained, with personal comfort, family moments, society's improvement, and collaboration. These words represent the upper layer of the consequences which resulted in the display of their personal values. The cases of the three emergent leaders' behaviours being analyzed here disclosed that they are all strong personalities who share prominent principles,

Table 3. Hierarchical classification of values

Values	Frequency
Personal Integrity	2
Security	2

self-awareness, and they value their personal integrity high. Furthermore, they all anticipate a high degree of security that Alpha is willing to provide them. Following this, the three emergent leaders also considered satisfaction, happiness, protection of the environment, improvement, and trust building as major personal values. Considering the high results throughout their experience, their high appreciation towards Alpha, and the comparison made in terms of financial rewards, it seems that the company covers the majority of their personal values.

Solutions and Recommendations

In this section, we discuss the results of our empirical study and present a set of distinct recommendations which will enhance team coherence and will thereby improve team efficiency, whilst considering the limitations which arise from the working context and the research methods employed. These recommendations will be informed by the literature review and our research findings.

DISCUSSION

Alpha is an organization with a global presence; its product ideas are generated in the USA, where research and innovation thrive, while manufacturing is outsourced to Asian countries where labour costs are low. Thus, GVTs are a common phenomenon within this organization. In this study, we interviewed managers with substantial virtual team experience.

The laddering technique revealed the interviewees' personal values and justified their preferred leadership styles. Some of the values emerged can be associated with theories on charismatic leadership (Conger & Kanungo, 1987; Shamir *et al.*, 1993). Charismatic leaders engage in proactive social influence (Person D) and share ideological values such as promotion of the company (Person

B), the protection of the environment (Person B), family happiness (Person D) or personal integrity (Person A). The interviewees typically follow a transactional leadership style, whereby they seek to develop a two-way beneficial relationship (Bass, 1998), and this is justified by the fact that they aim for rewards upon completion of a project. Most importantly, Alpha e-leaders make use of multiple leadership styles, as they try to adjust to each group (situational leadership), be authoritative (with reference to the Japanese – Person D), and learn from the outcome (learning-centred leadership – Persons A, B and E).

We also find that Alpha e-leaders combine different leadership styles simultaneously. Person D, for instance, being engaged in numerous GVTs, endeavours to adjust his leadership style to the idiosyncrasy of each group, while he suggestively notes that Japanese employees work better under authoritarian practices.

Overall, however, there seems to be an agreement that leadership should be shared as the project unfolds, and therefore, it is inevitable that multiple leaders are accountable for the same project. The findings indicate different instances where leadership could be shared; this could be, for example, shared among the different countries where members are based (e.g. example given by Person A) or by different sub-group leaders (e.g. Person B).

A critical parameter that allows them to reach their objectives is the opportunities they have in drawing upon different communication media to choose from for their virtual interactions. Several communication channels have been mentioned and, in some instances, these have been categorized based on their efficiency and level of interactivity. For example, e-meetings are held via pioneering interactive technologies such as the *Beta* or the *Delta* systems, and we therefore argue that these technologies importantly contribute to the GVTs achieving their goals. Despite that, there seems to be a type of technophobia or lack of technological expertise (Persons A, D), and they still consider important face-to-face meetings, especially when personal issues arise (Person E).

Cultural diversity is also an issue in Alpha, albeit the fact that they communicate with Anglophone virtual colleagues (mostly from the USA) heavily reduces culture-related hurdles. Nonetheless, they have developed ways to overcome such difficulties, for example by sending emails for confirmation of what has been already said or agreed (Person E). Alpha e-leaders are usually accepted by the rest of the team, while emergent e-leaders make sure they represent their team's views in order to be fully accepted (Person B). Yet, there are instances where the leader has not been accepted, and for this, Persons C and E suggest that an e-leader has to be managerially and technically skilful.

IMPLICATIONS FOR PRACTICE

This project is restricted to the idiosyncrasy of the examined case study, and this would partially prevent us from drawing general recommendations that would apply to each virtual organization. However, we set out a number of points that would be of considerable value to managers and organizations:

- By following a pragmatic approach, beneficial changes will be brought about, both for the individual employee's expectations and the company's macro-economic objectives. Thus, by embracing the appropriate strategies and adjusting them to situational variables (such as company culture, etc.) an e-leader can achieve high quality results.
- The research showed that computer-mediated communication cannot be effectively utilized in GVTs, unless members have been adequately trained. Therefore, organizations – regardless of industry and content – should not only invest in the infrastructure *per se*, but they should equally

invest in their human assets (e.g. employee selection and training).

- Given the qualities that describe the successful e-leader and despite the severe limitation of the context of the paper, virtual organizations should engage in recruiting and promoting the right people who are capable to handle geographical dispersion; in other words, there is a certain set of criteria that a person has to satisfy in order to overcome virtual hurdles, and companies should filter out future e-leaders, based not on stereotypes, but rather on empirical studies.

FUTURE TRENDS

While our goal here is to inform the modern business arena on how to improve their leadership styles and practices, the future seems rather unpredictable due to the constant technological advances and the exigency for efficiency at global level. Leadership is much changed with the advent of instant communication technologies that operate globally, and this chapter could prove useful to a number of organizations, when appropriately studied. Subsequent to our recommendations, we cite the following limitations in order to measure the viability and the degree of applicability and implementation of our models.

- The examined sample, in the main, recurrently participates in projects with the same virtual partners; this connotes a high degree of intimacy which leads to the development of trust and well-established relationships. Short-term GVTs have not been explored here.
- The small sample size importantly limits the generalizability and applicability of our models. Also, because of the nature of the research, the outcome relied upon subjective interpretation of the results. Further

research is needed, and we discuss this below.

From our empirical study, several research opportunities, which could expand the academic and working knowledge of virtual leadership, emerge. On the other hand, leadership is not the one and only variable that impacts GVTs' potency and operation, and thus, the future of the book's theme could expand to a wider exploration of issues that affect the modern digital enterprise. Concerning our chapter's future, researchers could move on and provide solutions applicable to a wider spectrum of GVTs. The research opportunities we have identified can be summed up as follows:

- Future researchers could focus on the plethora of different types of GVTs, varying in length and project types, as well as on different industries and departments. Employment of longitudinal research methodology, for example, could offer a better insight and could shift knowledge on e-leadership from the exploratory to the descriptive and explanatory phases. This would critically aid in understanding the phenomenon of e-leadership and in suggesting new avenues concerning a very wide range of virtual activities.
- This study initiated an exploration of the factors that motivate virtual actors to spearhead their teams, either *a priori* or emergently. However, only three of the interviewees have experienced the role of an emergent leader, and thusly, only three ladders were formulated here (Appendix). Therefore, research should examine a larger sample of leaders and should not only expand on the leaders who have acted emergently, but also on the values that determine *a priori* assigned leaders' behaviours.

- Lastly, e-leadership was here studied by looking at two parameters – distribution and motivation. This by no means embraces every single aspect of the phenomenon, and as a result, this chapter is unable to provide successful recommendations in isolation. Considering the relative immaturity of the topic, future research should seek to adapt the majority of the theories on collocated leadership to the uniqueness of the digital enterprise, and form a set of principles which organizations will be able to follow in order to deploy successful GVTs.

CONCLUSION

Drawing on Alpha's experiences, we agree with existing literature that traditional leadership practices are not always suitable to GVTs, though our data also indicated that these may be seen as appropriate, depending on the situation. Shared leadership was found as the most popular e-leadership style, though the way this is adopted seems to vary. Finally, as our dataset has been limited, we would encourage researchers to extend research in this field, by juxtaposing the theme as entailed in the *'Future Trends'* section of our chapter.

ACKNOWLEDGMENT

We are grateful to Alpha and its employees for their participation in this study.

REFERENCES

Alavi, M., & Yoo, Y. (1997). *Is learning in virtual teams real?* (working paper). Boston, MA: Harvard Business School.

Bal, D. J., Wilding, R., & Gundry, J. (2000). Virtual teaming in the agile supply chain. *The International Journal of Logistics Management, 10*(2), 71–82. doi:10.1108/09574099910806003

Bell, B. S., & Kozlowski, S. W. J. (2002). A typology of virtual teams: Implications for effective leadership. *Group & Organization Management, 27*(1), 14–49. doi:10.1177/1059601102027001003

Bourne, H., & Jenkins, M. (2005). Eliciting managers' personal values: An adaptation of the laddering interview method. *Organizational Research Methods, 8*(4), 410–428. doi:10.1177/1094428105280118

Burns, J. M. (1978). *Leadership*. New York, NY: Harper and Row.

Caulat, G. (2006). Virtual leadership. *The Ashridge Journal*. Retrieved June 20, 2007, from http://www.ashridge.com/360

Collins, J. (1998). Level five leadership: The triumph of humility and fierce resolve. *Harvard Business Review*, (January): 66–79.

Conger, J. A., & Kanungo, R. N. (1987). Toward a behavioral theory of charismatic leadership in organizational settings. *Academy of Management Review, 12*(4), 637–647. doi:10.2307/258069

Daft, R. L., & Lengel, R. H. (1986). Organizational information requirements, media richness, and structural design. *Management Science, 32*(5), 554–571. doi:10.1287/mnsc.32.5.554

De Hoogh, A. H. B., Den Hartog, D. N., Koopman, P. L., Thierry, H., Van den Berg, P. T., Van der Weide, J. G., & Wilderom, C. P. M. (2005). Leader motives, charismatic leadership, and subordinates' work attitude in the profit and voluntary sector. *The Leadership Quarterly, 16*, 17–38. doi:10.1016/j.leaqua.2004.10.001

DeRosa, D. M., Hantula, D. A., Kock, N. F., & D'Arcy, J. (2004). Trust and leadership in virtual teamwork: A media naturalness perspective. *Human Resource Management, 43*(2-3), 219–232. doi:10.1002/hrm.20016

DeSanctis, G., & Poole, M. S. (1997). Transitions in teamwork in new organizational forms. *Advances in Group Processes, 14*, 157–176.

Duarte, D. L., & Snyder, N. T. (1999). *Mastering virtual teams: Strategies, tools, and techniques that succeed*. San Francisco, CA: Jossey-Bass.

Fidler, B. (1997). School leadership: Some key ideas. *School Leadership & Management, 17*(1), 23–27. doi:10.1080/13632439770140

Gengler, C. E., & Reynolds, T. J. (1995). Consumer understanding and advertising strategy: Analysis and strategic translation of laddering data. *Journal of Advertising Research, 35*(4), 19–33.

Gillham, B. (2000). *The research interview*. London: Continuum.

Goodbody, J. (2005). Critical success factors of global virtual teams. *Strategic Communication Management, 9*, 18–21.

Gutman, J. (1982). A means-end chain model based on consumer categorization processes. *Journal of Marketing, 46*(2), 60–72. doi:10.2307/3203341

Handy, C. (1995). Trust and the virtual organization: How do you manage people whom you do not see? *Harvard Business Review, 73*, 40–48.

Hargrove, R. (1998). *Mastering the art of creative collaboration*. New York: McGraw-Hill Companies.

Henry, J. R., & Hartzler, M. (1998). *Tools for virtual teams*. Milwaukee, WI: ASQ Quality Press.

Jarvenpaa, S. L., Knoll, K. A., & Leidner, D. E. (1998). Is anybody out there? Antecedents of trust in global virtual teams. *Journal of Management Information Systems, 14*(4), 29–64.

Jarvenpaa, S. L., & Leidner, D. E. (1999). Communication and trust in global virtual teams. *Organization Science*, *10*(6), 791–815. doi:10.1287/orsc.10.6.791

Jolly, J. P., Reynolds, T. J., & Slocum, J. W. (1988). Application of the means-end theoretic for understanding the cognitive bases of performance appraisal. *Organizational Behavior and Human Decision Processes*, *41*, 153–179. doi:10.1016/0749-5978(88)90024-6

Kaboli, A., Tabari, M., & Kaboli, E. (2006). *Leadership in virtual teams*. Paper presented at the Sixth International Symposium on Operations Research and Its Applications, Xinjiang, China.

Kayworth, T. R., & Leidner, D. E. (2002). Leadership effectiveness in global virtual teams. *Journal of Management Information Systems*, *18*(3), 7–40.

Kerber, K. W., & Buono, A. F. (2004). Leading a team of change agents in a global corporation: Leadership challenges in a virtual world [white paper]. Adapted from K. W. Kerber & A. F. Buono, Intervening in virtual teams: Lessons from practice. In A. F. Buono (Ed.), *Creative consulting: Innovative perspectives on management consulting*. Greenwich, CT: Information Age Publishing.

Lipnack, J., & Stamps, J. (1997). *Virtual teams: Reaching across space, time and organizations with technology*. New York: John Wiley and Sons.

Lipnack, J., & Stamps, J. (2000). *Virtual teams: People working across boundaries with technology* (2nd ed.). New York: John Wiley and Sons.

Macbeath, J. (1998). *Effective school leadership: Responding to change*. London: Paul Chapman.

Malhotra, A., Majchrzak, A., & Rosen, B. (2007). Leading virtual teams. *The Academy of Management Perspectives*, *21*, 60–70.

Markus, M. L. (1994). Electronic mail as the medium of managerial choice. *Organization Science*, *5*(4), 502–527. doi:10.1287/orsc.5.4.502

McClelland, D. C., & Burnham, D. (1976). Power is the great motivator. *Harvard Business Review*, *54*, 100–110, 159–166.

McKee, T. W. (2004). *Motivating your very busy volunteers*. Retrieved September 2, 2007, from http://www.worldvolunteerweb.org/getnews/news2.cfm?ArticlesID=572

Mehra, A., Smith, B. R., Dixon, A. L., & Robertson, B. (2006). Distributed leadership in teams: The network of leadership perceptions and team performance. *The Leadership Quarterly*, *17*, 232–245. doi:10.1016/j.leaqua.2006.02.003

Panteli, N. (2002). Richness, power cues and email text. *Information & Management*, *40*, 75–86. doi:10.1016/S0378-7206(01)00136-7

Pavitt, C. (2004). *Small group communication: A theoretical approach* (3rd ed.). Retrieved June 15, 2004, from http://www.udel.edu/communication/pavitt/bookindex.htm

Powell, A., Piccoli, G., & Ives, B. (2004). Virtual teams: A review of current literature and directions for future research. *The Data Base for Advances in Information Systems*, *35*(1), 6–36.

Reynolds, T. J., & Gutmann, J. (1988). Laddering theory, method, analysis, and interpretation. *Journal of Advertising Research*, *18*(1), 11–31.

Saunders, M., Lewis, P., & Thornhill, A. (2007). *Research methods for business students* (4th ed.). Essex, UK: FT Prentice Hall.

Senge, P. (1990). *The fifth discipline: The art and practice of the learning organisation*. New York: Doubleday.

Shamir, B. (1999). Leadership in boundaryless organizations: Disposable or indispensable? *European Journal of Work and Organizational Psychology*, *8*(1), 49–71. doi:10.1080/135943299398438

Shamir, B., House, R. J., & Arthur, M. B. (1993). The motivational effects of charismatic leadership: A self-concept based theory. *Organization Science*, *4*(4), 577–594. doi:10.1287/orsc.4.4.577

Snow, C. C., Miles, R. E., & Coleman, H. J. (1992). Managing 21st century network organizations. *Organizational Dynamics*, *20*(3), 5–20. doi:10.1016/0090-2616(92)90021-E

Staples, D. S., Hulland, J. S., & Higgins, C. A. (1999). A self-efficacy theory explanation for the management of remote workers in virtual organizations. *Organization Science*, *10*(6), 758–776. doi:10.1287/orsc.10.6.758

Townsend, A. M., DeMarie, S. M., & Hendrickson, A. R. (1998). Virtual teams: Technology and the workplace of the future. *The Academy of Management Executive*, *12*(3), 17–29.

Tyran, K. L., Tyran, C. K., & Shepherd, M. (2003). Exploring emergent leadership in virtual teams. In C. B. Gibson & S. G. Cohen (Eds.), *Virtual teams that work: Creating conditions for virtual team effectiveness* (pp. 183-195). San Francisco, CA: Jossey-Bass.

Vogel, D., van Genuchten, M. L. D., Verveen, S., van Eekout, M., & Adams, A. (2001). Exploratory research on the role of national and professional cultures in a distributed learning project. *IEE Transactions on Professional Communication*, *44*(2), 114–125. doi:10.1109/47.925514

Wright, K. J. T. (1970). Exploring the uniqueness of common complaints. *The British Journal of Medical Psychology*, *41*, 221–232.

Yin, R. K. (2003). *Case study research: Design and methods* (3rd ed.). London: Sage.

Yoo, Y., & Alavi, M. (2004). Emergent leadership in virtual teams: What do emergent leaders do? *Information and Organization*, *14*, 27–58. doi:10.1016/j.infoandorg.2003.11.001

Zigurs, I. (2003). Leadership in virtual teams: Oxymoron or opportunity? *Organizational Dynamics*, *31*(4), 339–351. doi:10.1016/S0090-2616(02)00132-8

APPENDIX

Figure 4.

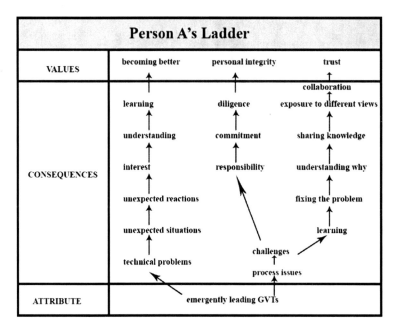

Figure 5.

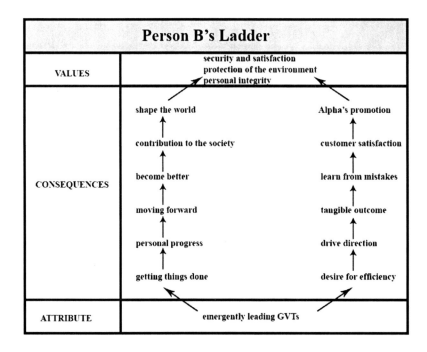

Figure 6.

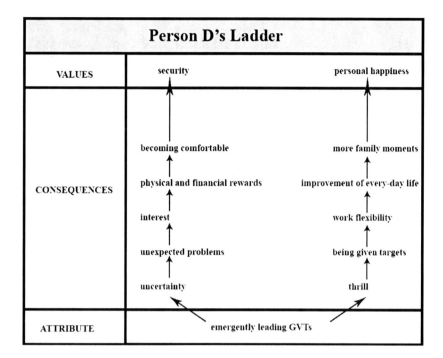

Section 3
Implications for Training and Development

Chapter 12
The Application of Blended Action Learning to Leadership Development
A Case Study

Kate Thornton
Victoria University of Wellington, New Zealand

Pak Yoong
Victoria University of Wellington, New Zealand

ABSTRACT

This chapter describes the use of blended action learning in a professional development context. Action learning is a process that involves small groups of learners working on issues or problems they face in their every day work with the support of a facilitator. Although action learning sets most often meet face-to-face, ICT is increasingly being used to support or in some cases replace traditional set meetings, thus providing a 'blended' approach. Action learning is a potentially empowering process that encourages reflection and questioning and promotes shifts in workplace practice. The role of the action learning facilitator appears to be a key element in the success of this approach. The purpose of this chapter is to describe a case study of a blended action learning process designed to support leadership development and discuss the subsequent implications and emerging trends.

INTRODUCTION

Blended action learning is a process that involves small groups or sets of learners working on issues or problems in face-to-face settings with the use of ICT to support some of the interactions. This chapter describes a case study in which participants, who were teachers in the New Zealand Early Childhood Education (ECE) sector, both met face-to-face in facilitated workshops and interacted online. The online interactions allowed for ongoing reflection, discussion and the sharing of knowledge and resources related to leadership back at their respective workplaces. The open source software MOODLE[1] was the enabling technology used in this study and the ICTs used include email, online

DOI: 10.4018/978-1-60566-958-8.ch012

reflective journals, forum discussions including online forums, and chat sessions. The group used an action learning process to learn about themselves as leaders and to work collaboratively on issues and challenges related to their leadership roles. Preliminary data from this study suggests that blended action learning groups are a very effective model for use in leadership development. Some of the benefits of this model are that it: allows for an intensive professional learning experience while not requiring a large amount of scheduled meeting time; encourages both individual and shared reflection; supports participants to identify and take action on issues that they face in their everyday work; and builds communities of practice through the sharing of knowledge and the building of strong networks. Both the action learning process and the role of the action learning facilitator in the face-to-face and virtual learning environments will be described and analysed in this chapter.

BACKGROUND

Leadership in ECE

There is no commonly accepted definition or understanding of what leadership in the ECE sector involves. This situation has been attributed to the "complexity of the field and the wide variety of program types" (Schomberg, 1999, p. 215). Rodd (2001, p. 10) has argued that "leadership is a contextual phenomenon, that is, it means different things to different people in different contexts". Scrivens (2003), drawing on Southworth's (2002) work, agrees. She has contended that "there is not just one way to be a leader" and that "leadership will vary from culture to culture and situation to situation" (p. 30). The diversity of the sector makes a common understanding of the notion of leadership problematic.

There has been debate about the similarities and differences between leadership in ECE and in the school sector or corporate world. Although some characteristics of leadership such as vision, courage and ethics; consideration of work culture; and productive work style (Kagan & Hallmark, 2001) appear to be universal, several writers have identified and discussed major differences between leadership in early childhood and in other settings. Henderson-Kelly and Pamphilon (2000, p. 9), in a discussion of the relevance of generic leadership and management language and practices to childcare, have commented that "many ideas provided structure and affirmation to the children's services leaders' work; however, an equal number provided contradictions". Kagan and Hallmark (p. 8) have claimed that "the intimacy, flexibility, diversity and individualization of early childhood programmes create a decidedly different leadership context than the formality, uniformity, rigidity, and bureaucratization that has been conventionally associated with the corporate setting". Many of the commonly accepted definitions of leadership are not appropriate for early childhood settings because of the more collaborative way early childhood teachers work and the lack of a hierarchical structure in the profession (Morgan, 1997).

More recent literature has minimized the differences between ECE and the wider field of education. Rodd (as cited in Ebbeck & Waniganayake, 2003) has stated that "being a leader is not at all different from being a leader in any other field. Effective leadership, be it of a large multi-national company or a child-care centre, requires certain attitudes, attributes and skills" (p. 22). The more recent literature on conceptions of leadership in the wider field of educational leadership such as distributed leadership (Hargreaves and Fink, 2003; Harris, 2003; Lambert, 2003) suggest frameworks more in line with the collaborative leadership approaches favoured in the ECE sector, so it appears the differences are becoming less significant.

A study exploring notions of leadership in the New Zealand Centres of Innovation programme found that leadership in these centres was characterised by courage, commitment and collaboration (Thornton, 2005). The Centres of Innovation programme is a Government funded initiative designed to "help improve quality in early childhood education services by demonstrating competent practice and innovation" (Meade, 2003). A definition of leadership developed as a result of this study is "working collaboratively in a learning community towards a shared vision" (Thornton, p. 93). This definition emphasises the collaborative nature of leadership in the ECE field as it is through group interaction that change occurs and visions are realised.

Approaches to Leadership Development

Traditional approaches to leadership development have involved removing individuals from their work contexts and training them in the skills deemed to be necessary for effective leadership. Marquardt (2004a) has suggested that many leadership programmes are ineffective because experts rather than practitioners are seen as the source of knowledge and "little, if any, of the knowledge ever gets transferred to the workplace" (p. 31). The lack of opportunities for reflection and self-questioning in many leadership development programmes has also been noted (Dotlich, Noel & Walker, 2004). Raelin (2004) cautions against detaching leadership learning from leadership practice. He suggests that typical approaches to leadership development such as the 'list approach', where training is designed to teach people a set list of leadership attributes, or the 'position approach', where leadership development is targeted only at people in certain positions in an organisation, are unlikely to have long-term benefits for either the individual or the organisation. This is because these approaches remove people from real-life situations so that learning is not contextualised, and promote singular rather than collective approaches to leadership. Other authors such as Southworth (2005), and Walker and Dimmock

(2005) also emphasise the importance of context in leadership development, suggesting that much leadership development is too generic and may lack relevance for individuals. West-Burnham (2003), writing from an educational leadership perspective, suggests a range of strategies that need to be in place for leadership learning to occur. These include:

- learning activities that are based on problem-solving in real-life situations;
- reflection on actual experiences based on appropriate feedback;
- challenge derived from new ideas, confronting performance etc.;
- coaching to help mediate the perceived gap between actual and desired performance;
- the creation of a community of practice to support the above (p. 58).

Paterson and West-Burnham (2005) describe a leadership programme for new head teachers called New Visions that has been operating successfully in England since November 2000. This programme, which has been extensively evaluated, uses a mixture of "active, collaborative and dialogic approaches" (p. 108). Several areas that are not usually provided for in leadership development are addressed in this programme, including time for analysis and reflection, opportunities for interacting with peers, and advice and support from more experienced leaders. Three fields of knowledge, the knowledge of individual head teachers, the knowledge informed by research and theory, and the knowledge created within the community of head teachers, guide the learning in this programme. Activities within the programme have been "designed to extend, deepen and connect these three fields of knowledge" (p. 115). A number of features of this programme offer a useful model for leadership development. These include: the value put on the personal knowledge and experience of these leaders and the opportunities for them to articulate this and develop shared knowledge; the focus on deep and profound learning which is achieved principally through reflective practice and approaches such as action learning; and the development of communities of practice that offer opportunities for support both individual and collaborative learning. Paterson and West-Burnham also report on other studies highlighting the importance of interacting with peers in leadership programmes with the most beneficial types of support shown to be networking and personal discussions with other leaders and critical friendships.

One of the key challenges faced by teachers in the ECE sector in New Zealand is having ready and relevant access to ongoing professional development, particularly leadership development. The lack of leadership development programmes has been identified as a key issue in ECE internationally (Muijs, Aubrey, Harris & Briggs, 2004). Studies in a number of different countries report a lack of preparation for leadership roles and a lack of training opportunities particularly at national levels (Kagan & Bowman, 1997; Nupponen, 2006; Rodd 2006). The lack of support for leadership training and professional development has also been suggested as a contributing factor to the low profile leadership has in the sector (Ebbeck & Waniganayake, 2003). Initial teacher education programmes are aimed at developing capable and competent teachers and although there are many similarities between good teaching and good leading, there is general agreement that those in leadership roles need to be further supported through the provision of appropriate training and professional development opportunities (Bloom & Bella, 2005; Geoghegan, Petriwskyj, Bower & Geoghegan, 2003; Hard, 2004; Rodd, 2001; Smith, 2005). Muijs et al. (2004) suggest that the consequences of a lack of leadership training programmes will be that those in leadership positions are unprepared for their leadership and management responsibilities. They state that there is a compelling reason for "investing substantially in leadership research

and development" (p. 167) and suggest that this is long overdue.

Because of the nature of the work environment, many senior ECE teachers feel isolated in their leadership roles and have few opportunities to engage in professional development that allows them to learn new theory, reflect on their practice and discuss issues and challenges with others in similar roles. Leadership development opportunities are limited and a shortage of qualified teachers means that taking time away from work to attend courses is difficult. One way of overcoming this challenge is to design professional development packages that involve using ICT, allow for participation within the workplace, and provide opportunities to locate other peer educators who may be facing similar practitioner challenges. Blended action learning supports this work-based learning and this approach will now be explained

Action Learning

Action learning has been described as "a continuous process of learning and reflecting that happens with the support of a group or 'set' of colleagues, working on real issues, with the intention of getting things done" (McGill & Brockbank, 2004, p.11). Marquardt (2004b) has identified six components of an effective action learning process: an action learning group; a problem, challenge or issue; a questioning and reflective learning process; the ability of group members to act on the problem; a commitment to personal learning; and an action learning coach or facilitator. Action learning groups meet regularly and participants take turns to discuss the issue or problem they are working on. The other group members ask questions aimed at clarifying the nature of the problem and also practice reflective listening. This action learning set process has been described as "shared reflection on individual perceptions of problems" and the group deliberations are seen to lead to the social construction of knowledge (Bird, 2006, p.3).

The empowering nature of action learning has been emphasised by several writers. Morgan (1983) suggests that action learning is "concerned with empowering people in the sense that they become critically conscious of their values, assumptions, actions, interdependences, rights, and prerogatives so that they can act in a substantially rational way as *active* partners in producing their own reality" (in Howell, 1997, p. 9). The potential of action learning to empower learners to be confident and courageous and to act in the light of their experiences has also been promoted (Morris, 1997). Marsick and O'Neil (1999) believe that action learning enables people to achieve more control of their own learning and more conscious of driving forces in themselves that can influence future directions. Action learning encourages a focus on real life rather than theoretical problems. This focus results in participants finding workable solutions to problems or challenges they face in the workplace and developing teamwork and leadership skills in the process (Raelin, 2000).

Blended Action Learning

Although action learning groups most often meet face-to-face, ICT is increasingly being used to support or in some cases replace traditional set meetings. Various technologies that have been used in blended action learning include email, audio and video conferencing and text-based discussions. The term 'blended action learning' is an adaptation of 'blended learning' which describes the combination of traditional face-to-face classroom interactions and online learning activities to support a learning environment (Davis and Fill, 2007). Blended action learning sets operate differently from other online groups such as online communities of practice because of their smaller group size and more formal nature. For this reason, it is important that the virtual medium used in blended action learning allows for the discussion, questioning and shared support that occurs in face-to-face action learning sets (Bird

2006). Advantages of using ICT to support action learning and in particular leadership development include that asynchronous interactions encourage in-depth reflection and that participants receive ongoing support from other set members and can raise and discuss pressing issues online without having to wait for face-to-face meetings. The importance of some face-to-face contacts between set members in order that participants get to know each other and that a feeling of trust develops within the group has been emphasised by a number of authors (Bird 2006; Powell 2003; Roche & Vernon 2003). This is not only seen to be important initially but throughout the life of the action learning group.

BLENDED ACTION LEARNING CASE STUDY

The case study that will be used to illustrate the blended action learning process involved the formation of an action learning group comprised of teachers from different services in the New Zealand ECE sector. The group used action learning processes to learn about themselves as leaders and to work collaboratively on issues and challenges related to their leadership roles. The reflection and questioning processes involved in action learning fits well with the literature on effective leadership development that promotes problem-solving in real-life situations and reflection on actual experiences. Marquardt (2004b) suggests that action learning is particularly effective in leadership development as it encourages the development of a number of important leadership competencies such as emotional intelligence and the ability to reflect, question and problem solve. He believes action learning differs from other leadership training in that the leaders are learning in context and solving real problems and that participants rather than teachers or facilitators are seen as the source of knowledge.

The action learning group consisted of six participants from a variety of services who will be identified by the letters A to F. The first author of this chapter was the facilitator of this group which was one of two such groups formed as part of her PhD study. This case study is divided into several stages in order to illustrate the activities and interactions involved in setting up and facilitating blended action learning groups.

Stage 1: Initial Face-to-Face Interactions

The group met initially for a full day session where they got to know each other, became familiar with the action learning process, considered recent literature and thinking on leadership, reflected on their own leadership journey and aspirations and became familiar with the ICT tools that would be used in the research study. We consider this initial face-to-face meeting to be crucial for the sustainability of this group as the trust building exercises used during the day were instrumental in enhancing the subsequent frank and honest online discussions regarding leadership development. The importance of starting the group with a face-to-face meeting was mentioned by several people:

I thought the all day meeting at the beginning was really good. It was a really good way to get to know people and form relationships. Because you were there the whole day, you really got a good chance to get to know people. (A)

I think it was an absolute stroke of genius to have us meet first before we went online and it's definitely been really helpful to meet face-to-face throughout the process. (D)

The action learning process known as triads (McGill & Brockbank, 2004) that was used in this first meeting was commented on by participants. This process involves one person (the presenter) discussing their task, problem or issue and be-

ing questioned by another group member (the enabler) in a process that allows them to redefine their problem and decide on some action steps. A third person, the observer, listens to the session and then gives feedback. Participants' comments on this process included the following:

I found splitting into two groups and using the Observer, Enabler and Presenter roles very helpful. It was also great to have a turn at each different role as I now feel more comfortable at using the Enabler role myself after practising. This scenario allowed me to come up with solutions that I can now put into place. (A)

The group activity was the highlight of the day for me as it was such a useful process. I found being the enabler first a challenge (but a good one) because I do like to know how to do something before I give it a go, but I'm glad I didn't have a choice to opt out and once I got started I got into the swing of things and saw how I can use this strategy in other ways too - particularly working with our teachers and helping them reflect and problem solve for themselves. (F)

Stage 2: A Series of Blended Interactions

(a) Online interactions

Online interactions using MOODLE began after the first meeting and included the keeping of online reflective journals, forum discussions initiated by participants and chat sessions. The online reflective journals provided an opportunity for participants to reflect in writing on their leadership goals and on the issues they faced in their every day work. These journals were only accessible to the facilitator who made comments and posed questions in order to help the participants work through issues they were facing in their leadership practice.

The value of keeping an online reflective journal was commented on:

I did really like the online journals. I think again for me because it's written and I do think a lot as I write, I think also having it shared with you was good again in that you're accountable, but also your questions did raise other questions and other points and I think that's really useful. (F)

The reflective journal was really valuable though it might have been partly because your responses were really useful. (C)

These findings support the literature that emphasises the benefits of reflective journalling to workplace learning. Cyboran (2005) suggests that online journalling encourages both knowledge transfer and workplace innovation. In this research study participants were able to clarify their ideas in their reflective journals before sharing them more widely.

Participants were also encouraged to initiate and contribute to different forums. These included: forums in which participants' learning goals were shared and discussed; forums in which discussions were held on resources participants had come across or on leadership related articles posted on the website; forums that allowed for the sharing of ideas on leadership practices including interviewing, mentoring and coaching, conflict resolution and organisation and time management; and online action learning forums, which will be discussed below. The forums were seen to be useful for sharing knowledge and ideas about leadership practices.

I find them really useful. I feel like the things that people write there and that I write there are a bit more considered. I think that you get some really useful feedback and ideas and questions and things in that context (C)

Chat sessions were held twice weekly as not all participants could be available at the same time. The chat was seen as the least useful technology in terms of the learning process, but was seen to be important in terms of the social presence aspect of the group.

I thought chat was the least useful in solving problems and issues and things like that but it was still good to keep in touch – it kept the relationship side of it going. (A)

The chats I did think were useful for keeping everyone in touch. I really did think that they had a place for that reason if not for any kind of leadership learning really. (F)

Overall participants valued all of the technologies used as they saw them as having different purposes.

They're all really important and they're important in different ways for different things. (D)

It's such a subtle but powerful combination of learning strategies and support strategies. (F)

The online interactions alternated with face-to-face follow-up sessions over the next few months as shown in figure 1 below. The first follow-up meeting was held just a month after the first face-to-face meeting. At this meeting, following a catch up of personal highlights, the action learning process continued. Participants were asked to report back on their leadership goals and the progress they had made towards achieving these. Three participants presented their individual issue or problem and the other group members asked questions of the presenter in order to assist them in identifying future actions. The participants who were not presenting in depth gave a brief update on their progress at this meeting. In the second

Figure 1. Timeline of interactions of the first leadership action learning group

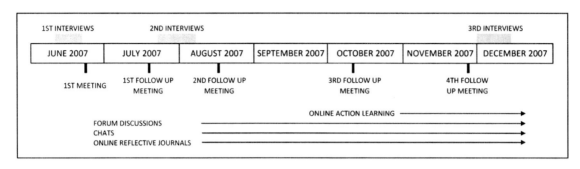

follow-up meeting, those participants who did not present at the first follow up meeting had a turn. At the third face-to face meeting participants chose to work on personality differences and leadership styles and only brief updates on progress were given. Although data collection stopped after the fourth follow-up meeting, the group chose to keep meeting throughout 2008.

This blended approach of alternating face-to-face and online interactions was valued by participants.

It's a good combination, because the face-to-face does makes it a bit more real (C)

The mix of the online and the face-to-face was really, really important because I think one without the other wouldn't have worked so well, I think you needed both kinds of contact to work. The personal contact helped build relationships and that sense of trust. (F)

Being part of a small and close group was another important aspect of this model of leadership development. Trust between group members developed quickly and a confidentiality agreement meant that participants felt able to share personal issues related to their practice. Several participants commented on how they enjoyed both being able to talk about their work and hearing other perspectives.

There aren't that many people you can talk to about your work in this role so I think it's a really useful outlet for everybody. (C)

It's happened several times throughout the process for me that someone's said something online, written something online, said something here and it's just turned my perception of the thing around a different way. (D)

THE ACTION LEARNING PROCESS

The action learning process begun at the face-to-face meetings was continued online after the second follow-up meeting. Online action learning forums involved participants identifying and describing a specific issue they were grappling within a forum space. Over the course of about a week, the facilitator and other participants asked questions in order to help the group member reflect on their situation.

One of the action learning online forums is presented in Table 1 to give an idea of the process.

The final comment from this blended action learning forum (bolded above) illustrates the value of the questioning process in helping group members identify action steps. Another participant who used this process to work through an issue

Table 1.

C	**Can I get critique of my decisions in this role?** Where can I get true critique of my ideas and actions in this role? I feel like I am flying unguided, and I think I would benefit from some more decision making input from others (management committee, assistant supervisor, ...) Everyone just agrees with me all the time!!! I wonder whether this is simply a phenomenon of the role, or if it is a signal I am giving off that says, "Don't worry, I have everything under control." I would like people (particularly the committee) to engage more with what I suggest, and to problematise before agreeing with me.
Kate	Hi C, Some questions for you to ponder: In what ways do you currently seek feedback from the committee and assistant supervisor? Do you give them time to consider new ideas/suggestions before committee meetings? (Thinking of different personality types here - some people need time to think things through) Kate
C	Hi Kate, These are very good questions (you're pretty good at this activity, aren't you? ☺ The first question has really made me think. I think the only way I really ask for feedback from the committee is at meetings. I write a topic on the agenda, explain my view on it in the meeting, then everyone agrees with me. Which brings me to your second question: I don't give them time to consider my ideas before the meetings! I read that you can type up a list of notes to hand out before staff meetings. This prepares people, and also saves time going over boring house-keeping details like dates to remember. I have suggested this to the teachers and am going to try it before the next staff meeting. Perhaps I should try this with the management committee too? As for the assistant supervisor, I am getting more comfortable in asking her for feedback- we have started to really settle into a working partnership in the past week or so. She is definitely the type to need time to process things before responding, so giving her my ideas in advance of a face-to-face would be useful too I think. Thanks, from C.
A	Do you actually ask them "What do you think about ....? Or "How do you feel about...?' A
C	Hi A, I do ask those questions, but I am beginning to realise that I justify my own idea or solution first. I will explain the situation, explain what I think needs to be done and why, and then ask, "What do you think about this?" I can see that this isn't a good way to get real engagement in the issues from people. I wonder: should I be holding back my ideas for longer? Perhaps I should simply explain the situation and not give any ideas at first. This would be a more genuine way to ask for input. I am a little conflicted with this idea though, because I like meetings to move along at a good pace. Also, sometimes I know more about the situation because of the role I'm in, and I want feedback on my ideas rather than a whole new set of ideas. Is this a fair comment? From C.
D	Hi C, I am intrigued about your idea of writing notes before staff meetings. Have you tried it? If so how did it work? And, just to satisfy my curiosity, how often do you meet as a staff, and how long do you meet for? As I read through this forum, I noticed that most have asked you about gaining feedback internally, from those within your organisation. This is my instinct too - when I read your question, I replied in my mind, "Have you asked for feedback?" This feedback is really helpful, as it is given by those who really understand the situation from the inside. There are two comments I would like to add (not really reflective questions, but they may be reflective comments!): firstly that some people feel uncomfortable offering this sort of feedback, fearing it might offend. Have you assured those you want feedback from that it is OK for them to do so, and that you will receive it in an objective manner? Secondly, my experience is that some members of my management group agree with me a lot because they respect that I am offering a professional opinion within a context they might not be trained in. Would this be the case for any of your management committee? I hope that helps! D ☺
B	Hi C, Perhaps you appear to be so confident that people don't think to question what you are saying, if you openly asked for their opinion on an issue before giving your opinion do you think they might give you a different view point. B C just re-read first part and gosh you have mentioned already about letting them comment first!!!! Also could you not say I am seeking an opinion on my idea, B
C	Thanks B, that's a good phrase to use: seeking opinions on my idea. I can see that it would be good to sometimes ask the committee for ideas first, and sometimes more appropriate to just ask for feedback on my ideas. Thanks everyone for the action-learning/prompting. **In hindsight, I feel a bit silly that I didn't come up with some of that stuff without this process! But I guess that's the beauty: the questioning shows us we kind of already know the answers ourselves.** I'm not sure whether I'm supposed to wrap this forum up at any particular point, but I feel like I've got what I needed out of it now. Cheers! From C.

involving conflict between staff members in her absence commented:

Thanks again for your thought provoking questions; they have really helped me to think this all through! (D)

It took participants some time to become confident in using the action learning approach. Some participants found it difficult at first not to be able to offer solutions to other people, although they soon saw the value of the questioning process.

I found it really rewarding in the end. At first I felt a bit frustrated by for one thing, not being able to offer suggestions which I desperately wanted to do, so it took a lot of effort to hold back on and also when I posed a question or a problem not being just offered some solutions or some people's advice., I don't know it just kind of felt awkward at first but after going through it a few times I do now see the value of coming to your own conclusions because the questions are really prompting it's not like you really get there on your own. (C)

That action learning process I did find very useful. And again practising that skill of not answering people's questions for them or giving advice but questioning them was interesting, watching other people learn those skills as well. (F)

This process encouraged the participants to engage in reflection, both individual and shared.

I like the fact that it makes us reflect a lot more (B)

Reflection really helps. I guess we've got the reflective journal just for yourself then you've got that shared reflection thing as well so you've got 2 forms of reflection (F)

Having to write rather than just share verbally in a face-to-face situation was seen to encourage deeper reflection.

Writing that stuff down makes you reflect a lot about what you're doing yourself and gives you ideas to think on. (B)

As I start to write I start to think and my thinking is quite externalised and as I start to think and reflect some things come out that I've surprised myself. (D)

The value of having to write reflections, rather than just discussing issues verbally, is supported by the literature that suggests text-based discussion formats encourage deeper and more meaningful reflection (Bird 2006; Friesen & Clifford 2003). Other advantages of the online aspects of this approach to leadership development include that it encouraged deeper reflection on issues facing participants, and that what is written in terms of journal entries, goals and discussions was able to be revisited.

The overall experience was described by participant D as "probably the most valuable professional development I've had" and she went on to say "it really has developed my leadership skills in 6 months like I've never been developed before and it will continue to do so".

THE FACILITATOR'S ROLE

The action learning facilitator or coach has the task of facilitating the group learning process. The facilitator may be a set group member or an external person. The advantage of having an external facilitator is that this person can allow group members to be fully involved at each session and ensure the focus stays on the learning rather than the problem, which according to Marquardt (2004a) tends to happen in self-facilitating sets.

According to McGill and Brockbank (2004), the facilitator has a significant guidance role in the early stages of a set but should eventually allow the set members to take over responsibility for how the set operates.

McGill and Brockbank (2004) suggest that set facilitators need to be skilled in active listening, managing emotions, challenging participants and showing empathy. The various roles a set facilitator may take have been described in different terms by different authors. Marquardt (2004b) describes the roles a facilitator may take in a set meeting as: catalyst for the action learning process; mirror for group reflection; and role model for the listening and questioning skills needed by the group. Bennett (1997) divides the tasks of a set facilitator into process roles, academic roles, interpersonal roles and validation roles. According to Bennett, process roles aid in the effectiveness of the action learning process and may include initiating tasks, liaising between set members and managing procedures. Academic roles include acting as a mentor, expert, innovator or tutor according to the needs of the group. Interpersonal roles help group interactions and may take the form of negotiating, supporting and motivating and validation roles may include challenging and evaluating progress. Action learning interventions rather than roles are discussed by O'Neil (1997). She suggests that facilitators intervene in the action learning process in a variety of ways such as: asking naïve questions that lead to a reframing of understandings; fostering critical reflection; releasing and enhancing capacity; and enabling learning.

The changed role of the online facilitator as compared to the face-to-face facilitator has been acknowledged by several authors. Gray (1999) suggests that the use of virtual technology changes the role from "the provider of knowledge to facilitators and designers of learning methods" (p. 10). Bird (2006, p. 9) also comments on the changed role of the facilitator, suggesting, that there is movement from "a skilled, face-to-face, listener" to a "reflective online discourse analyser".

Key Role Dimensions of the Facilitator

From this study, we found the blended action learning facilitator role had three important aspects: providing a structure and process that enable learning; acting as a critical friend; and being a role model. These three aspects will be discussed in the following sections.

(a) Provider of a Structure for Leadership Learning

This aspect of the blended action learning facilitator role includes providing a process and clarifying expectations. Heron's work on modes of facilitation is useful in reflecting on this aspect of the facilitator role. Heron (1999) describes three modes of facilitation: the hierarchical mode; the cooperative mode; and the autonomous mode. In the hierarchical mode, the learning process is directed by the facilitator, in the cooperative mode it is shared between the facilitator and participants and in the autonomous mode, the participants take control of the learning process. In this research study, the facilitator operated somewhere between the hierarchical and cooperative modes. According to McGill and Brockbank (2004), it is appropriate for the facilitator to adopt the hierarchical mode in the early stages of an action learning group when the participants are learning about the action learning process. The design of the website and the facilitation of the face-to-face action learning group meetings were examples of the facilitator acting in the hierarchical mode, however, over time there was movement towards the cooperative mode. Examples of the facilitator sharing power with group members include their instigation of a range of forum discussions and their questioning role in the blended action learning forums.

The movement from the hierarchical towards the cooperative mode was noted by participants as the quote below shows:

Particularly at the beginning you were the leader of the group and that's become kind of less obvious as we've gone along which is what you deliberately set out to do. (D)

The importance of the facilitator keeping participants on track and providing a structured process was commented on by different participants. When asked how I² encouraged participation, responses included:

Keeping us on task - because I'm sure we could get well off task if someone didn't keep us on track. Discussions sometimes get sidetracked. (A)

Prompting and reminding is an important part of your role that I think is pretty essential, if there wasn't somebody to remind people to participate and motivate people to remember to contribute, it wouldn't work at all I don't think.(C)

Frequent communication, prompt responses to posting and flexibility were also appreciated by participants.

I think there's been a really high level of communication from you and that's really important. (D)

It's definitely more motivating to put something up when you know that you are going to get some sort of response even if it's just a line and because everybody else is not necessarily that confident posting responses to everyone all the time. You always have something to say about it, not just "yes, yes very good" it is something constructive each time. (C)

Providing technical support was also seen to be important particularly for those who were struggling with the technology.

(b) Critical Friend

The term critical friend commonly refers to a professional relationship that offers both support and challenge and appears to be very applicable to the blended action learning facilitator role. Costa and Kallick (1993) define a critical friend as a "trusted person who asks provocative questions, provides data to be examined though another lens, and offers critique of a person's work as a friend" (p. 50). Expanding on the analogy of providing a different view of one's practice, these authors also suggest that critical friends are "willing to provide new lenses through which learners can refocus on their work" (Costa & Kallick, 1995, p. 154). There is possibly an inherent tension between the roles of critic and friend; however the concept of a critical friend is seen to be more complex than the simple balance between the two potentially contrasting roles as it is the combination of these roles that provides richness.

Establishing a Critical Friend Relationship

Factors that help the establishment of critical friendships have been identified as clarity of roles, a willingness to engage, and the establishment of trust and credibility (Swaffield, 2007). Clarity of roles and expectations was very important in this study and was established in a number of ways particularly at the initial face-to-face meetings. A willingness to engage was obviously a key to the success of the relationships and in general terms, the more willing participants were to engage in the action learning process, the stronger the critical friend relationship became. The importance of establishing of trust in a successful critical friend relationship has been emphasised by a number of authors (Costa & Kallick, 2003; Leitch & Williams, 2006; Swaffield, 2005; 2007). Without trust, critique will not be accepted and reflected on and therefore learning will be limited. Trust between the facilitator and participants was initially developed in the face-to-face interactions. The first interview which took place before the group met started the process of building trust and this was continued over the life of the group. The following comments were made in during the final interviews about the importance of the facilitator building strong relationships in order to facilitate learning:

Forming strong relationships with us in the beginning was important, so building that trust and that privacy and friendship. (A)

It's always respectful and that makes a huge difference and that allows us especially as head teachers to trust in you and if you don't have trust then you have nothing. I trust in the fact that I can write and say anything to you about anyone and I know that it's not going to go any further, that you'll be honest with us in a way that we can cope with. (B)

Critical Friend Competences and Competencies

A number of roles taken by critical friends that have been identified in the literature are relevant to the role of the online facilitator in this case study. These include supporting reflection, questioning, and supporting development (Swaffield, 2007), and acting as rapport builder, mirror, resource provider and match maker (Kember et al. 1997). In addition to these roles, a number of behaviours, skills and qualities needed by effective critical friends have also been identified. These include respect, empathy, thoughtfulness, listening, questioning and managing conflict (MacBeath, 1998; Swaffield, 2005; 2007). These competences and competencies concur with the skills and qualities identified as important for action learning facilitators which include self-awareness, courage, authenticity and listening skills (Marquardt, 2004),

management of emotions in oneself and others, and empathy (McGill & Brockbank, 2004). Various comments by participants have identified that a number of these were exhibited by the facilitator in this study.

The importance of the facilitator having strong interpersonal and leadership skills was commented on by participants.

It wasn't just your theoretical knowledge; I think it was your knowledge of people as well. I do actually think you're quite wise about people. (D)

I think facilitators have to have an ability to interact on a really high level with people so their own leadership skills have to be very honed and very high because when you're dealing with leaders and you're trying to help leaders then you have to be a damned good leader yourself in a very subtle way. (B)

The ability of the facilitator to form strong relationships with individual participants in order to effectively work with them was also valued.

I think that at times the questions you asked or the statements you made ... were being deliberately engineered to me because you knew who I was and knew things about me about how I respond or how I would think depending on the way you wrote it or what you wrote. I do feel really strongly that you knew who I was and the information you offered on a theoretical basis and also the information you offered about people was engineered towards who I am. (D)

The role of the facilitator in helping broker relationships between participants (equivalent to Kember et al.'s (1997) notion of match making) was also significant. This was done through role modelling and encouraging the sharing of both personal and professional information and perspectives.

An enabler for me was setting up those relationships first because setting up the beginnings of that trust was really helpful, so when I write online I know who I'm writing to or who I'm conversing with. (A)

You have a very relaxed but efficient way of working with us that's also set the tone for the group and how we treat each other. (F)

Encouraging reflection is seen to be a particularly crucial aspect of the role of the critical friend. Costa and Kallick (1993) suggest that both parties in the critical friendship should reflect and write. They argue that this changes the relationship from a traditional feedback situation in that the learner reflects on the feedback rather than having to respond or make decisions based on the feedback as is usually the case. The importance of writing is also emphasised by Barth (2001) who suggests that "when we write, we become responsible for our words and ultimately become more thoughtful human beings" (p. 39). This statement applies to both the facilitator and the participants in this study as having to respond in writing encouraged more considered responses. In this study, the online reflective journal was a particularly useful tool for encouraging reflection through a critical friendship. The role of the critical friend in encouraging reflection has been likened to that of a sounding board and a mirror as they are able to offer a different perspective from that of the centre leader (Swaffield, 2005). The following quotes illustrate how the action learning group process encouraged reflection in this case study.

I feel I am reflecting a lot more on my leadership styles and how they affect others these days. (A)

I have reflected so much since doing this course on my leadership and how to deal with others. (B)

Questioning is a key feature of an action learning facilitator's role and is also important in the role of critical friend. Socratic questioning has been signalled as important in both the action learning facilitator and critical friend roles. Socratic questioning aims to enable the speaker to "struggle with the issue under consideration, challenging embedded paradigms, encouraging consideration of possibilities, without restricting the range of possible solutions, and without providing a ready-made solution" (McGill & Brockbank, 2004).

Examples of this type of questioning are given below.

Facilitator responses to action learning forums:

How would you personally like to deal with conflict differently?

What happens when people have different views on a subject? When are you able to discuss different views as a team without people feeling uncomfortable?

Facilitator responses to online journal entries:

What is holding you back do you think?

How can you encourage her to take more responsibility?

(c) Role Model

As the action learning process was new to participants, the role modelling of the listening and questioning skills was an important aspect of the blended action learning facilitator's role.

You use the action learning techniques all the time, like when I write a reflective journal you seldom ever give an answer instead of a question, you almost always write your response in the form of a question which does really encourage more reflection. (C)

The encouragement of the development of new leadership skills and the role modelling of these different skills by the facilitator was also seen to be important.

It's that whole coaching style, not giving the answers. I think you just naturally do want to solve people's problems and you've only heard one side of the story. So that's been good because I've kind of taken it on board a bit more for myself instead of thinking "oh you could do this or you could try this", I've taken a step back. (A)

The coaching - getting us to look at things ourselves and find our own answers, also teaching us how to coach was really good and having to actually sit there and do it that first day was a really good way of learning it. (A)

Some participants also found they could transfer these skills to other situations.

Apart from the questions being really good they've also taught me a way to deal with other people. Just by reading your questions it's helped me learn how to question as well. (F)

FUTURE TRENDS AND EMERGING ISSUES

A number of issues emerged out of this case study. Some of these relate to the use of technology and others to the role of the blended action learning group facilitator. Some participants had problems accessing and using the online site. These access and confidence issues have implications for the

use of blended action learning as an approach to leadership development and need to be discussed and addressed when forming blended action learning groups.

This case study highlights a number of important aspects of the blended action learning group facilitator's role. This person needs to provide a clear structure for the blended learning process and support individuals in their use of the online site. The importance of the facilitator taking the role of a critical friend and both supporting and challenging the learning of participants is also paramount. Interpersonal skills that allow the facilitator to form close and trusting relationships with and between the participants are essential as is the ability to question appropriately and encourage reflection.

Although this study focuses on the use of blended action learning to support leadership development in the ECE sector, this approach may also have potential in other forms of professional development. Future research could focus on the use of blended action learning groups in different sectors of the education system or with different areas of professional learning. The use of different technologies such as Skype and Chatterbox that allow for online conversations could also be investigated.

CONCLUSION

Blended action learning groups appear to be an appropriate vehicle for supporting leadership development in the New Zealand ECE sector. Some of the benefits of this approach are that it: allows for an intensive professional learning experience while not requiring a large amount of scheduled meeting time; encourages both individual and shared reflection; supports participants to identify and take action on issues that they face in their everyday work; and builds communities of practice through the sharing of information and the building of strong networks. The combination of online learning and face-to-face interactions has several advantages over traditional forms of professional development including that it involves participants travelling less and taking less physical time away from their workplaces. The use of blended action learning also means that issues that come up can be addressed immediately either through the online reflective journal or a forum or chat discussion. In professional development groups that meet only face-to-face, there is usually no on-going support and no opportunity to discuss issues that arise between meetings. The action learning facilitator has an important role in the ensuring the success of blended action learning groups by acting as an enabler, critical friend and role model. Blended action learning groups facilitated by people willing to both support and challenge learning have much potential for enhancing professional practice in a variety of contexts.

REFERENCES

Bennett, R. (1997). Effective set advising. In A. Mumford (Ed.), *Action learning at work* (pp. 179-182). Aldershot, UK: Gower.

Bird, L. (2006). *Action learning sets: The case for running them online*. Retrieved May 5, 2006 from http://www.coventry.ac.uk/iped/papers/downloads/workbasedlearningwksp4jan2006/LenBirdActionLearningSetsOnline.doc

Bloom, P. J., & Bella, J. (2005). Investment in leadership training - the payoff for early childhood education. *Young Children, 2005*(January), 32–40.

Costa, A., & Kallick, B. (1993). Through the lens of a critical friend. *Educational Leadership, 51*(2), 49–51.

Costa, A., & Kallick, B. (1995). Through the lens of a critical friend. In A. Coster & B. Kallick (Eds.), *Assessment in the learning organization: Shifting the paradigm* (pp. 153-156). Alexandria, VA: ASCD.

Cyboran, V. (2005). Fostering workplace learning through online journaling . *Performance Improvement, 44*(7), 34–39. doi:10.1002/pfi.4140440709

Davis, H., & Fill, K. (2007). Embedding blended learning in a university's teaching culture: Experiences and reflections. *British Journal of Educational Technology, 38*(5), 817–828. doi:10.1111/j.1467-8535.2007.00756.x

Dotlich, D., Noel, J., & Walker, N. (2004). *Leadership passages*. San Francisco: Jossey-Bass.

Ebbeck, M., & Waninganayake, M. (2003). *Early childhood professionals: Leading today and tomorrow*. Sydney, Australia: MacLennan & Petty.

Friesen, S., & Clifford, P. (2003). *Working across different spaces to create communities of practice in teacher professional development*. Paper presented at the mICTE 2003 Multimedia, Information and Communication Technologies Conference, Badajoz, Spain.

Geoghegan, N., Petriwskyj, A., Bower, L., & Geoghegan, D. (2003). Eliciting dimensions of leadership in educational leadership in early childhood education. *Journal of Australian Research in Early Childhood Education, 10*(1), 12–21.

Gray, D. (1999). *Work-based learning, action learning and the virtual paradigm*. Retrieved May 5, 2006, from www.leeds.ac.uk/educol/documents/00001260.htm

Hard, L. (2004). How leadership is understood in early childhood education and care. *Journal of Australian Research in Early Childhood Education, 11*(1), 123–131.

Hargreaves, A., & Fink, D. (2003). Sustaining leadership. In B. Davies & J. West-Burnham (Eds.), *Handbook of educational leadership and management* (pp. 435-450). London: Pearson Education.

Harris, A. (2003). Teacher leadership: A new orthodoxy. In B. Davies & J. West-Burnham (Eds.), *Handbook of educational leadership and management* (pp. 44-50). London: Pearson Longman.

Henderson-Kelly, L., & Pamphilon, B. (2000). Women's models of leadership in the childcare sector. *Australian Journal of Early Childhood, 25*(1), 26–31.

Heron, J. (1999). *The complete facilitator's handbook.* London: Kogan Page.

Howell, F. (1997). Action learning and action research in management education and development. In A. Mumford (Ed.), *Action learning at work* (pp. 375-385). Aldershot, UK: Gower.

Kagan, S., & Bowman, B. (1997). Leadership in early care and education: Issues and challenges. In S. Kagan & B. Bowman (Eds.), *Leadership in care and education* (Vol. 3-8). Washington, DC: NAEYC.

Kagan, S., & Hallmark, L. (2001). Cultivating leadership in early care and education. *Child Care Information Exchange, 140,* 7–12.

Kember, D., Tak-Shing, H., Bick-Har, L., Lee, A., Ng, S., & Yan, L. (1997). The diverse role of the critical friend in supporting educational action research projects. *Educational Action Research, 5*(3), 463–481. doi:10.1080/09650799700200036

Lambert, L. (2003). Shifting conceptions of leadership: Towards a redefinition of leadership for the 21st century. In B. Davies & J. West-Burnham (Eds.), *Handbook of educational leadership and management.* London: Pearson Longman.

Leitch, R., & Williams, C. (2006). *Being and having a critical friend.* Paper presented at the CCEAM Conference, Cyprus. Retrieved May 27, 2008, from http://www.toplinisis.com/conference/CCEAM/wib/index

MacBeath, J. (1998). 'I didn't know he was ill': The role and value of the critical friend. In L. Stoll & K. Myers (Eds.), *No quick fixes: Perspectives on schools in difficulty.* London: Falmer Press.

Marquardt, M. (2004a). Harnessing the power of action learning . *Training & Development,* (June): 26–32.

Marquardt, M. (2004b). *Optimizing the power of action learning.* Mountain View, CA: Davies-Black.

Marsick, V., & O'Neil, J. (1999). The many faces of action learning. *Management Learning, 30*(2), 159–176. doi:10.1177/1350507699302004

McGill, I., & Brockbank, A. (2004). *The action learning handbook.* London: RoutledgeFalmer.

Meade, A. (2003). *ECE centres of innovation in New Zealand.* Paper presented at the Leadership and Management in the Early Years Conference, Pen Green Leadership Centre, Corby, North Hamptonshire.

Morgan, G. (1997). *What is leadership? Walking around a definition.* Boston: Center for Career Development in Early Care and Education.

Morris, J. (1997). Minding our Ps and Qs. In M. Pedler (Ed.), *Action learning in practice* (3rd ed., pp. 49-59). Aldershot, UK: Gower.

Muijs, D., Aubrey, C., Harris, A., & Briggs, M. (2004). How do they manage? *Journal of Early Childhood Research, 2*(2), 157–169. doi:10.1177/1476718X04042974

Nupponen, H. (2006). Leadership concepts and theories. *Australian Journal of Early Childhood, 31*(1), 43–50.

O'Neil, J. (1997). Set advising: More than just process consultancy. In M. Pedler (Ed.), *Action learning in practice* (3rd ed., pp. 243-255). Aldershot, UK: Gower.

Paterson, F., & West-Burnham, J. (2005). Developing beginning leadership. In M. Coles & G. Southworth (Eds.), *Developing leadership: Creating the schools of tomorrow* (pp. 108-126). Maidenhead, Berkshire, UK: Open University Press.

Powell, J. (2001). Using learning styles and action learning, over the Internet, to drive learning for innovation in small and medium enterprises - a case study from construction. Retrieved May 15, 2006, from http://www.portlandpress.com/pp/books/online/vu/pdf/vu_ch8.pdf

Raelin, J. (2000). *Work-based learning: The new frontier of management development*. Upper Saddle River, NJ: Prentice Hall.

Raelin, J. (2004). Don't bother putting leadership into people. *The Academy of Management Executive, 18*(3), 131–135.

Roche, V., & Vernon, M. (2003). Developing a virtual learning community of managers in rural and remote health services, Retrieved May 5, 2006, from http://www.abc.net.au/rural/rural-health2003/stories/s799695.htm

Rodd, J. (2001). Building leadership expertise of early childhood professionals. *Journal of Early Childhood Teacher Education, 22*, 9–12.

Rodd, J. (2006). *Leadership in early childhood* (3rd ed.). Crows Nest NSW, Australia: Allen & Unwin.

Schomberg, R. (1999). Leadership development in early childhood education. *Journal of Early Childhood Teacher Education*, 215–219.

Scrivens, C. (2003). Educational leadership: What might we learn from research in schools? *Early Education, 31*, 29–35.

Smith, M. (2005). Strategies for successful fellowships: Nurturing early childhood leaders. *Young Children, 2005*(January), 12–18.

Southworth, G. (2002). What is important in educational administration: Learning-centred school leadership. *New Zealand Journal of Educational Leadership, 17*, 5–9.

Southworth, G. (2005). Overview and conclusions. In M. Coles & G. Southworth (Eds.), *Developing leadership: Creating the schools of tomorrow* (pp. 158-173). Maidenhead, Berkshire, UK: Open University Press.

Swaffield, S. (2005). No sleeping partners: Relationships between head teachers and critical friends. *School Leadership & Management, 25*(1), 43–57. doi:10.1080/1363243052000317082

Swaffield, S. (2007). Light touch critical friendship. *Improving Schools, 10*(3), 205–219. doi:10.1177/1365480207077845

Thornton, K. (2005). *Courage, commitment and collaboration: Notions of leadership in the New Zealand ECE 'Centres of Innovation'*. Unpublished master's thesis, Victoria University of Wellington, Wellington.

Walker, A., & Dimmock, C. (2005). Developing leadership in context. In M. Coles & G. Southworth (Eds.), *Developing leadership* (pp. 80-94). Maidenhead, Berkshire, UK: Open University Press.

West-Burnham, J. (2003). Learning to lead. In B. Davies & J. West-Burnham (Eds.), *Handbook of educational leadership and management* (pp. 57-59). London: Pearson Education.

ENDNOTES

[1] Moodle is an online learning management system (www.moodle.org). It has been adapted for online community interactions for this study.

[2] The first person 'I' refers to the lead author of this chapter.

Chapter 13

Assessment Strategies for Servant Leadership Practice and Training in the Virtual Organization

Darin R. Molnar
CEO, eXcolo Research Group, USA

ABSTRACT

Leadership in the virtual organization presents unique opportunities and challenges for the manager. Some researchers consider management in the virtual organization to be comprised mainly of challenges while others see it as the opportunity to realize competitive advantage in the global marketplace. Several leadership approaches offer interesting options for the manager within the context of the virtual organization. One standout approach that has gained increasing popularity over the last 30 years is servant leadership in which the leader is servant first. Those managers in virtual organizations who have committed to a practice of servant leadership recognize the need for assessment instruments to help them understand the level of perceived servant leadership characteristics among organizational members under their guidance. This understanding acts as a foundation for training within this context. With this in mind, Laub's Organizational Leadership Assessment (OLA) offers a reliable survey instrument accepted by the servant leadership practice community. The OLA is easily administered to virtual organization members as a set of Web pages and can be used in conjunction with complementary, third-party data sets such as the World Values Survey database. Future directions for the assessment of servant leadership in the virtual organization include the potential modification of the OLA, as well as the creation of survey instruments to be used in conjunction with it.

INTRODUCTION

The practice and training of organizational members as servant leaders in the virtual organization is conducted under the same constraints as any other leadership approach (Bass & Stogdill, 1990; Burns, 1982). An important aspect of any leadership practice is the efficient and effective administration of survey tools to gauge the perceptions of organizational members. This helps managers hone their

DOI: 10.4018/978-1-60566-958-8.ch013

practice in ways that increase its efficacy in order to serve the organizational members under their guidance. In the case of the virtual organization, servant leaders are presented with the logistical challenge of assessing the perceptions of members in a widely distributed organization. Laub's (1999) Organizational Leadership Assessment (OLA) instrument offers a reliable tool that is widely accepted by the servant leadership research community. As an introduction to ways in which a servant leader may enhance her practice by using the OLA, this chapter introduces servant leadership and its practice, covers the opportunities and challenges of practicing servant leadership in the virtual organization. It discusses the OLA in greater depth and explains how the OLA might be used in the virtual organization with original and third-party data sets to assess the perceptions of organizational members regarding the level of servant leadership practiced by organizational members. This will help managers better understand the groups they manage and allow them to tailor training programs as necessary. As a forward-looking conclusion, future directions for the assessment of servant leadership in the virtual organization using the OLA, along with complementary instruments, are offered.

SERVANT LEADERSHIP

Greenleaf's (1970) publication of *The Servant as Leader* represents a Kuhnian paradigm shift in the truest sense of the term. Kuhn (1996) presents the notion that new ideas arise not from a single prophet in the wilderness, but rather from a groundswell of knowledge and research which most often culminates in a seminal publication, or publications, representing both a consolidation of knowledge and the opening of a new knowledge gateway through which others may pass. The creator of the seminal publication is often quite new to the discipline. This is where the Greenleaf story diverges from the Kuhnian concept of paradigm

shift, though paradigm shift it most certainly was. Robert K. Greenleaf presented the idea of servant leadership after he had retired from AT&T where he held various leadership positions for forty years (Frick, 2004).

Greenleaf claims to have come upon the idea of servant leadership after reading Hesse's (2003) *Journey to the East* in which one of the characters, Leo, plays a central role as guide to a group of Europeans traveling in Asia. After a long and arduous journey in which several characters lose their lives, the main character of the book discovers that Leo, the seemingly insignificant servant of the troupe, is actually "the titular head of the Order, its guiding spirit, a great and noble leader" (Greenleaf, 1977/2002, p. 58). At the time of Greenleaf's epiphany, the United States was still in the throes of the social discord and violence created by the Vietnam War. Greenleaf eventually published what has become the seminal book on servant leadership, *Servant Leadership: A Journey into the Nature of Legitimate Power and Greatness* (Greenleaf, 1977/2002). One of Greenleaf's fundamental goals was to create a better society by asking the rhetorical question of students he taught at Dartmouth, Harvard, and MIT: "Who is standing in the way of a larger consensus on the definition of the better society and paths to reaching it?" (Greenleaf, 1977/2002, p. 58). In the intervening years between the publication of *The Servant Leader: A Journey into Legitimate Power and Greatness* and now, we have seen an explosion of servant leadership publications, seminars, conferences, and university programs in the United States and abroad. Servant leadership has finally become a positive force in making our society more patient, understanding, and compassionate by transforming how leaders and managers in all sectors perform their duties and train their followers. At the foundation of this burgeoning shift is an understanding of the importance of values and the role they play in shaping the behaviors of leaders and organizational members whose initial desire is to serve others.

At the very heart of servant leadership praxis is a willingness to lead by first serving others:

It begins with the natural feeling that one wants to serve, to serve first. Then conscious choice brings one to aspire to lead. The person is sharply different from one who is leader first, perhaps because of the need to assuage an unusual power drive or to acquire material possessions. For such, it will be a later choice to serve-after leadership is established. The leader-first and the servant-first are two extreme types. Between them are shadings and blends that are part of the infinite variety of human nature (Greenleaf, 1977/2002, p. 27).

This quote from Greenleaf speaks to the personal values of the servant leader and how those values affect his or her view of what it means to lead others. Fortunately, the principles of servant leadership have been constructed upon a solid foundation of virtue ethics that extends from the works of Aristotle (1911/1998) to contemporary times (Annas, 2003; Hookway, 2003; Murphy, 1999; Slote, 2003, Solomon, 2003; Whetstone, 2001). An ethic based upon principles of virtue emphasizes the moralistic character and personal comportment of the agent. In the case of servant leader as agent, the practitioner is required to ask, "What sort of person am I?" whenever confronted with a situation requiring an ethical decision. This stands in contrast to various other normative ethics which prompt the agent to ask questions such as, "How should I behave in this situation in order to maximize the good and minimize the harm for all parties involved?" The servant leader will rely upon intrinsic and deep-seated moral characteristics to make decisions in an ethical manner. In this way, servant leadership is a way of being in which the practitioner is constantly monitoring and adjusting his own functional leadership attributes and behaviors (i.e., ways of doing) with the goal of fulfilling the role of true servant leader.

For every way of being there exists one or more ways of doing, and servant leadership is no exception. Before construction of practice guidelines may begin, a measurement strategy should be created to capture and quantify outcomes. Such a strategy must be highly reliable with solid internal consistency and verifiability for researchers while offering a stable standard, or set of standards, that is repeatable within multiple, competing research contexts. The first step in this construction process is the identification and definition of characteristics that are capable of informing the theory, hypotheses, discipline, field, or study. Several good efforts have been made within quantitative and qualitative methodics to identify fundamental behavioral and character attributes of servant leaders (Dennis & Bocarnea, 2005; Dennis & Winston, 2003; Laub, 1999; Page & Wong, 2000; Russell, 2000; 2001; Russell & Stone, 2002; Spears, 2004). The most notable of these efforts at this time are those by Spears (2004), Dennis and Bocarnea (2005), Page and Wong (2005), Russell and Stone (2002), and Laub (1999).

The assessment of servant leadership has been problematic since its introduction into the leadership and management literatures. This stems from two facts: (a) servant leadership is a relatively new approach to leading and managing people and an assortment of assessment instruments has not yet amassed and (b) to this point in time servant leadership has been an inherently qualitative approach. The first factor is an understandable dynamic of a new field of study while the second presents a unique challenge. Because servant leadership is a way of being, the practitioner is constantly considering and honing her own functional leadership attributes. When combined with assessment in the context of the virtual organization, the task of assessing servant leadership practice can become daunting. Fortunately, assessment approaches exist that make this task easier for managers.

SERVANT LEADERSHIP IN THE VIRTUAL ORGANIZATION

Organizational leadership has been a vigorously discussed topic within the academic community since the early part of the 20th century (Taylor, 1918/1998; Weber, 1947). As the emphasis on the organization as a hierarchical, bureaucratic structure shifted to more flexible forms with less centralized control structures within the leadership literature, new ways of thinking about and analyzing the roles and activities of leaders emerged (Bass & Stogdill, 1990; Burns, 1982). Granted, these new approaches to leadership research were not created exclusively by new organizational forms, yet they were certainly influenced by the need to study organizational leadership and management in a new light. Now, in the early part of the 21st century, these new forms are often heavily influenced by innovative economic forms and technologies available for the analysis of both the structure and management of organizations. Argandoña (2003, p. 3) recognizes three basic features of the new economy: "(1) a knowledge- and information-based change, (2) which is taking place in real time on a planetary scale (globalization), and (3) which entails a new, flexible, network –based business organization." One of these new change-driven forms is the virtual organization.

A popular assumption about the virtual organization *per se* is that it is composed only of geographically dispersed members. As organizations have adapted to new work environments, virtual teams have gained increasing importance as a management structure at the local level. Arnison and Miller (2002) remind us virtual organizations as dispersed teams "could include any team that uses technology to collaborate for a common purpose with the support of the organisation and with the necessary technology to enable the team to reach its goals" (p. 169). This flexible definition speaks to the often transient nature of this type of organization. Temporary virtual project work

teams fall under this definition and represent a nimble approach to product development, yet this chapter is concerned with the more stable form of the virtual organization, one that lasts longer than the duration of a project and whose lifetime is considered theoretically perpetual. Hence, the virtual organization under consideration here may range in size from the few members who comprise a startup company to a global virtual powerhouse with hundreds of thousands of members scattered across the globe. Regardless of its size, the virtual organization is now an accepted organizational form. This makes the assessment of servant leadership practice in the context of the virtual organization an important part of ensuring its continued success.

Like any innovation, the virtual organization presents opportunities and challenges for managers. Minimal personal interaction, group member accountability and accessibility issues, lack of traditional control mechanisms, performance management logistics, and cross-cultural contexts are just a few of the challenges leaders face in this new world. Personal qualities typically reinforced through daily contact and by example are much harder for leaders to effect in a virtual environment. This makes it vastly more difficult for managers to establish the trust relationships so necessary for the creation and ongoing maintenance of successful training programs. On the other hand, Silbergh and Lennon (2006) and Shekhar (2006) see member perception of the effectiveness of virtual organizations and the highly dispersed nature of the form as grounds for competitive advantage on a global scale. Ultimately, the success of the virtual organization is based upon outcomes realized from leadership characteristics, behaviors, and practices such as strategic thinking, goal setting, positive motivation, and general ethical environment. One particularly effective approach which relies upon all of these, as well as virtue ethics and the personal ethical comportment of the leader, is servant leadership. The distributed nature of the virtual organization requires an ethic

Table 1. Spears' ten servant leadership characteristics

Listening	Listening, coupled with regular periods of reflection, is essential to the growth of the servant-leader.
Empathy	The servant-leader strives to understand and empathize with others.
Healing	Learning to heal is a powerful force for transformation and integration.
Awareness	General awareness, and especially self-awareness, strengthens the servant-leader.
Persuasion	The servant-leader seeks to persuade others rather than to coerce compliance.
Conceptualization	The ability to look at a problem (or an organization) from a conceptualizing perspective means that one must think beyond day-to-day realities.
Foresight	Foresight is a characteristic that enables the servant-leader to understand the lessons from the past, the realities of the present, and the likely consequences of a decision for the future.
Stewardship	Servant-leadership, like stewardship, assumes first and foremost a commitment to serving the needs of others.
Commitment to the growth of people	Servant-leaders believe that people have an intrinsic value beyond their tangible contributions as workers.
Building community	Servant-leadership suggests that true community can be created among those who work in businesses and other institutions.

Note: Adapted from Spears, L. C. (2004). The understanding and practice of servant-leadership. In L. C. Spears & M. Lawrence (Eds.), *Practicing servant leadership: Succeeding through trust, bravery, and forgiveness* (pp. 9-24). San Francisco: Jossey-Bass.

that is transparent and trusting, rather than opaque and controlling, and servant leadership answers such a call.

QUALITATIVE APPROACHES TO SERVANT LEADERSHIP PRACTICE ASSESSMENT

As the former director of *The Greenleaf Center for Servant-Leadership* and now the *Spears Center for Servant-Leadership*, Larry Spears carries considerable weight whenever addressing servant leadership topics, of which he is an expert acknowledged across the world. He identifies 10 characteristics of servant leadership in Table 1 below. These characteristics have been widely accepted within the servant leadership academic and practice communities.

In a similar vein, Russell and Stone (2002) offer two complementary lists of servant leadership attributes. These two lists are described by Russell and Stone as (a) *functional* because their classification "primarily results from their repetitive prominence in the literature" (2002, p. 146)

and (b) *supporting* with regard to the functional attributes. The two lists are presented in Table 2 below. The functional attributions are "operative qualities, characteristics, and distinctive features belonging to leaders and observed through specific leader behaviors in the workplace" (Russell & Stone, 2002, p. 146). The accompanying attributes are secondary characteristics intended to complement the functional list. There exists no correlation between the functional and accompanying attributes; they are merely counterparts which Russell and Stone consider fundamental parts of two basic servant leadership models.

In a summary to their literature review, Russell and Stone assert that "since values are the core beliefs that determine an individual's principles, they are the independent variables in a model of servant leadership. The dependent variable is manifest servant leadership" (2002, p. 153). They suggest two models of servant leadership. Model 1 describes "the relationship between leader attributes and manifest servant leadership" (p. 153) while Model 2 "is a more encompassing model for servant leadership" (p. 153). Model 2 includes considerations of organizational culture, behav-

Table 2. Russell and Stone's servant leadership functional and accompanying attributes

Functional Attributes	Accompanying Attributes
Vision	Communication
Honesty	Credibility
Integrity	Competence
Trust	Stewardship
Service	Visibility
Modeling	Influence
Pioneering	Persuasion
Appreciation of others	Listening
Empowerment	Encouragement
	Teaching
	Delegation

Note: Adapted from Russell, R. F., & Stone, A. G. (2002). A review of servant leadership attributes: Developing a practical model. *Leadership and Organization Development Journal, 23*(3), 145-157.

iors, and performance in a systemic loop structure. The accompanying attributes act as intervening variables in both models which serve to raise and modify the functional attributes. Regardless of the model, the primary goal of Russell and Stone is to construct the groundwork for further discussion and dialogue centered on the establishment of additional servant leadership theoretical and practice frameworks, not for training program development.

PAGE AND WONG'S SERVANT LEADERSHIP MEASUREMENT INSTRUMENTS

Page and Wong have developed several servant leadership measurement instruments aimed at self-assessment and the measurement of both positive and negative leadership characteristics (Page, 2004; Page & Wong, 2005; Wong & Page, 2003; Wong & Page, 2005; Wong, Page, & Rude, 2005). The research at the core of these instruments is a qualitative literature review combined with their own experience putting servant leadership principles into practice (Page & Wong, 2000). Their efforts have resulted in 12 servant leader-

ship categories: integrity, humility, servanthood, caring for others, empowering others, developing others, visioning, goal setting, leading, modeling, team building, and shared decision-making. Other researchers (Dennis & Winston, 2003) have taken pains to apply quantitative statistical techniques to Page and Wong's work in the interest of creating a tractable servant leadership measurement scale. Dennis and Winston's (2003) principal component factor analysis "indicates that Page and Wong's instrument measures three of the 12 purported factors and while it did not represent all 12, this scale represents a potential tool with positive implications for training new and existing leaders" (Dennis & Winston, 2003, p. 456). This instrument clearly holds promise, yet lacks the maturity and quantitative methodological rigor sought by so many practicing managers, especially those hoping to use the tool as a training aid.

QUANTITATIVE APPROACHES TO SERVANT LEADERSHIP PRACTICE ASSESSMENT

While qualitative approaches to assessing servant leadership are an important part of construct-

Table 3. Patterson's servant leadership constructs

Construct	Description
Agapao Love	To love in a social or moral sense
Humility	The ability to keep one's accomplishments and successes in perspective
Altruism	Helping others selflessly just for the sake of helping
Vision	Necessary to good leadership
Trust	Speaks to leader morality and competence
Service	A mission of responsibility to others
Empowerment	Entrusting power to others

Note. Adapted from Patterson, K. A. (2003). Servant leadership: A theoretical model. *Dissertation Abstracts International, 64* (02), 570. (UMI No. 3082719).

ing a viable practice, many managers are more comfortable with quantifying results. A popular approach involves the administration of a survey instrument to a sample population followed by application of statistical methods and procedures to attempt hypothesis disproof. Such instruments already exist with more in development. Here, we will examine Dennis and Bocarnea's (2005) and Laub's (1999) instruments in greater depth, paying special attention to the utility of Laub's Organizational Leadership Assessment (OLA) instrument as a way to understand the level of servant leadership in the interest of refining servant leadership training strategies and tactics within the virtual organization context.

DENNIS AND BOCARNEA'S SERVANT LEADERSHIP ASSESSMENT INSTRUMENT

Dennis and Bocarnea (2005) build upon Dennis' (2004) study to create a servant leadership assessment instrument based upon Patterson's (2003) theory of servant leadership. Dennis and Bocarnea base their instrument solely upon Patterson's (2003) "component constructs underlying the practice of servant leadership" (p. 15) detailed in Table 3.

Dennis and Bocarnea's study constructs a proposed servant leadership characteristic set; it uses the Delphi (i.e., panel-of-experts) method for settling upon a final survey item list gathered from follower data. By conducting a factor analysis with Oblimin rotation, Dennis and Bocarnea (2005) "sought to answer the following question: Can the presence of Patterson's servant leadership concept be assessed through a written instrument?" (p. 610). In the end, they are only able to verify five of Patterson's seven servant leadership constructs, eliminating the *altruism* and *service* factors.

THE ORGANIZATIONAL LEADERSHIP ASSESSMENT INSTRUMENT

Laub's creation of the OLA[1] marks a significant contribution to the development of a reliable, internally consistent, and quantifiable servant leadership characteristics scale. Several researchers have utilized the OLA in a range of disciplines from school effectiveness to law enforcement to job satisfaction (Braye, 2001; Drury, 2004; Hebert, 2003; Herbst, 2004; Irving, 2005; Ledbetter, 2004; Miears, 2005; Molnar, 2007; Thompson, 2004). Laub recognizes within the servant leadership scholarly community "a significant lack of quan-

Assessment Strategies for Servant Leadership Practice and Training in the Virtual Organization

titative research, as we are still in the early stages of study in this new field; and there is a need for tools to assist in ongoing research" (1999, p. 34). This was an accurate statement in 1999 and still rings true today.

Laub's response to the recognition of the need for more quantitative servant leadership research is to develop a three-phase study composed of a Delphi panel, a pilot study, and a cross-sectional survey consisting of a sample drawn from 41 organizations distributed throughout the world. The Delphi panel is composed of 14 recognized experts in the field. Factor analysis of Laub's study results produced six categories of servant leadership: (a) values people, (b) develops people, (c) builds community, (d) displays authenticity, (e) provides leadership, and (f) shares leadership. The discovery of these factors is important for several reasons and will be more fully explored later.

In his doctoral dissertation study, Laub (1999) initially develops 74 survey questions using the Delphi panel technique. This technique ensures qualitative research design rigor (Malterud, 2001; Morgan & Smircich, 1980; Munck, 1998, Tobin & Begley, 2004), which is important during the early design phase of a survey instrument. The origins of this method lie in the Rand Corporation's early efforts at forecasting military probabilities covering scenarios such as large-scale bombing attacks against the United States (Helmer, 1975, p. xix). Linstone and Turoff (1975) offer a concise definition of the method: "Delphi may be characterized as a method for structuring a group communication process so that the process is effective in allowing a group of individuals, as a whole, to deal with a complex problem" (p. 3). Thus, the Delphi technique is considered an iterative, facilitated, expert group communication process that is, at its heart, a qualitative effort. In this way, Laub's initial efforts at creating a quantitative servant leadership assessment instrument are grounded in the qualitative realm. This is not the last time we will observe the qualitative and quantitative

Figure 1. Example items from the organizational leadership assessment instrument

In general, people within this organization…
1. Trust each other
2. Are clear on the key goals of the organization
3. Enjoy people
4. Are non-judgmental – they keep an open mind
5. Respect each other

domains engaged in a relationship in which one needs the other and vice versa.

The OLA uses a Likert-type scale that ranges from one for "Strongly Disagree" to five for "Strongly Agree" (see Figure 1 for organization level examples) with six additional questions designed to assess job satisfaction for a total of 80 survey questions. After deciding the survey took too much time to complete, Laub settled upon 60 servant leadership characteristic questions plus the job satisfaction questions for a total of 66 questions (Laub, 1999). Seven demographic, or control variable, questions are included. These questions are intended to assess respondents' categorical responses under gender, age, level of education, type of organization, number of years with the organization, present position with the company, and ethnic origin. These variables are important for researchers because they allow research question and hypothesis testing based upon statements such as, "Gender affects a participant's view of his/her role within the organization." Such statements are important because they tie more general statements about servant leadership at the organizational level to organizational members.

Laub is able to use the factor analysis statistical technique with his study data to discover the six sub-scores mentioned above: (a) values people, (b) develops people, (c) builds community, (d) display authenticity, (e) provides leadership, and (f) shares leadership. By creating an instrument that "has been developed in such a way that it can be taken by anyone, at any level, within an organization, work group or team" (Laub, 1999, p. 49), the resulting instrument effectively and accurately measures the servant leadership characteristics of respondents at three levels: (a) top management, (b) management, and (c) workforce/staff. As a quantitative approach, Laub's OLA is an instrument of high quality and reliability that is quickly becoming the *de facto* standard among servant leadership researchers for measuring servant leadership characteristics in a quantitative way.

PUTTING THE OLA TO USE

Laub's OLA is an effective instrument in the context of the virtual organization in which a researcher administers it to a sample population drawn from that organization. Several researchers have conducted similar studies with great success (Braye, 2001; Hebert, 2003; Ledbetter, 2004; Miears, 2005; Molnar, 2007; Thompson, 2004), and more continue to incorporate the OLA into their work every day. Because the OLA is comprised of 60 items using a Likert-type scale with an upper bound of five, the measure of the quintessential servant leader is 300 (60x5). This allows a researcher several opportunities for good, solid statistical analyses. For instance, the mean, median, and mode and total counts by category are easily accomplished. A good researcher will make use of the OLA's demographic (control) variables to run the Analysis of Variance (ANOVA) technique with the goal of determining whether any of the demographic variables might influence the servant leadership scores of the respondents. As an example, one may discover whether gender influences the group's servant leadership practice. This is accomplished using a statistics software package such as SPSS. In such a scenario, the researcher would use the ANOVA function of SPSS to include the gender variable with the mean servant leadership scores for the entire sample. The

result would be the discovery of possible influence by one of the genders (for humans, male and female) upon the practice of servant leadership in that particular sample. This example assumes the researcher has the time and resources to pursue such a data collection regimen.

In the likely event that time and money act as study constraints, the researcher may use the OLA and Laub's (1999) doctoral dissertation study as guides for creation of their own servant leadership index from a secondary data set. Such a data set might come from the researcher's own organization (e.g., a prior study/human resources department) or from a third-party. Useful for such a study is Hebert's (2004) doctoral dissertation. Her study includes a factor analysis of Laub's six sub-scores in which she produces a single factor, servant leadership. This finding is important for two reasons: (a) it compresses multiple servant leadership meta-characteristics into a single factor and (b) it allows other researchers to rely upon her work to define servant leadership characteristics within foreign datasets. An example of this might involve the creative use of Hebert's compression technique in conjunction with the World Values Survey (World Values Survey, 2008) database. In some ways, the World Values Survey (WVS) represents the ultimate virtual organization. This longitudinal study is comprised of demographic and values data from 80 countries located on all six inhabited continents of the world. It has been conducted in waves starting in 1981, the last taking place over the course of 2005 and 2006. The point is well taken when the WVS Web site states that "the most important product of this project may be the insight that it produces concerning changes at the individual level that are transforming social, economic and political life" (World Values Survey, 2008).

Along with plentiful demographic information, the values data points of the WVS consist of survey items such as, "For each of the following, indicate how important it is in your life. Would you say it is…" The values choices for this item are family, friends, leisure time, politics, work, and religion with Likert-type scale answers that include very important, rather important, not very important, and not important at all. Hundreds of similar items exist in the survey and can vary from wave to wave. Though some items may be included in the survey for all of the waves, not all of the questions are asked by interviewers during the administration of each wave. This can create interesting gaps for the researcher interested in discovering how values change over time for a particular country or group of countries (e.g., region of the world), yet this is not uncommon for a study of this scope and size. As a way of building a unique "servant leadership index" over several of the WVS items, a researcher will decide which items to include in their fabricated index. This is where the relationship between quantitative and qualitative data decisions rises again. In this case, the researcher will use Laub's OLA sub-scores, (a) values people, (b) develops people, (c) builds community, (d) displays authenticity, (e) provides leadership, and (f) share leadership, combined with Hebert's compression of them into the single "servant leadership" factor to make determinations about which WVS variables to include in their own, unique servant leadership index. Once several variables are chosen and a determination regarding which of the five data sets to use is made, the researcher will use a statistical package such as SPSS to run the Cronbach's Alpha statistical technique to decide whether the chosen variables measure the same construct (i.e., internal reliability), servant leadership. In this way, the researcher has made a qualitative determination about which quantitative values to use. He has also then used a quantitative technique to establish the reliability of the new "instrument" before using other quantitative techniques such as ANOVA and Pearson's Correlation Coefficient (Pearson's r) to determine correlations between variables.

In the context of a virtual organization, a survey instrument such as the OLA can be created as a set of Web pages that capture the item answers to a database. Since the OLA covers three levels of an organization, (a) top management, (b) management/supervisory, and (c) workforce/ staff, it would be instructive to administer the survey over time to see if and how member views of the level of organizational servant leadership have changed. Such recognition in organizational member perceptions is an important part of maintaining a vibrant servant leadership practice. As the mean OLA score for the virtual organization shifts up or down, it will become the task of the leader-manager to understand why such a shift is taking place and create a plan for how to modify organizational dynamics to correct or enhance it. Regardless of the direction of the shift, it will have been the careful and conscientious administration of the OLA that made its recognition possible.

FUTURE DIRECTIONS

The ideas presented here regarding the use of Laub's (1999) OLA constitute a short introduction to the use of such an instrument as a training assessment and program preparation tool in the context of the virtual organization. Laub originally administered the OLA to traditional organizations, yet there is nothing inherently "traditional" in the tool that prevents its use by servant leadership practitioners in virtual organizations. The OLA is an excellent resource for the preparation of training programs by providing clear understanding of the level of servant leadership within the organization. One opportunity for further refinement of the OLA might involve the reduction of the number of items presented by the instrument. Reducing the number of items while retaining its practical efficacy would make the OLA more attractive to organizational members and managers alike. Research into the creation of complementary instruments that consider an individual organizational member's servant leadership practice would hold enormous utility for managers, as well. Finally, a comparison study of OLA results from traditional and virtual organizations would provide information about servant leadership practice in the virtual organization, as well as valuable research details about differences that might exist between administering such a tool in the two environments. Regardless of the context in which the OLA is used, it is a valuable tool for managers to conduct both pre- and post-training assessments of the virtual organization.

REFERENCES

Annas, J. (2003). The structure of virtue. In M. DePaul & L. Zagzebski (Eds.), *Intellectual virtue: Perspectives from ethics and epistemology* (pp. 15-33). New York: Oxford University Press, Inc.

Argandoña, A. (2003). The new economy: Ethical issues. *Journal of Business Ethics, 44*, 3–22. doi:10.1023/A:1023226105869

Aristotle. (1998). *Nicomachean ethics* (D. P. Chase, Trans.). Mineola, NY: Dover Publications, Inc.

Arnison, L., & Miller, P. (2002). Virtual teams: A virtue for the conventional team. *Journal of Workplace Learning, 14*(4), 166–173. doi:10.1108/13665620210427294

Bass, B. M., & Stogdill, R. M. (1990). *Bass and Stogdill's handbook of leadership: Theory, research, and managerial applications* (3rd ed.). New York: Simon & Schuster.

Braye, R. H. (2001). Servant-leadership: Belief and practice in women-led businesses. *Dissertation Abstracts International, 61*(07), 2799. (UMI No. 9981536).

Burns, J. M. (1982). *Leadership.* New York: HarperCollins Publishers.

Dennis, R. S., & Bocarnea, M. (2005). Development of the servant leadership assessment instrument. *Leadership and Organization Development Journal, 26*(8), 600–615. doi:10.1108/01437730510633692

Dennis, R. S., & Winston, B. E. (2003). A factor analysis of Page and Wong's servant leadership instrument. *Leadership and Organization Development Journal, 24*(8), 455–459. doi:10.1108/01437730310505885

Drury, S. L. (2005). Employee perceptions of servant leadership: Comparisons by level and with job satisfaction and organizational commitment. *Dissertation Abstracts International, 65*(09), 3457. (UMI No. 3146724).

Frick, D. M. (2004). *Robert K. Greenleaf: A life of servant leadership.* San Francisco: Berrett-Kohler Publishers.

Greenleaf, R. K. (1970). *The servant as leader.* Indianapolis, IN: The Greenleaf Center for Servant Leadership.

Greenleaf, R. K. (2002). *Servant leadership: A journey into the nature of legitimate power and greatness* (25th anniversary ed.). New York: Paulist Press.

Hebert, S. C. (2004). The relationship of perceived servant leadership and job satisfaction from the follower's perspective. *Dissertation Abstracts International, 64*(11), 4118. (UMI No. 3112981).

Helmer, O. (1975). Foreword. In H. A. Linstone & M. Turoff (Eds.), *The Delphi method: Techniques and applications.* Reading, MA: Addison-Wesley Publishing Company.

Herbst, J. D. (2004). Organizational servant leadership and its relationship to secondary school effectiveness. *Dissertation Abstracts International, 64*(11), 4001. (UMI No. 3110574).

Hesse, H. (2003). *Journey to the east* (H. Rosner, Trans.). New York: Picador USA.

Hookway, C. (2003). How to be a virtue epistemologist. In M. DePaul & L. Zagzebski (Eds.), *Intellectual virtue: Perspectives from ethics and epistemology.* New York: Oxford University Press.

Irving, J. A. (2005). Servant leadership and the effectiveness of teams. *Dissertation Abstracts International, 66*(04), 1421. (UMI No. 3173207).

Kuhn, T. S. (1996). *The structure of scientific revolutions* (3rd ed.). Chicago: Chicago University Press.

Laub, J. A. (1999). Assessing the servant leadership organization: Development of the Servant Organizational Leadership Assessment (OLA) instrument. *Dissertation Abstracts International, 62*(02), 308. (UMI No. 9921922).

Ledbetter, D. S. (2004). Law enforcement leaders and servant leadership: A reliability study of the organizational leadership assessment. *Dissertation Abstracts International, 64*(11), 4200. (UMI No. 3110778).

Linstone, H. A., & Turoff, M. (Eds.). (1975). *The Delphi method: Techniques and applications*. Reading, MA: Addison-Wesley Publishing Company.

Malterud, K. (2001). Qualitative research: Standards, challenges, and guidelines. *Lancet, 358,* 483–488. doi:10.1016/S0140-6736(01)05627-6

Miears, L. D. (2005). Servant-leadership and job satisfaction: A correlational study in Texas Education Agency Region X public schools. *Dissertation Abstracts International, 65*(09), 3237. (UMI No. 3148083).

Molnar, D. R. (2007). Serving the world: A cross-cultural study of national culture dimensions and servant leadership. *Dissertation Abstracts International, 68/05*, 139. (UMI No. AAT 3266277).

Morgan, G., & Smircich, L. (1980). The case for qualitative research. *Academy of Management Review, 5*(4), 491–500. doi:10.2307/257453

Munck, G. L. (1998). Canons of research design in qualitative analysis. *Studies in Comparative International Development, 33*(3), 18–45. doi:10.1007/BF02687490

Murphy, P. E. (1999). Character and virtue ethics in international marketing: An agenda for managers, researchers, and educators. *Journal of Business Ethics, 18*(1), 107–124. doi:10.1023/A:1006072413165

Page, D., & Wong, P. T. (2000). A conceptual framework for measuring servant-leadership. In S. B.-S. K. Adjibolosoo (Ed.), *The human factor in shaping the course of history and development* (pp. 1-16). Latham, MD: University Press of America.

Popper, K. (2002). *The logic of scientific discovery* (J. Fried & L. Fried, Trans.). New York: Routledge.

Russell, R. F. (2001). The role of values in servant leadership. *Leadership and Organization Development Journal, 22*(2), 76–89. doi:10.1108/01437730110382631

Russell, R. F., & Stone, A. G. (2002). A review of servant leadership attributes: Developing a practical model. *Leadership and Organization Development Journal, 23*(3), 145–157. doi:10.1108/01437730210424

Shekhar, S. (2006). Understanding the virtuality of virtual organizations. *Leadership and Organization Development Journal, 27*(6), 465–483. doi:10.1108/01437730610687755

Silbergh, D., & Lennon, K. (2006). Developing leadership skills: Online versus face-to-face. *Journal of European Industrial Training, 30*(7), 498–511. doi:10.1108/03090590610704376

Slote, M. (2003). Agent-based virtue ethics. In S. Darwall (Ed.), *Blackwell readings in philosophy: Virtue ethics* (pp. 203-226). New York: Oxford University Press.

Solomon, D. (2003). Virtue ethics: Radical or routine? In M. DePaul & L. Zagzebski (Eds.), *Intellectual virtue: Perspectives from ethics and epistemology* (pp. 57-80). New York: Oxford University Press.

Spears, L. C. (2004). The understanding and practice of servant-leadership. In L. C. Spears & M. Lawrence, *Practicing servant leadership: Succeeding through trust, bravery, and forgiveness* (pp. 9-24). San Francisco: Jossey-Bass.

Taylor, F. W. (1998). *The principles of scientific management*. New York: Dover Publications.

Thompson, C. H. (2006). The public school superintendent and servant leadership. *Dissertation Abstracts International, 66*(09). (UMI No. 3190501).

Tobin, G. A., & Begley, C. M. (2004). Methodological rigor within a qualitative framework. *Methodological Issues in Nursing Research, 48*(4), 388–396.

Weber, M. (1947). *The theory of economic organization* (A. Henderson & T. Parsons, Trans., T. Parsons, Ed.). New York: The Free Press.

Whetstone, J. T. (2001). How virtue fits with business ethics. *Journal of Business Ethics, 33*, 101–114. doi:10.1023/A:1017554318867

World Values Survey. (2008). *World values survey: The world's most comprehensive investigation of political and sociocultural change.* Retrieved June 25, 2008, from http://www.worldvalues-survey.org/

ENDNOTE

¹ You may find complete information about obtaining and using the instrument at Dr. Jim Laub's OLAgroup Web site at http://www.OLAgroup.com.

Chapter 14
Online Networks Can Support the Rise of Virtual Leaders:
An Actor–Network Theory Analysis

Annick Janson
Victoria University of Wellington, New Zealand

ABSTRACT

The actor network theory (ANT) as first proposed by Latour (1984) describes the emergence of socio-technical systems through interaction patterns between network participants as a means of harnessing technological and human factors. This research extended ANT to investigate how self-selected leaders spontaneously emerged in a virtual environment, using the online medium to gain legitimacy and coverage. Thematic analysis of online postings and interviews outlined how participants: 1) tested and developed virtual leadership competencies for the first time; 2) seized the opportunity to raise their personal profile even when geographically isolated; 3) made purposeful process and content contributions and; 4) developed online networking competencies. Since emergent leadership is simultaneously enabling of and enabled by acts of virtual communication, it is important for organisations to learn to identify virtual leaders. Virtual leaders may rise and contribute to the organisation through communication channels other than those typically used by conventional leaders – hence potentially requiring a different set of communication and network building skills.

INTRODUCTION

This research investigated how self-selected leaders spontaneously emerged in a virtual environment using the online medium to gain legitimacy and coverage. While conventional leadership has been studied extensively, 'virtual leadership' is a novel phenomenon, developing alongside technology. The questions of how virtual environments may be used to grow constructive participation, and the motives for so doing, are increasing in significance for a broad range of contexts. This research extends the Actor-Network Theory (ANT) proponed by Latour (1987) to account for virtual network development

DOI: 10.4018/978-1-60566-958-8.ch014

and describe the online behaviours of their actors. This chapter aims to characterize how ANT processes may be 'virtualised'. The virtual leadership building model is proposed to explain how these processes were carried out, and collaboration and trust fostered early on in online relationships. The chapter also illustrates what the contribution of technology may be in facilitating the development of novel types of leadership.

BACKGROUND

Virtual Leadership

The eighties saw a flurry of research reporting conflicting results as to the ability of computer mediated communication channels to support meaningful interaction (Wellman, Quan-Haase, Witte, & Hampton, 2001), covering aspects of both technical and people capabilities of systems. The role of existing key leadership figures (for instance managers, group owners, facilitators) was theorized as critical because of their ability to direct action aimed at shaping communication patterns in their organizations.

Identified leaders were studied in virtual community research. Blanchard and Markus (2002) noted that participants' sense of community fluctuated with the level of their involvement within the community and the perceived benefits from participation and contribution. For instance participants in health related support groups that reported receiving informational support, also exchanged emotional support in an ongoing manner. In such instances, the roles of community managers included some clear boundaries of responsibilities, with the long term survival of the online community identified as a direct function of their contribution. On the other hand, their motivations for contributions were shown to be intrinsically related to their roles. One such established leader, for instance, characterised her feeling as a need to "give back" to a group that had contributed so much to her (p.6).

In the work organizational context, it is virtual teams, rather than general online groups or communities that were studied. The role of existing leaders such as managers of 'virtual' organisations was viewed as fundamental in building trust and mutual understanding (Van der Smagt, 2000) thus generally reinforcing online group cohesion to improve virtual group functioning (DeSanctis & Monge, 1999). Studies of virtual team facilitators involving participants enrolled in a virtual facilitation programme, crossing boundaries of time, space and culture (Pauleen & Yoong, 2001a) described the facilitators' use of information and communication technology to build effective team work relationships. Pauleen and Yoong (2001b) concluded that training needs be aimed at helping virtual facilitators gain the necessary experience and understanding to work in various online and offline environments. Pauleen and Yoong (2004) further outlined relationship building as the key social process at work in virtual team facilitation and concluded that their Action Research design promoted learning and reflection for the virtual facilitators. These results support previous findings that emphasise the quality of online facilitation as a potential enabling factor, with the group leadership and its skill at online communication under study (Durnell Cramton & Orvis, 2003; James & Rykert, 1998; Klein & Kleinhanns, 2003). The latter view the role of the facilitator as maintaining the social dynamics of the discussion and as moderating content to increase and encourage online participation, together with its leadership connection (Gibson & Manuel, 2003).

Studying the email use-patterns of emerging leaders in virtual teams, Yoo and Alavi (2002) concluded that contemporary leaders need to master the art of online communication if they are to extend their sphere of influence in their organisations. The authors note that this is a paradigm shift as most management development programs emphasise conventional communication modes and little attention, if any, is given to computer mediated communication. Special curricula would need to be developed to treat in depth the subject of computer mediated communication mastery in order for potential leaders to learn how to emerge and become accepted as such in an online environment.

In a study where MBA participants were asked to form virtual teams (Lewis Tyran, Tyran & Shepherd, 2003), trust appears to act as a mediating variable for team performance. While the authors found no relationship at first between emergent leadership and team performance, after isolating the trust variable, the teams that performed better had either an emergent leader who was trusted to perform the task at hand or there were high trust levels among team members. Team members described emergent leaders as displaying the ability to inspire them. Leaders' communication abilities were important, but most important were the emergent leaders' skills at conveying their ideas and inspiration through the written medium, since emails were the primary communication mode for the teams. Hence, the electronic medium for the virtual collaboration did appear to make a difference in the type of self-selected leaders ("the characteristics of electronic media used in a virtual team setting may influence the type of leader who emerges" p. 189). The authors conclusions reinforce earlier findings (Jarvenpaa & Leidner, 1999; Molina & Yoong, 2003; Yoong & Galluppe, 2001) that trust and virtual effectiveness are intimately connected. Furthermore, Lewis Tyran, Tyran and Shepherd (2003) make recommendations to aspiring emerging virtual leaders that are similar to the those made by Schindler and Thomas (1993) to aspiring online facilitators – foster an online climate of trust and model trustworthiness.

There is a dearth of literature describing the experiences and motivation of leaders and their perceptions of the advantages to participating in online groups (Avolio, Kahai, & Dodge, 2000). While it has been shown that in real world, i.e. non-virtual environments, team performance and team members' satisfaction are positively influenced by leadership (Bass, 1990; Hackman, 1990), theories of virtual leadership are in their infancy. Little is known about virtual leaders, or 'e-leaders' as coined by Avolio and Kahai (2003) and most of the literature addresses virtual leaders within pre-existing teams (Alavi & Yoo, 1997; Yoo & Alavi, 1996). Few studies of emerging virtual leadership explored the experiences at leading through online channels of their emergent leaders (Lewis Tyran, Tyran & Shepherd, 2003). Researching those individuals who self-selected as leaders of an online group, as opposed to having been placed in a "leading" position from the start, would add value to both researchers of online group development as well as designers of leadership development programmes.

Actor-Networks: Where People and Technology Interplay

Actor Network Theory describes the emergence of socio-technical systems through interaction patterns between network participants as their ways of harnessing technological and human factors. In order to do this, ANT uses the traces remaining (interactions, texts, exchanges) while the network is being constructed. This is one reason why ANT is particularly suited to the study of innovation, which is typically made up of a complex web of intricate activities and interactions.

Actor Network Theory is able to provide a unique lens through which to study innovation networks and their development. ANT focuses on the processes through which collective projects are carried out, describing short segments of a longer term process, as they differentially affect the development of the whole project. ANT views the heterogeneous make up of actor-networks (from social and technical material) as a central factor in their sustainability (Latour 1991; Joerges & Czarniawska 1998). Hence, ANT contrasts with innovation diffusion models, which focus primarily on the characteristics of the innovation itself.

Actor-Network Theory extended the role of agency to non-human actors beyond human ones. According to ANT, an actor is "something that acts to which activity is granted by others. An actor is accepted to be the source of an action, regardless of its status as human or non-human" (Doolin & Lowe 2002, p. 70). Latour (1987; 1996) for instance, extended the role of agency to actors mostly ignored until recently in social and organisational analyses. Texts record codified rules or commands such as directing, committing, authorizing or informing. Online postings in a virtual group thus played a recognisable role in group interactions by either reflecting or impacting the actions taken by human actors. Actor-Network Theory analyses extended networks constituted from agents such as humans, texts, machines or technologies in the groups under study. The ANT framework will provide the theoretical framework for the network development analysis in the present research.

Translations and Inscriptions: The 'Active Ingredients' of Actor-Networks

'Translations' and 'inscriptions' are the mechanisms through which actors contribute their individual strengths to the network and reach their objectives. Design is translation, according to ANT; designers' function is to control the iterative process whereby interests and needs of users are translated into a solution (or system). In turn, when participants adopt the technology as inscribed, they further translate the system into their respective operational contexts. Designers compose scenarios as programs of action for users, making implicit or explicit assumptions about the skills needed to act and the capability of the system. In this way they define roles to be played by actors in the network. As soon as programs of actions are inscribed into a piece of technology, the technology becomes recognised as an actor offering its inscribed program of action on its users (Latour, 1991).

In virtual environments, different platforms have been designed to allow for certain types of communication (synchronous and asynchronous communication, for instance, necessitate different capabilities and availabilities from users); similarly discussion lists and web-based bulletin boards provide very different virtual communication experiences and support different virtual patterns of interaction. Additionally, technologies inscribe either weak/flexible or strong/inflexible programs of action for users (Hanseth & Monteiro, 1998). Hanseth and Monteiro give the example of a hammer as the former and the assembly line of Chaplin's "Modern Times" as the latter. In the current work environment, emails are strong inscriptions because of their prevalence in today's workplace, where so much communication is done by email, whereas web-based bulletin boards are weaker from that respect, because most still require users to manually go onto the websites and check whether any new messages are received (as opposed to getting an email in one's inbox). E-mail list servers, thus, are associated with strong programs of action because so many knowledge workers are online most of the working day. Hence, the strength of a program of action in the present example is determined by a complex interplay between humans and technology in both the prevalence of the communication medium and the ease of access from the actors' perspective.

According to Actor Network Theory, inscribing behaviour into actor-networks is how an actor might reach an objective. There are short term (i.e. to make potent decisions and raise support to implement them in iterative stages) and long term objectives (i.e. to succeed in the design and implementation of a system). Networks also develop by accumulating the strength of their inscriptions, through iterative processes. Actors of the network may seek to inscribe their interest (setting up virtual communication channels) through the process of translation (trying out various software and virtual platforms). Inscriptions often turn out unsuccessful in the sense that their scenarios are not followed, the intentions of the designer not fulfilled. To increase the likelihood that an inscription may succeed, it is necessary to increase its strength. A key insight is that it is nearly impossible to know beforehand whether an inscription is strong enough to fulfil its role - it remains each time an open, empirical question needs addressing through trial and error ('usability testing' in technology lingo). There are two ways to increase the strength of an inscription: the first is the superimposing of inscriptions, i.e. adding inscriptions from the start, rather than waiting for the trial and error process to show results, and the second one is to expand the network: In ANT terms, enroll new actors and technologies, and look for new, as yet unused, material to into which to inscribe scenarios. Through the process of translation, each actor contributes specific resources to the activity and robustness of the network.

Latour (1991) offers a concrete illustration of the mutual effects of inscriptions and translations, taken from the tourism industry. Hotels need to ensure that guests leave their room keys at the front desk while checking out. According to Actor Network Theory, they need to inscribe the desired pattern of behaviour into an actor-network and solve the question of how to inscribe it and into what. As in a typical trial and error experiment, hotel management had to test the strength of different inscriptions. This was done by creating an artefact in the form of a sign behind the counter requesting all guests to return the key when leaving to enrolling a human door-keeper actor, back to an artefact in the form of a key with a metal knob. Through incremental increases of weight of the knob, the desired behaviour was finally achieved. In ANT's terms, it is through a succession of translations, that the hotels' interests were finally inscribed into a network strong enough to create the desired behaviour from their guests. Another way to describe translations is as negotiations during which actors construct definitions and meanings together and assign and receive roles

in the pursuit of individual and collective objectives (Law, 1992; Singleton & Michael, 1993). Translation is successful at the point where actors accept the roles defined and attributed to them in the network (Callon, 1986) and power relations are used to explain how social relations are actively used to sustain the actor-networks. Translation and inscriptions mechanisms were recorded and analysed following the methodology described in the next section.

METHOD

Interpretive research typically begins with the assumption that access to reality takes place through social constructions. The methodology for the present research was interpretive in an attempt to understand phenomena through the meaning that people assign to them, beginning with the assumption that access to reality takes place through social constructions such as language, consciousness and shared meanings (Kaplan & Maxwell, 1994). Interpretivists usually do not predefine dependent and independent variables; they rather generate rich descriptions for the phenomena under investigation. Sensemaking processes in organisations, for example, emphasise that knowledge is not an entity to be transferred; rather it is created, enacted and transformed through interactive social networking patterns as part of a larger sensemaking process. Over the last decade, interpretivism has made significant contributions to qualitative research conducted on information-based collaborative processes (Walsham, 1995).

Potential participants were identified in the six months preceding the study as experts in their fields (business, virtual communities and innovation) as well as innovators and entrepreneurs at various stages of their ventures. They were identified through consultations with individuals in the private, public and academic sector. Participants were reached through a) direct request,

b) referrals and c) self referral from participants who read about the study in the media (Collins, 2001; Foreman, 2002; Peek, 2002). Potential participants were also pointed to the Project's webpage where they could register general interest and leave contact details. The 54 innovators who agreed to contribute, participated in a 36 week long online conversation, through an email-based system delivering emails in participants' inboxes in real time (ListServer®) and a web-based virtual environment (Webcrossing ®) for the remainder of the manipulation.

Recorded inscriptions are materials in variable forms (texts but also images or databases) central to the construction of knowledge and essential to enable action at a distance, because they can travel over time (Latour & Woolgar, 1991). In the context of the present study, inscriptions play a central role. Likewise, Preece and Rogers (Preece & Rogers, 2002) note that discourse analyses in online groups (distributed e-mail discussion lists or bulletin boards) are valid and useful data to understand online participants' perspectives. Online postings ("computer-based artefacts" according to the ANT), face to face conversations and individual interviews were thus recorded.

In total, online conversations were collated during eight months, through which participants shared their views on the potential contribution of a virtual communication channel for business purposes. A total of 653 online messages and four hours of face-to-face interviews with the online community manager were analysed thematically (Owen, 1984), uncovering the ANT developmental stage as follows.

RESULTS

Emergence of the Actor-Network ('How?')

Well suited for Information Systems research (Tatnall & Gilding 1999), Actor Network Theory conceptualises series of events and activities as becoming linked together by a translation carried out by members of the network. This process was recorded as a historical analysis and texts were analysed thematically as summarised in Figure 1. The figure describes subthemes, definitions and sample quotes from each major theme, which will be elaborated upon throughout the Results section.

The analysis describes how actors are called upon to join the forming network and aligned to follow the development of the different stages of the network (Callon, 1994) problematisation, interressement, enrolment and mobilization as described in Figure 2.

PROBLEMATISATION STAGE: RAISING AWARENESS

The initial stage of network development include actors engaging other actors through the process of "problematisation", i.e. defining a problem for which the solution lies in the expertise that the very actor-network being formed will organise (Latour, 1987; 1993; 1999). Failure to engage in one of the stages can provide some indications as to why certain projects fail or succeed, such as the Information Technology projects described earlier in the introduction. In the present study, problematisation activities will be identified in interaction focusing on innovators' isolation and difficulties to connect to an appropriate peer group, for instance.

One way for actors to start the lengthy enrolment process was to look for others to partake in the network development and "problematise" (Callon, 1994; Latour, 1987) the issue under scrutiny. Thematic analyses of message contents show that the actors "problematised" the issue of lack of effective communication means for innovators. They identified two main barriers preventing the growth of online networks – time and trust. They described, on the one hand not having

Figure 1. Participants' perceived enabling factors to online collaboration

Primary and (when applicable) secondary theme
Networking (Benefits of networking)
Definition and sample quote
D: Building and maintaining a network of business contacts Q: Business networking is an essential part of business – we need other people to reach further than our own networks. Cultivating networks that will take you to the places you need to go is an art that is mastered by those who have reached the highest business achievement (E)
Primary and (when applicable) secondary theme
Networking (Networking modes)
Definition and sample quote
D: Online collaboration has advantage compared to face to face collaboration Q: Until recently, face to face situations were the main stage for networking situations. Telephone calls are difficult to place here – in a way there are not face to face situations (…). Now we can interact online and get to know a person, their advice, their reactions to others before deciding whether we want to develop the business relation and – why not – partner injoint ventures (W)
Primary and (when applicable) secondary theme
Networking (Online roles)
Definition and sample quote
D: Online roles participants choose, (e.g., leader vs. lurker) influence their networking ability Q: It is up to each participant to decide what role they want to play online as this will affect the value added they get from their connections… and the amount of networking they will do (J)
Primary and (when applicable) secondary theme
Motivation (Business success)
Definition and sample quote
D: The value attributed to online participation contributing to business success Q: Online collaboration is a huge factor of business success – you can ask a question and receive an answer within minutes, which can save heaps of money (W)
Primary and (when applicable) secondary theme
Motivation (Social entrepreneurship)
Definition and sample quote
D: Participation in the Virtual Network in order to contribute to a positive cause Q: I guess I can call myself a "Social Entrepreneur" as a life choice (…) the network gave me a golden opportunity to achieve a dream of contribution (E)
Primary and (when applicable) secondary theme
Community belonging (Individual perspective)
Definition and sample quote
D: The sense of being part of a group of like-minded people Q: Even when I was anowed under the online network provided opportunity to spend a few minutes and interact with colleagues to ask a question or contribute by giving other sides… That is just the time I can spare. This online network is a great idea—the support of the group might give me the confidence and energy to carry on – and perhaps raise the funding that will make it possible (L)
Primary and (when applicable) secondary theme
Community belonging (Community identity)
Definition and sample quote
D: Defining the characteristics of the community Q: It is important we define ourselves and our goals so that other innovators can join the group. Who are we and what do we stand for – this is what needs to be formulated (S)

continued on following page

Figure 1. continued

Primary and (when applicable) secondary theme
Communication channels
Definition and sample quote
D: Communicating online as one means of communication
Q: We need to get use to online communication as the interest is here to stay and getting proficient at online exchanges is an important part of getting ready for the future (D)
Primary and (when applicable) secondary theme
Storytelling
Definition and sample quote
D: Sharing stories of virtual networking where online communication resulted in tangible benefit
Q: I posted a request online and within minutes has the critical business information I needed from trusted source – my online network (W)
Primary and (when applicable) secondary theme
Building online trust
Definition and sample quote
D: Using the online medium to carryout activities that help others trust us
Q: How can we alleviate online trust issues? Perhaps concerns on activities that build online trust keep our word when we say we are going to do something and build the "trust credit" that we have (A)

Figure 2. The developmental stage of the actor-network

Actor Network developmental stages	
Group activities Online group conversations on email listserve for core group initiation Online postings on email listserve to reach outside the core group	ANT Processes Problematisation: defining a problem for which the solution is the very innovation process in which the actors are engaged in Interressement: engaging in activites to persuade other actors to join in pursuit
Face to face dialogues and individual interviews	Enrolment: distributing roles in the network
Widening the network through web-based bulletin board postings	Mobilisation: building on the result on the enrolment process at which point actors and processes become manageable entities noticeable and usable at government level

enough time to devote to online communication because of work pressure and, on the other hand, debating whether they could trust virtual and invisible correspondents. They created a sense of urgency as clearly articulated by one participant to legitimise the development of the very project they were involved in.

Teaching people commercialisation skills should be our top priority. What we need are mechanisms – such as virtual communication projects as this one – through which this can be achieved most effectively. It is not urgent; it is an emergency if we want to make any difference in the country's wealth creation efforts (Anthony)

As actors engaged others, they defined the problems, thus shaping as a solution the very actor-network being formed.

INTERRESSEMENT STAGE: PERSUADING OTHERS TO JOIN

Interressement is a set of actions performed by one or more actors to try to persuade others to identify with their goals. An alliance is built by enrolling allies into an aligned network. One of the main ideas behind the Actor Network Theory is that such allies include humans as well as technologies. In this sense, technology designers and innovators also design roles for humans, such as users, support people, and anyone using technology to fulfil roles. Making the technology work includes making the human actors play the role designed for them. In the present study, interressement activities will be identified in the actions taken by innovators to rally other participants toward a common goal.

Interressement is a series of actions executed by one or more actors to try and persuade others (as described in action planning below) to identify with a common goal. Optimising factors discussed by participants as they brainstormed possible ways to circumvent these obstacles were factors that enhance virtual communication to business' ends (or as the term emerged during the conversations 'active virtual networking'). As participants defined the group and their common aims they identified and discussed 'virtual networking' as a potential benefit of online collaboration. Hence, when the added value was articulated, group belonging and participation was seen as beneficial to participants. This is further explained in the wider context of the Actor Network Theory as how actors enacted the network activity. As a nucleus of interested innovators formulated their first ideas about forming the online network, they turned to other, potential like-minded or complementary individuals and started enrolment processes with

them. It should be noted that the email listserve contributions doubled in the first six weeks of this stage as compared previous contributions. Amongst discussions that took place online, about 70% of the contents were about reinforcing one another in the opinion that participants could help with the problem identified that innovators were isolated and might subscribe to an online community if there was one created for them. The other 30% of the messages were about describing themselves, their businesses and more general conversation.

Out of the networking theme and its subthemes, what emerged as a major interressement issue was defining the "active virtual networking" phenomenon so coined by one leader (William) and described below. 'Active virtual networking' includes elements of the enabling factors described above with the addition of the intent of the participants to purposely and actively seek to enlarge their network of business connections for the benefit of achieving better results in their business. One significant added value of an online networking mechanism was exemplified shortly after Woody joined the online group. Another participant was actively looking for a business contact in Singapore and Woody was able to instantly recommend a very able former colleague of his. The recommendation made online led to successful transactions for the participant who later recognised this had resulted in large saving in time and money for his company. "In these instances, electronic mail is an efficient tool to activate already established world-wide contacts" (Bill)

One instance where a targeting mechanism is vital is in "filling the chasm between Sales and Marketing", which is, according to one participant, not well addressed in today's innovation scene. He shared with other actors how his company was filling precisely this niche and how "one has to have contacts in remote parts and have the ability to activate online networks in order to make things happen" (Justin). Other participants described the need for innovators to make targeted business contacts that will add value to their development and commercialisation efforts. One participant so described the development and aims of online targeted business contact-making activity:

The world is full of vast quantities of information and a key way we filter it is to get information from people we know and trust. Confidentiality is a key part of the real world networking process (...) when finding out about things in your social network efficiently, for example people looking for staff, looking for someone to help with marketing, looking to invest etc... The issue with previous attempts at online networking tools is that there is not enough incentive to get people to participate (or) solve specific problems for people. As we have found if you are motivated (e.g. looking for a job or trying to find staff) then you will use it and build your network (Chris)

This participant went on affirming that, to be effective, 'active virtual networking' needs to be as closely aligned to real world networks as possible. Hence, participants invested time and care in building online the case for 'active online networking' as a significant interressement challenge.

ENROLMENT PROCESS: DISTRIBUTING ROLES

Enrolment happens with the distribution and allocation of roles in the network. This process involves the gradual emergence of the network as constituted with the intention to find the appropriate actors who will produce the specific knowledge needed, and all this in a complex sequence of connected actions. In the context of an online group, this would happen as interest is seen in specific topics. At that point, actors other than the original ones would be sought after to join the group by original members thinking the new recruits can contribute. In the present study, enrolment mechanisms will be identified in role

distribution amongst the actors, for instance.

Leaders (key actors in ANT terminology) were recognised and legitimised by the group. It was agreed that one participant (William) would continue to administer the online network, deal with membership enquiries and spearhead the network development. William was also offered to oversee the website with technical assistance from the researcher's technical team. William was one of the proponents for the summit and had put out clear signs of his interest to lead the group. He explained in online postings that in his opinion the network needed to identify a spokesperson to interact with other organisations. Interaction with other organisations included the networking area - the second area in which roles were discussed. Activity through the website was showing promising signs of potential linkages that were held up as illustrating the potential of the actor-network. Links with other government officials and offices were being forged and reported to the group at the summit. Some members of these organisations and others were already approaching network participants and showing interest in collaborating in some common tasks. This was seen as encouraging given that publicity had been limited.

A third component of the interaction between the online network and other organisations was the strategy that the network should adopt in prioritising which organisations to approach and form strategic alliances with. Initial contacts with nationwide networks took place. There was common agreement that the target audiences of some of the groups were highly compatible and mutual interressement were evoked at the summit that would eventually impact on mobilisation. Since other interest groups need access to grassroots, and that the actor-network needed access to these interest groups' offshore knowledge networks, joint press releases were issued. The actor-network action points (from group dialogues, administration, networking and growing the network through alliances) were concerned with components of the enrolment processes that ANT identifies as part of the actor-network formation. What is expected to occur at the enrolment stage is that actors allocate roles to each other or get allocated roles by others. In this case, roles related to group functioning, as described below, were distributed in the following areas.

Interaction with elements external to the network brought about discussion about what would the differentiating factors be for actors that were part of the original core group as opposed to newly enrolled actors. Core members agreed that the original online interaction listserve platform would be used for core group members' communication and that the new website would also include special areas for them. The membership whiteboard was such a space. "Gold Members" were invited to go to this area on the site and profile themselves or their business ventures for greater visibility. Individual evaluations carried out at the end of the face to face meeting in a group setting and also during individual interviews are presented below.

MOBILISATION STAGE: TAKING ACTION

Mobilisation is the end result of the enrolment process at which point actors and processes become manageable entities noticeable and usable at some official level – such as government level. This is the case, for example, with emerging groups becoming recognised by government officials as new stakeholders. In the present study, mobilisation was identifiable in the form of government or official recognition of the network formed.

The launching of the network's website coincided with the release of a research report on national entrepreneurship levels (Frederick & Carswell, 2001) and organisers of the website were asked to host online discussions on topics of relevance to the research report. Accordingly, some publicising of the online events was carried out, in partner websites and bookmarks with the

network URL were distributed at contemporary conferences. Following acceptance and legitimacy from group members, focal actors continued to seek legitimacy from government officials. This network grew to offer a nationwide ongoing virtual communication forum with a growing membership. Activities organised and planned by the group facilitating new projects included online fora, online mentoring events and applications for funding. Since inhibitors to the long-term success of such ventures relate to the ability of the group to sustain and fund ongoing interaction, success in obtaining such funding put it in a good position to extend the network: repeated meetings with public servant and engagement with government bodies have finally produced the desired result of recognition and funding. Obtaining Government funding was a definite sign of recognition at the highest level.

Hence the mobilisation stage unfolded as a result of the enrolment process - started at the previous stages - when official bodies accepted the existence of the actor-network and took it into account at higher levels, such as government level.

Virtual Leadership Rise through Online Networking

The data used to identify online leaders was triangulated to ensure reliability. In the present study, observing the actors meant collecting data relevant to understanding what different roles they each wanted to adopt during the network development. Identifying leaders was done in a variety of ways through observing the nature of their contributions. This was done through a process type of observation, often involving the recording of a number of postings or by way of another numerical representation of online activity. These tentative conclusions were checked against pre and post information: leaders' early identification was validated "in retrospect" as they were called upon to take the network through its next organisational development phase involving wider societal recognition.

A focal actor, in ANT terms, was formally chosen to carry through the group's decision and bring the online network to new interaction levels and nationwide exposure. This focal actor did indeed carry that role through, meeting with government officials and becoming a recognised player in the government's agenda of growth and innovation. This actor reinforced the formation of the network by providing a conduit (Kimble, Hildreth & Wright. 2000) to legitimise the self selected leaders, and reinforced patterns and decisions made online.

The other way actors' contributions were analysed was through observing the content of their contribution, i.e. the way they communicated that encouraged others to follow or steered the network in particular directions. Data analysis pointed to 'virtual networking' as one factor differentiating between the different types of online group members – leaders, participants and lurkers. These had dramatically different beliefs and actions about virtual networking. They differentiated themselves in the amount of personal benefit or added value they perceived they would gain from posting. Active contributors to the online discussions, self selected leaders and participants viewed virtual networking as added value to their participation in the online group. Interview analysis of actors showed that virtual networking was also a factor in lurkers' decisions to not post. The network leaders took upon themselves to build their own networks. Each had different stories and motivations attached to this activity: one participant described his inability to rely on his organisation's networks; another described how his organisation was sending mixed messages about participating in network activities. A third knowledge worker who exercised professional activities "in isolation" from a home-office described his rise to leadership as follows:

I had lots of ideas on how to lead the group but it only dawned on me slowly that I could take on the direction of the online network. I had tried to set up online groups in previous settings before, including my own business website, but could not gather momentum. This time was different, each little success led to the next one, people responded well to my leadership, in ways that even surprised me. In retrospect, I am glad I put in the extra effort! There is more intellectual property in the... network meetings than in all other professional meetings I have participated in recently (W: 171).

Another participant described himself as a geographically isolated expatriate:

*It was absolutely great to be able to participate in the... network from anywhere in the world! I would **never** have been able to feel so involved if it hadn't been for the virtual channels. In return the... network gave me a golden opportunity to achieve a dream of contribution to my country (E: 169)...*

Virtual networking was found to play an important role for all participants – even members' decisions to not participate were coloured by their underlying lack of belief in the effectiveness of virtual networking. Leaders, on the other hand, were passionate about the positive impact of virtual networking and recounted their impetus for driving the group forward was partially due to their deep beliefs on the positive impact of virtual networking.

Online Environments to Nurture Virtual Leadership Rise: Technology Matters

Early experiences at using specific technology or software influence users' experience, hence analysis of network formation and analysis necessarily benefits from collection of narratives from human actors. It follows, therefore, that such research should study each level, individual, group and organisation, and consider the interplay between them.

The ANT patterns of actor collaboration through the traces (interactions, texts and exchanges) left on the network showed how certain focal actors (leaders) self-selected via one technology (an email listserve) better than through another (a web-based bulletin board). In ANT terms, the email listserve environment allowed for stronger inscriptions for the initial stages of actor-network emergence, where complex decision making processes are at work. This may have been because of the real time impact of messages appearing in participants' email inboxes, as opposed to participants having to make special efforts to log on to the web-based bulletin board to check what the latest activity has been. Similarly, actor-network theorists include in their analysis, interactions between human and non-human actors, such as technology (Certina, 1997; Law, 2000; Whitley, 1999). Latour (1991) for instance, refers to some software impact as "technoscience" and analyses its characteristics. In this light, the characteristics of the web-based bulletin board, i.e. accumulation of organisational electronic memory, were not "strong" (Rose, 1997; Rose & Truex, 2000) enough to engage participants in spite of the manufacturer's claims. For this early stage of online group emergence, it was not appropriate. The web-based bulletin board technology had stronger agency though, when online interaction was aimed at the wider target population. In line with Law (1991) and Knights & Murray (1994) who consider that the ordering of actor-networks is "sociotechnical", the present analysis indicates that social and technical aspects seemed to make differential contributions at different stages in the emergence of the network.

Network leaders indeed outlined that technology could act either as an ally (identified in the study as "enabling" factors) or as an impediment (identified in the study as "constraining" factors).

As each factor emerged in the discussion and participants categorised it as either an enabler or constraint, the actors included that factor in their translations (design processes of the future online platform). Leaders effectively used the virtual environment to facilitate trust formation, gathering commitment to collaborate and organise a pivotal face to face meeting. The group discussed online engagement issues that can be organised into three meta-themes: community belonging, communication channels and networking strategy. The virtual leaders who were the designers of the final technology platform also used inscriptions (to assign roles to participants through their use of the technology). Examples of inscriptions are the various roles that can be played in the online network forum in its present form, where the administrator gives different levels (and access rights) to different participants, according to their centrality in the forum. In this sense, technology designers and innovators also design roles for humans, such as users, support people, or others using their technology to fulfil their roles. Making the technology work included making the human actors play the role designed (inscribed) for them. This exemplifies the way ANT theorists (Latour, 1991) conceived translations and inscriptions acting together as balancing mechanisms for network development, being constantly redefined through use of the technology.

Proposing an Integrative Model of Virtual Leadership Emergence

The model developed below, extends the above findings and shows how web-based interaction has the potential to increase social interaction thus has the potential to make significant difference to the future wealth of organizations (Prusak & Cohen, 2001; Stewart, 2001).

Figure 3 depicts the factors at work in virtual leadership building, as they appear throughout the findings of the present research. It is represented in a pyramidal shape as a basis from which to design the leaders' and lurkers' online participation model of Figure 4.

The series of factors influential in the rise of virtual leaders in the group will be explained together with the next figure. Figure 4 is a model developed to represent the rise of virtual leaders in the Innovators Online Network as perceived by group participants.

In building the integrative model, the time and trust inhibiting factors to online collaboration were recorded first because they were the first encountered. These are presented in the model as 'barriers to online collaboration'. While the obstacles to online group collaboration are well documented (Ardichvili, Page & Wentling, 2002) the present research adds to the knowledge in this field, embedded in participants' strategies to overcome these obstacles. For instance, time factors seemed to lose some of their constraining value as relevance of online interaction increased. Similarly, trust inhibiting factors decreased as trust building activities were offset to add to the "enhancing factors to online collaboration" level of the model. From this level on, the model shows how leaders and all

other participants perceived their roles and what motivated the roles they chose. The lurkers are shown as playing a minor role while the rest of the participants, leaders included, could identify benefits to online collaboration. At a higher level in the model is the representation of the in-depth analyses, showing that means of overcoming these obstacles were uncovered. This happened as participants articulated an added value of online participation: virtual networking. To the leaders there were important benefits to be gained from virtual networking: the opportunity to contribute, even from afar to their homeland, gained them legitimacy thus raising their local profile. Figure 4 shows how active participants used the online channel to evaluate their networking habits, even to consider developing new ones to harness online power (Janson & Roper, 2004). Other than those benefits that accrued on the personal and professional level, there were further implications in that virtual leaders can have an impact extending into society at large.

Leaders identified in the present research displayed characteristics of social entrepreneurship: "people who realize where there is an opportunity

Figure 3. Factors at work in virtual leadership building

Social result
Personal result
Phenomenon
Action
Motivation
Actors
Novel barriers uncovered
Enhancing factors to online collaboration
Barriers to online collaboration

Figure 4. Virtual leadership as perceived by group members

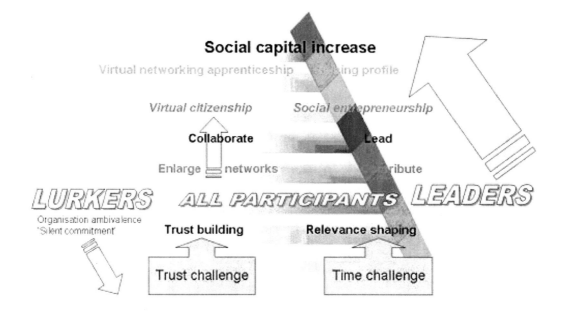

to satisfy some unmet need that the state …. will not or cannot meet, and who gather together the necessary resources (generally people, often volunteers, money and premises) and use these to 'make a difference'" as coined by Thompson, Alvy and Lees (2000, p.328). According to them, social entrepreneurs can either carry out social benefit type activities through traditional means or use creative and innovative means during their problem-solving process. As noted earlier, the virtual leaders identified in the present research bear the characteristics of social entrepreneurs, an old idea but also a newly researched phenomenon. This research extends the social entrepreneurship theory by describing the motivation at work planning for social entrepreneurs, and as happened in the present research, to strive to increase social capital (Nahapiet & Goshal, 1998). The motivations that leader participants reported were concurrent with such definitions of social entrepreneurs. In a wider perspective, it is suggested to extend social entrepreneurship theory, and propose that virtual leadership has the potential to facilitate social capital building using yet untapped resources

(Leadbeater, 1997). As advanced by the latest research on virtual leaders (Yoo & Alavi 1996; Yoo & Alavi 2002) it would be expected that the phenomena of emergent leadership has duality (Giddens, 1999), meaning that emergent leadership is simultaneously enabling of and enabled by acts of virtual communication.

DISCUSSION AND PRACTITIONER ANALYSIS: WHY IS IT IMPORTANT TO UNDERSTAND VIRTUAL LEADERSHIP?

The following section proposes a number of topics about essence and process for discussion in the organisational context. The observations made from the theoretical standpoint of the Actor-Network Theory might be significant for practitioners, established and aspiring leaders to consider if they aim to harness the potential inherent in the virtual leadership phenomenon.

1. Why identify virtual leaders? It is important for organisations to learn to identify virtual leaders because they can rise and contribute to the organisation through communication channels other than those typically used by conventional leaders. As shown in the present study, group members simultaneously build up a commitment to their ideas, with cohesiveness to carry out team projects and high levels of internal motivation to put these into practice throughout online interaction. In the present case, emerging virtual leaders helped the network gain government recognition and funding. The identification of these leaders carries with it the potential to uncover new social entrepreneurs while building momentum to reach the action stages sooner.

2. How can potential virtual leaders be identified? Practitioners can use the results of the present study to understand the characteristics of the different stages of Actor Network development and identify potential future virtual leaders by observing the actors at work in the organisation's virtual environments. As described earlier, leaders used the problematisation stage to engage others by pointing to the predicament of innovators, perceived as isolated and in need of a common platform on which to interact. The interressement stage followed during which specific actions were performed by either of the focal actors, i.e. identified leaders, to convince others that their goals were worthy of pursuit. One example of interressement activity was that of establishing alliances with certain groups whose objectives were in line with those of the actors, such as in the reported efforts to establish ongoing relationships with a newly formed expatriates association. Next, virtual leaders used the enrolment stage to distribute and allocate roles in the network. The above findings outlined the gradual emergence

of the network as an ongoing self-selection system during which leaders stirred the group to locate the appropriate actors that created the knowledge and momentum needed at each stage. This self selection process was a long string of - sometimes small - actions connected together (Callon, 1986). Finally the mobilisation and last stage of the actor-network development marked the end of the enrolment process at which point actors (in this case leaders) and processes (such as communication platforms) became manageable bodies recognised at government level. This indeed happened as the online network gained official legitimacy by becoming recognised by government officers as a new stakeholder group.

Practitioners can learn to recognize and participate in online activity that acts as 'virtual' mobilization, and in particular learn to read through shared emails or discussion groups produced and disseminated through organizational intranets. Practitioners can ask themselves how virtual networking can be used in their organization to develop a 'virtual' type of interressement, i.e. appropriate to the online medium. As shown above, what actors produced to gain credibility was often one and the same that strengthened the network.

3. How can established and aspiring organizational leaders use this knowledge? To established leaders it may be significant to know that virtual channels can help identify upcoming leadership in organisations. Additionally, once this mechanism is identified, it can be harnessed to help leadership grow where needed within groups or organisations or conversely, be recognised early enough to be suppressed. The above research showed that virtual leaders had specific motivations to raise their profile – not only for personal gain but in terms of an altruistic desire to contribute to national growth. Established leaders may ask themselves in what areas

of activity does their organization need help with projects that could be carried out by leaders identified via virtual channels.

To aspiring leaders it may bring a sense of control to appreciate the **process** of how they might rise. This may provide release in frustrating situations where leadership positions are being distributed to others – perhaps looking inaccessible. In such cases, aspiring leaders might ask themselves in what matters they wish to contribute and in which areas they are passionate enough to invest energy and cause impact. Virtual channels may offer 'sandbox situations' where people can exercise new skills to reach others and initiate action. Cyberspace is where followers can have 'real' impact by choosing 'virtual' leaders to follow. Virtual leaders are not necessarily offered roles or positions – they are often chosen by their followers by the latter's decision to respond to their call to action, perhaps in new democratic processes. Since followers choose those who are already demonstrating leadership, does this mean that cyberspace may be a more merit-based environment? It is certainly one where aspiring leaders have more control over their destiny – because they can act without having to wait to be asked. If they problematise, create interessement, enrol a core group of actors and mobilise wider audiences of followers, they are able to go through the development stages of actor-networks. Because these leaders need to create their impact through virtual channels, they need to call on different communication skills than those needed to rise to the challenges of the face to face world. We know for instance, from the transformational leadership literature (Avolio & Luthans, 2005) that high impact leadership involves trust building from the very early stages onwards. Trust building is also one likely precursor to authentic leadership development. Similarly, leaders may need to understand how to inscribe behaviour into the network that corresponds to or builds on followers' own motivation.

FUTURE TRENDS

Given the increasing use of electronic communication within and across organizations it is clear that virtual leadership phenomena will increase in importance. The model described in the present study can serve as a basis for discussion but more research needs to be undertaken on self-selected online leaders and followers, on the differences between virtual and conventional leaders, particularly identifying what set of unique skills leaders in the virtual sphere need, to engage wide-ranging audiences with the potential benefits that they can help reap. Secondly research efforts could be targeted at identifying virtual leadership using online consultation tools. In particular, the question of the underlying mechanisms of the online rise of leaders should be investigated: do they, for instance, use interressement and enrolment mechanisms that downplay technological constraints to stress its enabling effects? Thirdly, there is a need to uncover the protocols and potential of 'active networking' and construct an integrated model of the networking experience – face-to-face and online – as a foundation for sustainable business success and collective capacity building.

A different point of interest is the stark contrast between the online presence of people who come to the fore through virtual means and established leaders (who seemingly rarely post or participate actively – aside from speeches written by their speechwriters). There may be an inverse relationship between leadership level and potential added value from virtual networks: might established leaders have more to lose from online participation that to gain? Might the opposite be true for virtual leaders who have all to gain and little to lose from online interaction? Leadership scholars explain why the paradigm is no longer a command and control one, but rather one in which authentic and transformational leaders capture passions and hearts (Avolio & Luthans, 2006). If so, what is the significance of the paradigm shift? What is the more specific virtual paradigm? The virtual world offers striking new possibilities for distributed leadership but we yet have to identify and analyse its added value from more working examples of this phenomenon.

CONCLUSION

Preece and Maloney-Krichmar (2003) reported that there have been major advances supporting technology/software online interaction since the ubiquity of web since the early 1990's. In their opinion, it is not the technological performance advances that are most significant, rather the way the technology is being used and who is using it. The present study reemphasises that analyses for online groups must take into account the humans-technology interplay. The contribution of this chapter was to distil how an actor network engages with people and technology and how some of its actors used the online environment to become leaders.

While Actor Network Theory was not specifically developed to apply to computerised networks and to account for online behaviours, we asked the question whether ANT processes can be 'virtualised'. The virtual leadership building model facilitates understanding as to how these processes are carried out online. Virtual leaders used online discussion groups to problematise, while a Listserve environment seemed to have worked better to rally people around issues than a web-based discussion group. Trust building was an activity singled-out by participants as an important stage in initial network formation.

As proposed, the online leaders virtualised the process of enrolment. All participants' motivation, at this stage, revealed that engaging in the online network had ulterior motives, and these were the enlargement of their networks. Virtual leaders invested energy to show their followers that collaboration would indeed lead to them achieving these goals, thus pre-empting followers' "what's in it for me?" questions. These leaders, however,

had additional motivations: to contribute to the greater good of national innovation.

As one would expect in actor-network formation, the political activity of certain participants, and that of the leaders in particular, strengthened the size of the network and the relationships between actors. The network leaders enrolled resources and commitments to ensure the longevity of the network, and revised core group structure. Leaders also attended to the non-human network actors by ensuring the network is accessible by most computerized systems and provided with ongoing support.

Leadbeater (1997) stressed that there is a need to develop innovative forms of generating social capital and noted that social entrepreneurship is the future engine for real societal change. Since social entrepreneurs use social interaction to foster the latter, it is important, on the one hand, to help social entrepreneurs rise through novel channels, and on the other hand, to learn to identify them in the spheres in which they operate.

REFERENCES

Alavi, M., & Yoo, Y. (1997). *Leadership emergence in virtual team environments.* Boston: Harvard University.

Ardichvili, A., Page, V., & Wentling, T. (2002, September). *Motivation and barriers to participation in virtual knowledge-sharing communities of practice.* Paper presented at the OKLC Conference, Athens.

Avolio, B. J., & Kahai, S. (2003). Adding the e to e-leadership: How it may impact your leadership. *Organizational Dynamics, 31*(4), 325–338. doi:10.1016/S0090-2616(02)00133-X

Avolio, B. J., Kahai, S. S., & Dodge, G. E. (2000). E-leadership: Implications for theory, research and practice. *The Leadership Quarterly, 11*(4), 615–668. doi:10.1016/S1048-9843(00)00062-X

Avolio, B. J., & Luthans, F. (2006). *The high impact leader*. New York: McGraw-Hill.

Bass, B. M. (1990). *Handbook of leadership*. New York: Free Press.

Blanchard, A. L., & Markus, M. L. (2002, January). *Sense of virtual community: Maintaining the experience of belonging*. Paper presented at the 35th Hawai International Conference on Systems Sciences.

Callon, M. (1986). The sociology of an actor-network: The case of the electric vehicle. In M. Callon, J. Law, & A. Roip (Eds.) *Mapping the dynamics of science and technology: Sociology of science in the real world* (pp. 19-34).

Callon, M. (1994). Is science a public good? *Science, Technology & Human Values, 19*(4), 395–424. doi:10.1177/016224399401900401

Certina, K. (1997). Sociality with objects: Social relations in postsocial knowledge societies. *Theory, Culture & Society, 14*(4), 1–30. doi:10.1177/026327697014004001

Collins, S. (2001). Expert help a mouse click away. *The New Zealand Herald*. Auckland, New Zealand.

DeSanctis, G., & Monge, P. (1999). Communication processes for virtual organizations. *Organization Science, 10*(6), 693–703. doi:10.1287/orsc.10.6.693

Doolin, B., & Lowe, A. (2002). To reveal is to critique: Actor-network theory and critical information systems research. *Journal of Information Technology, 17*, 69–78. doi:10.1080/02683960210145986

Durnell Cramton, C., & Orvis, K. L. (2003). Overcoming barriers to information sharing in virtual teams. In C. B. Gibson & S. G. Cohen (Eds.), *Virtual teams that work: Creating conditions for virtual teams effectiveness* (pp. 214-230). San Francisco: Jossey-Bass.

Foreman, M. (2002). Virtual networking for Kiwi entrepreneurs. *The Independent*. Auckland, New Zealand.

Frederick, H. H., & Carswell, P. J. (2001). *Global entrepreneurship monitor: New Zealand*. Auckland, New Zealand: New Zealand Centre for Innovation and Entrepreneurship.

Gibson, C. B., & Manuel, J. A. (2003). Building trust: Effective multicultural communication processes in virtual teams. In C. B. Gibson & S. G. Cohen (Eds.), *Virtual teams that work: Creating conditions for virtual teams effectiveness* (pp. 59-86). San Francisco: Jossey-Bass.

Giddens, A. (1999). *The third way: The renewal of social democracy*. Malden, MA: Polity Press.

Hackman, J. R. (1990). *Groups that work (and those that don't)*. San Francisco: Jossey-Bass.

Hanseth, O., & Monteiro, E. (1998). *Understanding information infrastructure*. Retrieved January, 29, 2004, from http://heim.ifi.uio.no/~oleha/Publications/bok.html

James, M., & Rykert, L. (1998). *From workplace to workspace: Using email lists to work together*. Retrieved January, 12, 2004, from http://www.idrc.ca/books/848/index_e.html

Janson, A., & Roper, J. (2004, March). *Identify virtual leaders to increase social capital: Information-based approach as a vehicle for social entrepreneurship engagement*. Paper presented at the International Sustainable Development Research Conference, Manchester, UK, Erpen-Environment.

Jarvenpaa, S. L., & Leidner, D. E. (1999). Communication and trust in virtual teams. *Organization Science, 10*(6), 791–815. doi:10.1287/orsc.10.6.791

Joerges, B., & Czarniawska, B. (1998). The question of technology, or how organizations incribe the world. *Organization Studies, 19*(3), 363–385. doi:10.1177/017084069801900301

Kaplan, B., & Maxwell, J. A. (1994). Qualitative research methods for evaluating computer information systems. In J. G. Anderson, C. E. Aydin, & S. J. Jay (Eds.), *Evaluating health care information systems: Methods and applications* (pp. 45-68). Thousand Oaks, CA: Sage.

Kimble, C., Hildreth, P., & Wright, P. (2000). Communities of practice: Going virtual. In Y. Malhotra. (Ed.), *Knowledge management and business model innovation* (pp. 220-234). Hershey, PA: Idea Group Publishing.

Klein, J. A., & Kleinhanns, A. (2003). Closing the gap in virtual teams. In C. B. Gibson & S. G. Cohen (Eds.), *Virtual teams that work: Creating conditions for virtual teams effectiveness* (pp. 381-400). San Francisco: Jossey-Bass.

Knights, D., & Murray, F. (1994). *Managers divided: Organization politics and information technology management.* Chicester, UK: Wiley.

Latour, B. (1987). *Science in action: How to follow scientists and engineers through society.* Cambridge, MA: Harvard University Press.

Latour, B. (1991). Technology is society made durable. In J. Law (Ed.), *A sociology of monsters: Essays on power, technology and domination.* London: Routledge.

Law, J. (1991). Introduction: Monsters, machines and sociotechnical relations. In J. Law (Ed.), *A sociology of monsters: Essays on power, technology and domination.* London: Routledge.

Law, J. (1992). Notes on the theory of the actor-network: Ordering, strategy and heterogeneity. *Systems Practice, 5*(4), 379–393. doi:10.1007/BF01059830

Law, J. (2000). *Networks, relations, cyborgs: On the social study of technology.* Retrieved December 23, 2003, from http://www.comp.lancs.ac.uk/sociology/soc042jl.html

Leadbeater, C. (1997). *The rise of the social entrepreneur.* London: Demos.

Lewis Tyran, K., Tyran, C. K., & Shepherd, M. (2003). Exploring emerging leadership in virtual teams. In C. B. Gibson & S. G. Cohen (Eds.), *Virtual teams that work: Creating conditions for virtual teams effectiveness* (pp. 183-195). San Francisco: Jossey-Bass.

Molina, M., & Yoong, P. (2003). Knowledge sharing in a co-opetitive environment: The case of business clusters. *Journal of Information and Knowledge Management, 2*(4), 1–23.

Nahapiet, J., & Goshal, S. (1998). Social capital, intellectual capital and the organizational advantage. *Academy of Management Review, 23*(2), 242–266. doi:10.2307/259373

Pauleen, D. F., & Yoong, P. (2001a). Facilitating virtual team relationship via Internet and conventional communication channels. *Internet Research: Electronic networking applications and policy, 11*(3), 190-202.

Pauleen, D. F., & Yoong, P. (2001b). Relationship building and the use of ICT in boundary-crossing virtual teams: A facilitator's perspective. *Journal of Information Technology, 16*(4), 205–220. doi:10.1080/02683960110100391

Pauleen, D. F., & Yoong, P. (2004). Studying human-centered IT innovation using a grounded action learning approach. *Qualitative Report, 9*(1), 137–160.

Pedler, M., Burgoyne, J. G., & Boydell, T. (2003). *A manager's guide to leadership.* Maindenhead, UK: McGraw-Hill.

Peek, S. (2002). Virtual networks link entrepreneurs to skills. *RE: THINK Supplement to the Sunday Star Times.*

Preece, J., & Maloney-Krichmar, P. (2003). Online communities. In J. Jacko & A. Sears (Eds.), *Handbook of human-computer interaction* (pp. 596-620). Mahwah, NJ: Lawrence Erlbaum Associates Inc.

Preece, J., & Rogers, Y. (2002). *Interaction design: Beyond human-computer interaction.* New York: John Wiley & Sons.

Prusak, L., & Cohen, D. (2001). *In good company: How social capital makes organizations work.* Boston: Harvard Business School Press.

Rose, J. (1997). Soft systems methodology as a social science research tool. *Systems Research and Behavioral Science, 14*(4), 249–258. doi:10.1002/(SICI)1099-1743(199707/08)14:4<249::AID-SRES119>3.0.CO;2-S

Rose, J., & Truex, D. (2000). Machine agency as perceived autonomy. In R. Baskerville, J. Stage, & J. I. DeGross (Eds.), *Organizational and social perspectives on information technology.* Boston: Kluwer.

Schindler, P. L., & Thomas, C. C. (1993). The structure of interpersonal trust in the workplace. *Psychological Reports, 73,* 563–573.

Singleton, V., & Michael, M. (1993). Actor-networks and ambivalence: General practitioners in the UK cervical screening programme. *Social Studies of Science, 23,* 227–264. doi:10.1177/030631293023002001

Stewart, T. (2001). *The wealth of knowledge: Intellectual capital and the 21th century organisation.* New York: Currency Doubleday.

Tatnall, A., & Gilding, A. (1999, January). *Actor-network theory and information systems research.* Paper presented at the ACIS 99 Conference, Wellington, Victoria University of Wellington.

Thompson, J., Alvy, G., & Lees, A. (2000). Social entrepreneurship: A new look at the people and the potential. *Management Decision, 38*(5), 328–338. doi:10.1108/00251740010340517

Van der Smagt, T. (2000). Enhancing virtual teams: Social relations vs. communication technology. *Industrial Management & Data Systems, 100*(4), 148–156. doi:10.1108/02635570010291766

Walsham, G. (1995). The emergence of interpretivism in IS research. *Information Systems Research, 6*(4), 376–394. doi:10.1287/isre.6.4.376

Wellman, B., Quan-Haase, A., Witte, J., & Hampton, K. N. (2001). Does the Internet increase, decrease, or supplement social capital? Social networks, participation, and community commitment. *The American Behavioral Scientist, 45*(3), 436–456. doi:10.1177/00027640121957286

Whitley, E. A. (1999). *Habermas and the non-humans: Towards a critical theory for the new collective.* Retrieved December 23, 2003, from http://www.keele.ac.uk/depts/stt/cstt2/papers/whitley.htm

Yoo, Y., & Alavi, M. (1996). *Emergence of leadership and its impact on group performance in virtual team environments: A longitudinal field study.* Paper presented at the International conference on information systems, Cleveland, Ohio.

Yoo, Y., & Alavi, M. (2002). *Electronic mail usage patterns of emergent leaders in distributed teams.* Retrieved February 2, 2004, from www.weatherhead.cwru.edu/sprouts/2002/020309.pdf

Yoong, P., & Galluppe, B. (2001). Action learning and groupware technologies: A case study in GSS facilitation research. *Journal of Information Technology and People, 14*(1), 78–90. doi:10.1108/09593840110384780

Section 4
Additional Selected Readings

Chapter 15
Leadership in Technology Project Management

Ralf Müller
Umeå School of Business, Sweden & BI Norwegian School of Management, Norway

ABSTRACT

This chapter addresses project managers' leadership styles, mainly from the perspective of technology projects. It starts by defining and outlining the need for leadership, and then describes the historical schools and the recent schools of leadership theory. Subsequently the focus turns to current leadership research in project management, and its related theories. Subsequently, the personality profiles of successful project managers in different types of projects are presented. The chapter ends with some managerial and theoretical implications, as well as scholarly challenges for further research and future developments in this area.

INTRODUCTION

Leadership and management are terms often used interchangeably in day-to-day business. There are, however, significant differences between the two.

Management refers to the *professional administration of business concerns or public undertakings* (Oxford Concise Dictionary, 1995). It is often related to guidance and coordination of people towards a defined goal, through a person granted management authority by higher levels in an organization's hierarchy.

Contrarily, leadership is defined as *a relationship through which one person influences the behavior of other people* (Mullins, 1996). Discussions on leadership often refer to the sum of traits, behaviors and characteristics of people being followed by others, independent of their formal authority in an organization. Bennis and

Nanus (1985) define management and leadership and the difference thereof as:

To manage means to bring about, to accomplish, to have responsibility for, to conduct. Leading is influencing, guiding in direction, course, action, and opinion. This distinction is crucial. Managers are people who do things right and leaders are people who do the right things.

Parry (2004) showed that with increasingly higher levels in a corporate hierarchy the need for management decreases, whereas the need for leadership increases.

The project management literature, for example the International Project Management Association's (IPMA) Competence Baseline (IPMA, 2007, p. 86), refers to leadership as:

Leadership involves providing direction and motivating others in their role or task to fulfill the project's objectives. It is a vital competence for project managers.

This definition identifies leadership as a key competence for project managers.

The mission of the chapter is to provide insight into the current state of leadership research and contemporary leadership theories and their relevance for project management. The chapter shows the fit of different leadership styles with different types of projects, and its relation to project success.

The Role of Leadership in the Project Management Literature

While the management tasks of project managers are well described, leadership is rarely addressed in the project management literature. Sometimes team roles are applied to leadership styles, such as the well known Myers-Briggs, FIRO-B, Belbin, or 16PF (Bryggs-Myers, 1995; Schultz, 1955; Belbin, 1986; Cattell *et al*, 1970 respectively). However,

there is little correlation between competencies of leaders and commonly identified team roles and behaviors (Dulewicz & Higgs, 2005), even though many of these are used as part of the recruitment process of managers and executives. Team roles are different from leadership styles, and only very few team roles and personality factors are correlated with leadership performance, according to Dulewicz and Higgs (2005):

1. **Belbin:** Only the roles of resource investigator and team worker are correlated to performance as a leader. The coordinator and implementer roles are weakly correlated to performance as a leader.
2. **16PF:** Extroverts and more emotionally stable individuals are likely to be better leaders. There is also some correlation with some of the other factors.

To understand the leadership role of project managers, we now turn to the literature on leadership, and then describe contemporary research results in leadership research in project management, and finish with theoretical and practical implications thereof.

LEADERSHIP LITERATURE

A comprehensive review of the literature on leadership theory and its relation to project management can be found in (Turner & Müller, 2006). The following is a summary thereof.

By doing a chronological review of leadership literature two classical theories of leadership can be found, dating back to 500 and 300 BC. More recently an early work on the function of the leader, and six different schools of leadership were developed. Research on leadership in project management was only addressed in recent years. All are described in the in the following.

As early as 500 BC Confucius identified the virtues (*de*) of effective leaders, which were *jen* (love), *li* (proper conduct), *xiao* (piety), *zhang rong* (the doctrine of the mean). Already this text showed the importance of interpersonal factors for effective leadership. Two hundred years later Aristotle (300 BC) developed these into the three steps of good leadership, which were:

1. **Pathos:** First build relationships with those being led
2. **Ethos:** Then sell the moral vision
3. **Logos:** Then and only then persuade by logic to manage actions

He showed that effective leaders follow the three steps above, whereas managers go straight in with the logos.

Interestingly, 2,300 years later most of the marketing and sales training in the industry still follows these steps.

Leadership Theories in the 20th Century

Among the first writers on the function in leaders was Barnard (1938). He identified both managerial and emotional functions for executive managers, which he called cognitive and cathectic functions respectively, where:

- Cognitive functions relate to guiding, directing, as well as constraining choices and actions of those being delegated a task
- Cathectic functions relate to emotional and motivational aspects of goal setting, and developing faith and commitment to a larger moral purpose

This is similar to Aristotle's view of pathos, ethos, and logos. Today, the cognitive roles are often associated with a transactional, and the cathectic roles with a transformational leadership style.

Over the last seventy years six main schools of leadership theory developed, (Handy, 1982; Partington, 2003; Dulewicz and Higgs, 2005):

1. The trait school
2. The behavioral or style school
3. The contingency school
4. The visionary or charismatic school
5. The emotional intelligence school
6. The competency school

The Trait School

This school was popular up to the 1940s. It assumes that effective leaders posses common traits, and that leaders are born not made or developed. The traits of effective leaders were clustered into three main areas:

- **Abilities:** Hard management skills
- **Personality:** Such as self-confidence and emotional variables
- **Physical appearance:** Including size and appearance

More recently

- Kirkpatrick and Locke (1992) identified six traits of effective leaders:
  o Drive and ambition
  o The desire to lead and influence others
  o Honesty and integrity
  o Self-confidence
  o Intelligence
  o Technical knowledge
- Turner (1999) identified seven traits of effective project managers:
  o Problem solving ability
  o Results orientation
  o Energy and initiative
  o Self-confidence
  o Perspective

o   Communication
o   Negotiating ability

So the traits school has been subject of interest for project management even in recent times.

The Behavioral or Style School

This school was popular from the 1940s to the 1960s. According to this school, effective leaders adopt certain styles of behaviors, which can be learned. So that effective leaders can be developed. Theories in this school often characterize managers or leaders against a few parameters, and place them on a continuum or in a two-dimensional matrix. Examples are, for instance, Blake and Mouton (1978), Tannenbaum and Schmidt (1958), Adair (1983), Hershey and Blanchard (1988), Slevin (1989). The parameters include:

1.   Concern for people or relationships
2.   Concern for production
3.   Use of authority
4.   Involvement of the team in decision-making (formulating decisions)
5.   Involvement of the team in decision-taking (choosing options)
6.   Flexibility versus the application of rules

The Contingency School

In the 1960s and 1970s, this school became popular (see Krech *et al*, 1962; Fiedler, 1967; House, 1971; Robbins, 1997). Aim was to identify effective leadership behavior in different situations. So the understanding of leadership moved away from universal theories to situational contingency theories. These theories typically:

1.   Assessed the characteristics of the leader
2.   Evaluated the situation in terms of key contingency variables
3.   Aimed for identification of a match between the leader and a particular situation.

Especially popular became the path-goal theory by House (1971). It suggests that a leader must help the team find its path to their goals and then help them in the process to achieve their goals. Leadership behaviors identified here were directive, supportive, participative, and achievement-oriented. To identify the best match with a situation these four behaviors were matched against environmental and subordinate factors, which include environmental factors such as: task structure, formal authority system; as well as workgroup factors such as; subordinate factors, locus of control, experience, and perceived ability.

Another popular contingency theory was developed by Fiedler (1967). He recommends different leadership styles, depending on the favorability of the leadership situation. Here favorability is determined by the relationship between leader and those being led (level of trust), the structure of the task (clearness of task and instructions), and position power. He distinguishes between task oriented and participative leadership. A least-preferred-coworker (LPC) score is used for assigning team members to leaders depending on a particular leadership situation. In very favorable and very unfavorable situations **task oriented leaders** (having a low LPC score) are assigned to achieve effectiveness through a directive and controlling style. In moderately favorable situations **participative leaders** (high LPC score) are assigned for high effectiveness through interpersonal relationship orientation.

Frame (1987) suggested four contingent leadership styles for project managers as appropriate at different stages of the project life-cycle and with different team structures, Table 1.

The Visionary or Charismatic School

Popular during the 1980s and 1990s, this school derived from research on effective leadership in organizational change projects. Representative for this school is the transactional and transformational leadership style theory (Bass, 1990), in:

Table 1. Leadership styles, project team types and the project life-cycle

Leadership style	Stage	Team type	Team nature
Laissez-faire	Feasibility	Egoless	Experts with shared responsibility
Democratic	Design	Matrix	Mixed discipline working on several tasks
Autocratic	Execution	Task	Single discipline working on separate tasks
Bureaucratic	Close-out	Surgical	Mixed working on a single task

1. Transactional leadership:
   - Team members are rewarded for achievement of specific performance targets.
   - Managers mainly get involved when things are not going according to plan.
2. Transformational leadership:
   - Managers use charisma and vision, plus pride, respect and trust in team and task.
   - Managers set high expectations, inspire and motivate by providing intellectual stimulation, and challenging team members with new ideas and approaches.
   - Team members are allowed to be creative in problem solving.
   - Managers consider the individual, showing respect and personality.

Different combinations of the two styles are appropriate in different situations. As mentioned above, the transactional style refers to Barnard's cognitive roles and Aristotle's *logos*. The transformational style resembles Barnard's cathectic roles, as well as Aristotle's *pathos* and *ethos*.

Keegan and den Hartog (2004) took this school into the world of project management. They hypothesized that project managers mainly use transformational leadership styles, but could not find empirical support for their hypothesis. However, Dominick, Artonson and Lechler (2007) found a correlation between transformational style and project success. So transformational style contributes to success, but is not necessarily more often used than transactional style. Turner and Müller (2006) identified transactional style for simple engineering projects and transformational style in more complex projects.

The Emotional Intelligence School

Since the late 1990s, the Emotional Intelligence School became increasingly popular. This school assumes a reasonable level of intelligence among all managers, so that it is not the intellectual intelligence that differentiates success of leaders, but their emotional response to situations. So a leader's emotional intelligence has a greater impact on success as a leader and the performance of the team than the intellectual intelligence (Goleman, Boyatzis & McKee, 2002). They identified four dimensions of emotional intelligence, based on nineteen underlying competencies: these are listed and described in the Appendix.

Six management styles for different leadership situations derived from that. Each style is associated with a different leadership competencies profile. Of those six styles, four (visionary, coaching, affiliative, and democratic) are applicable for situations requiring a medium to long-term perspective. These styles foster resonance among the team members and improve team performance when used in appropriate circumstances. The other two (pacesetting and commanding) are applicable for turnaround or recovery situations with a short tem perspective. These styles can foster dissonance and need to be used with care. Thus, Goleman *et al* (2002), and later on others, showed a contingency between situational particularities and appropriate leadership styles.

The Competency School

Since the late 1990s, the emphasis has been to identify the competencies of effective leaders. Following Boyatzis (1982) and Crawford (2003) competences are:

• Knowledge
• Skills
• Personal characteristics

that allow to deliver superior results.

So competence covers personal characteristics, (traits as understood by the traits school and emotional intelligence), knowledge and skills, (including intelligence and problem solving ability as well as management skills).

While, at first glance, this looks like a return to the trait approach, it differs from earlier schools by:

• The underlying assumption that competencies can be learned. Therefore leaders can be made or developed, not just born.
• The assumption that different combinations of competencies will lead to different leadership styles. These styles then are appropriate for different situations. Examples are transactional leaders in circumstances of low complexity and transformational leaders in circumstances of high complexity.
• Not being a singular new school, but encompassing all the earlier schools

The competence school shows that different competence profiles are appropriate in different circumstances, covering the trait, contingency, visionary & charismatic, as well as the emotional intelligence school.

Types of Competence

Dulewicz and Higgs (2005) found that the majority of researchers in the competency school identified up to four different types of competencies that impact leadership performance. These are:

1. Cognitive competencies
2. Emotional competencies
3. Behavioral competencies
4. Motivational competencies

Cognitive competencies are associated with Confucius's *li* and Barnard's cognitive functions. Emotional, behavioral and motivational competencies are associated with Confucius's *ren* and *yi,* and Barnard's cathectic functions.

Based on their research, analyses, and literature review Dulewicz and Higgs (2005) identified fifteen leadership competencies. These are categorized in seven emotional (EQ) competencies, three intellectual (IQ) ones and five managerial (MQ) ones, Table 2.

By tabulating their identified competences against those suggested by others, Dulewicz and Higgs found quite strong support in the literature. They go on to show that intellectual competence (IQ) accounts for 27% of leadership performance, managerial competence (MQ) accounts for 16%, and emotional competence (EQ) accounts for 36%. Emotional competence is therefore the most significant, but the other two are important as Barnard and Confucius suggested (Dulewicz & Higgs, 2000).

Contemporary Research in Project Management Related Leadership

Relationship Between Personality, Project Type and Project Success

A study by Dvir, Sadeh and Malach-Pines (2006) showed tentative support for the hypotheses that projects are more successful if personality

Table 2. Fifteen leadership competencies as suggested by Dulewicz and Higgs (2005)

Group	Competency
Intellectual (IQ)	1. critical analysis and judgement 2. vision and imagination 3. strategic perspective
Managerial (MQ)	4. engaging communication 5. managing resources 6. empowering 7. developing 8. achieving
Emotional (EQ)	9. self-awareness 10. emotional resilience 11. motivation 12. sensitivity 13. influence 14. intuitiveness 15. conscientiousness

characteristics match project profiles, and that project managers are more attracted to and more successful with projects that fit their personality. The researchers used a four dimensional model of project complexity, pace, novelty and technology to classify projects and identify associated leadership styles during project initiation and recruiting of team members, as well as for different structures, processes, and tools.

Leadership Competences of Successful Project Managers in Different Types of Projects

The importance of leadership competencies for project success in different types of projects was investigated by Turner and Müller (2006). They used the Leadership Development Questionnaire (LDQ) developed by Dulewicz and Higgs (2005) as part of the competency school of leadership.

Here intellectual leadership competencies (IQ) are understood as the rational capabilities of the project manager. Managerial leadership competencies (MQ) as the competencies to lead teams towards pre-defined goals. It allows the leader to

adjust the amount of management and control to the expectations of those being led. This includes open communication and the ability to manage people, empower and develop them, as well as giving them a sense of achievement. Emotional leadership competencies (EQ) set the right tone and social relationship. These were measured as the degree of a project manager's awareness and ability to manage their own feelings and their appearance to other people.

EQ competencies correlated positively with success across all types of projects. Strategic perspective (IQ), however, was negatively related to project success. There were also two exceptions: on successful mandatory projects and projects under a fixed price contract MQ is stronger related to project success than EQ. These are project types where managers cannot negotiate project scope. So they have to rely on their managerial competences to lead the project team and deliver the project as required.

At the more detailed level they identified different combinations of the underlying 15 competencies in successful projects of different type. These are described next.

Engineering and Construction Projects

Three of the 15 leadership competencies shown in Table 4 correlate positively with success. They explain 43% of the variance in success measures for these projects.

These competencies are:

- **Conscientiousness**, an emotional competency, where the project manager displays clear commitment to a course of action in the face of challenges and matches 'words and deeds' in encouraging others to support the chosen direction.
- **Interpersonal sensitivity**, another emotional competency, where the project manager is aware of, and takes account of, the needs and perceptions of others in arriving at decisions and proposing solutions to problems and challenges
- **Engaging communication**, a managerial competency, where the project manager is approachable and accessible, engages others and wins their support through communication tailored for each audience.

So a sense of duty and good interpersonal communication are the project managers' leadership attributes contributing to project success in engineering and construction projects.

Information Technology and Telecommunication Projects

The important competencies correlating positively with success are once again engaging communication, plus:

- **Self-awareness**, an emotional competency, where the project manager is aware of his or her own feelings and able to recognize them
- **Developing resources**, a managerial competency, where project managers encourage

others to take on ever more demanding tasks, roles, and accountabilities. He or she develops others' competencies and invests time and effort in coaching them.

This combination explains 21% of success in these projects. The 'soft' factors make IT projects successful. Finding the right 'tone' with others, together with good control over their own feelings, and helping project team members to take on challenging tasks, are the attributes of successful leadership in these projects.

Organizational Change Projects

Another set of competencies influences success in organizational change projects and explains 17% of success in these projects. Here again, engaging communication is important, but also:

- **Motivation**, an emotional competency, where the project manager shows drive and energy to achieve clear results and make an impact

Therefore, actively creating the required dynamics for change, together with accommodation of those involved helps organizational change projects to be successful.

However, one competency correlates negatively with success in all types of projects:

- **Vision and imagination**, an intellectual competency, where the project manager is imaginative and innovative, with a clear vision of the future. He or she foresees the impact of changes on implementation issues and business realities.

Visionary and imaginative leaders are without doubt needed for projects to succeed. So this role should be assumed by the project sponsor, who by default sets the vision and projected end-state of a project and its outcome.

Having identified the leadership dimensions correlated with project success in different types of projects (Müller & Turner, 2007) the researchers also identified the extent the different leadership dimensions are expressed (from low to high) within successful project managers (Müller & Turner, 2006). For that they looked at managers of projects with above average performance and identified the leadership profile of these managers for three different types of projects, Figure 1.

The competency most strongly expressed in successful project managers is conscientiousness. All other profile dimensions differ by project type.

Differences Between Functional Managers and Project Managers

This study by Dulewicz, Turner and Müller (2006) identified the differences between leadership profiles of line (or functional) managers and project managers.

Project managers scored higher than line managers on:

- Critical analysis (IQ)
- Conscientiousness (EQ)
- Sensitivity (EQ)

Line managers scored higher than project managers on:

- Communication (MQ)
- Developing (MQ)

The study showed also differences in explained leadership performance, depending on line or project manager role.

- For project managers leadership success is explained to 21% by EQ dimensions, 22% by IQ dimensions, and 30% by MQ dimensions
- For line (functional) managers leadership performance is explained to 36% by EQ, 27% by IQ, and 16% by MQ dimensions.

Requirement for EQ and IQ leadership competencies are higher and for MQ competencies lower in line management functions.

Figure 1. Leadership competency profiles of successful project managers

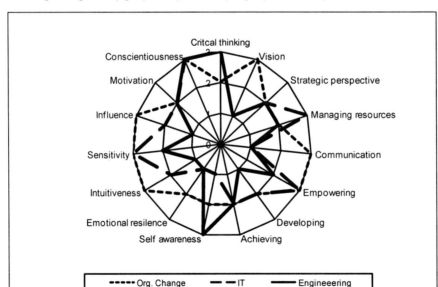

Agile Project Managers' Leadership Competencies

Porthouse and Dulewicz (2007) investigated the differences in leadership competencies between project managers using Agile/Scrum approaches and line managers. These projects are managed using more interactive and team-based approaches than traditional project management methodologies, because of a shift in management style from controlling to facilitating and the use of self organizing teams. They found:

- Intuitiveness and sensitivity significantly higher in Agile project managers
- Motivation and emotional resilience significantly lower in Agile project managers

Then they compared Agile/Scrum project managers with international project managers from the Turner and Müller (2006) study. They found:

- Intuitiveness, communication, development significantly higher in Agile project managers
- Motivation and conscientiousness significantly lower in Agile project managers

Thirteen of the 15 leadership dimensions (Table 4) correlated with success in Agile/Scrum projects: These were all except intuitiveness and vision & imagination.

Leadership performance was explained to 40% by EQ dimensions, 19% MQ dimensions, and only 4% by IQ dimensions (the latter being insignificant).

Leadership profiles in different types of complexity

By taking further their original study on leadership competences and their relationship with success in different project types, Müller, Geraldi and Turner (2007) looked into the different leadership profiles for success in projects of different types of complexity. The complexity model was adopted from Geraldi and Adlbrecht (2007) and consisted of three main dimensions for complexity:

- **Complexity of fact:** Structural complexity, including measures for the amount of information to analyse, or the number of organizations and people involved in a project

- **Complexity of faith:** Uncertainty, including measures for severity and frequency of scope changes, level of immaturity of the project team, and level of multi-disciplinarity

- **Complexity of interaction:** Inter-personal relationships, with measures for level of transparency in the team and level of internationality

The results were drawn mainly from IT projects. They show different leadership profiles for projects with different types of complexity, Figure 2.

Projects dominated by either complexity of faith or interaction require relatively small expressions of the leadership dimensions. Successful managers of projects dominated by complexity of fact are stronger in achievement, emotional competencies and management of resources.

They found that:

- In any type of complexity project managers must show their commitment through high levels of conscientiousness
- High levels of complexity of fact requires achievement competency (MQ) from the project manager
- High levels of complexity of fact require strong emotional and interpersonal skills

They also conclude that projects with tangible outcomes, such as in construction or engineering, demand achievement competencies. Projects with intangible outcomes, such as IT or organizational change, demand competencies in interpersonal sensitivity.

FUTURE TRENDS

The importance of leadership on the side of the project manager is a young subject in the project management area. It was not until 2006 that major studies identified the fit between different leadership styles and project success in different types of projects, thus until the project manager was identified as a key success factor. With the momentum gained in current years, leadership in project management will be addressed both from a research as well as from a practitioner perspective.

Near Term Implications for Practitioners

Leadership will increasingly become part of project manager education and training. Assessments of leadership styles and their fit or development towards an organization's project types will increase, allowing for better project results.

The approach described above allows existing project managers to develop their own leadership competencies to make them fit for their particular project type. After taking the LDQ assessment, they can use the information on the relevant dimensions for project success and the 'target' profile of successful project managers to identify the gap between their own profile and that of successful managers. By taking into account which leadership dimensions correlate with success in their particular project type, they then identify and prioritize training needs for their own development.

Human resource departments will most likely make use of LDQ or similar assessment tools to

Figure 2. Leadership profiles of successful managers of IT projects of different type of complexity

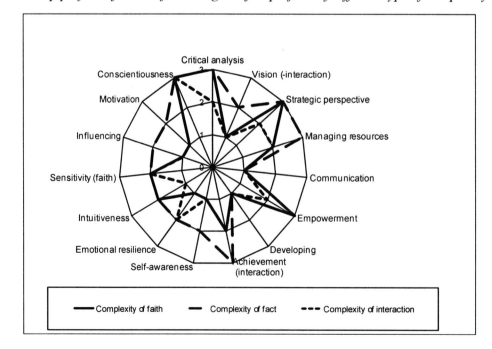

Table 3. Reoccurring dimensions of leadership

	People	*Vision*	*Process*
Confucius 500BC	Jen	Xiao	Li
Aristotle 300BC	Pathos	Ethos	Logos
Dulewicz & Higgs 2005	EQ	IQ	MQ

identify best suitable candidates for their projects, or use the above profiles as targets for development of their workforce.

Near Term Implications for Academia

The research on leadership's importance and impact on projects will continue. While writing this chapter, the Project Management Institute (PMI) decided to sponsor a further study on the development of project managers' emotional competencies for better project results. This trend will continue. Possible areas to investigate in the coming years include the different requirements for leadership training for line and project managers, as well as managers of different types of projects and in different cultures. A better understanding of these implications will allow for development of improved interaction and collaboration in international, virtual, and cross-industry teams. This will impact the ability to manage long-term projects successfully and sustainably.

Along with that, leadership competence will be accepted into the project management bodies of knowledge as a complement to existing management competences, thus contribute to a balance of 'hard' and 'soft' factors for the management of projects.

CONCLUSION

This chapter gave an overview of leadership theories and current research results on leadership in projects. The degree of influence of different

leadership competences on success in different types of projects was shown, together with the presence of leadership competencies in managers of successful projects of different type.

By going back 2,500 years to the classic writings on leadership and reviewing the six schools of leadership theories of the last 70 years we see three main dimensions of leadership pervading all work, from ancient to recent times. These are people, vision, and process, Table 3.

While this bears the question of how far we have come within the last 2,500 years, it also shows the need to continue to research, to understand and apply new learning in the area. Its importance should not be underestimated, as this *new science of human relationship* (Goleman, 2006) comes close to a *DNA of leadership*, which can migrate continually.

ACKNOWLEDGMENT

Parts of this chapter were written jointly with Prof. Rodney Turner of the Graduate School of Management in Lille, France.

REFERENCES

Adair, J. (1983). *Effective deadership: A self-development manual.* Adershott, UK: Gower.

Barnard, C. I. (1938). *The functions of the executive.* Cambridge, MA: Harvard University Press.

Bass, B.M. (1990). From transactional to transformational leadership: Learning to share the vision. *Organisational Dynamics, 18*(3), 19-31.

Belbin, R. M. (1986). *Management teams.* London: Heinemann.

Bennis, W., & Nanus, B. (1985). *Leaders: The strategies for taking charge.* New York: Harper and Row.

Blake, R. R., & Mouton, S. J. (1978). *The new managerial grid.* Houston, TX: Gulf.

Boyatzis, R. E. (1982). *The Competent Manager: a model for effective performance.* New York, NY: Wiley.

Briggs-Myers, I. (1992). *Gifts differing.* Palo Alto, CA: Consulting Psychologists Press.

Cattell, R. B., Eber, H. W., & Tatsuoka, M. M. (1970). *Handbook for the 16PF.* Illinois: IPAT.

Crawford, L. H. (2003). Assessing and developing the project management competence of individuals. In J. R. Turner, (Ed.), *People in project management.* Aldershot, UK: Gower.

Dominick, P., Aronson, Z., & Lechler, T. (2007). Transformational leadership and project success. In R. R. Reilly (Ed.), *The human side of project leadership,* (pp. 1-30). Newton Square, PA: Project Management Institute.

Dulewicz, V., & Higgs, M. J. (2000). Emotional intelligence: a review and evaluation study. *Journal of Managerial Psychology, 15*(4), 341–368.

Dulewicz, & Higgs, M. (2005). Assessing leadership styles and organisational context. *Journal of Managerial Psychology, 20*(1), 105-123.

Dulevicz, V., Turner, J. R., & Müller, R. (2006). *Assessment of project managers using the leadership dimensions questionnaire: An international study* (Henley Working Paper Series). Henley Management College, Henley-on-Thames, UK.

Dvir, D., Sadeh, A., & Malach-Pines, A. (2006). Project and project managers: The relationship between project manager's personality, project types and project success. *Project Management Journal, 37*(5), 36-48.

Fiedler, F. E. (1967). *A theory of leadership effectiveness.* New York: McGraw-Hill.

Frame, J. D. (1987). *Managing projects in organizations.* San Francisco: Jossey Bass.

Geraldi, J., & Adlbrecht, G. (2007). On faith, fact, and interaction in projects. *Project Management Journal, 38*(1), 32-43.

Goleman, D. (2006). *Social intelligence: The new science of human telationships.* London: Hutchinson.

Goleman, D., Boyatzis, R., & McKee, A. (2002). *The new leaders.* Boston: Harvard Business School Press.

Handy, C. B. (1982). *Understanding organizations.* London: Penguin

Hershey, P., & Blanchard, K. H. (1988). *Management of organizational behaviour,* 5th ed. Englewood Cliffs, NJ: Prentice Hall.

House, R. J. (1971). A path-goal theory of leader effectiveness. *Administrative Science Quarterly,* September, 321-338.

IPMA (2007). *ICB: IPMA competence baseline Version 3.0.* In C. Caupin, H. Knöpfl, G. Koch., H. Pannenbäcker, F- Pérez-Polo, & C. Seabury (Eds.), Njkerk, The Netherlands: International Project Management Association.

Keegan, A. E., & Den Hartog, D. N. (2004). Transformational leadership in a project-based environment: a comparative study of the leadership styles of project managers and line managers. *International Journal of Project Management, 22*(8), 609-618.

Kirkpatrick, S. A., & Locke, E. A. (1991). Leadership traits do matter. *Academy of Management Executive,* March, 44-60.

Krech, D., Crutchfield, R. S., & Ballachey, E. L. (1962). *Individual in society.* New York: McGraw-Hill.

Müller, R., Geraldi, J., & Turner, J. R. (2007, September). *Linking complexity and leadership competences of project managers.* Paper presented at IRNOP VIII Conference (International Research Network for Organizing by Projects), Brighton, UK.

Müller, R., & Turner, J. R. (2006). Leadership competences and their successful application in different types of project. In L. Ou & R. Turner (Ed.), *Proceedings of IRNOP VII (International Research Network for Organizing by Projects),* Northwestern Polytechnic University, Xi'an, China.

Müller, R., & Turner, J. R. (2007a). Matching the project manager's leadership style to project type. *International Journal of Project Management, 25*(1), 21-32.

Müller, R., & Turner, J. R. (2007b).The influence of project managers on project success criteria and project success by type of project. *European Management Journal, 25*(4), 289-309.

Mullins, L. J. (1996). *Management and organizational behavior.* London: Pitman.

Oxford Concise Dictionary (1995). 9th edn. UK: Oxford University Press.

Parry, K. (2004). *The seven sins and the seven virtues of leadership: Which path do we follow?* (The Leading Matters Symposium Series). Centre for Leadership & Management in Education, Graduate School of Management, Griffith University, Australia, Griffith University EcoCentre.

Partington, D. A. (2003). Managing and leading. In J. R. Turner (Eds.), *People in project management.* Aldershott, UK: Gower.

Porterhouse, M., & Dulewicz, V. (2007). *Agile project managers' leadership competencies* (Henley Working Paper Series). Henley Management College, Henley-on-Thames, UK.

Robbins, S. P. (1997). *Essentials of organizational behaviour.* Englewood Cliffs, NJ: Prentice Hall.

Schultz, W. C. (1955). *FIRO: A three dimensional theory of interpersonal behaviour.* New York: Holt, Rinehart, Winston.

Slevin, D. P. (1989). *The Whole Manager.* New York, NY: Amacom.

Tannenbaum, R. & Schmidt, K. H. (1958). How to choose a leadership style. *Harvard Business Review*, March-April.

Turner, J. R. (1999). *The handbook of project-based management: Improving the processes for achieving strategic objectives.* London: McGraw-Hill.

Turner, J. R., & Müller, R. (2006). *Choosing appropriate project managers.* Newton Square, PA: Project Management Institute.

KEY TERMS AND DEFINITIONS

Behavioral or Style School: A school of leadership theories which assumes that effective leaders adopt certain styles of behaviors, which can be learned. So that effective leaders can be developed.

Competency School: A school of leadership theories which encompasses all earlier schools. It is multidimensional and includes the personal characteristics, knowledge and skills of the leader. The competency school assumes that different competence profiles are appropriate in different circumstances.

Contingency School: A school of leadership theories which assumed that effective leadership occurs through a particular leadership style which fits the idiosyncrasies of a situation.

Emotional Intelligence School: A school of leadership theories that emphasizes the social interaction between people. It assumes that the leader's emotional response to a situation has more impact on the success than the intellectual capabilities of the leader.

Emotional Leadership Competencies (EQ): A group of behavioral and motivational competencies of leaders for handling themselves and their relationships.

Intellectual Leadership Competencies (IQ): A group of cognitive competencies encompassing intelligence in form of critical analysis, strategic perspective, vision and imagination.

Leadership: A relationship through which one person influences the behavior of other people (Mullins, 1996).

Leadership Profile: The specific combination of the expression of the 15 leadership competencies in the personality of an individual.

Managerial Leadership Competencies (MQ): A group of cognitive leadership competencies encompassing the knowledge and skills of management functions.

Management: Professional administration of business concerns or public undertakings (Oxford Concise Dictionary, 1995)

Project Types: A categorization of projects, typically by project purpose or project attributes. Often done in order to prioritize projects, or to assign resources and develop or assign appropriate capabilities to manage the projects of a particular category.

Trait School: A school of leadership theories which assumes that effective leaders posses common traits, and that leaders are born not made or developed.

Visionary or Charismatic School: A school of leadership theories which emphasizes the balance between concern for relationships and concern for process and its different combinations in different situations

APPENDIX

Emotional Intelligence (EI)	EI dimension	Underlying competency	Description
Personal competencies	Self-awareness	Emotional self-awareness	• read and understand your emotions • recognize their impact on job performance and relationships.
		Accurate self-assessment	• realistically evaluate your strengths and limitations
		Self-confidence	• keep a realistically positive sense of self-worth
	Self-management	Self-control	• keep disruptive emotions and impulses under control
		Transparency	• be honest, authentic, and have integrity
		Initiative	• have a sense of efficacy and seize opportunities as they arise
		Adaptability	• adjust to changing situations and overcome obstacles
		Optimism	• view setbacks as opportunities instead of threats
		Achievement	• set realistic goals and seek for performance improvements
Social competencies	Social awareness	Empathy	• sensing a wide range of emotional signals • understanding others' perspectives • taking an active interest in their concerns
		Organizational awareness	• read the currents of organizational life • build social networks • navigate politics
		Service	• recognize and meet customers' needs
	Relationship management	Influence	• sending clear, convincing, and well-tuned messages
		Inspiration	• inspire and move people with a compelling vision
		Catalyst for change	• challenge the status quo and champion the new order

Chapter 16
The Language of Leaders:
Identifying Emergent Leaders
in Global Virtual Teams

Simeon J. Simoff
University of Technology, Sydney, Australia

Fay Sudweeks
Murdoch University, Australia

ABSTRACT

Virtual teams and their leaders are key players in global organizations. Using teams of workers dispersed temporally and geographically has changed the way people work in groups and redefined the nature of teamwork. Emergent leadership issues in computer-mediated communication are vital today because of the increasing prevalence of the virtual organization, the flattening of organizational structures, and the corresponding interest in managing virtual groups and teams. This chapter examines the communication behaviors of participants in two different case studies to determine if number, length, and content of messages are sufficient criteria to identify emergent leaders in asynchronous and synchronous environments. The methodology used can be embedded in collaborative virtual environments as a technology for identifying potential leaders in organizational and educational environments.

INTRODUCTION

Identifying competent leaders is a crucial component in building high performing teams that operate in global, cross-functional, and cross-cultural environments. During the different phases of team development, leaders may need to take different roles (Kolb, 1999). For instance, in an early stage, leadership skills may involve understanding individual differences, work styles, and cultural nuances. In later stages, leaders may assume a peer relationship with team members. In any of the roles, leaders communicate with the other team members. If a team collaborates over the Internet, then we can observe that communication. Our assumption is that emergent leaders can be identified through their communication patterns. We address our assumption focusing on *communication behaviors* of participants in two different case studies to determine if number, length, and content of messages are sufficient criteria to identify emergent leaders in both synchronous and asynchronous environments. We pose the following research questions:

- How will leadership be reflected in communication patterns and communication style among team members; in other words, what is the language of leaders?
- Are there differences in these patterns/trends in different scenarios?
- Can we facilitate technologically the identification of leaders in virtual teams, based on the patterns of their communication?

In this chapter, we initially provide background research that frames the context of the problem. Then we present our approach, based on a complementary explorative data analysis (CEDA) research methodology developed by the authors for conducting Internet research (Sudweeks & Simoff, 1999). We examine the patterns of communication of leaders in two different case studies of online teamwork. The case studies complement each other in terms of activity scenarios and text-based communication modes. One case study is a group of autonomous and diverse individuals using an asynchronous communication medium over a relatively long period of time, while the other case study is a group of individuals using a synchronous communication medium and bound by the communication network for a short period of time. Finally, we present technological solutions for enabling leader identification in virtual environments along with some concluding discussions.

BACKGROUND

The formation of global virtual teams has changed the way people work in groups and redefined the nature of teamwork (Lipnack & Stamps, 1997; Mabry, 2002; Meier, 2003). A global virtual team is defined as teams of workers dispersed temporally and geographically which are assembled using a combination of telecommunications and information technologies to accomplish an organizational task (Townsend, DeMarie, & Hendrickson, 1998). Members of such teams work and interact in various modes, using a diverse set of computer-mediating technologies (Maher, Simoff, & Cicognani, 2000). In the climate of enterprise globalization, such virtual teams are essential components in the enterprise "toolbox" to remain competitive (Maznevski & Chudoba, 2000). Research on communication in virtual teams is less well documented (Furst, Blackburn, & Rosen, 1999). However, understanding the elements of group dynamics of virtual teams is of crucial importance in facilitating and managing these teams.

Leadership is acknowledged as a key element in virtual team dynamics and is well researched (Cascio & Shurygailo, 2003; Zaccaro & Bader, 2003; Zigurs, 2003), yet less is studied about how leadership activities influence group collaborative processes (Avolio, Kahai, & Dodge, 2000; Cascio & Shurygailo, 2003; Pauleen & Yoong, 2001; Zaccaro & Bader, 2003; Zigurs, 2003). Emphasizing the paucity of research on leadership in virtual teams, Misiolek and Heckman (2005) provide a broad and up-to-date overview of the literature on virtual teams in organizational context.

Addressing leadership in virtual teams is an essential part of an in-depth study of virtual team dynamics and analysis of their development (Sudweeks, 2004). Leadership issues in virtual teams remain vital today because of the increasing prevalence of the virtual organization, the flattening of organizational structures, and the corresponding interest in managing virtual groups and teams. In this chapter, we distinguish between *assigned* leadership and *emergent* leadership. An assigned leader is an individual who is assigned to a position of leadership. An emergent leader is an individual who is not assigned to a leadership position, who has the same status as other team members initially, but who gradually emerges as a leader through the support and acceptance of the team over a period of time (Guastello, 2002). The establishment of emergent leaders is a result of their actions and their communication behaviors, which include being involved, informed, firm but seeking the opinion of others, and initiating new ideas (Fisher, 1974). Leaders emerge according to the needs of the group (Myers, Slavin, & Southern, 1990) and usually exhibit the following characteristics: (1) participate early and often; (2) focus on communication quality as well as quantity; (3) demonstrate competence; (4) create social structures (Avolio et al., 2000); and (5) help build a cohesive team (Hackman & Johnson, 2000).

Earlier research in leadership in face-to-face environments shows that leaders are identified by high participation rates in discussions (Mullen, Salas, & Driskell, 1989; Regula & Julian, 1973; Sorrentino & Boutillier, 1975). McCroskey and Richmond (1998) related effective leadership to "talkativity." However, Yoo and Alavi (2002) proposed that, because of the reduced awareness of social presence and social context, the receiver of a message via computer-mediated communication (CMC) pays more attention to the message than the messenger. This observation led Yoo and Alavi to study emergent leaders in virtual teams. They found that, in asynchronous communication, emergent leaders could be identified by the number, length, and content of messages. Not only did emergent leaders send more messages and longer messages, their messages were more task oriented than other team members.

Misiolek and Heckman (2005) studied patterns of emergent leadership behavior in distributed virtual teams based on an analysis of interactions between college seniors, captured during a two-week course of a virtual collaboration exercise. The authors conducted a content analysis of the interactions using a coding scheme derived from behaviorally based leadership theory. The two-week period may not necessarily be sufficient time for the development of emergent leaders. However, the analysis is an interesting attempt to employ behaviorally based and functional theories of leadership to the analysis of leadership in virtual teams.

CASE STUDIES

The first case study (Case Study 1) was a two-year collaborative research project conducted by an international group of volunteer researchers, most of whom had never met either online or offline. This is different from the majority of the studies of leadership in virtual teams, where usually there has been at least one face-to-face session (Avolio et al., 2000; Misiolek & Heckman, 2005; Pauleen, 2003). The collaborative activity of the group was the collection and analysis of data from electronic discussion groups. Computer-mediated *asynchronous communication* was used for coordination, participant recruitment, distribution of information, formulation and discussion of policies, decision making, encouragement, and technology transfer. The number of members varied at any one time, but 143 people were consistently involved in the project. Two participants were assigned leadership roles, and they took on the facilitating task of encouraging the group to work together interdependently in a collaborative manner.

The second case study (Case Study 2) involved a group of 18 students engaged in collaborative learning in nine one-hour workshops over a four-month period. The workshops required substantial preparation, both individually and collaboratively. The workshops were held in a WebCT chat room

Table 1. Feature summary of the two case studies

Feature	Case Study 1	Case Study 2
Medium	E-mail	Chat room
Mode	Asynchronous	Synchronous
Duration	2 years	4 months
Leadership	Assigned	Appointed
Formation	Spontaneous	Predefined
Meetings	Unstructured	Structured
Purpose	Research project	Workshop series
No. of participants	143	19
Location of participants	Global	Mostly Australia
Age group	20-65	Mostly 20-30
Process	Unstructured	Structured

and were part of a unit of study. Although the participants lived within a 100 km range of the university, the majority of the students had never met either online or off-line. For each workshop, a tutor participated and a different student was appointed as a moderator. Moderators were required to lead the group discussions and facilitate learning through discussion of set readings.

The two case studies therefore differed in the features listed in Table 1. To some extent they complement each other, allowing an exploration of various facets of emergent leadership both in asynchronous and synchronous online scenarios.

RESEARCH METHODOLOGY

Research in virtual teams is part of what constitutes Internet research. The replication of Internet field research is difficult, if not impossible, for two main reasons (apart from the usual problems of the environment and human nature itself constantly changing). On a *technological* level, the Net is perpetually changing its configuration and supporting technology. On an *interaction* level, the difficulties in replication come from

the creative aspect of language use and the evolution of computer media. Apart from standard clichés, sentences are rarely duplicated exactly, yet each variation is generally comprehended. It follows that experiments involving text generation can rarely be repeated. Furthermore, studies of virtual teams have been usually conducted under controlled experimental conditions which may not present an accurate picture of the reality of virtuality. The problems can come from the following factors: (1) subjects are an atypically captive audience who would probably behave differently in a laboratory than they would in a real-world setting; (2) groups studied in experiments tend to be unrealistically small; and (3) an almost natural inclination of experimental design is to compare CMC with a face-to-face standard (Rafaeli & Sudweeks, 1997, 1998), a comparison that may be misleading.

The CEDA methodology—developed by Sudweeks and Simoff (1999), further extended by Riva and Galimberti (2001) as complementary explorative multilevel data analysis (CEMDA), and revised in Sudweeks (2004)—has developed multi-method research design principles in order to address the abovementioned issues. Hence, the methodology applied to each case study follows the

Figure 1. Research methodology and communication model: (a) the composition principles of a CEDA-compliant study (Adapted from Sudweeks & Simoff, 1999); (b) representing activities in virtual environments (Adapted from Simoff & Maher, 2000)

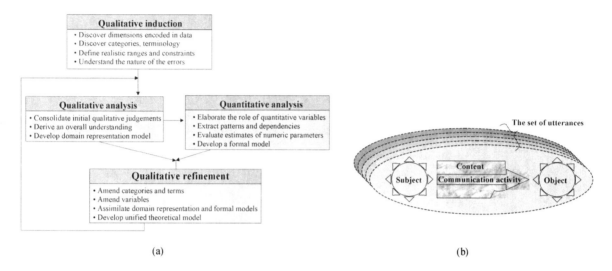

(a)   (b)

CEDA approach. The methodological composition principles are illustrated in Figure 1a.

The integrated data sets include a variety of sources including participant observations and archived electronic discussions. Throughout the duration of each study, one of the authors was participating and observing communication processes within both case studies, thus providing richness of data (Witmer, 1997). Observation assisted in discovering the underlying assumptions and dimensions of which group participants may have been unaware (Hammersley & Atkinson, 1983).

In Case Study 1, team members posted more than 1,000 e-mail messages while collaborating on their project. In Case Study 2, students engaged in nine hours of synchronous discussions, which were automatically logged and downloaded by one of the authors.

To be able to compare the results of two dissimilar case studies, the communication was viewed as *sets of utterances*. The communication model for the analysis of virtual design teams, proposed by Simoff and Maher (2000), is based on the premise that each communication activity

is composed of: (1) a subject who performs the communication event; (2) the content of the communication event; and (3) an object(s) to whom the communication event is addressed. In other words, in an utterance, a subject is communicating content to an object. Formally, each utterance can be represented as ⟨Subject, Object, Content⟩ which is defined as a SOC-triple. Hence an utterance can be denoted as: $u_i = \langle s_i, o_i, c_i \rangle$, where s_i, and o_i denote the corresponding subject and object in utterance u_i, respectively, and c_i is the content of utterance u_i. This model of an utterance provides a common timeless representation for both asynchronous and synchronous communication as illustrated in Figure 1b. Communication within a particular time window is represented as a sequence U of SOC-triples u_i, $U = u_1, u_2,..., u_n$, where n denotes the *length* of the sequence of utterances. A *communication pattern* in our terms is a subsequence $U_{kl} = u_k,..., u_l$, where $U_{kl} \subset U$ and $k < l$. In this framework, communication patterns can be grouped into three classes: (1) *content-independent patterns*—these patterns are statistics or utterance sequences that can be derived without consideration of the content of the

Figure 2. Representing the interactions via listserv and via a chat room as a set of utterances, (a) inter-actions via listserv media, (b) interactions via a chat room

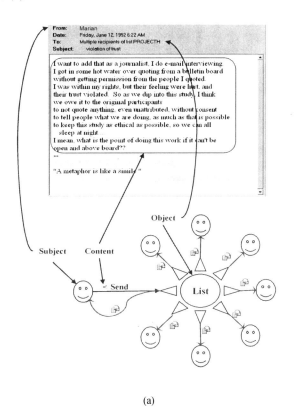

(a)

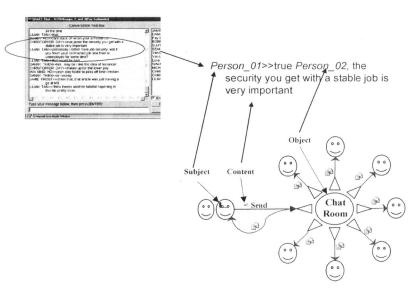

(b)

utterances; (2) *content-dependent patterns*—these patterns are statistics or utterance sequences that can be derived from an analysis of labeled communication sequences, where the labels belong to a predefined coding scheme, and each utterance is labeled according to its content; and (3) *content-based patterns*—these patterns consist of various text statistics, term clusters, contingency analyses, and taxonomies of words, which are derived from a text analysis of the utterance content.

This general model is applicable in text-based CMC to communication activities in both asynchronous environments and synchronous environments. In an initial analysis, the data was segmented into utterances—that is, each communication event (e-mail message or chat turn) was converted into utterances on the basis of one object (receiver) per utterance. The object in a communication utterance could be the whole group, part of the group, or an individual. The approach applied to both case studies is illustrated in Figure 2. Thus the e-mail messages and chat room logs

were converted to 1,345 utterances for Case Study 1 and 4,547 utterances for Case Study 2.

To enable content-dependent analysis, all utterances were coded using an open hierarchical coding scheme (Table 2) designed to investigate increasing levels of detail with the possibility for consistent extension. The coding features included five categories: management, reflection, content, style, and interactivity. Coding of the data was performed by three independent coders using Excel spreadsheets. Each coder was given a copy of the coding scheme with examples of each variable and then trained on a sample data. A level of accuracy was set and coders began coding when that standard of accuracy was attained.

ANALYSIS

The descriptive statistics of the utterances in both case studies is presented in Table 3. In Case Study 1, where each of the utterances represents

Table 2. Open hierarchical coding scheme

Level 1	Level 2	Level 3
Management	Formal Management	
	Informal Management	
Reflection	Awareness	
	Environment	
Content	Social	Chat, Agree, Disagree
	Emotional	Argumentative, Supportive
	Conceptual	Idea, Clarification, Acceptance, Rejection
	Task	Clarification, Acceptance, Rejection, Instruction
Style	Negative	
	Humor	
	Asking	
	Positive	
Interactivity	All	
	Part of a Group	
	Person	

a communication act via an e-mail message, the average length of an utterance is 776 characters (~120 words) whereas the average length of an utterance in Case Study 2 is 45-50 characters (~9-11 words). The distribution of utterances in both cases contains a number of extreme cases far from the average, which is indicated by the differences between the mean and the other measures of location—the median and the mode. The data sets in both case studies are positively (right) skewed. In Case Study 1, the range of utterance length is from 3 characters (1 word) to almost 16,000 characters (2,818 words), whereas the range of utterance length in Case Study 2 varies from 1 character to 909 characters. The maximum range across the groups is fairly consistent, varying between 663 and 909 (112-163 words). The distributions of utterance lengths in both case studies are heterogeneous, as indicated by the relatively large value of the heterogeneity factor.

Case Study 1

The activity levels of 143 participants were initially analyzed in terms of: (1) number of utterances; (2) total number of words; (3) average utterance length; and (4) task-related utterances sent. Figure 3 illustrates the total number of utterances over the entire period of Case Study 1. The utterance level is organized into five intervals. The first bin [1, 10] of the lowest number of utterances accommodates the levels of activities of typical participants—that is, 78% of the group members. The remaining 22% of the group are spread across the other five bins. The two bins of the highest activity (more than 40 utterances), representing only eight participants (6% of the group), are highlighted.

Rather than using the whole data set of 143 participants, the 31 participants who were the most active on any of the four activity criteria (number of utterances, total number of words, average utterance length, activity-related utterances) were selected. These 31 participants generated 78% of

Table 3. Descriptive statistics of utterances for Case Studies 1 and 2

	Case Study 1	Case Study 2
Total number of utterances	1,343	4,547
In terms of characters		
Average utterance length	776	48
Median	401	34
Mode	37	3
Average deviation	679	35
Standard deviation	1,218	58
Range of the length	15,970	908
Minimum length	3	1
Maximum length	15,973	909
Characters (total)	1,0417,99	218,950
Characters (without spaces)	865,414	183,298
Heterogeneity	13	16
In terms of words		
Average utterance length	120	10
Median	67	7
Mode	7	1
Average deviation	117	7
Standard deviation	214	11
Range of the length	2,817	163
Minimum length	1	1
Maximum length	2,818	164
Words (total)	177,932	40,185
Heterogeneity	13	15

Figure 3. Activity levels of different participants

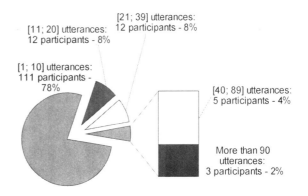

[11; 20] utterances: 12 participants - 8%

[21; 39] utterances: 12 participants - 8%

[1; 10] utterances: 111 participants - 78%

[40; 89] utterances: 5 participants - 4%

More than 90 utterances: 3 participants - 2%

Table 4. Comparison of eight participants who rated highest on (a) the number of utterances, (b) density of utterances, and (c) activity-related content criteria

Number			Density					Content	
Participant	*No. of utterances*		*Participant*	*Total no. of words*	*Participant*	*Average utterance length*		*Participant*	*Activity-related utterances*
Fay	160		Sheizaf	28,408	Jonathan	291		Fay	111
Sheizaf	101		Fay	22,994	Sheizaf	281		Jeff	71
Jeff	90		Jeff	16,770	Jeff	186		Sheizaf	61
Barbara	47		Jonathan	12,211	Jamie	183		Jonathan	35
Catherine	47		Barbara	6,863	Daniel	149		Barbara	33
Deborah	42		Eric	5,675	Barbara	146		Catherine	31
Jonathan	42		Nadia	3,960	Fay	144		Eric	25
Eric	40		Catherine	3,958	Eric	142		Deborah	21

| (a) | (b) | (c) |

the utterances throughout the project. The measures for the participants who rated highest on the four activity criteria are given in Table 4.

From these activity measures, participants were tentatively classified as one of three types:

- **Assigned leader** (participants who have been assigned as leader explicitly or implicitly at the beginning of the project);
- **Emergent leader** (participants who are identified as potential emergent leaders using the number of utterances, total number of words, average utterance length, and task-related utterance criteria); or
- **Participant** (participants who are identified as non-leaders).

With an appropriate combination of inductive techniques, a collection of attributes is used to ascertain which of these attributes are most important in characterizing the three participant types. The collection of attributes include the four activity criteria plus the number of utterances received by an individual and the number of task-related utterances received by an individual. Table 5 lists the set of six attributes which were used as candidates for defining *Participant Type*. In our classification problem *Participant Type* is the target ("dependent") variable, and the six attributes listed in Table 5 are the "independent" variables.

The analysis included two inductive techniques: (1) decision (classification) tree induction (Witten & Frank, 2000), that was run in an exploratory mode; and (2) visual clustering. First, the CART (Classification and Regression Trees) (Lewis, 2000) technique produced a classification tree of *Participant Type*. Guided by the derived classification tree, the second step, visual clustering (Miner3D), was performed. The major goal in looking at a decision tree model is to understand the attributes that are responsible for the phenomenon. The derived tree offers a description of the concept of *Participant Type* in terms of the six attributes.

Figure 4 shows the derived classification tree which isolates each of the three participant types: *assigned leaders; emergent leaders;* and *participants*. This induction technique shows that *Utterances* (number of utterances sent) is the primary attribute that splits the sample of participants into Assigned Leaders and the rest. At the next level,

Table 5. Attributes used for defining participant type

Attribute	Description
Utterances	Total number of utterances
Total Number of Words	Total number of words posted by an individual
Average Length in Words	Average length of utterances in words of an individual
TSK+CON(U)	Number of activity-related utterances sent by an individual
Addressed	Number of utterances of any variable addressed to an individual
TSK+CON(A)	Number of activity-related utterances addressed to an individual

Figure 4. The decision (classification) tree for Participant Type in Case Study 1

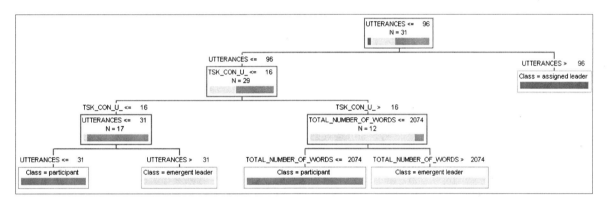

the attribute *TSK+CON(U)* (activity-related utterances sent by an individual) captures a significant portion of the leadership characteristics. At the next level, the *Utterances* and *Total Number of Words* attributes split the sample into emergent leader and participant classes. These three attributes partitioned the data to cover all participant types in Case Study 1.

The CART technique is then complemented by visual clustering. Visual clustering is the process of finding a partitioning of the data set into homogeneous sub-sets (clusters) (Keim & Ward, 2003). The key element in this technique is the mapping between the attributes and the corresponding visual features; in other words, this technique looks for groups of instances (individuals) that "belong together." Once the mapping is done, the visual clustering is an interactive

procedure. In our case, the procedure is guided by the results of the decision tree induction. As this is an unsupervised technique, the clusters are not known in advance.

Figures 5 and 6 show the results of visual cluster analyses performed on the data set of 31 participants and the six attributes listed in Table 5. Figure 5 shows the initial visualization of the data set. The X, Y, and Z axes are *Utterances, TSK+CON(U),* and *Total Number of Words* respectively. The value of the *Average Length in Words* attribute has been used to define the size of the spheres. Guided by the classification tree (Figure 4), in which the *Utterances* attribute splits the data at >31, *Utterance* is set to '32'. This setting filters out a cluster of 23 participants. The remaining nine individuals are shown in Figure 6. Again, guided by the classification tree, in which

Figure 5. Initial visualization of the data set

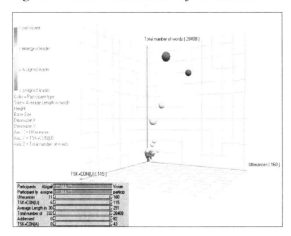

Figure 6. Clustering on Utterances attribute at value '32', TSK+CON(U) attribute at '17', and Total Number of Words *attribute at value '2075'*

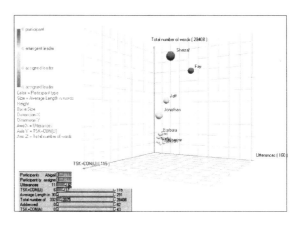

Figure 7. Enlargement of the emergent leaders identified in Figure 6

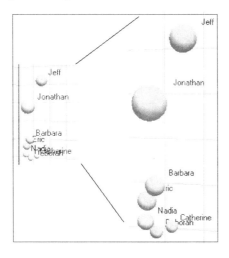

Figure 8. Clustering on Utterances *attribute at value '97' identifies assigned leaders*

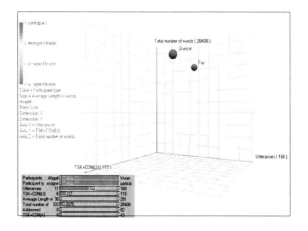

the *TSK+CON(U)* attribute splits the data at >16 and the *Total Number of Words* attribute at >2,074 (see Figure 4), these attributes are set at '17' and '2075' respectively in Figure 6. The same nine individuals remain—that is, two assigned leaders and seven emergent leaders.

Figure 7 is an enlargement of a section of Figure 6 showing the seven emergent leaders identified by name—that is, Jeff, Jonathan, Barbara, Eric, Catherine, Deborah, and Nadia. Figure 8 shows that when the *Utterances* attribute is set to '97'

(see Figure 4, which indicates that the *Utterances* attribute splits the data again at >96), Fay and Sheizaf are identified as assigned leaders.

Hence, the classification tree in Figure 4, visualized as clusters in Figures 5 to 8, shows that the attributes *Utterances*, *TSK+CON(U)* and *Total Number of Words* were able to split the sample of 31 active participants into three *Participant Types* as listed in Table 6.

Table 6. Assigned leaders, emergent leaders, and participants

Assigned Leaders	Emergent Leaders	Participants	
Fay	Jeff	Donna	Michael
Sheizaf	Jonathan	Marian	Daniel
	Barbara	Ben	Stuart
	Eric	David	Nicola
	Catherine	Vivian	Brad
	Deborah	Brent	Jamie
	Nadia	Sally	Marie
		Chloe	Andy
		Tom	Clive
		Sarah	Peter
		Carleen	Abigail

Figure 9. Engagement level of participants

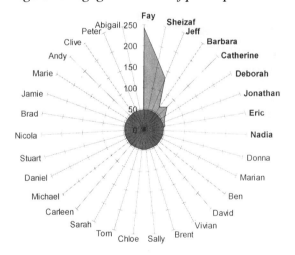

The descriptive statistics indicated four strong emergent leaders (Jeff, Barbara, Jonathan, and Eric) and two weaker candidates (Catherine and Deborah). When additional criteria were added and the data were analyzed with the CART and cluster tools, it was found that the *TSK-CON(U)* attribute (number of activity-related utterances) contributed to the identification of the same four

strong emergent leaders (Jeff, Barbara, Jonathan, and Eric) and another three (Catherine, Deborah, and Nadia). The engagement graph confirms the set of six emergent leaders identified by the descriptive statistics (Jeff, Barbara, Jonathan, Eric, Catherine, and Deborah), with Nadia at the highest end of the mean engagement level.

The combination of two attributes—*Utterances* and *Addressed*—also gives a measurement of the intensity of engagement for any participant. Figure 9 illustrates the engagement level for the 31 participants examined in the classification tree model. The circle in the middle of Figure 9 corresponds to the mean level of engagement across the data set of 31 participants. The graph illustrates the findings of CART (and visualized in Minder3D); that is, the two assigned leaders (Fay and Sheizaf) have the highest level of engagement, while six of the emergent leaders (Jeff, Catherine, Barbara, Deborah, Jonathan, and Eric) are above the mean level of engagement. Nadia has the next highest level of engagement and was identified in the CART procedure.

Thus, it has been demonstrated that the criteria used for descriptive statistics (number of utterances, total number of words, average utterance length, and activity-related utterances), classification tree and clustering (number of utterances sent, total number of words, average utterance length, activity-related utterances sent, number of utterances received, and activity-related utterances received), and the radar chart on engagement level (number of utterances and utterances received) all point to a set of leaders that emerged during the life of the group.

Case Study 2

As discussed earlier, the participants in Case Study 2 formed a community of learners in a series of nine workshops using synchronous interaction in a chat room. Each week a different student was appointed to moderate the discussions. Given that each student moderated just one workshop, each student would be expected to dominate discussions in one workshop only. Hence, it would be expected that the participation pattern of any one student would be a large number of utterances in one workshop and a smaller number of utterances in the remaining eight workshops. Therefore the contributions to the discussions from each participant were potentially equalized across the period of the nine workshops.

The number and density of utterances are effective criteria for measuring verbosity in participants. Figure 10 illustrates the activity level of different participants, measured as the total number of utterances over the entire period of Case Study 2. The appointed leader and Gail communicated most intensively (bin [500; 800]), with Doug and Lorna communicating more than the other 15 participants (bin [300; 499]).

Density of utterances is measured by total number of words throughout the workshop series and the average utterance length in words. Note that average number of words per utterance is not as informative as for Case Study 1 since the range for Case Study 2 is 1-10 words. What this measure does highlight is the very different style of communication in a synchronous vs. asynchronous environment. Utterances in a

Figure 10. Activity levels of different participants

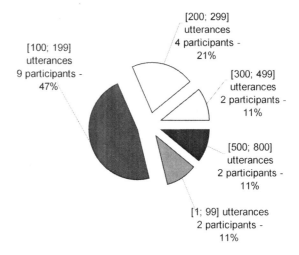

synchronous environment are short, acronyms or abbreviated.

When using the number of utterances criteria, the potential emergent leaders were Gail, Doug, Lorna, Henry, Kirk, Leah, and Joe, in order of most frequent utterances (see Table 7). When using the total number of words criteria, the potential emergent leaders were Gail, Doug, Henry, Duncan, and Lorna, in order of most words. When

Table 7. Comparison of eight participants who rated highest on different criteria: (a) the number of utterances, (b) density of utterances, and (c) activity-related content criteria

Number		Density				Content	
Participant	*No. of utterances*	*Participant*	*Total no. of words*	*Participant*	*Average utterance length*	*Participant*	*Activity-related utterances*
Fay	743	Gail	7,039	Gail	10	Fay	471
Gail	626	Fay	5,743	Henry	10	Gail	432
Doug	410	Doug	3,834	Duncan	10	Lorna	228
Lorna	317	Henry	2,688	Fay	8	Doug	225
Henry	256	Duncan	2,583	Leah	7	Henry	180
Kirk	225	Lorna	2,328	Donald	7	Leah	166
Leah	209	Joe	1,849	Kirk	6	Kirk	158
Joe	205	Kirk	1,807	Louis	6	Susan	133

(a)	(b)	(c)

Figure 11. The decision (classification) tree for participant type in Case Study 1

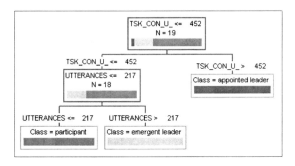

Figure 12. Visual clusters of data set of appointed leader, emergent leaders, and participants for Case Study 2

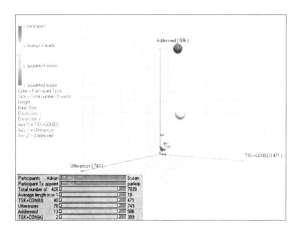

Figure 13. Clustering on Utterances *attribute at value '218'*

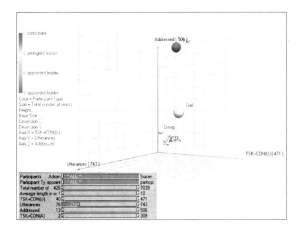

Figure 14. Engagement level of participants

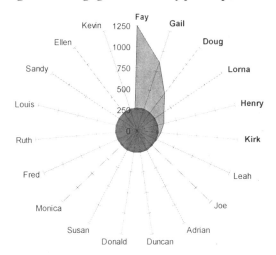

using the average utterance length, the potential emergent leaders were Gail, Henry, Duncan, Leah, and Donald, in order of longest average utterance. Adding task-related content as a criteria for identifying leadership characteristics refines the set of emergent leaders. Apart from the appointed leader, only Gail, Henry, and Kirk show evidence of emergent leadership. If any three of the four criteria are taken into account, then Doug, Lorna, and Leah are also contenders.

An expanded set of criteria was used to explore the emergent leadership within the group. Similar to Case Study 1, we reframed the problem as a classification task, classifying the group members as

one of the participant types—that is, (1) appointed leader; (2) emergent leader; or (3) participant. Note that in the case of synchronous communication, the total number of words was not depicted as a parameter in the emergent leadership classification model. The classification tree model is presented in Figure 11, and the results of the visual clustering are shown in Figures 12 and 13.

The descriptive statistics indicated three strong emergent leaders (Gail, Henry, and Kirk) and three weaker candidates (Doug, Lorna, and Leah). When additional criteria were added and the data were analyzed with CART and the visual cluster tools, it was found that the *Number of Utterances* attribute contributed to the identification of the same three strong emergent leaders (Gail, Henry, and Kirk) and two of the weaker candidates (Doug and Lorna). The engagement graph in Figure 14 confirms the set of five emergent leaders identified by the descriptive statistics, and the classification tree model and clustering.

DISCUSSION

The methodology for studying emergent leadership that has been used in both case studies led to the development of an overall approach and technology for facilitating the identification of emergent leadership from project and organizational scenarios where there is a record of the communication among the individuals involved. The operationalization of the approach that can

be embedded into CSCW systems is illustrated in Figure 15. Currently, the approach is focused on text-based communication data, including e-mail, chat transcripts, and communication transcripts generated from virtual environments. The collected communication data is segmented into utterances (as an utterance is considered as a data unit in the data set). In a collection of e-mail messages, the e-mail message is usually considered the organizing unit of the data. In our approach, during the data pre-processing, the sequence of e-mail messages is converted into a sequence of utterances. Each e-mail message may include one or more utterances. For example, a single message may include two or more utterances—one that addresses all team members on the list and a few utterances that address particular individuals. In practice, these and similar types of messages require segmentation into the corresponding separate utterance. The segmentation is implemented using rule-based techniques. The first set of rules is applied to the selection of messages that may potentially have several utterances.

Figure 15. Operationalization of leader identification approach into an embedded technology: (a) depicting the language of leaders, (b) depicting leaders via the three analysis streams

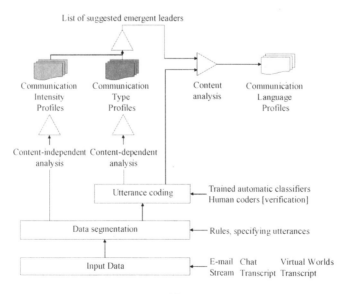

(a)

Figure 15. continued

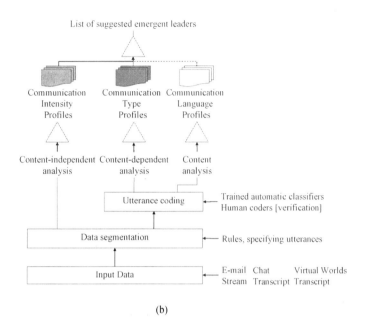

(b)

The rules applied at this stage are targeting specific constructs that identify separate utterances. Selected messages are then parsed to identify the split points. Then the splits are repacked as time-stamped SOC-triples. Technically, this is sufficient for the content-independent analysis algorithms (which include various descriptive statistics based on the presence of an utterance) and algorithms for depicting regular sequences of communicating subjects. Note that at this stage we do not consider whether high participation is a result of a high percentage of social utterances (in which case we may be looking for potential coordinator) or a high percentage of topic-related utterances (in which case we may be looking for a potential expert).

The content-dependent analysis requires labeling of the SOC-tripples following the coding schema presented in Figure 1. The automation of the process includes training of a classifier and then using it for labeling the utterances. Currently, a sample of the data set is selected as a training data, it is labeled manually and used for training

a classifier for the labels at a particular level of the coding schema. Classifiers are trained for coding at different levels, and the consistency between the levels is part of the selection process of the appropriate classifier. Then the rest of the data set (the unseen part) is run, and the classification output is used for the content-dependent analysis.

FUTURE TRENDS

The content analysis described in this chapter is currently being developed and incorporated in the system in a way that it caters for two research scenarios. Figure 15a shows the system which identifies the leaders based on the outcome of content-independent and content-dependent analysis. The list of leaders and the list of coded messages is then used to filter the leadership messages of different categories and investigated through text mining the "language" of leadership (including statistical features of the sentences, use of emoticons, spectrum across word length, the dictionaries for different categories, keywords in context analysis, and a semantic net of the concepts used). Figure 15b shows the other scenario for the system where the abovementioned text features are used to identify the list of leaders, complementing the other two methods.

The study reported here provides parameters that can be used to monitor CMC of team members in collaborative virtual environments for predicting emergent leaders within the groups. Emergent leaders may impact the group dynamics, and the prediction of potential leaders may assist smart project management in virtual organizations.

The findings of the research have been embedded in a technology that facilitates the identification of leaders based on transcripts of CMC. The application is useful in both the educational and organizational setting. Researchers in organizational science have increased their efforts in group development in organizations. These studies have been motivated by the increased flattening of organizational structures, which leads to the emergence of informal groups. Knowing the structure of such emergent groups and their emergent leaders is invaluable for company management. The development of methods that assist in identifying such structures and emergent leaders is directly related to the research work presented in this chapter.

Emergent leadership also plays an important role in collaborative learning. Group development is one of the key components of social constructivism in online (flexible) learning strategies. The approach presented in this chapter is appropriate for conducting a detailed study of social learning in flexible (computer-mediated) learning environments.

Current work is focused on the incorporation of the analysis of the activities in the virtual environment in the leadership identification methods. The work is based on pilot developments in mining collaborative virtual environments reported in Simoff and Biuk-Aghai (2003a, 2003b).

CONCLUSION

The increasingly global nature of business is associated with an increased role of virtual distributed teams that communicate electronically. If such virtual organizations are to be successful, they will have to ensure that aspects of team organization transfer. We have focused on emergent leadership, as it has received little attention within the literature when compared to other models of leadership (Kickul & Neuman, 2000).

We looked at the patterns of communication that indicate the emergence of leaders. Three criteria were added to the verbosity criteria to identify emergent leaders: number of utterances addressed to an individual, number of activity-related utterances sent by an individual, and number of activity-related utterances addressed to an individual. In both case studies, a non-parametric technique and a visual clustering procedure identified a small group of participants who emerged as leaders. The findings therefore suggest that frequency, density, content, and engagement level of communication contribute to identifying emergent leadership within virtual teams.

In Case Study 1, three attributes were instrumental in categorizing assigned leaders, emergent leaders, and participants: number of utterances sent, number of activity-related utterances sent, and total number of words. In Case Study 2, two attributes categorized appointed leaders, emergent leaders, and participants: number of activity-related utterances sent and number of utterances sent.

In both asynchronous and synchronous environments, there were several people who emerged as leaders—that is, emergent leadership functions were shared. Emergent leaders send more messages, but the messages are more likely to be task related. In other words, sheer volume of words does not make an emergent leader, but frequent messages with topic-related content does contribute to leadership qualities. These findings demonstrated that emergent leadership patterns were consistent in both synchronously and asynchronously mediated virtual teams.

REFERENCES

Avolio, B., Kahai, S. S., & Dodge, G. E. (2000). E-leadership: Implications for theory, research, and practice. *The Leadership Quarterly, 11*(4), 615-668.

Cascio, W. F., & Shurygailo, S. (2003). E-leadership and virtual teams. *Organizational Dynamics, 31*(4), 362-376.

Fisher, B. A. (1974). *Small group decision making: Communication and the group process.* New York: McGraw-Hill.

Furst, S., Blackburn, R., & Rosen, B. (1999). Virtual team effectiveness: A proposed research agenda. *Information Systems Journal, 9*(4), 249-269.

Guastello, S. J. (2002). *Managing emergent phenomena.* Mahwah, NJ: Lawrence Erlbaum.

Hackman, M. Z., & Johnson, C. E. (2000). *Leadership: A communication perspective.* Prospect Heights, IL: Waveland Press.

Hammersley, N., & Atkinson, P. (1983). *Ethnography: Principles in practice.* New York: Tavistock.

Keim, D., & Ward, M. (2003). Visualization. In M. Bertold & D. J. Hand (Eds.), *Intelligent data analysis* (2nd ed., pp. 403-427). Heidelberg, Germany: Springer.

Kickul, J., & Neuman, G. (2000). Emergent leadership behaviors: The function of personality and cognitive ability in determining teamwork performance and KSAS. *Journal of Business and Psychology, 15*, 27-51.

Kolb, D. C. (1999). *Team leadership.* Durango, CO: Lore International Group.

Lewis, R. J. (2000). An introduction to classification and regression tree (CART) analysis. In *Proceedings of the Annual Meeting of the Society for Academic Emergency Medicine,* San Francisco.

Lipnack, J., & Stamps, J. (1997). *Virtual teams: Working across space, time and organizations.* New York: John Wiley & Sons.

Mabry, E. A. (2002). Group communication and technology: Rethinking the role of communication modality in group work and performance. In L. R. Frey (Ed.), *New directions in group communication* (pp. 285-298). Thousand Oaks, CA: Sage.

Maher, M. L., Simoff, S. J., & Cicognani, A. (2000). *Understanding virtual design studios.* Heidelberg, Germany: Springer.

Maznevski, M. L., & Chudoba, K. M. (2000). Bridging space over time: Global virtual team dynamics and effectiveness. *Organization Science, 11*(5), 473-492.

McCroskey, J. C., & Richmond, V. P. (1998). Willingness to communicate. In J. C. McCroskey, J. A. Daly, M. M. Martin, & M. J. Beatty (Eds.), *Communication and personality: Trait perspectives* (pp. 119-131). Cresswell, NJ: Hampton Press.

Meier, C. (2003). Doing 'groupness' in a spatially distributed work group: The case of videoconferences at Technics. In L. R. Frey (Ed.), *Group communication in context: Studies of bona fide groups* (2nd ed., pp. 367-397). Mahwah, NJ: Lawrence Erlbaum.

Misiolek, N. I., & Heckman, R. (2005). Patterns of emergent leadership in virtual teams. In *Proceedings of the 38th Annual Hawaii International Conference on System Sciences (HICSS'05),* HI.

Mullen, B., Salas, E., & Driskell, J. E. (1989). Salience, motivation and artifact as contributions to the relation between participation rate and leadership. *Journal of Experimental Social Psychology, 25,* 545-559.

Myers, M. R., Slavin, M. J., & Southern, W. T. (1990). Emergence and maintenance of leadership among gifted students in group problem solving. *Roeper Review, 12*(4), 256-260.

Pauleen, D. J. (2003). Leadership in a global virtual team: An action learning approach. *Leadership and Organization Development Journal, 24*(3), 153-162.

Pauleen, D. J., & Yoong, P. (2001). Facilitating virtual team relationships via Internet and conventional communication channels. *Internet Research: Electronic Networking Applications and Policies, 11,* 190-202.

Rafaeli, S., & Sudweeks, F. (1997). Net interactivity. *Journal of Computer-Mediated Communication, 2*(4).

Rafaeli, S., & Sudweeks, F. (1998). Interactivity on the nets. In F. Sudweeks, M. McLaughlin, & S. Rafaeli (Eds.), *Network and Netplay: Virtual groups on the Internet* (pp. 173-190). Cambridge, MA: MIT Press.

Regula, C. R., & Julian, J. W. (1973). The impact of quality and frequency of task contributions on perceived ability. *The Journal of Social Psychology, 89,* 115-122.

Riva, G., & Galimberti, C. (2001). Complementary explorative multilevel data analysis—CEMDA: A socio-cognitive model of data analysis for Internet research. In G. Riva & C. Galimberti (Eds.), *Towards cyberpsychology: Mind, cognitions and society in the Internet age* (pp. 19-35). Amsterdam: IOS Press.

Simoff, S. J., & Biuk-Aghai, R. (2003a). Generation, transfer and utilisation of knowledge: Knowledge discovery and visualisation. In H. Hasan & M. Handzic (Eds.), *Australian studies in knowledge management* (pp. 184-238). Wollongong, Australia: University of Wollongong Press.

Simoff, S. J., & Biuk-Aghai, R. (2003b). Multimedia mining of collaborative virtual workspaces: An integrative framework for extracting and integrating collaborative process knowledge. In O. Zaiane, S. J. Simoff, & C. Djeraba (Eds.), *Min-ing multimedia and complex data* (pp. 168-186). Heidelberg, Germany: Springer.

Simoff, S. J., & Maher, M. L. (2000). Analyzing participation in collaborative design environments. *Design Studies, 21,* 119-144.

Sorrentino, R. M., & Boutillier, R. G. (1975). The effect of quantity and quality of verbal interaction on ratings of leadership ability. *Journal of Experimental Social Psychology, 11,* 403-411.

Sudweeks, F. (2004). *Development and leadership in computer-mediated collaborative groups.* PhD thesis, Communication Studies, Murdoch University, Australia.

Sudweeks, F., & Simoff, S. (1999). Complementary explorative data analysis: The reconciliation of quantitative and qualitative principles. In S. Jones (Ed.), *Doing Internet research* (pp. 29-55). Thousand Oaks, CA: Sage.

Townsend, A. M., DeMarie, S. M., & Hendrickson, A. R. (1998). Virtual teams: Technology and the workplace of the future. *Academy of Management Journal, 12*(3), 17-29.

Witmer, D. F. (1997). Communication and recovery: Structuration as an ontological approach to organizational culture. *Communication Monographs, 64,* 324-349.

Witten, I. H., & Frank, E. (2000). *Data mining: Practical machine learning tools and techniques with Java implementations.* San Francisco: Morgan Kaufmann.

Yoo, Y., & Alavi, M. (2002, Summer). Electronic mail usage pattern of emergent leaders in distributed teams. *Sprouts: Working Papers on Information Environments. Systems and Organizations, 2.*

Zaccaro, S. J., & Bader, P. (2003). E-leadership and the challenges of leading e-teams: Minimizing the bad and maximizing the good. *Organizational Dynamics, 31*(4), 377-387.

Zigurs, I. (2003). Leadership in virtual teams: Oxymoron or opportunity? *Organizational Dynamics, 31*(4), 339-351.

Chapter 17
Building Trust in Networked Environments:
Understanding the Importance of Trust Brokers

Tom E. Julsrud
Norwegian University of Science and Technology, Norway

John W. Bakke
Telenor Research & Innovation, Norway

ABSTRACT

As organizations grow and become multi-national, distributed work, that is, work where members are located in different sites, cities, or countries usually follows (Meyerson, Weick, & Kramer, 1996; Jarvenpaa & Leidner 1999; Zolin & Hinds 2002; Hossain & Wigand 2004; Panteli 2005). Yet such teams and groups have fewer opportunities to build social networks as is common in traditional groups, such as time spent together and frequent informal interaction. The "paradox of trust" in distributed work then, is that while trust is a need-to-have asset for distributed work groups, in particular for knowledge work, it is also difficult to foster due to the lack of physical co-location (Handy, 1995). This chapter argues that one way to deal with the paradox is to recognize the importance of trust as generated through individuals that have trustful ties that cross central boundaries, that is, trust brokers. Based on a relational approach to trust in groups as well as empirical studies of distributed work groups, we argue that trust brokers can help to establish trust quickly and make the group operate in more robust and sustainable ways.

INTRODUCTION

Over the last two decades, a rich stream of research has emphasized the importance of *trust* for large scale organizational processes as well as individual employees. As organizations become more and more knowledge-oriented, trust has moved to the center of attention as a supplement and also as a corrective for control as a coordinative mechanism. As recently argued by Adler and Heckscher (2006), this seems to be especially important for organizations that are engaged in innovations and knowledge-based work:

Knowledge work ... requires that each party offer something with no guarantee that they will get anything specific back in return. They must trust that the other has useful competence and knowledge that will help in their joint effort; that the other can understand her own ideas well enough to engage them productively. (p. 30)

Another aspect of modern organizations that may make trust even more critical for the functioning of organizations is the increase of more geographically dispersed physical structures. As organizations grow and become multi-national, *distributed work,*[1] that is, work where members are located in different sites, cities, or countries, usually follows. According to a recent Nordic study, every third Nordic manager in knowledge intensive businesses plans to reorganize their workplaces, and over 50% of these managers considered "distributed and mobile work" as a relevant option (Julsrud & Bakke, 2004).

There are several reasons for establishing and upholding distributed organizations: In addition to having distributed work as an instrument for establishing presence in different regions and markets, as in the case of regional offices, distributed work may also be a way of saving facilities costs and costs related to work travels. Setting up distributed work groups may also help organizations save expenses, as compared to the collocation of groups and employees. Distributed organizations may also be part of a strategy for developing new knowledge in teams by including people from various organizational units. Distributed groups by definition represent groups with participants situated in different physical settings and organizational and national cultures. To the extent that these people also include differences in knowledge and points of view, distributed work groups can be hubs for development of knowledge and in-

novations (Cummings, 2004). The challenge is to get such groups working together with a limited amount of physical contact, although supported by a diverse set of communication tools.

The Paradox of Trust in Distributed Work Groups

At a general level, the phenomenon of trust can be described as, "a willingness of a party to be vulnerable to actions of another party based on the expectations that the other will perform a particular action important to the trustor, irrespective of the ability to monitor or control that other party" (Mayer & Davis, 1995, p. 712). Whereas collaborating in distributed work groups is emerging as a common way of working, the ability to monitor or control the other party is drastically reduced, and, in essence, this is what makes trust a core asset for organizations practicing distributed work. There is a risk that distributed work may become fragmented if people cannot work together with a sense of comfort or if they feel that they must constantly use time and efforts on controlling the distant colleagues or employees. The "paradox of distributed work" is that while, in general, trust is a "need to have" asset for distributed work groups, in particular, for knowledge work, it is also difficult to foster due to the lack of physical co-location (Handy, 1995). Distance reduces the abilities to interact and to gradually develop trust over time. Even if interaction on Web-based infrastructures and software applications like e-mail and instant messaging (IM), as well as mobile communication provides rich opportunities for instant communication, it often lacks the differentiating cues that influences judgments about trustfulness[2] (Nissenbaum, 2004).

We will in this chapter argue that one way to deal with the paradox of trust in distributed work is to focus on the role of *trust brokers*. Based on a relational approach to trust in groups, we argue that trust can be enhanced by centrally located trust brokers that establish and sustain ties over distances and across boundaries. We will first clarify the concept of trust brokers, drawing on literature in the broad fields of social network analysis and organizational trust. We propose that trust brokering should be understood as an activity involving persistent elaboration of relations based on position in a social network. Next, we will describe trust-broker activities based on a case study of distributed workers within a large Nordic ICT-company. Deploying a combination of qualitative analysis and social network data, we found that trust brokers were important for the positive development of trust within this group. In the last section we will discuss how trust brokering mechanisms can be used strategically by organizations as a way of enhancing the development of trust in distributed groups.

The purpose of this study, then, is to demonstrate how certain qualities of the relations between actors play important roles in the establishment of trust in computer-mediated work environments and other forms of distributed work. The concept of trust brokering, we argue, is a key to understanding the construction of trust across distance.

A Note on the Methodology

This chapter is based on an empirical field study of distributed work groups in a Nordic ICT-company. Over a period of 15 months, a sample of five groups were followed closely. These groups worked in established, distributed work groups with employees situated in different places and countries, and they were also working together with people in other organizational units.

This study has been guided by an inductive approach, trying to understand how trust was built up in the groups over time (Eisenhardt, 1989; Ragin, 1994). In this process, in-depth interviews of participants were combined with formal questionnaires. The network techniques were applied to assist us in building an understanding of both the roles individuals had in the distributed social

networks and of the flow of information within the networks. Social networks were mapped by distributing a list of collaborators to each participant so that adjacency matrixes could be constructed. This approach contrasts and supplements much of the former research in this area, which, to a large extent has, had a focus on testing selected theoretical hypotheses.

One of the core findings from this inductive approach was that individual employees figured as important "nodes" active in the process of developing trust across the boundaries. We will here label this as *trust brokering*, and we will in this chapter explain further the mechanisms and activities involved with trust brokering.

TRUST BROKERING: CONCEPT AND DIMENSIONS

Trust brokering can be described as an activity, informally or formally, targeted at creating trustful relations between two or more groups[3]. As a working definition, we will here describe trust brokering as the active building of trust across distinct groups and/or subgroups, through the development of social relations. Trust brokering thereby refers to an activity within an organization, whereas the term trust broker refers to the corresponding role.

Reflecting the definition of trust cited above, trust brokering may be seen as an activity aiming at increasing positive expectations and reducing negative expectations about other parties in particular groupings. As indicated by the definition, trust brokering relates to trust building as an activity in the development of relations across distance between distinct social groups. In cases where distributed work is based on collaboration between employees belonging to multiple organizations, departments, or locations, the integration of such units becomes an important challenge. We will in this section explain how trust can be understood as a relational concept with cognitive and affective aspects and that trust brokering can be analyzed from its relational and positional aspects.

Cognitive and Affective Dimensions of Trust

Trust may be seen as a multidimensional construct with both cognitive and affective dimensions (Lewis & Weigert, 1995). The *cognitive dimension* refers to the calculative and rational characteristics demonstrated by trustees, such as reliability, integrity, competence, and responsibility. *Affect-based trust*, on the other hand, involves emotional elements and social skills of trustees.

The affective aspects of trust have in particular been studied in close relationships, but they have also been found to be important in work-related relationships (Boon & Holmes, 1991; McAllister, 1995). It has also been argued that in temporary and distributed groups the cognitive aspects are most important because there are fewer opportunities to develop affective ties (Jarvenpaa & Leidner, 1999; Kanawattanachai & Yoo, 2002; Meyerson et al., 1996). Yet recent studies of trust in organizations tends to emphasize the importance of also capturing the affective side of the concept (Kramer & Tyler, 1996). Hence the term trust brokering should strive to capture both cognitive and affective dimensions and we will in this article include both these dimensions.

A Relational Approach to Trust

When trust is defined as "a willingness of a party to be vulnerable to actions of another party based on the expectations that the other will perform a particular action important to the trustor, irrespective of the ability to monitor or control that other party" (Mayer, Davis, & Schoorman, 1995, p. 3), trust is defined as a relational concept, referring to characteristics of both the trustor and the trustee.

In actual studies, trust is nevertheless often seen as a characteristic of the trustee alone: Measures of individuals' trust levels may then be compared, or aggregated as a group characteristic, for example, when groups are rank-ordered according to the dimension of high trust/low trust (Jarvenpaa & Leidner, 1999; Kanawattanachai & Yoo, 2002; Piccoli & Ives, 2003).

In this article, where we investigate how trust-based relations develop within a group of distributed workers, we will deploy the relation-based approach to trust, also on the methodological level. This approach gives the benefits of exploring in depth the structure of relations within a group and the roles that are related to position in these networks. To reflect the cognitive and the affective aspects of trust, this chapter explores relations based on preferred collaboration partners when it comes to solving difficult work issues, as well as relations based on discussing a potential change of job situation. The affective and cognitive trust relations will be combined with relations based on both mediated and face-to-face daily interaction.

Two Aspects of Trust Brokering

The concept of trust brokering, as defined above, addresses two central issues: the establishment of trustful relationships and the "bridging" of formerly weakly connected groups or sub-groups within a larger structured network. While the first issue mainly has been elaborated by psychologically oriented studies of organizational trust (Kramer & Tyler, 1996; Lewicki & Bunker, 1996; Mayer et al., 1995; McKnight, Cummings et al., 1995), the latter has been discussed in particular within social network oriented approaches (Burt, 2005; Coleman, 1988; Granovetter, 1973; Kilduff & Tsai, 2003; Krackhardt & Kilduff, 2002). The "relational" and "positional" aspects of trust brokering, will be discussed briefly below.

Relational Aspects of Trust Brokering

A trust broker may be seen as an individual that actively seeks to establish trustful ties across groups with low levels of trust, whereas trust brokerage may be seen as the outcome of trust brokering activities or of activities that have the establishment of trust brokerage as a by-product.[4] In traditional network terms, trustful relations are usually described as "strong ties" (Granovetter, 1973; Krackhardt, 1992; Krackhardt & Brass, 1994). Strong ties are often found in denser social units like in families and between close friends or partners, while weaker ties exist between acquaintances. A strong tie is usually seen as a provider of more trustful relationships than a weak one. As argued by Mark Granovetter, the strength of ties is the outcome of "the combination of the amount of time, the emotional intensity, the intimacy (mutual confiding), and the reciprocal services that characterize the tie" (Granovetter, 1973, p. 1361). A wide range of research has indicated the value of having a broad network of weak ties. There are also studies exploring the more obvious phenomenon, that strong ties are also important. According to David Krackhardt (1992), the "strength of the strong ties" is that they help reduce risks in insecure environments and predict the behavior of others. This indicates a close conceptual relation between strong ties and trustful relation, and empirical studies corroborate that stronger ties usually are more trustful than weaker ties (Burt & Knez, 1996).

Few studies in the social network tradition have explored the activities that are involved in the development of trust and trustfulness between individuals. Although this issue has been developed and discussed within general studies of trust within organizations (Dirks & Ferrin, 2001; Kramer & Cook, 2004; Lewicki & Bunker, 1996; Mayer et al., 1995). Summing up different studies, Mayer and his colleagues proposes three central factors that influence the general trustworthiness of a person: ability, benevolence, and integrity (Mayer et al.). Ability refers to the competence and skills the party is believed to have or display on a certain task. If people are believed to have certain skills their trustworthiness is usually high. This is probably particularly important in situations involving knowledge-based work. Benevolence refers more directly to the expected motivation the trustee has to help or support the other party. In certain situations the relationship between the parties is of a kind that supports benevolence, such as between teacher and pupil. Thus benevolence refers to the particular role a party has and his relations to the trustor (i.e., the person that is to be trusted). And finally, the integrity of the trustor is believed to be important for the trustworthiness of a person. If the party is believed to adhere to a set of principles that has acceptance for the trustor, this affects the perceived integrity. But also knowledge about earlier achievements and actions may affect perceived integrity. Thus, the trustworthiness of a certain person builds on how a trustor understands the particular person's competence, intentions, and personal integrity.[5]

It is, however, important to note that these forms of understanding are not evolving in a social vacuum; they are affected by the particular context and the situation within which the relationships take place. Particular qualities of institutional systems like organizations and states will in most cases affect the willingness and possibilities to trust the other part (Mishira, 1996). Sudden changes in organizations can, for instance, create power differences and destabilize trust between individuals. Similarly, duration of interaction over time is believed to be important for the emergence of trustful relationships. Based on these three core concepts, one may say that contextual factors and interaction over time is likely to affect the understanding of the other part's ability, benevolence, and integrity.

Positional Aspects of Trust Brokering

Trust brokering is not only about developing trust between individuals but in particular about connecting individuals with low trust across boundaries. Social network studies have traditionally used the term "brokers" and "brokerage" to describe individuals who actively profit from connecting information and/or people belonging to different groups or networks (Boissevain, 1974; Burt, 2005; Cross & Prusak, 2002). Brokers are described as individuals who try to get personal advantages from negotiating information between parties. As described by Boissevain: "A broker is a professional manipulator of people and information who brings about communication for profit" (Boissevain, 1974).

In technical terms, the *information broker*, then, can be described as a person having an active transmitter role, mediating information between to two other roles; sources, and destinations. The information broker gets information or messages from one "source-node" and transmits it over to a "destination-node". Based on the position within these groups, the information broker can act as a coordinator, consultant, gatekeeper, representative, or liaison (Fernandez & Gould, 1994). Table 1 presents these different positions.

In all these positions, the information broker is active in transmitting or trading information between actors across the boundaries of two or more groups (or within a group). A high level of brokerage activities indicates a central position between two or three groups, which is fundamental for the exploitation of opportunities provided by the "structural holes," understood as gaps in the social worlds across which there are no current connections. According to Burt, these holes in the networks can be connected by savvy entrepreneurs who thereby gain control over the flow of information across these gaps (Burt, 2002, 2005).

A *trust broker* may in principle be located in every one of Fernandez and Gould's (1994) positions. Nevertheless, information brokerage

Table 1. Information broker positions (Based on Fernandez & Gould, 1994)

ROLE TYPE	DESCRIPTION
Coordinator	*Indicates brokerage within the same group*
Consultant	*Indicates brokerages where the broker belongs to one group, and the other two belong to a different group*
Gatekeeper	*The source node belongs to a different group than the broker and the destination node*
Representative	*Indicates that the destination node belongs to a different group than the broker and the source node*
Liaison	*Indicates that each node belongs to a different group*

and trust brokerage are in principle distinctively different since the latter is less focused on getting access to information and more oriented towards developing ties and relations across distances. This implies a difference of relational quality, as well as a difference of network structure; information brokerage in terms of self-interest is best achieved when there is only one connection between two network components (or groups) and the tension between these groups can be exploited at the maximum (Burt, 2005). Trust brokerage, on the other hand, will seek to develop more relations, and move towards a "closure" of networks. There is also an important difference related to motivation: The goal of trust brokering is to develop trustful relations, not to exploit information from different sources. Thereby, it is more driven by a motivation of creating a common understanding and identity within a group. The trust broker can, similar to the information broker, be positioned differently between groups, but the difference between source and destination is less important in trust brokerage, since it is always a question of brokering in both directions, since brokering is a bi-directional activity[6].

The trust broker then, as described, is a role in a network that is directed towards develop stronger relations between distant units, and to develop more cohesive structures within the group. An important element in the development of trustful relations in network theories may be the use of third parties, that is, individuals outside the dyad that can ensure the trustfulness of the other (Coleman, 1988; Granovetter, 1973). If persons B and C have a strong relationship, this can be used as a platform to develop trust further. If C also has a strong tie to A, C may display a middleman position between B and A that opens for trust brokering (See Figure 1). Given that A has an interest to establish or develop a trustful relation to B, person C can be used as transmitter or mediator of trust, ensuring that A is trustful and has good intentions. The trustworthiness B has to C then spills over to A. Related to the relational qualities described above, we can say that brokering involves the mediation of trustful relations in a network by acting as a middleman between more weakly connected nodes. It is in particular the integrity that can be affected by trust brokering; ensuring that the new person is trustworthy may affect the person's integrity.

An important point is that even though the role as a middleman can be performed in a passive way, there is an opportunity for C to act purposeful, as a trust-connector, when he is aware of the needs and capabilities of A and B. He will then not only act as a guarantor for the relationship, but will also create the new "triadic" unit, ABC. Trust brokers can enhance the denser network structures that are usually perceived as important for the establishment of common norms and security (Coleman, 1988). Compared to the two dyadic relationships AC and CB, the triad ABC will in most cases appear as a social unit with other properties than the dyad, which would more likely induce trust. According to general network theory, a triad is usually more likely to induce trust than a dyadic relationship (Krackhardt, 1999; Krackhardt & Kilduff, 2002; Wolff, 1950).

Summing Up

The discussion above demonstrates that trust brokering involves both relational and positional aspects. On the one hand, the performance of particular actions and communication help to build up trustfulness across boundaries. Central elements here are exposure and demonstration of individual integrity, ability, and/or benevolence. On the other hand, trust brokering involves the connecting of stronger ties within the group and, in particular, across boundaries. This could be done directly by elaborating on relations or indirectly by involving third parties. In addition, we have noted that relational trust in general involves both cognitive and affective aspects.

Figure 1. Inclusion of a third party (C) in a dyadic relation (A & B)

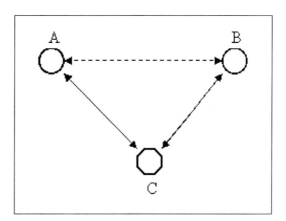

This general outline of trust brokering then suggests recognizing this as a position in network, but also as a position that requires particular actions to enhance relations and ties. One implication of this general attempt is to go beyond the strong structural approach that often is associated with network theories and to bring the individual back in using social network analyses in organizations (Kilduff & Corley, 2000).

DEVELOPMENT OF TRUST-BASED RELATIONS IN OMEGA

The case company, NOMO, is a Scandinavian ICT company with several thousand employees in more than 10 countries.[7] The company has experienced a significant growth in the last years, and investments, mergers, and acquisitions have made it one of the largest European companies within its business area.

Previously, the different national activities of NOMO were relatively independent, but when central divisions of NOMO were merged with ICT companies in Sweden and Denmark, closely interlinked forms of distributed work were initiated across both national and organizational boundaries.[8] A key motivation for the merger was to create synergies across the former divisions, while still keeping contacts with the respective local markets. The transformation from a national ICT company towards a larger multinational company created new challenges for the company. One manager in NOMO told us that "the main challenge for NOMO now is to get the different units work together as one company, not to keep on starting 'national wars' to get local advantages every time there is a potential conflict" (John, Norwegian HR-manager).

To understand more about collaboration within the multinational, distributed groups, a study of distributed work across the former organizational boundaries was launched. Five different distributed work groups were studied in depth over a period of 18 months.[9] We used evidence from one group of product developers, Omega, to illustrate how trust brokerage was important for the development of trust. The study started 15 months after the merger and involved structured analysis of interaction within the group, as well as qualitative interviews with the employees and managers involved.

We will first describe the development within the group during the study period before we turn to a closer description of the networks of trust we found within the group. We will then move on to discuss further some of the most essential nodes and relations within these networks; thus, we try to capture both the positional as well as the relational dimensions of trust brokering, as described in the former chapter

From Crisis to the Re-Establishment of Trust

The core task for the group of 17 developers on Omega was to develop new products for users of computer related services. They were not only located in two of the countries, Norway and Denmark, but they were also at different physical locations within the two countries. In total, people in the group were situated at four different locations (see Figure 2).

The interviews showed that the merged group had experienced a tough initial phase, characterized by numerous intrigues and conflicts. There were underlying conflicts about which product lines that were to be continued in the future. Many of the Danish employees felt their products were rejected in favor of the Norwegian product lines. The challenges were, however, not due to the increased distance between the product developers, but rather to a more complex organizational model where the local marketing units had been given more control of the product development. The product developers needed to establish relations

Figure 2. Location of employees in Omega (number of employees inside boxes)

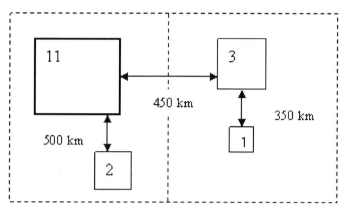

Omega-Norway   Omega-Denmark

with employees in market units in three countries to get resources for developing products. This proved to be difficult as long as the group did not manage to develop a common understanding.

The reorganization initially created a situation that seemed to make the group drift towards mistrust, rather than trust. Underlying much of the conflicts were changes of tasks in Denmark due to the merger. For many of the Danish employees, this was perceived as unpleasant changes, involving a lot of uncertainty. The product development group, which used to be a highly independent and strong unit within the former Danish firm, now experienced problems with being integrated in the larger and more complex NOMO. The understanding of the goals of the group as well as their individual task was low in the first period. In particular the Danish employees reported differences in understanding the new organizational model as well as their role in it.

We simply did not know what to do. All the old was taken away, and projects were closed. I will call this chaos, and very close to an untenable situation. Satisfaction surveys confirmed our problems, and all the "warning-lamps" were blinking. (Ronny, Danish employee)

The situation called for action and 12 months after the merger it was decided to reorganize the group by establishing minor, more specialized units within the groups. A new Norwegian leader (Torhild) was recruited from another division in NOMO, with an objective of facilitating the integration of the groups of developers in Denmark and Norway. When we conducted the interviews, the degree of satisfaction with the new structure was high. The reorganization of Omega was accompanied by changes in the larger NOMO group, involving clearer assignments of tasks, both within the Danish and the Norwegian group of product developers, and to the market units. Although problems with the market units persisted, most of the interviewees emphasized that the group was now moving in a more positive direction than before. Thus, 15 months after the merger, most employees expressed positive attitudes to the new Omega group.

There has been a dramatic improvement in our group during the last couple of months. We have now better people in our management group, and the motivation within the group is much higher. The roles and the responsibilities for the various tasks and assignments are now more clearly defined. (Kai, Norwegian employee)

According to Kai, this attitude was shared by most employees: The group had managed to re-orient their collaboration in a more positive direction.

Positional Aspects of Trust Brokering

In order to better understand the collaboration patterns and the relations within the group, a social network survey was conducted. The following two questions were used to capture cognitive and affective aspects of trust (C-trust and A-trust):

- Who in your group would you talk to if you needed a professional advice in your daily work?
- If you were planning to apply for a job similar to the one you have today, but in another company, whom would you prefer to discuss this with?

In addition, questions that captured the general daily and weekly interaction was used, including face to face communication, as well as the use of e-mails, telephone conversations, and text messages (SMS) on mobile phones (the enterprise deployed mobile phones as the primary work telephone):

- How often have you sent /received e-mails to/from this person the last 7 days?
- How often have you sent/received SMS to/from this person the last 7 days?
- How many mobile phone calls have you had with this person the last 7 days?
- How often have you been in contact with this person during the last 7 days?

All network data was gathered through retrospective reports of the frequency of communication.[10] The data was then coded as regular 1-mode social network data in sociomatrices for valued data. The data was used to conduct differ-

ent analysis, using UCINET software to further explore the trust network vis-a-vis other relational networks.[11] We will here refer to some of the findings and use the directed graphs to illustrate how certain persons in Omega were central in the two trust-based relational networks. We will, also use some simple measures on centrality and density of the networks. *Indegree* centrality indicates the number of incoming lines for each node in a node-by-node network, while *outdegree* centrality indicates the number of outgoing lines (Freeman, 1979). This is a frequently-sed indicator on prestige and popularity in valued networks and in this particular study it indicates whom the other in the group tends to trust. The *density* of a network is measured as the number of actual connections as a proportion of the maximal possible connection, going from 0 to 1.

The cognitive trust network had a dense structure, with connections criss-crossing the group, whereas the affective network was looser: For the C-trust network the density was 0.169, while for the affective trust network, the density was only 0.0542, showing that the general level of cognitive trust was much higher than the level of affective trust. This finding corroborates much former research on trust in distributed group, finding that across distance, cognitive trust is easier established than affective trust.

The head of the department, Torhild, proved to be central in both the trust networks and in the interaction-based network (Table 2 provides data on the degree of centrality for C-trust, A-trust, and daily interaction.) In the interviews, she was acknowledged for playing an important role in connecting the local units. The material also showed that a small group of other individuals with no formal positions proved to be central in these networks. In particular Kai and Martin figured as central in both the C-trust network and the interaction network. All the participants in the group knew someone whom they would trust to give them professional advice, indicating a certain amount of coherence in the group. Yet, when it

Table 2. Indegree and outdegree centrality indicators for position in the cognitive trust network (C-trust), affective trust network (A-trust) and the general interaction network in Omega

	C-trust		A-trust		Interaction	
	Indegree	Outdegree	Indegree	Outdegree	Indegree	Outdegree
Kai	12,00	3,00	0,00	0,00	6,00	4,00
Torhild	10,00	3,00	2,00	0,00	8,00	3,00
Martin	6,00	3,00	3,00	0,00	7,00	4,00
Knut	5,00	3,00	0,00	0,00	1,00	5,00
Kari	4,00	2,00	0,00	2,00	5,00	6,00
Marianne	3,00	2,00	2,00	2,00	3,00	1,00
Ronny	2,00	2,00	0,00	1,00	0,00	1,00
Daniel	1,00	3,00	1,00	0,00	1,00	5,00
Jørgen	1,00	3,00	0,00	0,00	1,00	1,00
Andreas	1,00	3,00	0,00	0,00	1,00	0,00
Emil	1,00	2,00	2,00	2,00	1,00	0,00
Erika	0,00	3,00	0,00	3,00	3,00	7,00
Heidi	0,00	3,00	1,00	1,00	3,00	1,00
Sissel	0,00	3,00	1,00	0,00	3,00	2,00
Simon	0,00	3,00	1,00	2,00	2,00	1,00
Liv	0,00	3,00	0,00	0,00	2,00	3,00
Mathias	0,00	2,00	-	-	2,00	7,00
MEAN	*2,71*	*2,56*	*0,813*	*0,813*	*3.00*	*3*
SD	*3,54*	*0,76*	*0.950*	*1.014*	*2.223*	*2,301*

comes to affective trust, 9 of the 17 employee did not consider anyone in the group as "trustworthy". In addition the nodes that tended to be central in the C-trust network did not appear as highly central in the A-trust network; Kai, for instance, was highly central in the cognitive network, but not included in the affective trust network. Emil, on the other hand, was trusted by two individuals in the group on the affective dimension, but only by one in the cognitive network. Other employees, like Heidi, only had indegree ties in the affective network.

Table 3. Degree of centrality for interaction through e-mail, mobile dialogues and SMS in Omega

Node	E-mail	Mobile	SMS	SUM
Knut	19	15	11	45
Martin	20	10	11	41
Torhild	24	8	7	39
Kai	17	12	9	38
Kari	19	8	5	32
Marianne	13	10	5	28
Erika	14	6	6	26
Jørgen	8	8	6	22
Sissel	14	3	3	20
Mathias	7	6	7	20
Liv	10	4	5	19
Simon	9	5	4	18
Ronny	8	6	4	18
Heidi	10	5	2	17
Daniel	9	3	5	17
Andreas	6	6	3	15
Emil	8	3	1	12
MEAN	11,889	6,941	5,529	
SD	5,801	3,244	2,746	

The indicators for daily interaction showed that Torhild, Martin, and Kai were the most central partners for communication within the group, as well as for the cognitive trust network. Of these three persons, Torhild and Martin were also central in the affective trust network (Table 2). An analysis of communication patterns through mediated channels of communication indicates that the affective trust network follows the cognitive trust networks closely.

A rough measure of the centrality of the network members can be established by looking at the aggregate level of communication, established by adding the incoming and outgoing lines for each partner in the network, while ignoring the direction of communication (Freeman, 1979).[12] Table 3 presents this measure of centrality for all three communication channels. The material shows interesting differences between the networks, based on e-mail, telephone conversations and text messages (SMS) on mobile phones: The manager, Torhild, was most central in the e-mail network, indicating that this perhaps was a more formal medium. Knut was active in the mobile communication interaction, including the use of SMS, even though he had very low centrality in the affective trust network. This is an indicator that interaction frequency is not necessarily closely linked to centrality in trust networks.

Figure 3. Affective and cognitive trust relations in the Omega-network (Danish employees white, Norwegian colored)

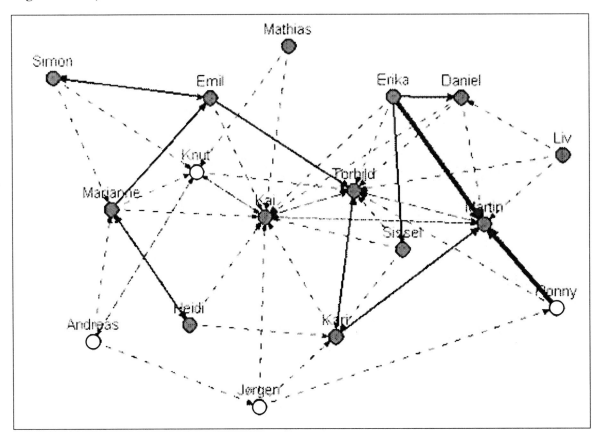

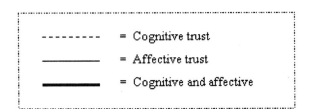

------- = Cognitive trust

———— = Affective trust

━━━━ = Cognitive and affective

The network survey indicated that the manager, Torhild, as well as Kai and Martin, were most central in the cognitive trust network. Knut, on the other hand, was central in the mediated information flow, but not in particular as a cognitive trust partner. The outdegree interaction table also suggested that he was a sender more than a receiver of information and messages. As illustrated in Figure 3, the centrality of Kai, Torhild, and Martin was based on their relations to both Danes and Norwegians. Two of the 12 persons seeking advice from Kai were from the Danish part of the group and three of the Norwegians would ask Knut for advice, even though he came from the Danish part of NOMO. As such, these could be considered as trust brokers along the cognitive dimension. When it comes to the affective trust relations, only Martin displayed ties that crossed the national boundary. He was the only person that filled the role as an affective trust broker in this group.

Relational Aspects of Trust Brokering

The network measures and the accompanying diagraph showed clearly that some nodes were more central in the interconnected networks of Omega. This finding confirms several earlier studies of social networks of teams and groups, where individual variations in centrality is common (Cross & Prusak, 2002; Cummings & Cross, 2003). Further, the study indicated that the cognitive and the affective dimensions of trust followed rather different tracks. While the cognitive and task-oriented type of trust was present among almost all the employees, the affective trust relation was more sparsely distributed. Interestingly we found that individuals who were central in the cognitive trust network were in some cases not included in the affective trust network. This suggests that we might have individuals that connected along affective or cognitive dimensions only, or along both dimensions.

To give a closer understanding of the relational dimensions of trust brokering, we will here focus on the activities of Kai and Martin, two Norwegian employees who appeared as central players having several connections to the distant units. Martin appeared as the most important trust broker in this group, as he also had affective bonds that crossed the organizational boundary. His close collaborator in Denmark, Ronny, expressed that the development of a strong relationship with Martin was something of a turning point for him, stating:

The fact that Martin now has joined the group with his high level of competence really makes me believe in this. He actually is the first Norwegian that I can say that I really trust. (Ronny, Danish employee)

The relations between these two employees had become an important tie that strengthened the relations not only between two employees but between different geographical units within Omega. It is worth noting, however, that Ronny emphasized Martin's competence and abilities as main reasons for trusting him. For Martin, frequent visits to Denmark, together with frequent communication by electronic media, appeared to be part of a deliberate effort to create a better climate of collaboration within the group:

I use much of my time on communication and on the establishment of a common understanding within the group. I must establish agreement, not by dictates but by communication. Our organization has not done enough to foster this type of understanding across the national boundaries. (Martin, Norwegian employee)

Kai had a particular central role in the cognitive trust network. It turned out that he had a significant advantage by speaking both languages fluently. He had lived in Denmark for long periods of time and he used his insights into culture and language actively to avoid conflicts and misunderstandings. He considered that he had a special responsibility to act as a mediator in the group, due to his ability to detect language-based misunderstandings:

I speak Danish with my collaborators in Denmark, and Norwegian with the collaborators in Norway. In many situations I become a mediator between the environments, and frequently I must change into a role of an "interpreter" in situations where I suspect that people misunderstand each other. (Kai, Norwegian employee)

Thus, Kai's bilingualism helped him to detect misunderstandings but perhaps also to strengthen his own integrity across the nationalities. The deliberate development of relations across the boundaries also involved active use of communication tools.

Kai told us that he had made a routine of calling his colleagues regularly just to hear "how things were going". One of these distant colleagues had recently experienced a critical conflict. He argued that the frequent telephone calls were important to better understand the colleagues' feelings:

I call the other colleagues in my groups often to hear how things are going. I want them to feel that there is interest for what they are doing. When I do not sit beside them and see their faces, I need to call them up and hear how things are going. You must 'read between the lines' to know how their actually are doing in their work.... Sometimes I also talk to others to get information about these issues. (Kai, Norwegian employee)

Martin and Kai were not only developing relations, they were also actively surveying and following up on the others' work within the group. Interestingly, Kai expressed that he actively used third parties to get a better understanding of other colleague's situation. The concern was, on the one hand, that of work-related control, since he was in the position of being the manager of a sub-unit. On the other hand, it was also related to concern about the well-being of his colleagues and an interest in "sorting out" problems in the group. Thus, aspects of control seemed to be intertwined with establishment of trustful relation in this case.[13] All in all, however, Kai and Martin had more interest for the group's activities and their colleagues work than most of the others in Omega. In addition to having an active attitude regarding the connection of ties across the local units, Kai and Martin also seemed to deliberately make use of existing relations on a broader scale. Both were employees who not only had longest records of working in the company, but also of working in different parts of the organization. This was important as Omega was highly dependent on collaboration with other groups within the larger NOMO system. Access to a wide network, then, was also clearly seen as an advantage by the others in the group. "Martin has experience from working in the market units. This gives him access to very rich networks of

contacts that is really useful to us now" (Erika, Norwegian employee).

Kai and Martin enjoyed high levels of trust, at least partly based on their experiences and wide network of contacts within the company. As far as we discovered, this was not used to keep the others at a distance, or to take credit of having exclusive access to central information and resources. Kai expressed that he tried to use help his Danish colleagues to develop their own network within the Norwegian part of the organization. In this way he, implicitly, saw himself as a stepping stone for Danish colleagues in order to develop relations in the Norwegian part of NOMO.

Collaboration across the two countries is difficult. One of my colleagues is coming to me on Thursday, and he has not been here for six months. He needs to get help to develop his networks of contacts in the Norwegian part of the organization. (Kai, Norwegian employee)

This indicates that mediation of relations, and potentially trustfulness, actually took place in the group.

Martin and Kai both reported being involved in trying to solve or moderate conflicts within the group as well as with partners outside the group. Kai emphasized that many conflicts seemed to be based on misunderstanding due to cultural and language differences. Martin, however, said that Norwegians in some situations had been complaining to him about others in the Danish part of the group, recognizing that he had stronger relations here than others. This situation also indicated that Martin operated as a "bridgehead" between the Danish and the Norwegian part of Omega, moderating conflicts.

It is noteworthy that Kai and Martin (as well as Torhild and Knut) developed different types of relations within the group. In a way they might be considered as a "team" of trust brokers, creating a common platform to develop trust across the group. The reorientation of Omega into smaller groups probably also helped the brokers to develop trust within the group based on a common set of tasks and common professional ideas and norms.

Summing Up

Our investigation of Omega found that some employees in the group were important for integrating the two former weakly connected sub-units and building trust within the group. These employees did not only play roles as central connectors, but also acted as trust builders in a network initially suffering from low trust relations. While there were several that figured as trust brokers along the cognitive dimension, affective trust brokers were more infrequent. In Omega only one employee had such a position.

Our qualitative inquiry provided evidence that these persons actually were supporting trustfulness within the group, and that their position as "trusting and trusted individuals" was vital for the development of trust within the group. This involved activities related to establishing and strengthening relations with colleagues at a distance, as well as exploitation of formerly established relations. Actions were also taken to moderate and solve conflicts within the group, and to deploy individual networks to help others to establish new relations: Even though most of the trust brokering was related to establishment of dyadic relations, indications of network building activities through third parties were evident.

THE EMERGENCE OF TRUST BROKERING IN MEDIATED ENVIRONMENTS

Trust brokering as such is not a new phenomenon. The existence of middlemen to enhance trust has been recognized as important and exploited actively for ages. In the beginning of the 20th century, the sociologist Georg Simmel wrote about the sociological significance of a "third element" in social relations. When a dyad was extended with a third person that acted as a neutral mediator, he argued that this tended to moderate conflicts and create a stronger focus on group based interest rather than individual needs (Wolff, 1950). The importance of using third parties to foster trust is also increasingly being recognized as important for trust development on cooperation and negotiations between companies (McEvily & Zaheer, 2004; Wall, Stark, et al., 2001). Yet this perspective is largely neglected in studies of trust in distributed groups.

As we have explained here, when such brokers succeed in lowering conflicts and establishing trust between two or more sub-groups, we can see this as trust brokering. There are reasons to believe that in current and emerging distributed organizations—as well as in temporal and time-limited organizations—trust brokering will become much more important. One reason for this is simply that distributed collaboration becomes more common. Often, however, this emerges in settings that challenge trust and trustfulness. As in the case of NOMO, the merger, or company acquisitions, initial conflicts and discomfort due to power differences and insecurity regarding future work tasks were created. Such settings call for an active approach to the development of trust, rather than a passive one expecting trust to emerge and develop over time as a result of regular interactions.

Another equally important issue is that changing competitive environments requires the rapid establishment of groups and teams, often with a limited time-frame. Despite the fact that groups may work over distance, collaboration—and trust—needs to be developed fast. Active trust brokering may here suggest a strategy for the development of trust in distributed groups and teams more efficiently than traditional approaches. Focusing on the network of relations opens for integration and trust building through a limited number of central connections rather than between all nodes in a network.

Finally, the issue of developing knowledge and common ideas in organizational environments is getting increasingly complex, as modern organizations tend to become more networked. In some cases this also represents a development of a "networked individualization" where the relations between individual employees are work tasks (Wellman, 2002; Wellman, Quan-Haase, Boase, Chen, Hampton, & Diaz, 2003). A high level of complexity makes it difficult for individuals to know or understand what others are doing. Trust brokers can in such organizations be central for connecting people with similar ideas and projects and make them work together. As such, trust brokering can be a key factor for transmission of tacit knowledge that usually depends on higher levels of trust (Hansen, 1999).

Implications for Further Research

Several contributions have recognized the challenge of developing trust in distributed groups, and different solutions have been suggested for remedying the difficulties. Research in this area tends to emphasize different facets of research as decisive for the trust building in the distributed groups. At least three central factors have been much studied: the timing of the interaction, the quality of the communication, and the duration of interaction in the group. The timing argument holds that face-to-face interaction should be regular during the lifetime of the group, or more intense in the beginning of the collaboration (Jarvenpaa & Leidner, 1999; Maznevski & Chudoba, 2000; Zolin & Hinds, 2002). The quality of interaction argument, on the other hand, emphasizes that changes in the communication content, in particular by the managers in the group, will support the trust development (Jarvenpaa & Leidner; Panteli, 2005). And finally, the duration argument argues that trust is enhanced by longer durations and time of interaction (Wilson, Straus, & McEvily,

2006). As an implication of these arguments, trust in distributed groups should develop in much the same way as in co-located groups, although it will take a longer time.

Within this chapter, distributed work groups are seen from a structural perspective. This approach helps us to see that trust development is largely established and sustained by a limited set of individual actors. The trust brokering argument holds that a closer focus on individual roles and their relations within a social network represents a supplementary and more detailed perspective on the development of trust in distributed groups. Rather than seeing the group as one closed unit, it provides a more fine-grained analysis of trust as a product of particular relational positions and patterns within a network of distributed workers. This is a novel approach to studies of distributed work group, and we believe that it should be further explored.

Although the concept of trust brokering has been explored through an inductive, and small scale study, both the identified phenomenon and the concept seem to refer to generic organizational processes. Therefore, we believe that it has value as a description of mechanisms of developing trust, in particular for distributed settings where trust processes are challenged and contested. As a theoretical concept it is rooted in social network theory, as well as in general theories about development of relational trust in organizations. Yet it reflects a wider stream of research over the last decades focusing on the value of doing "boundary work" to connect individual groups to larger units.[14]

Still, the concept needs to be further clarified and compared to other network related role descriptions such as hubs, central connectors, and boundary spanners, as well as gate-keepers. More empirically oriented studies focusing on trust brokering activities, as well as on the impact of such activities on trust within the groups would be of interest. Our study of Omega suggests that trust brokering activities seems to be highly dependent on multiple communication channels, as well as a deliberate use of face-to face interaction. It would, however, be of interest to know more about the use of media for support trust brokering activities. Variations in the use of communication channels, suggested that different communication media were used for different purposes and to support different kinds of relations and ties. In this chapter we have also suggested that trust brokering based on affective and cognitive bonds follow rather different tracks. It would be interesting to explore further the similarities and dissimilarities between these two dimensions of trust brokering.

A further exploration of the role of trust brokers on distributed groups can also be developed in a more methodological direction, utilizing more sophisticated techniques for detecting and analyzing trust brokers and brokering mechanisms. Within the area of social network studies several paths are optional, including the use of positional role analysis and traditional broker indicators (Borgatti & Foster, 2003; Breiger, 2004; Fernandez & Gould, 1994; Hanneman, 2001). The nature of trust brokering as described here, however, may in particular be to call for a combination of quantitative and qualitative network studies, focusing on both structural aspects as well as the individuals work to establish and sustain social relations in distributed networks.

Implications for Organizations

We have used this case study as a tool for developing the concept of trust brokering, based on the observation that individuals may facilitate collaboration and networking within a distributed organization, where trust is seen as something that, to a certain degree, can be actively addressed. The idea of trust in distributed groups as affected by brokerage allows for a more active approach to trust in organizations. This position is somewhat contrary to the view that trust is a by-product of other activities (Elster, 1983); instead, trust bro-

kering may be seen as "functional equivalent" to trust emerging over time (Giddens, 1994). The concept of trust brokering also shows an affinity to the concept of *active trust*, trust that has to be energetically treated and sustained (Beck & Beck-Gernsheim, 1994).

One practical implication is that organizations may actively assign individuals as trust brokers when setting up distributed work groups. This might include giving them particular and formal responsibilities and resources to develop relations, or one may take effort to enhance the development of social relations more indirectly through enhanced social interactions. Where the goal of traditional approaches would seek to develop trust on a broad scale, the trust-brokerage approach would emphasize the need for a few, but strong, relations across the boundaries. An alternative strategy is to develop the groups around existing relations where trust exists in advance. If there are pre-existing trusting relations spanning across the distant groups, this may kick-start the development of trust within the group.

A central issue for the development of trust in distributed networks is how to stimulate the development of trustful and stronger ties. For companies wanting to develop ties across boundaries and distances, the establishment of meeting places, communities, and fora where relations and networks can develop, becomes important strategy elements. Trust brokers can be central in the planning and development of such meeting places, and they can support them in the development of boundary-crossing relations and structures. Collaboration in projects might be one example of such fora, but more informal arrangements can also be introduced, such as professional interest groups.

Trust brokering should, however, not be seen as a highly fixed role description within a group. As emphasized by the definition suggested in this article, we see this as an ongoing activity. This implies that trust brokering activities may be performed by several persons in a group, shifting over time. Neither should this necessarily be seen as a formalized role; brokering activities will in most groups take place when there is a need to develop trust and someone feels obliged or called to support the development of a group.

Organizations should, however, be aware of the risks that may be ascribed to the trust brokers. Earlier studies of individuals located in boundary-crossing positions suggest that this can be a vulnerable position, where there are risks of being targets of cross pressure and role conflicts (Friedman & Podolny, 1982; Krackhardt, 1999). A higher awareness of the actions and processes involved in trust brokering might help to avoid negative consequences, such as overwork, stress, or burnout.

CONCLUDING REMARKS

A trusting relationship is usually characterized by having positive expectations about other parties' actions and doings, with few options of controlling this directly. We have argued that in settings where options for interaction, observation, and control diminish, like distributed work, and work in time-limited teams, trust becomes more vital. This is particularly critical for groups and organizations that are engaged in knowledge-based work, with high interdependencies in the tasks and high degrees of uncertainty. While regular interaction over time may enhance this, the particular setting of distributed work makes this difficult to achieve. This is what has been described as "the paradox of trust" in distributed work (Handy, 1995).

This chapter has argued that the development of trust in distributed groups can be strengthened by trust brokers who work actively to connect employees and build (or thereby building) trust across distributed groups. By studying a case of distributed product developers as a network of relations, we found that both cognitive and affective relational trust was facilitated by trust brokers, centrally located between two national

operations. Their active development of stronger relations within the group seemed to enhance the trust within the group, and helped to solve "the paradox of trust" in the distributed group of product developers. Thus, the answer to the difficulties of enhancing trust is not necessarily to develop more trust on a general basis among all the involved employees. Another option is to enhance the development of trust through a limited number of centrally located trust brokers.

REFERENCES

Adler, P. S., & Heckscher, C. (2006). Towards collaborative community. In P. Adler & C. Heckscher (Eds.), *The firm as a collaborative community* (pp. 11-105). New York: Oxford University Press.

Beck, U., & Beck-Gernsheim, E. (1994). *Individualization*. London: Sage.

Bernhardt, H. R., Killworth, P., et al. (1982). Informant accuracy in social network data V. *Social Science Research, 11,* 30-66.

Boissevain, J. (1974). *Friends of friends. Networks, manipulators and coalitions.* Oxford: Basil Blackwell.

Boon, S.D. & Holmes, J. G. (1991). The dynamics of interpersonal trust: resolving uncertainty in the face of risk. In R. A. Hinde & J. Groebel (Eds.), *Cooperation and Presocial Behavior.* (pp. 190-211). Cambridge, UK: Cambridge University Press.

Borgatti, S. P., Everett, M.G., et al. (2002). *Ucinet 6 for windows.* Harvard: Analytic Technologies.

Borgatti, S. P., & Foster, P. C. (2003). The network paradigm in organizational research: A review and typology. *Journal of Management, 6*(23), 991-1013.

Breiger, R. (2004). The analysis of social networks. In M. Hardy & A. Bryman (Eds.), *Handbook of data analysis.* London: Sage.

Brown, H. G., Poole, M. S., et al. (2004). Interpersonal traits, complementarity and trust in virtual collaboration. *Journal of Management of Information Systems, 20*(4), 115-137.

Burt, R. (2005). *Brokerage and closure. An introduction to social capital.* New York: Oxford University Press.

Burt, R., & Knez, M. (1996). Trust and third-party gossip. In R. M. Kramer & T. R. Tyler (Eds.), *Trust in organizations. Frontiers of theory and research* (pp. 68-89). Thousand Oaks: Sage.

Cohen, D. & Prusak, L. (2001). *In good company: How social capital makes organizations works.* Boston, MA: Harvard Business School Press.

Coleman, J. (1988). Social capital in the creation of human capital. *American Journal of Sociology, 94*, 95-120.

Cross, R., & Prusak, L. (2002). The people who make organizations go or stop. *Harvard Business Review, 80*(6), 104-112.

Cummings, J. N. (2004). Work groups, structural diversity, and knowledge sharing in a global organization. *Management Science, 50*(3), 352-364.

Cummings, J. N., & Cross, R. (2003). Structural properties of work groups and their consequences for performance. *Social Networks, 25*, 197-210.

Dirks, & Ferrin (2001). The role of trust in organizational settings. *Organizational Science, 4*(12), 450-467.

Eisenhardt, K. M. (1989). Building theories from case study research. *Academy of Management Review, 14*(4), 532-550.

Elster, J. (1983). *Sour grapes: Studies in the subversion of rationality.* Cambridge, MA: Cambridge University Press.

Fernandez, R. M., & Gould, R. V. (1994). A dilemma of state power: Brokerage and influence in the national health policy domain. *American Journal of Sociology, 99*, 1455-91.

Friedman, R. A., & Podolny, J. (1982). Differentiation of boundary spanning roles: Labor negotiations and implications for role conflict. *Administrative Science Quarterly, 1*(37), 28-47.

Giddens, A. (1994). Risk, trust, reflexivity. In *Reflexive Modernization.* U. Beck, A. Giddens, & S. Lash (Eds.), Cambridge, UK: Polity Press, 184-197.

Granovetter, M. S. (1973). The strength of weak ties. *American Journal of Sociology, 81*, 1287-1303.

Handy, C. (1995). Trust and the virtual organization. How do you manage people whom you not see? *Harvard Business Review, 73*(3), 40-50.

Hanneman, R. (2001). *Introduction to social network methods.* Department of Sociology, University of California, Riverside.

Hansen, M. (1999). The search-transfer problem: The role of weak ties in sharing knowledge across organization subunits. *Administrative Science Quarterly, 44*, 82-111.

Haragadon, A. B. (1998). Firms as knowledge brokers: Lessons in pursuing continuous innovation. *Management Review, 40*(3), 209-227.

Hartley, C., Brecht, M., et al. (1977). Subjective time estimates of work tasks by office workers. *Journal of Occupational Psychology, 50*, 23-36.

Hossain, L., & Wigand, R. (2004). ICT enabled virtual collaboration through trust. *Journal of Computer-Mediated Communication, 10*(1).

Jarvenpaa, S. L., & Leidner, D. E. (1999, Nov-Dec). Communication and trust in global virtual teams. *Organisational Science, 10*, 791-815.

Julsrud, T., Bakke, J. W., et al. (2004). *Status and strategies for the knowledge intensive Nordic workplace.* Oslo, Norway: Nordic Innovation Center.

Julsrud, T., Schiefloe, P. M., et al. (2006). *Networks and trust in distributed groups.* University of Trondheim: NTNU.

Julsrud, T. E. & Schiefloe, P. M. (2007). Trust and stability in distributed work groups: A social network perspective. *International Journal of Networking and Virtual Organisations.* Forthcoming.

Kanawattanachai, P., & Yoo, Y. (2002). Dynamic nature of trust in virtual teams. *Strategic Information Systems, 11,* 187-213.

Kilduff, M., & Corley, K. G. (2000). Organizational culture from a network perspective. In N. Ashkanasy, C. P. M. Wilderom, & M. F. Peterson (Eds.), *Handbook of organizational culture and climate* (pp. 211-221). New York: Sage.

Kilduff, M., & Tsai, W. (2003). *Social networks and organizations.* London: Sage.

Krackhardt, D. (1992). The strength of strong ties: The importance of philos in organizations. In N. Nohria & R. Eccles (Eds.), *Network and organizations: Structure, form and action* (pp. 216-239). Boston: Harvard University Press.

Krackhardt, D. (1999). The ties that torture: Simmelian tie analysis in organizations. *Research in the Sociology of Organizations, 16,* 183-210.

Krackhardt, D., & Brass, D. (1994). Intraorganizational networks. In S. Wasserman & J. Galaskiewicz (Eds.), *The micro side. Advances in social network analysis* (pp. 207-229). Thousand Oaks, CA: Sage.

Krackhardt, D., & Kilduff, M. (2002). Structure, culture and simmelian ties in entrepreneurial firms. *Social Networks, 3*(24), 279-290.

Kramer, R. M., & Cook, K. S. (2004). Trust and distrust in organizations: Dilemmas and approaches. In R. M. Kramer & K. S. Cook (Eds.), *Trust and distrust in organizations. Dilemmas and approaches* (pp. 1-17). New York: Russel Sage Foundation.

Kramer, R. M., & Tyler, T. R. (1996). Whither trust. In R. M. Kramer & T. R. Tyler (Eds.), *Trust in organizations: Frontiers of theory and research.* Thousand Oaks, CA: Sage Publications.

Lave, J., & Wenger, E. (1991). *Situated learning. Legitimate peripheral participation.* Cambridge, UK: Cambridge University Press.

Lewicki, R. L., & Bunker, B. B. (1996). Developing and maintaining trust in work relationships. In R. Kramer & T. Tyler (Eds.), *Trust in organizations. Frontiers of theory and research.* Thousand Oaks, CA: Sage.

Lewis, J. D., & Weigert, A. (1985). Trust as a social reality. *Social Forces 63*(4), 967-985.

Marchington, M., Grimshaw, D. (Eds.). (2005). *Fragmenting work. Blurring organizational boundaries and disordering hierarchies.* Oxford: Oxford University Press.

Mayer, R. C., Davis, J. H., et al. (1995). An integrated model of organizational trust. *Academy of Management Review, 3*(20), 709-734.

Maznevski, M. L., & Chudoba, K. M. (2000). Bridging space over time: Global virtual team dynamics and effectiveness. *Organizational Science, 11*(5), 473-492.

McAllister, D. J. (1995). Affect- and cognition-based trust as foundations for interpersonal cooperation in organizations. *Academy of Management Journal, 1*(38), 24-59.

McEvily, B., & Zaheer, A. (2004). Architects of trust: The role of network facilitators in geographical clusters. In R. M. Kramer & K. S. Cook (Eds.), *Trust and distrust in organizations. Dilemmas and approaches* (pp. 189-213). New York: Russel Sage Foundation.

McKnight, D. H., Cummings, L. L., et al. (1995). *Trust formations in new organizational relationships* (Information and Decision Sciences Workshop). University of Minnesota.

Meyerson, D., Weick, K., et al. (1996). Swift trust and temporary groups. In R. Kramer & R. Tyler (Eds.), *Trust in organizations. Frontiers of research and theory* (pp. 166-195). Thousand Oaks, CA: Sage.

Mishira, A. K. (1996). Organizational response to crisis: The centrality of trust. In R. M. Kramer & T. R. Tyler (Eds.), *Trust in organizations: Frontiers of theory and research* (pp. 261-287). Thousand Oaks, CA: Sage.

Nissenbaum, H. (2004). Will security enhance trust online, or supplant it? In R. M. Kramer & K. S. Cook (Eds.), *Trust and distrust in organizations. Dilemmas and approaches* (pp. 155-185). New York: Russel Sage Foundation.

O'Leary, M., Orlikowski, W., et al. (2002). Distributed work over the centuries. Trust and control in the Hudson Bay Company. In P. Hinds & S. Kiesler (Eds.), *Distributed work.* Cambridge, MA: MIT Press.

Panteli, N. (2005). Trust in global virtual teams. *Ariadne 43.* Retrieved April 2007 from http://www.ariadne.ac.uk/issue43/panteli/

Piccoli, G., & Ives, B. (2003). Trust and the unintended effects of behavior control in virtual teams. *MIS Quarterly, 27*(3), 365-395.

Podolny, J., & Baron, J. (1997). Resources and relationships, social networks and mobility in the workplace. *American Sociological Review, 62,* 673-693.

Ragin, C. A. (1994). *Constructing social research.* Thousand Oaks, CA: Sage.

Star, S. L., & Griesmer, J. (1989). Institutional ecology, "translation" and boundary objects: Amateurs and professionals in Berkley's Museum of Vertebrate Zoology. *Social Studies of Science, 19,* 387-420.

Wall, J. A., Stark, J. B., & Standifer, R. L. (2001). A current review and theory development. *Journal of Conflict Resolution, 45*(3), 370-391.

Wasserman, S., & Faust, K. (1994). *Social network analysis. Methods and applications.* New York: Cambridge University Press.

Wellman, B. (2002). Little boxes, globalization, and networked individualism? In M. Tanabe, P. v. d. Besselaar, & T. Ishida (Eds.), *Digital cities II: Computational and sociological approaches* (pp. 10-25). Berlin: Springer.

Wellman, B., Quan-Haase, A., Boase, J., Chen, W., Hampton, K., Diaz, I., et al. (2003) The social affordances of the internet for networked individualism. *Journal of Computer Mediated Communication, 8*(3). Retrieved April 2007 from http://www.ascusc.org/jcmc/vol8/issue3/wellman.html

Wenger, E. (1998). *Communities of praxis. Learning, meaning and identity.* Cambridge: Cambridge University Press.

Wilson, J. M., Straus, S. G., et al. (2006). All in due time: The development of trust in computer-mediated and face-to-face teams. *Organizational Behavior and Human Decision Processes, 99,* 16-33.

Wolff, K. H. (Ed.). (1950). *The sociology of Georg Simmel.* New York: The Free Press.

Zolin, R., & Hinds, P. (2002). Trust in context: The development of interpesonal trust in geographically distributed work teams (CIFE Working Paper). S. University. Stanford, Center for Integrated Facility Engineering.

ENDNOTES

[1] There is no single way to define distributed work groups. We will here follow Zolin and Hinds and define this in a general way, as group-based work where members are located in different cities or countries, supported by use of information and communication technology (2002).

[2] This discussion of networked environments has even wider implications, since the development of organizations and organizational units with more limited timeframes presents challenges quite similar to the "paradox of trust" in distributed work.

[3] The term has been used by former authors to coin individual actors work to integrate different units. For instance, Cohen and Prusak (2001) describe this as "someone who vouch for people and make introductions to help spread trust throughout an organization" (p. 35). The term "network facilitators" has been described by McEvily and Zaheer (2004) as organizations and institutions deliberately and intentional act to promote and sustain trust (p.208). The term "knowledge brokers" has in a similar way been applied to describe organizations that support innovation by connecting, recombining, and transferring to new contexts otherwise disconnected pools of ideas (Haragadon, 1998).

[4] On the concept of by-products of social activities, see Elster (1983).

[5] In addition, there are also factors related to the trustor (the person that are going to trust the other part) that affects the perceived trustworthiness of a person. The term "propensity to trust" is usually used to denote the general willingness of a party to trust others (Mayer et al., 1995; Brown, Poole, et al., 2004). Not only differences in personalities but also individual experiences and values can affect the willingness to trust others in general.

[6] The idea of structural holes has been criticized for not paying sufficient attention to content of the relations. Analyzing different types of relations in a high technological engineering company, Podolny and Baron found that structural holes were advantageous for strategic network content, but not for relations involving social support and trustfulness (1997).

[7] Please note that all names are pseudonyms, as well as the names of the group (Omega) and the organization (NOMO)

[8] In technical terms, the Norwegian unit acquired the Swedish and Danish units, but the term *merger* was commonly used, both by the interviewees and in internal publications; hence this term is used throughout the presentation of the case.

[9] Results from this study are reported elsewhere (Julsrud, Schiefloe, et al., 2006).

[10] Such self-reported frequency data are not expected to be objectively accurate, but are expected to allow comparison across relations, and to indicate relative strength of interactions within a group (Hartley, Brecht, et al., 1977; Bernhardt, Killworth, et al., 1982)

[11] Closer description of social network measures and techniques can be found in Wassemann and Faust (1994) and in the UCINET software manuals (Borgatti, Everett, et al., 2002).

[12] We will here prefer symmetrical rather than directional ties to reduce complexity in the presentation, even though this represents a reduction in the richness of the empirical material. A more thorough analysis of the mediation of the social relation should, however, analyze directional as well as symmetrical ties.

[13] This point is elaborated explicitly by O'Leary and his colleagues in an historical analysis of trust and control in the Hudson Bay Company (O'Leary, Orlikowski, et al., 2002)

[14] Related terms include boundary spanning agents in the field of intra organizational networks (Friedman & Podolny, 1982; Marchington & Grimshaw, 2005), legitimate peripheral participation in the field of communities of practice (Lave & Wenger, 1991; Wenger, 1998), and boundary objects related to actor network theory (Star & Griesmer, 1989).

Compilation of References

Adair, J. (1983). *Effective deadership: A self-development manual.* Adershott, UK: Gower.

Adler, P. S., & Heckscher, C. (2006). Towards collaborative community. In P. Adler & C. Heckscher (Eds.), *The firm as a collaborative community* (pp. 11-105). New York: Oxford University Press.

Aguinis, H., Ansari, M. A., Jayasingam, S., & Aafaqi, R. (2008). Perceived entrepreneurial success and social power. *Management Research, 6,* 121–137. doi:10.2753/JMR1536-5433060204

Aguinis, H., Nesler, M. S., Quigley, B. M., Lee, S., & Tedeschi, J. T. (1996). Power bases of faculty supervisors and educational outcomes for graduate students. *The Journal of Higher Education, 67,* 267–297. doi:10.2307/2943845

Alavi, M. (1994). Computer-mediated collaborative learning: An empirical evaluation. *MIS Quarterly, 18*(2), 159–174. doi:10.2307/249763

Alavi, M., & Yoo, Y. (1997). *Is learning in virtual teams real?* (working paper). Boston, MA: Harvard Business School.

Alavi, M., & Yoo, Y. (1997). *Leadership emergence in virtual team environments.* Boston: Harvard University.

Albino, V., Garavelli, A., & Gorgoglione, M. (2004). Organization and technology in knowledge transfer. *Benchmarking: An International Journal, 11*(6), 584–600. doi:10.1108/14635770410566492

Allen, T. (1967). Communications in the research and development laboratory. *Technology Review, 70,* 31–37.

Allen, T. (1977). *Managing the flow of technology: Technology transfer and the dissemination of technological information within the r&d organization.* Cambridge, MA: MIT Press.

Amar, A. D. (2001). Motivating knowledge workers to innovate: A model integrating motivation dynamics and antecedents. *European Journal of Innovation Management, 4,* 126–132. doi:10.1108/14601060110399289

Amar, A. D. (2002). *Managing knowledge workers: Unleashing innovation and productivity.* Westport, CT: Quorum books.

Ambrosio, J. (2000). *Knowledge management mistakes.* Retrieved November 23, 2005, from http:/ www.computerworld.com/industrytopics/energy/story/ 0, 10801,46693,00.html

Ancona, D., & Caldwell, D. (1992). Bridging the boundary: External activity and performance in organizational teams. *Administrative Science Quarterly, 37*(4), 634–665. doi:10.2307/2393475

Ancona, D., Malone, T., Orlikowski, W., & Senge, P. (2007). In praise of the incomplete leader. *Harvard Business Review, 2007*(February), 92–100.

Annas, J. (2003). The structure of virtue. In M. DePaul & L. Zagzebski (Eds.), *Intellectual virtue: Perspectives from ethics and epistemology* (pp. 15-33). New York: Oxford University Press, Inc.

Ansari, M. A. (1990). *Managing people at work: Leadership styles and influence strategies.* Newbury Park, CA: Sage.

Ansari, M. A., Aafaqi, R., & Oh, S. H. (2008). *Social power and leader-member exchange: The impact of power distance orientation in the Malaysian business context.* Unpublished manuscript, University of Lethbridge, Canada.

APQC. (2000). *Building and sustaining communities of practice: Final report. Research report.* Houston, TX: American Productivity and Quality Center.

Aranda, E. K., Aranda, L., & Conlon, K. (1998). *Teams: Structure, process, culture, and politics.* Upper Saddle River, NJ: Prentice Hall.

Ardichvili, A., Page, V., & Wentling, T. (2002, September). *Motivation and barriers to participation in virtual knowledge-sharing communities of practice.* Paper presented at the OKLC Conference, Athens.

Ardichvili, A., Page, V., & Wentling, T. (2003). Motivation and barriers to participation in virtual knowledge-sharing communities of practice. *Journal of Knowledge Management, 7*(1), 64–77. doi:10.1108/13673270310463626

Argandoña, A. (2003). The new economy: Ethical issues. *Journal of Business Ethics, 44*, 3–22. doi:10.1023/A:1023226105869

Aristotle. (1998). *Nicomachean ethics* (D. P. Chase, Trans.). Mineola, NY: Dover Publications, Inc.

Arnison, L., & Miller, P. (2002). Virtual teams: A virtue for the conventional team. *Journal of Workplace Learning, 14*(4), 166–173. doi:10.1108/13665620210427294

Asllani, A., & Luthans, F. (2003). What knowledge managers really do: An empirical and comparative analysis. *Journal of Knowledge Management, 7*, 53–66. doi:10.1108/13673270310485622

Avolio, B. (1999). *Full leadership development: Building the vital forces in organizations.* Thousand Oaks, CA: Sage.

Avolio, B. J., & Kahai, S. (2003). Adding the e to e-leadership: How it may impact your leadership. *Organizational Dynamics, 31*(4), 325–338. doi:10.1016/S0090-2616(02)00133-X

Avolio, B. J., & Luthans, F. (2006). *The high impact leader.* New York: McGraw-Hill.

Avolio, B. J., Kahai, S. S., & Dodge, G. E. (2000). E-leadership: Implications for theory, research and practice. *The Leadership Quarterly, 11*(4), 615–668. doi:10.1016/S1048-9843(00)00062-X

Avolio, B., & Kahai, S. (2003). Adding the "e" to e-leadership: How it may impact your leadership. *Organizational Dynamics, 31*(4), 325–338. doi:10.1016/S0090-2616(02)00133-X

Avolio, B., Kahai, S. S., & Dodge, G. E. (2000). E-leadership: Implications for theory, research, and practice. *The Leadership Quarterly, 11*(4), 615-668.

Awad, E. M., & Ghaziri, H. M. (2004). *Knowledge management.* Upper Saddle River, NJ: Prentice Hall.

Awazu, Y., & Desouza, K. C. (2004). The knowledge chiefs: CKOs, CLOs and CPOs. *European Management Journal, 22*(3), 339–344. doi:10.1016/j.emj.2004.04.009

Axelson, M. (2002). Smartwear. *Australian CPA, 72*(4), 62–64.

Bachman, J. G., Smith, C. G., & Slesinger, J. A. (1966). Control, performance and satisfaction: An analysis of structural and individual effects. *Journal of Personality and Social Psychology, 4*, 127–136. doi:10.1037/h0023615

Badham, R., Couchman, P., & McLoughlin, I. P. (1997). *Implementing vulnerable socio-technical change projects. Innovation, organizational change and technology.* London: ITB Press.

Bal, D. J., Wilding, R., & Gundry, J. (2000). Virtual teaming in the agile supply chain. *The International Journal of Logistics Management, 10*(2), 71–82. doi:10.1108/09574099910806003

Bales, R. (1950). *Interaction process analysis.* Cambridge, MA: Addison Wesley.

Barge, J. K., & Hirokawa, R. Y. (1989). Toward a communication competency model of group leadership. *Small Group Behavior, 20*(2), 167–189. doi:10.1177/104649648902000203

Barnard, C. I. (1938). *The functions of the executive.* Cambridge, MA: Harvard University Press.

Barry, D. (1991). Managing the bossless team: Lessons in distributed leadership. *Organizational Dynamics, 20,* 31–47. doi:10.1016/0090-2616(91)90081-J

Bass, B. M. (1990). *Bass and Stodgill's handbook of leadership.* New York: Free Press.

Bass, B. M. (1990). *Handbook of leadership.* New York: Free Press.

Bass, B. M., & Stogdill, R. M. (1990). *Bass and Stogdill's handbook of leadership: Theory, research, and managerial applications* (3rd ed.). New York: Simon & Schuster.

Bass, B. M. (1990). From transactional to transformational leadership: Learning to share the vision. *Organisational Dynamics, 18*(3), 19-31.

Beck, U., & Beck-Gernsheim, E. (1994). *Individualization.* London: Sage.

Becker, A., Carte, T., & Chidambaram, L. (2006). Shared realms of consideration in virtual teams: Some field-based experiences. In *Proceedings of the Americas Conference on Information Systems*, Acapulco, Mexico.

Beijerse, R. P. (1999). Questions in knowledge management: Defining and conceptualizing a phenomenon. *Journal of Knowledge Management, 3*(2), 94–109. doi:10.1108/13673279910275512

Belbin, R. M. (1986). *Management teams.* London: Heinemann.

Bell, B. S., & Kozlowski, S. W. J. (2002). A typology of virtual teams: Implications for effective leadership. *Group & Organization Management, 27*(1), 14–49. doi:10.1177/1059601102027001003

Bell, B. S., & Kozlowski, S. W. J. (2002). A typology of virtual teams: Implications for effective leadership. *Group & Organization Management, 27*(1), 14–49. doi:10.1177/1059601102027001003

Bennett, N., Wise, C., Woods, P., & Harvey, J. (2003). *Distributed Leadership.* Nottingham, UK: National College for School Leadership.

Bennett, R. (1997). Effective set advising. In A. Mumford (Ed.), *Action learning at work* (pp. 179-182). Aldershot, UK: Gower.

Bennis, W., & Nanus, B. (1985). *Leaders: The strategies for taking charge.* New York: Harper and Row.

Berge, Z. L., & Collins, M. P. (2000). Perceptions of e-moderators about their roles and functions in moderating electronic mailing lists. *Distance Education, 21*(1), 81–100. doi:10.1080/0158791000210106

Berner, E. S., & Adams, B. (2004). Added value of video compared to audio lectures for distance learning. *International Journal of Medical Informatics, 73*(2), 189–193. doi:10.1016/j.ijmedinf.2003.12.001

Bernhardt, H. R., Killworth, P., et al. (1982). Informant accuracy in social network data V. *Social Science Research, 11,* 30-66.

Beveren, J. V. (2002). The model of knowledge acquisition that refocuses knowledge management. *Journal of Knowledge Management, 6*(1), 18–22. doi:10.1108/13673270210417655

Binney, D. (2001). The knowledge management spectrum - understanding the KM landscape. *Journal of Knowledge Management, 5*(1), 33–42. doi:10.1108/13673270110384383

Bird, L. (2006). *Action learning sets: The case for running them online.* Retrieved May 5, 2006 from http://www.coventry.ac.uk/iped/papers/downloads/workbasedlearningwksp4jan2006/LenBirdActionLearningSetsOnline.doc

Blake, R. R., & Mouton, S. J. (1978). *The new managerial grid.* Houston, TX: Gulf.

Blanchard, A. L., & Markus, M. L. (2002, January). *Sense of virtual community: Maintaining the experience of belonging.* Paper presented at the 35th Hawai International Conference on Systems Sciences.

Blau, P. M. (1964). *Exchange and power in social life.* New York: John Wiley & Sons.

Bligh, M., Pearce, C. L., & Kohles, J. (2006). The importance of self and shared leadership in team based knowledge work: Toward a meso-level model of leadership dynamics. *Journal of Managerial Psychology, 21,* 296–318. doi:10.1108/02683940610663105

Bloom, P. J., & Bella, J. (2005). Investment in leadership training - the payoff for early childhood education. *Young Children, 2005*(January), 32–40.

Bogdanowicz, M. S., & Bailey, E. K. (2002). The value of knowledge and the value of the new knowledge worker: Generation X in the new economy. *Journal of European Industrial Training, 26,* 125–129. doi:10.1108/03090590210422003

Boissevain, J. (1974). *Friends of friends. Networks, manipulators and coalitions.* Oxford: Basil Blackwell.

Boon, S.D. & Holmes, J. G. (1991). The dynamics of interpersonal trust: resolving uncertainty in the face of risk. In R. A. Hinde & J. Groebel (Eds.), *Cooperation and Presocial Behavior.* (pp. 190-211). Cambridge, UK: Cambridge University Press.

Borgatti, S. P., & Foster, P. C. (2003). The network paradigm in organizational research: A review and typology. *Journal of Management, 6*(23), 991-1013.

Borgatti, S. P., Everett, M.G., et al. (2002). *Ucinet 6 for windows.* Harvard: Analytic Technologies.

Bourne, H., & Jenkins, M. (2005). Eliciting managers' personal values: An adaptation of the laddering interview method. *Organizational Research Methods, 8*(4), 410–428. doi:10.1177/1094428105280118

Bower, J. L., & Gilbert, C. G. (2007). How managers' everyday decisions create or destroy your company's strategy. *Harvard Business Review, 2007*(February), 72–79.

Boyatzis, R. E. (1982). *The Competent Manager: a model for effective performance.* New York, NY: Wiley.

Bradshaw, P., Powell, S., & Terrell, I. (2004). Building a community of practice: Technological and social implications for a distributed team. In P. Hildreth & C. Kimble (Eds.), *Knowledge networks: Innovation through communities of practice* (pp. 184-201). Hershey, PA: Idea Group Publishing.

Braye, R. H. (2001). Servant-leadership: Belief and practice in women-led businesses. *Dissertation Abstracts International, 61*(07), 2799. (UMI No. 9981536).

Breiger, R. (2004). The analysis of social networks. In M. Hardy & A. Bryman (Eds.), *Handbook of data analysis.* London: Sage.

Briggs-Myers, I. (1992). *Gifts differing.* Palo Alto, CA: Consulting Psychologists Press.

Brown, A. E., & Grant, G. G. (2005). Framing the frameworks: A review of IT governance research. *Communications of the AIS, 15,* 696–712.

Brown, C. (1997). Examining the emergence of hybrid IS governance solutions: Evidence from a single case site. *Information Systems Research, 8*(1), 69–94. doi:10.1287/isre.8.1.69

Brown, C. V. (1999). Horizontal mechanisms under differing IS organization contexts. *MIS Quarterly, 23*(3), 421–454. doi:10.2307/249470

Brown, C., & Magill, S. L. (1994). Alignment of the IS functions with the enterprise: Toward a model of antecedents. *MIS Quarterly, 18*(4), 371–403. doi:10.2307/249521

Brown, H. G., Poole, M. S., & Rodgers, T. L. (2004). Interpersonal traits, comlementarity and trust in virtual collaboration. *Journal of Management Information Systems, 20*(4), 115–137.

Brown, H. G., Poole, M. S., et al. (2004). Interpersonal traits, complementarity and trust in virtual collaboration. *Journal of Management of Information Systems, 20*(4), 115-137.

Brown, J. S., & Duguid, P. (2000). *The social life of information.* Boston: Harvard University Press.

Brown, J., & Duguid, P. (1998). Organizing knowledge. *California Management Review, 40*(3), 90–111.

Burke, K., & Chidambaram, L. (1999). How much bandwidth is enough? A longitudinal examination of media characteristics and group outcomes. *MIS Quarterly, 23*(4), 557–580. doi:10.2307/249489

Burke, R. J., & Wilcox, D. S. (1971). Bases of supervisory power and subordinate job satisfactions. *Canadian Journal of Behavioural Science, 3*, 183–193. doi:10.1037/h0082260

Burns, J. M. (1978). *Leadership*. New York, NY: Harper and Row.

Burns, J. M. (1982). *Leadership*. New York: HarperCollins Publishers.

Burns, P. (2001). Report on a virtual action learning set. *Action Learning News, 20*(2), 2–7.

Burt, R. (2005). *Brokerage and closure. An introduction to social capital.* New York: Oxford University Press.

Burt, R., & Knez, M. (1996). Trust and third-party gossip. In R. M. Kramer & T. R. Tyler (Eds.), *Trust in organizations. Frontiers of theory and research* (pp. 68-89). Thousand Oaks: Sage.

Callon, M. (1986). The sociology of an actor-network: The case of the electric vehicle. In M. Callon, J. Law, & A. Roip (Eds.) *Mapping the dynamics of science and technology: Sociology of science in the real world* (pp. 19-34).

Callon, M. (1994). Is science a public good? *Science, Technology & Human Values, 19*(4), 395–424. doi:10.1177/016224399401900401

Carroll, J.-M., Neale, D.-C., Isenhour, P.-L., Rosson, M.-B., & McCrickard, S. (2003). Notification and awareness: Synchronizing task-oriented collaborative activity. *International Journal of Human-Computer Studies, 58*, 605–632. doi:10.1016/S1071-5819(03)00024-7

Carroll, J.-M., Neale, D.-C., Isenhour, P.-L., Rosson, M.-B., & McCrickard, S. (2003). Notification and awareness: Synchronizing task-oriented collaborative activity. *International Journal of Human-Computer Studies, 58*, 605–632. doi:10.1016/S1071-5819(03)00024-7

Carte, T. A., & Chidambaram, L. (2004). A capabilities-based theory of technology deployment in diverse teams: Leapfrogging the pitfalls of diversity and leveraging its potential with collaborative technology. *Journal of the AIS, 5*(11-12), 448–471.

Cascio, W. F. (1999). Virtual workplaces: Implications for organizational behavior. In C. L. Cooper & D. M. Rousseau (Eds.), *Trends in organizational behavior: The virtual organization*. Chichester, England: Wiley.

Cascio, W. F., & Shurygailo, S. (2003). E-leadership and virtual teams. *Organizational Dynamics, 31*(4), 362-376.

Cascio, W., & Shurygailo, S. (2003). E-leadership and virtual teams. *Organizational Dynamics, 31*(4), 362–376. doi:10.1016/S0090-2616(02)00130-4

Castro, M. (2004). *The community of practice ecosystem: On competition, cooperation, differentiation, and the role of blogs* [Electronic Version 0.9]. Retrieved July 5, 2004, from http://www.knowledgeboard.com/lib/1567

Castro, M. (2006). *Revisiting communities of practice: From fisherman guilds to the global village.* Paper presented at the 3rd European Knowledge Management Network Summer School, Madrid, Spain. Retrieved February 29, 2008, from http://www.knowledgeboard.com/item/2713

Cattell, R. B., Eber, H. W., & Tatsuoka, M. M. (1970). *Handbook for the 16PF.* Illinois: IPAT.

Caulat, G. (2006). Virtual leadership. *The Ashridge Journal.* Retrieved June 20, 2007, from http://www.ashridge.com/360

Certina, K. (1997). Sociality with objects: Social relations in postsocial knowledge societies. *Theory, Culture & Society, 14*(4), 1–30. doi:10.1177/026327697014004001

Charan, R. (1976). Classroom techniques in teaching by the case method. *Academy of Management Review*, (3): 116–123. doi:10.2307/257280

Chau, P. Y. K., & Tam, K. Y. (1997). Factors affecting the adoption of open systems: An exploratory study. *MIS Quarterly, 21*(1), 1–24. doi:10.2307/249740

Chen, L. (2004). *An examination of relationship among leadership behavior, knowledge sharing, and organizational marketing effectiveness in professional service firms that have been engaged in strategic alliances.* Unpublished doctoral dissertation, Nova Southeastern

University (Proquest Digital Dissertation Abstract, 3125998, 303).

Chong, S. C. (2006). KM implementation and its influence on performance: An empirical evidence from Malaysian multimedia super corridor (MSC) companies. *Journal of Information and Knowledge Management, 5*(1), 21–37. doi:10.1142/S0219649206001293

Chong, S. C. (2006). KM critical success factors: A comparison of perceived importance vs implementation in Malaysian ICT companies. *The Learning Organization, 13*(3), 230–256. doi:10.1108/09696470610661108

Chua, A. (2006). The role of technology in supporting communities of practice. In E. Coakes (Ed.), *Encyclopedia of communities of practice in information and knowledge management* (pp. 447-452). Hershey, PA: Idea Group Reference.

Chua, A., & Lam, W. (2005). Why KM projects fail: A multi-case analysis. *Journal of Knowledge Management, 9*(3), 6–17. doi:10.1108/13673270510602737

Chyung, S. Y., & Vachon, M. (2005). An investigation of the profiles of satisfying and dissatisfying factors in e-learning. *Performance Improvement Quality, 18*(2), 97–103.

Clawson, V. K., & Bostrom, R. P. (1996). Research-driven facilitation training for computer-supported environments. *Group Decision and Negotiation, 5*(1), 7–29.

Coakes, E., & Clarke, S. (2006). The concept of communities of practice. In E. Coakes (Ed.), *Encyclopedia of communities of practice in information and knowledge management* (pp. 92-96). Hershey, PA: Idea Group Reference.

Cohen, D. & Prusak, L. (2001). *In good company: How social capital makes organizations works.* Boston, MA: Harvard Business School Press.

Coleman, J. (1988). Social capital in the creation of human capital. *American Journal of Sociology, 94,* 95-120.

Collins, J. (1998). Level five leadership: The triumph of humility and fierce resolve. *Harvard Business Review,* (January): 66–79.

Collins, S. (2001). Expert help a mouse click away. *The New Zealand Herald.* Auckland, New Zealand.

Conger, J. A., & Kanungo, R. N. (1987). Toward a behavioral theory of charismatic leadership in organizational settings. *Academy of Management Review, 12*(4), 637–647. doi:10.2307/258069

Conger, J. A., & Pearce, C. L. (2003). A landscape of opportunities: Future research on shared leadership. In C. L. Pearce & J. A. Conger (Eds.), *Shared leadership: Reframing the hows and whys of leadership* (pp. 285-303). Thousand Oaks, CA: Sage.

Conger, J. A., Spreitzer, G., & Lawler, E. E. (Eds.). (1999). *The leader's change handbook.* San Francisco: Jossey-Bass.

Conger, J., & Toegel, G. (2003). Action learning and multirater feedback: Pathways to leadership development. In S. Murphy & R. Riggio (Eds.), *The future of leadership development* (pp. 133-151). Mahwah, NJ: Lawrence Erlbaum Associates.

Connelly, C. E., & Kelloway, E. K. (2003). Predictors of employee's perception of knowledge sharing cultures. *Leadership and Organization Development Journal, 24*(5), 294–301. doi:10.1108/01437730310485815

Connerley, M. L., & Mael, F. A. (2001). The importance and invasiveness of student team selection criteria. *Journal of Management Education, 25,* 471–494. doi:10.1177/105256290102500502

Cordery, J., Soo, C., Kirkman, B., Rosen, B., & Mathieu, J. (in press). Leading parallel global virtual teams: Lessons from Alcoa. *Organizational Dynamics.*

Cordoba, J., & Robson, W. (2006). Understanding communities of practice to support collaborative research. In E. Coakes (Ed.), *Encyclopedia of communities of practice in information and knowledge management* (pp. 558-564). Hershey, PA: Idea Group Reference.

Cosley, D., Frankowski, D., Kiesler, S., Terveen, L., & Riedl, J. (2005, April 2-7). *How oversight improves member-maintained communities.* Paper presented at the SIGCHI 2005 Conference on Human factors in Computing Systems, Portland, Oregon, USA.

Costa, A., & Kallick, B. (1993). Through the lens of a critical friend. *Educational Leadership, 51*(2), 49–51.

Costa, A., & Kallick, B. (1995). Through the lens of a critical friend. In A. Coster & B. Kallick (Eds.), *Assessment in the learning organization: Shifting the paradigm* (pp. 153-156). Alexandria, VA: ASCD.

Cox, A. (2005). What are communities of practice? A comparative review of four seminal works. *Journal of Information Science, 31*, 527–540. doi:10.1177/0165551505057016

Cox, J. F., Pearce, C. L., & Perry, M. L. (2003). Toward a model of shared leadership and distributed influence in the innovation process. In C. L. Pearce & J. A. Conger (Eds.), *Shared leadership: Reframing the hows and whys of leadership* (pp. 48-76). Thousand Oaks, CA: Sage.

Cragg, P., & King, M. (1993). Small firm computing: Motivators and inhibitors. *MIS Quarterly*, 47–59. doi:10.2307/249509

Cramton, C. D. (2001). The mutual knowledge problem and its consequences for distributed collaboration. *Organization Science, 12*(3), 346–371. doi:10.1287/orsc.12.3.346.10098

Cramton, C. D. (2001). The mutual knowledge problem and its consequences for distributed collaboration. *Organization Science, 12*(3), 346–371. doi:10.1287/orsc.12.3.346.10098

Cramton, C. D. (2002). Finding common ground in dispersed collaboration. *Organizational Dynamics, 30*, 356–367. doi:10.1016/S0090-2616(02)00063-3

Cramton, C. D. (2002). Finding common ground in dispersed collaboration. *Organizational Dynamics, 30*, 356–367. doi:10.1016/S0090-2616(02)00063-3

Cranefield, J., & Yoong, P. (2007). Inter-organisational knowledge transfer: The role of the gatekeeper. *International Journal of Knowledge and Learning, 3*(1), 121–138. doi:10.1504/IJKL.2007.012604

Cranefield, J., & Yoong, P. (2007). The role of the translator/ interpreter in knowledge transfer environments. *Journal of Knowledge and Process Management, 14*(2), 95–103. doi:10.1002/kpm.271

Crawford, C. B. (2005). Effects of transformational leadership and organizational position on knowledge management. *Journal of Knowledge Management, 9*(6), 6–16. doi:10.1108/13673270510629927

Crawford, L. H. (2003). Assessing and developing the project management competence of individuals. In J. R. Turner, (Ed.), *People in project management.* Aldershot, UK: Gower.

Creswell, J. W. (1998). *Qualitative inquiry and research design.* Thousand Oaks, CA: Sage Publications.

Cross, R., & Prusak, L. (2002). The people who make organizations go - or stop. *Harvard Business Review, 80*(6), 104–112.

Cross, R., & Prusak, L. (2002). The people who make organizations go or stop. *Harvard Business Review, 80*(6), 104-112.

Cross, R., Parker, A., Prusak, L., & Borgatti, S. P. (2001). Knowing what we know: Supporting knowledge creation and sharing in social networks. *Organizational Dynamics, 30*(2), 100–120. doi:10.1016/S0090-2616(01)00046-8

Cummings, J. N. (2004). Work groups, structural diversity, and knowledge sharing in a global organization. *Management Science, 50*(3), 352-364.

Cummings, J. N., & Cross, R. (2003). Structural properties of work groups and their consequences for performance. *Social Networks, 25*, 197-210.

Cyboran, V. (2005). Fostering workplace learning through online journaling . *Performance Improvement, 44*(7), 34–39. doi:10.1002/pfi.4140440709

Daassi, M. (2006). *La conscience collective au sein des équipes virtuelles: Déterminants, mesure set nature dynamiques.* Unpublished doctoral dissertation, University of Grenoble, France.

Daassi, M. (2006). *La conscience collective au sein des équipes virtuelles: Déterminants, mesure set nature dynamiques.* Unpublished doctoral dissertation, University of Grenoble, France.

Daassi, M., & Favier, M. (2005). Groupware and team aware. In S. Dasgupta (Ed.), *Encyclopedia of virtual communities and technologies*. Hershey, PA: Information Science Reference.

Daassi, M., & Favier, M. (2005). Groupware and team aware. In S. Dasgupta (Ed.), *Encyclopedia of virtual communities and technologies*. Hershey, PA: Information Science Reference.

Daassi, M., Daassi, C., & Favier, M. (2005). Integrating visualization techniques in groupware interfaces. In S. Dasgupta (Ed.), *encyclopedia of virtual communities and technologies*. Hershey, PA: Information Science Reference.

Daassi, M., Daassi, C., & Favier, M. (2005). Integrating visualization techniques in groupware interfaces. In S. Dasgupta (Ed.), *encyclopedia of virtual communities and technologies*. Hershey, PA: Information Science Reference.

Daassi, M., Jawadi, N., Favier, M., & Kalika, M. (2006). An empirical investigation of trust's impact on collective awareness development in virtual teams. *Int. J. Networking and Virtual Organisations, 3*(4), 378–394. doi:10.1504/IJNVO.2006.011867

Daft, R. L., & Lengel, R. H. (1986). Organizational information requirements, media richness, and structural design. *Management Science, 32*(5), 554–571. doi:10.1287/mnsc.32.5.554

Dansereau, F., Cashman, J., & Graen, G. B. (1973). Instrumentality theory and equity theory as complementary approaches in predicting the relationship of leadership and turnover among managers. *Organizational Behavior and Human Performance, 10*, 184–200. doi:10.1016/0030-5073(73)90012-3

Darroch, J. (2003). Developing a measure of knowledge management behaviors and practices. *Journal of Knowledge Management, 7*, 41–54. doi:10.1108/13673270310505377

Davenport, T. H. (1999). *Human capital: What it is and why people invest it.* San Francisco, CA: Jossey-Bass.

Davenport, T. H., & Prusak, L. (1998). *Working knowledge: How organizations manage what they know.* Boston, MA: Harvard Business School Press.

Davenport, T. H., & Prusak, L. (2000). *Working knowledge.* Cambridge, MA: Harvard Business School Press.

Davenport, T., & Prusak, L. (1998). *Working knowledge: How organizations manage what they know.* Boston: Harvard Business School Press.

Davis, D. D. (2004). The tao of leadership in virtual teams. *Organizational Dynamics, 33*, 47–62. doi:10.1016/j.orgdyn.2003.11.004

Davis, D. D., & Bryant, J. L. (2003). Influence at a distance: Leadership in global virtual teams. In W. H. Mobley & P. W. Dorfman (Eds.), *Advances in global leadership* (Vol. 3, pp. 303-340). Oxford, UK: Elsevier.

Davis, F. D. (1989). Perceived usefulness, Perceived ease of use, and user acceptance of information technology. *MIS Quarterly, 13*(3), 319–340. doi:10.2307/249008

Davis, H., & Fill, K. (2007). Embedding blended learning in a university's teaching culture: Experiences and reflections. *British Journal of Educational Technology, 38*(5), 817–828. doi:10.1111/j.1467-8535.2007.00756.x

Day, C. (2003). What successful leadership in schools looks like: Implications for policy and practice. In B. Davies & J. West-Burnham (Eds.), *Handbook of educational leadership* (pp. 87-204). London: Pearson Education.

Day, C., & Harris, A. (2002). Teacher leadership, reflective practice, and school improvement. In K. Leithwood & P. Hallinger (Eds.), *Second international handbook of educational leadership and administration* (pp. 957-978). Dordrecht, The Netherlands: Kluwer Academic Publishers.

De Hoogh, A. H. B., Den Hartog, D. N., Koopman, P. L., Thierry, H., Van den Berg, P. T., Van der Weide, J. G., & Wilderom, C. P. M. (2005). Leader motives, charismatic leadership, and subordinates' work attitude in the profit and voluntary sector. *The Leadership Quarterly, 16*, 17–38. doi:10.1016/j.leaqua.2004.10.001

De Long, D. W., & Fahey, L. (2000). Diagnosing cultural barriers to knowledge management. *The Academy of Management Executive, 14*(4), 113–129.

De Rooij, J., Verburg, R., Andriessen, E., & Den Hartog, D. (2007). Barriers for shared understanding in virtual teams: A leader perspective. *The Electronic Journal for Virtual Organizations and Networks, 9*, 64–77.

de Vreede, G. J., Boonstra, J., & Niederman, F. (2002). What is effective GSS facilitation? A qualitative inquiry into participants' perceptions. In *Proceedings of the 35th Annual Hawaii International Conference on System Sciences, 2002* (pp. 616-627).

Dennis, A. R., Kinney, S. T., & Hung, Y.-T. C. (1999). Gender differences in the effects of media richness. *Small Group Research, 30*, 405–437. doi:10.1177/104649649903000402

Dennis, A. R., Kinney, S. T., & Hung, Y.-T. C. (1999). Gender differences in the effects of media richness. *Small Group Research, 30*, 405–437. doi:10.1177/104649649903000402

Dennis, R. S., & Bocarnea, M. (2005). Development of the servant leadership assessment instrument. *Leadership and Organization Development Journal, 26*(8), 600–615. doi:10.1108/01437730510633692

Dennis, R. S., & Winston, B. E. (2003). A factor analysis of Page and Wong's servant leadership instrument. *Leadership and Organization Development Journal, 24*(8), 455–459. doi:10.1108/01437730310505885

DeRosa, D. M., Hantula, D. A., Kock, N. F., & D'Arcy, J. (2004). Trust and leadership in virtual teamwork: A media naturalness perspective. *Human Resource Management, 43*(2-3), 219–232. doi:10.1002/hrm.20016

DeSanctis, G., & Monge, P. (1999). Communication processes for virtual organizations. *Organization Science, 10*(6), 693–703. doi:10.1287/orsc.10.6.693

DeSanctis, G., & Poole, M. S. (1997). Transitions in teamwork in new organizational forms. In B. Markovsky (Ed.), *Advances in group processes* (Vol. 14, pp. 157-176). Greenwich, CT: JAI Press.

DeSanctis, G., & Poole, M. S. (1997). Transitions in teamwork in new organizational forms. *Advances in Group Processes, 14*, 157–176.

Desouza, K. C., Jayaramam, A., & Evaristo, R. (2002). *Knowledge management in non-collocated environments: A look at centralized vs. distributed design approaches.* Paper presented at the HICSS.

Dfouni, M. (2002). *Knowledge leaders' critical issues: An international Delphi studies.* Unpublished master's thesis, Concordia University, Montreal, Canada (Proquest Digital Dissertation Abstract, MQ77669, 211).

Dineen, B. R., & Noe, R. A. (2003). The impact of team fluidity and its implications for human resource management research and practice. *Research in Personal and Human Resource Management, 22*, 1–38. doi:10.1016/S0742-7301(03)22001-6

Dirks, & Ferrin (2001). The role of trust in organizational settings. *Organizational Science, 4*(12), 450-467.

Doll, W. J., & Torkzadeh, G. (1987). The relationship of MIS steering committee to size of firm and formalization of MIS planning. *Communications of the ACM, 30*(11), 972–978. doi:10.1145/32206.32213

Dominick, P., Aronson, Z., & Lechler, T. (2007). Transformational leadership and project success. In R. R. Reilly (Ed.), *The human side of project leadership,* (pp. 1-30). Newton Square, PA: Project Management Institute.

Doolin, B., & Lowe, A. (2002). To reveal is to critique: Actor-network theory and critical information systems research. *Journal of Information Technology, 17*, 69–78. doi:10.1080/02683960210145986

Dotlich, D., Noel, J., & Walker, N. (2004). *Leadership passages.* San Francisco: Jossey-Bass.

Dourish, P., & Bellotti, V. (1992). Awareness and coordination in shared workspace. In . *Proceedings of the, CSCW92*, 107–114.

Drew, S. (2003). Strategic uses of e-commerce by SMEs in the east of England. *European Management Journal, 21*(1), 79. doi:10.1016/S0263-2373(02)00148-2

Drucker, P. (1993). *Post-capitalist society*. Oxford, UK: Butterworth Heinemann.

Drucker, P. F. (1959). *Landmarks of tomorrow*. New York: Harper.

Drucker, P. F. (1993). *Post-capitalist society*. New York: Harper Business.

Drury, S. L. (2005). Employee perceptions of servant leadership: Comparisons by level and with job satisfaction and organizational commitment. *Dissertation Abstracts International, 65*(09), 3457. (UMI No. 3146724).

Duarte, D. L., & Snyder, N. T. (1999). *Mastering virtual teams: Strategies, tools, and techniques that succeed*. San Francisco: Jossey-Bass Publishers.

Duarte, D. L., & Snyder, N. T. (1999). *Mastering virtual teams: Strategies, tools, and techniques that succeed*. San Francisco, CA: Jossey-Bass.

Dubé, L., Bourhis, A., & Jacob, R. (2006). Towards a typology of virtual communities of practice. *Interdisciplinary Journal of Information, Knowledge, and Management, 1*, 69–93.

Dubé, L., Bourhis, A., & Jacob, R. (2006). Towards a typology of virtual communities of practice. *Interdisciplinary Journal of Information, Knowledge, and Management, 1*, 69–93.

Dubrovsky, V., Kiesler, S., & Sethna, B. (1991). The equalization phenomenon: Status effects in computer-mediated and face-to-face decision making groups. *Human-Computer Interaction, 6*(2), 119–146. doi:10.1207/s15327051hci0602_2

Dulevicz, V., Turner, J. R., & Müller, R. (2006). *Assessment of project managers using the leadership dimensions questionnaire: An international study* (Henley Working Paper Series). Henley Management College, Henley-on-Thames, UK.

Dulewicz, & Higgs, M. (2005). Assessing leadership styles and organisational context. *Journal of Managerial Psychology, 20*(1), 105-123.

Dulewicz, V., & Higgs, M. J. (2000). Emotional intelligence: a review and evaluation study. *Journal of Managerial Psychology, 15*(4), 341–368.

Durnell Cramton, C., & Orvis, K. L. (2003). Overcoming barriers to information sharing in virtual teams. In C. B. Gibson & S. G. Cohen (Eds.), *Virtual teams that work: Creating conditions for virtual teams effectiveness* (pp. 214-230). San Francisco: Jossey-Bass.

Dvir, D., Sadeh, A., & Malach-Pines, A. (2006). Project and project managers: The relationship between project manager's personality, project types and project success. *Project Management Journal, 37*(5), 36-48.

Earl, M., & Scott, I. (1998). *What on Earth is a CKO?* London: London Business School Press.

Ebbeck, M., & Waninganayake, M. (2003). *Early childhood professionals: Leading today and tomorrow*. Sydney, Australia: MacLennan & Petty.

Efimova, L., & Hendrick, S. (2005). *In search for a virtual settlement: An exploration of Weblog community boundaries*. Updated version of a paper presented at the Communities and Technologies Conference 2005. Retrieved September 3, 2008, from https://doc.telin.nl/dsweb/Get/Document-46041/weblog_community_boundaries.pdf

Ein-Dor, P., & Segev, E. (1982). Organizational context and MIS structure: Some empirical evidence. *MIS Quarterly, 6*(3), 55–69. doi:10.2307/248656

Eisenhardt, K. M. (1989). Building theories from case study research. *Academy of Management Review, 14*(4), 532-550.

Elangovan, A. R., & Jia, L. X. (2000). Effects of perceived power of supervisor on subordinate work attitudes. *Leadership and Organization Development Journal, 21*, 319–328. doi:10.1108/01437730010343095

Elster, J. (1983). *Sour grapes: Studies in the subversion of rationality*. Cambridge, MA: Cambridge University Press.

Ensley, M. D., Hmieleski, K. M., & Pearce, C. L. (2006). The importance of vertical and shared leadership within new venture top management teams: Implications for the performance of startups. *The Leadership Quarterly, 17,* 217–231. doi:10.1016/j.leaqua.2006.02.002

Erchul, W. P., Raven, B. H., & Ray, A. G. (2001). School psychologists' perceptions of social power bases in teacher consultation. *Journal of Educational & Psychological Consultation, 12,* 1–23. doi:10.1207/S1532768XJEPC1201_01

Escriba-Moreno, M. A., Canet-Giner, M. T., & Moreno-Luzon, M. (2008). TQM and teamwork effectiveness: The intermediate role of organizational design. *The Quality Management Journal, 15*(3), 41–59.

Evaristo, R. (2003). The management of distributed projects across cultures. *Journal of Global Information Management, 11,* 58–70.

Fedor, D. B., Ghosh, S., Caldwell, S. D., Maurer, T. J., & Singhal, V. R. (2003). The effects of knowledge management on team members' rating of project success and impact. *Decision Sciences, 34,* 513–539. doi:10.1111/j.1540-5414.2003.02395.x

Fernandez, R. M., & Gould, R. V. (1994). A dilemma of state power: Brokerage and influence in the national health policy domain. *American Journal of Sociology, 99,* 1455-91.

Fidler, B. (1997). School leadership: Some key ideas. *School Leadership & Management, 17*(1), 23–27. doi:10.1080/13632439770140

Fiedler, F. E. (1967). *A theory of leadership effectiveness.* New York: McGraw-Hill.

Fink, D. (2005). Developing leaders for their future not our past. In M. Coles & G. Southworth (Eds.), *Developing leadership: Creating the schools of tomorrow* (pp. 1-20). Maidenhead, UK: Open University Press.

Fischer, G. (2001). Communities of interest: Learning through the interaction of multiple knowledge systems. In *Proceedings of the 24th Annual Information Systems Research Seminar In Scandinavia (IRIS'24), Ulvik, Norway* (pp. 1-14).

Fisher, B. A. (1974). *Small group decision making: Communication and the group process.* New York: McGraw-Hill.

Fluss, D. (2002). Why knowledge management is a "dirty" word. *Customer Interface, 15*(2), 40–41.

Fontaine, M. (2001). Keeping communities of practice afloat: Understanding and fostering roles in communities. *Knowledge Management Review, 4*(4), 16–21.

Foreman, M. (2002). Virtual networking for Kiwi entrepreneurs. *The Independent.* Auckland, New Zealand.

Fornell, C., & Larcker, D. F. (1981). Evaluating structural equation models with unobservable variables and measurement error. *JMR, Journal of Marketing Research, 18*(1), 39–50. doi:10.2307/3151312

Forstenlechner, I., & Lettice, F. (2007). Cultural difference in motivating global knowledge workers. *Equal Opportunities International, 26*(8), 823–833. doi:10.1108/02610150710836154

Frame, J. D. (1987). *Managing projects in organizations.* San Francisco: Jossey Bass.

Frederick, H. H., & Carswell, P. J. (2001). *Global entrepreneurship monitor: New Zealand.* Auckland, New Zealand: New Zealand Centre for Innovation and Entrepreneurship.

Frick, D. M. (2004). *Robert K. Greenleaf: A life of servant leadership.* San Francisco: Berrett-Kohler Publishers.

Friedman, R. A., & Podolny, J. (1982). Differentiation of boundary spanning roles: Labor negotiations and implications for role conflict. *Administrative Science Quarterly, 1*(37), 28-47.

Friesen, S., & Clifford, P. (2003). *Working across different spaces to create communities of practice in teacher professional development.* Paper presented at the mICTE 2003 Multimedia, Information and Communication Technologies Conference, Badajoz, Spain.

Friesen, S., & Clifford, P. (2003). *Working across different spaces to create communities of practice in teacher professional development.* Paper presented at the mICTE 2003 Multimedia, Information and Communication Technologies Conference, Badajoz, Spain.

Fulk, J., & De Sanctis, G. (1995). Electronic communication and changing organizational forms. *Organization Science, 6*, 337–349. doi:10.1287/orsc.6.4.337

Furst, S., Blackburn, R., & Rosen, B. (1999). Virtual team effectiveness: A proposed research agenda. *Information Systems Journal, 9*(4), 249-269.

Gal, Y. (2004). The reward effect: A case study of failing to manage knowledge. *Journal of Knowledge Management, 8*(2), 73–83. doi:10.1108/13673270410529127

Gambetta, D. (1988). *Trust: Making and breaking cooperative relations.* Oxford, England: Basic Blackwell.

Gambetta, D. (1988). *Trust: Making and breaking cooperative relations.* Oxford, England: Basic Blackwell.

Gapp, R. (2002). The influence the system of profound knowledge has on the development of leadership and management within an organization. *Managerial Auditing Journal, 17*(6), 338–342. doi:10.1108/02686900210434131

Gefen, D., & Ridings, C. (2002). Implementation team responsiveness and user evaluation of customer relationship management: A quasi-experimental design study of social exchange theory. *Journal of Management Information Systems, 19*(1), 47–69.

Gengler, C. E., & Reynolds, T. J. (1995). Consumer understanding and advertising strategy: Analysis and strategic translation of laddering data. *Journal of Advertising Research, 35*(4), 19–33.

Geoghegan, N., Petriwskyj, A., Bower, L., & Geoghegan, D. (2003). Eliciting dimensions of leadership in educational leadership in early childhood education. *Journal of Australian Research in Early Childhood Education, 10*(1), 12–21.

Geraldi, J., & Adlbrecht, G. (2007). On faith, fact, and interaction in projects. *Project Management Journal, 38*(1), 32-43.

Gerber, B. (1995, Apr)... *Training. Minneapolis, 32*(Iss. 4), 36.

Gibson, C. B., & Manuel, J. A. (2003). Building trust: Effective multicultural communication processes in virtual teams. In C. B. Gibson & S. G. Cohen (Eds.), *Virtual teams that work: Creating conditions for virtual teams effectiveness* (pp. 59-86). San Francisco: Jossey-Bass.

Gibson, C., & Cohen, S. (Eds.). (2003). *Virtual teams that work: Creating conditions for virtual team effectiveness.* San Francisco: Jossey-Bass.

Giddens, A. (1994). Risk, trust, reflexivity. In *Reflexive Modernization.* U. Beck, A. Giddens, & S. Lash (Eds.), Cambridge, UK: Polity Press, 184-197.

Giddens, A. (1999). *The third way: The renewal of social democracy.* Malden, MA: Polity Press.

Gillham, B. (2000). *The research interview.* London: Continuum.

Gladstein, D. L. (1984). Groups in context: A model of task group effectiveness. *Administrative Science Quarterly, 29*(4), 499–517. doi:10.2307/2392936

Goldstein, I. L., & Ford, J. K. (2002). *Training in organizations: Needs assessment, development and evaluation* (4th ed.). Florence, KY: Wadsworth Publishing.

Goleman, D. (2004). What makes a leader? *Harvard Business Review*, 82–91.

Goleman, D. (2006). *Social intelligence: The new science of human telationships.* London: Hutchinson.

Goleman, D., Boyatzis, R., & McKee, A. (2002). *The new leaders.* Boston: Harvard Business School Press.

Gongla, P., & Rizzuto, C. R. (2001). Evolving communities of practice: IBM Global Services experience. *IBM Systems Journal, 40*(4), 842–862.

Goodbody, J. (2005). Critical success factors for global virtual teams. *Strategic Communication Management, 9*, 18–21.

Goodbody, J. (2005). Critical success factors of global virtual teams. *Strategic Communication Management, 9*, 18–21.

Gove, S., Clark, M. A., & Boyd, B. (1999). *Moving metaphors: Recipes for teaching management via ex-*

periential exercises. Paper presented at the Academy of Management Annual Meeting.

Grabowski, M., & Roberts, K. H. (1999). Risk mitigation in virtual organizations. *Organization Science, 10*(6), 704–721. doi:10.1287/orsc.10.6.704

Grandon, E., & Pearson, J. M. (2003). Strategic value and adoption of electronic commerce: An empirical study of Chilean small and medium businesses. *Journal of Global Information Technology Management, 6*(3).

Granovetter, M. S. (1973). The strength of weak ties. *American Journal of Sociology, 81*, 1287-1303.

Grant, H., & Crutchfield, L. (2008). The hub of leadership: Lessons from the social sector. *Leader to Leader, 48*, 45–52. doi:10.1002/ltl.280

Grant, R. M. (1996). Towards a knowledge-based theory of the firm. *Strategic Management Journal, 17*, 102–122.

Gray, B. (2004). Informal learning in an online community of practice. *Journal of Distance Education, 19*(1), 20–35.

Gray, D. (1999). *Work-based learning, action learning and the virtual paradigm.* Retrieved May 5, 2006, from http://www.leeds.ac.uk/educol/documents/00001260.htm

Gray, D. (1999). *Work-based learning, action learning and the virtual paradigm.* Retrieved May 5, 2006, from www.leeds.ac.uk/educol/documents/00001260.htm

Gray, P. H. (2001). The impact of knowledge repositories on power and control in the workplace. *Information Technology & People, 14*(4), 368–384. doi:10.1108/09593840110411167

Greenleaf, R. K. (1970). *The servant as leader.* Indianapolis, IN: The Greenleaf Center for Servant Leadership.

Greenleaf, R. K. (2002). *Servant leadership: A journey into the nature of legitimate power and greatness* (25th anniversary ed.). New York: Paulist Press.

Gronn, P. (2002). Distributed leadership. In K. Leithwood & P. Hallinger (Eds.), *Second international handbook of educational leadership and administration* (pp. 653-

696). Dordrecht, The Netherlands: Kluwer Academic Publishers.

Guastello, S. J. (2002). *Managing emergent phenomena.* Mahwah, NJ: Lawrence Erlbaum.

Gutman, J. (1982). A means-end chain model based on consumer categorization processes. *Journal of Marketing, 46*(2), 60–72. doi:10.2307/3203341

Gutwin, C., Greenberg, S., & Roseman, M. (1996). Workspace awareness in real-time distributed groupware: Framework, widgets, and evaluation. In *Proceedings of the HCI'96 Conference on People and Computers XI, Computer-Supported Cooperative Work.*

Gutwin, C., Greenberg, S., & Roseman, M. (1996). Workspace awareness in real-time distributed groupware: Framework, widgets, and evaluation. In *Proceedings of the HCI'96 Conference on People and Computers XI, Computer-Supported Cooperative Work.*

Hacker, M., & Lang, J. D. (2000). Designing a performance measurement system for a high technology virtual engineering team. *International Journal of Agile Management Systems, 2*(3), 225–232. doi:10.1108/14654650010356130

Hackman, J. R. (1990). *Groups that work (and those that don't).* San Francisco: Jossey-Bass.

Hackman, M. Z., & Johnson, C. E. (2000). *Leadership: A communication perspective.* Prospect Heights, IL: Waveland Press.

Hambley, L., O'Neill, T., & Kline, T. (2007). Virtual team leadership: Perspectives from the field. *International Journal of e-Collaboration, 3*(1), 40–64.

Hammersley, N., & Atkinson, P. (1983). *Ethnography: Principles in practice.* New York: Tavistock.

Handy, C. (1995). Trust and the virtual organization. How do you manage people whom you not see? *Harvard Business Review, 73*(3), 40-50.

Handy, C. B. (1982). *Understanding organizations.* London: Penguin

Hanneman, R. (2001). *Introduction to social network methods.* Department of Sociology, University of California, Riverside.

Hansen, M. (1999). The search-transfer problem: The role of weak ties in sharing knowledge across organization subunits. *Administrative Science Quarterly, 44,* 82-111.

Hansen, M. T., Nohria, N., & Tierney, T. (1999). What's your strategy for managing knowledge? *Harvard Business Review, 77*(March-April), 106–116.

Hanseth, O., & Monteiro, E. (1998). *Understanding information infrastructure.* Retrieved January, 29, 2004, from http://heim.ifi.uio.no/~oleha/Publications/bok.html

Haragadon, A. B. (1998). Firms as knowledge brokers: Lessons in pursuing continuous innovation. *Management Review, 40*(3), 209-227.

Hard, L. (2004). How leadership is understood in early childhood education and care. *Journal of Australian Research in Early Childhood Education, 11*(1), 123–131.

Hargreaves, A., & Fink, D. (2003). Sustaining leadership. In B. Davies & J. West-Burnham (Eds.), *Handbook of educational leadership and management* (pp. 435-450). London: Pearson Education.

Hargrove, R. (1998). *Mastering the art of creative collaboration.* New York: McGraw-Hill Companies.

Harragon, A., & Sutton, R. (1997). Technology brokering and innovation in a product development firm. *Administrative Science Quarterly, 42,* 716–749. doi:10.2307/2393655

Harris, A. (2003). Teacher leadership: A new orthodoxy. In B. Davies & J. West-Burnham (Eds.), *Handbook of educational leadership and management,* (pp. 44-50). London: Pearson Longman.

Harris, A. (2004). Distributed leadership and school improvement. *Educational Management Administration & Leadership, 32*(1), 11–24. doi:10.1177/1741143204039297

Hart, R. K., & Mcleod, P. L. (2003). Rethinking team building in geographically dispersed teams: One message at a time. *Organizational Dynamics, 31*(4), 352–361. doi:10.1016/S0090-2616(02)00131-6

Hartley, C., Brecht, M., et al. (1977). Subjective time estimates of work tasks by office workers. *Journal of Occupational Psychology, 50,* 23-36.

Hebert, S. C. (2004). The relationship of perceived servant leadership and job satisfaction from the follower's perspective. *Dissertation Abstracts International, 64*(11), 4118. (UMI No. 3112981).

Helmer, O. (1975). Foreword. In H. A. Linstone & M. Turoff (Eds.), *The Delphi method: Techniques and applications.* Reading, MA: Addison-Wesley Publishing Company.

Henderson-Kelly, L., & Pamphilon, B. (2000). Women's models of leadership in the childcare sector. *Australian Journal of Early Childhood, 25*(1), 26–31.

Henry, J. R., & Hartzler, M. (1998). *Tools for virtual teams.* Milwaukee, WI: ASQ Quality Press.

Herbst, J. D. (2004). Organizational servant leadership and its relationship to secondary school effectiveness. *Dissertation Abstracts International, 64*(11), 4001. (UMI No. 3110574).

Heron, J. (1999). *The complete facilitator's handbook.* London: Kogan Page.

Hersey, P., & Blanchard, K. (1982). *Management of organizational behaviour* (4th ed.). Englewood Cliffs, NJ: Prentice-Hall.

Hersey, P., & Blanchard, K. (1982). *Management of organizational behavior: Utilizing human resources.* Englewood Cliffs, NJ: Prentice Hall.

Hershey, P., & Blanchard, K. H. (1988). *Management of organizational behaviour,* 5th ed. Englewood Cliffs, NJ: Prentice Hall.

Herzberg, F. (1968). One more time: How do you motivate employees? *Harvard Business Review, 46*(1), 53–63.

Hesse, H. (2003). *Journey to the east* (H. Rosner, Trans.). New York: Picador USA.

Hildreth, P. M., Kimble, C., & Wright, P. (2000). Communities of practice in the distributed international environment. *Journal of Knowledge Management, 4*(1), 27–38. doi:10.1108/13673270010315920

Hinds, P. J., & Weisband, S. (2003). Knowledge sharing and shared understanding in virtual teams. In C. B. Gibson & S. G. Cohen (Eds.), *Virtual teams that work: Creating conditions for virtual team effectiveness* (pp. 21-36). San Francisco: Jossey-Bass.

Hinds, P. J., & Weisband, S. (2003). Knowledge sharing and shared understanding in virtual teams. In C. B. Gibson & S. G. Cohen (Eds.), *Virtual teams that work: Creating conditions for virtual team effectiveness* (pp. 21-36). San Francisco: Jossey-Bass.

Hinkin, T. R., & Schriesheim, C. A. (1989). Development and application of new scales to measure the French and Raven (1959) bases of social power. *The Journal of Applied Psychology, 74*, 561–567. doi:10.1037/0021-9010.74.4.561

Hislop, D. (2003). Linking human resource management and knowledge management via commitment. *Employee Relations, 25*(2), 182–202. doi:10.1108/01425450310456479

Hoch, J. E. (2007). *Shared and vertical leadership in product development teams.* Paper presented at the International Workshop on Teamwork (IWOT), Copenhagen, Denmark.

Holden, N. J. (2004). *National culture and diversity of knowledge-sharing styles.* Paper presented at the KMAP 2004, Taipei, Taiwan.

Holden, N., & Von Kortzfleisch, H. (2004). Why cross-cultural knowledge transfer is a form of translation in more ways than you think. *Knowledge and Process Management, 11*(2), 127–137. doi:10.1002/kpm.198

Hooijberg, R. (1996). A Multi-Directional approach toward leadership: An extension of the concept of behavioral complexity. *Human Relations, 49*(7), 917–946. doi:10.1177/001872679604900703

Hookway, C. (2003). How to be a virtue epistemologist. In M. DePaul & L. Zagzebski (Eds.), *Intellectual virtue: Perspectives from ethics and epistemology.* New York: Oxford University Press.

Hossain, L., & Wigand, R. (2004). ICT enabled virtual collaboration through trust. *Journal of Computer-Mediated Communication, 10*(1).

House, R. J. (1971). A path-goal theory of leader effectiveness. *Administrative Science Quarterly, 16*, 321–339. doi:10.2307/2391905

House, R. J., & Aditya, R. N. (1997). The social scientific study of leadership: quo vadis. *Journal of Management, 23*(3), 409–473. doi:10.1177/014920639702300306

House, R. J., & Aditya, R. N. (1997). The social scientific study of leadership: quo vadis. *Journal of Management, 23*(3), 409–473. doi:10.1177/014920639702300306

Howell, F. (1997). Action learning and action research in management education and development. In A. Mumford (Ed.), *Action learning at work* (pp. 375-385). Aldershot, UK: Gower.

Hoy, W. K., & Miskel, C. G. (1987). *Educational administration: Theory, research, and practice* (3rd ed.). New York: Random House.

Hoyt, C. L., & Blascovich, J. (2003). Transformational and transactional leadership in virtual teams and physical environments. *Small Group Research, 34*(6), 678–715. doi:10.1177/1046496403257527

Hoyt, C. L., & Blascovich, J. (2003). Transformational and transactional leadership in virtual teams and physical environments. *Small Group Research, 34*(6), 678–715. doi:10.1177/1046496403257527

Humes, M., & Reilly, A. H. (2007). Managing intercultural teams: The eorganization exercise. *Journal of Management Education, 32*(1), 118. doi:10.1177/1052562906294988

Hummel, J., & Lechner, U. (2002). *Social profiles of virtual communities.* Paper presented at the 35th Annual Hawaii International Conference on System Sciences, 2002.

Hunt, J. G., & Osborn, R. N. (1982). Toward a macro-oriented model of leadership: An odyssey. In J. G. Hunt, U. Sekaran, & C. A. Schriesheim (Eds.), *Leadership: Beyond establishment views* (pp. 196-221). Carbondale, IL: Southern Illinois University Press.

Huszczo, G. E. (1996). *Tools for team excellence*. Palo Alto, CA: Davies-Black.

Iacovou, C. L., Benbasat, I., & Dexter, A. S. (1995). Electronic data interchange and small organizations: Adoption and impact of technology. *MIS Quarterly, 19*(4), 465–485. doi:10.2307/249629

IPMA (2007). *ICB: IPMA competence baseline* Version 3.0. In C. Caupin, H. Knöpfl, G. Koch., H. Pannenbäcker, F- Pérez-Polo, & C. Seabury (Eds.), Njkerk, The Netherlands: International Project Management Association.

Irving, J. A. (2005). Servant leadership and the effectiveness of teams. *Dissertation Abstracts International, 66*(04), 1421. (UMI No. 3173207).

IT Governance Institute. (2003). *Board briefing on IT governance*. Retrieved May 3, 2007, from http://www.itgi.org

Ivancevich, J. M., & Donnely, J. H. (1970). Leader influence and performance. *Personnel Psychology, 23*, 539–549. doi:10.1111/j.1744-6570.1970.tb01371.x

Ives, B. (2008). *Tomoye: Bringing Web 2.0 to communities of practice*. Retrieved June 16, 2008, from http://www.theappgap.com/tomoye-bringing-web-20-to-communities-of-practice.html

Jago, A. G. (1982). Leadership: Perspectives in theory and research. *Management Science, 28*(3), 22. doi:10.1287/mnsc.28.3.315

James, K., Mann, J., & Creasy, J. (2007). Leaders as lead learners. *Management Learning, 38*(1), 79–94. doi:10.1177/1350507607073026

James, M., & Rykert, L. (1998). *From workplace to workspace: Using email lists to work together*. Retrieved January, 12, 2004, from http://www.idrc.ca/books/848/index_e.html

Janson, A., & Roper, J. (2004, March). *Identify virtual leaders to increase social capital: Information-based approach as a vehicle for social entrepreneurship engagement*. Paper presented at the International Sustainable Development Research Conference, Manchester, UK, Erpen-Environment.

Janz, B. D., & Prasarnphanich, P. (2003). Understanding the antecedents of effective knowledge management: The importance of knowledge-centered culture. *Decision Sciences, 34*(2), 351–384. doi:10.1111/1540-5915.02328

Jarvenpaa, S. L., & Leidner, D. E. (1999). Communication and trust in global virtual teams. *Organization Science, 10*(6), 791–815. doi:10.1287/orsc.10.6.791

Jarvenpaa, S. L., Knoll, K. A., & Leidner, D. E. (1998). Is anybody out there? Antecedents of trust in global virtual teams. *Journal of Management Information Systems, 14*(4), 29–64.

Jarvenpaa, S. L., Knoll, K., & Leidner, D. E. (1998). Communication and trust in global virtual teams. *Journal of Computer-Mediated Communication, 3*(4).

Jarvenpaa, S. L., Knoll, K., & Leidner, D. E. (1998). Is there any body out there? Antecedents of trust in global virtual teams. *Journal of Management Information Systems, 14*(4), 29–64.

Jawadi, N., Daassi, M., Kalika, M., & Favier, M. (2007). Virtual teams: The role of leadership in trust management. In L.-L. Brennan & V.-E. Johnson (Eds.), Computer-mediated relationships and trust: Managerial and organizational effects (pp. 34-45). Hershey, PA: Information Science Reference.

Jawadi, N., Daassi, M., Kalika, M., & Favier, M. (2007). Virtual teams: The role of leadership in trust management. In L.-L. Brennan & V.-E. Johnson (Eds.), Computer-mediated relationships and trust: Managerial and organizational effects (pp. 34-45). Hershey, PA: Information Science Reference.

Jayasingam, S. (2001). *Entrepreneurial success, gender, and bases of power*. Unpublished master's thesis, Penang, University Science Malaysia.

Jayasingam, S., Jantan, M., & Ansari, M. A. (2008). Influencing knowledge workers: The power of top management. In *Proceedings of the Knowledge Management International Conference 2008 (KMICE '08)*, Langkawi, Malaysia.

Jeyaraj, A., Rottman, J., & Lacity, M. J. (2006). A review of the predictors, linkages, and biases in IT innovation adoption research. *Journal of Information Technology, 21*(1), 1–23. doi:10.1057/palgrave.jit.2000056

Joerges, B., & Czarniawska, B. (1998). The question of technology, or how organizations incribe the world. *Organization Studies, 19*(3), 363–385. doi:10.1177/017084069801900301

Johnson, C. M. (2001). A survey of current research on online communities of practice. *The Internet and Higher Education, 4*(1), 45–60. doi:10.1016/S1096-7516(01)00047-1

Johnson, T. R., Zhang, J., Tang, Z., Johnson, C., & Turley, J. (2004). Assessing informatics students' satisfaction with a Web-based courseware system. *International Journal of Medical Informatics, 73*(2), 181–187. doi:10.1016/j.ijmedinf.2003.12.006

Jolly, J. P., Reynolds, T. J., & Slocum, J. W. (1988). Application of the means-end theoretic for understanding the cognitive bases of performance appraisal. *Organizational Behavior and Human Decision Processes, 41*, 153–179. doi:10.1016/0749-5978(88)90024-6

Jong, J. P. J., & Hartog, D. N. D. (2007). How leaders influence employee's innovative behavior. *European Journal of Innovation Management, 10*(1), 41–64. doi:10.1108/14601060710720546

Julsrud, T. E. & Schiefloe, P. M. (2007). Trust and stability in distributed work groups: A social network perspective. *International Journal of Networking and Virtual Organisations*. Forthcoming.

Julsrud, T., Bakke, J. W., et al. (2004). *Status and strategies for the knowledge intensive Nordic workplace*. Oslo, Norway: Nordic Innovation Center.

Julsrud, T., Schiefloe, P. M., et al. (2006). *Networks and trust in distributed groups*. University of Trondheim: NTNU.

Jung, D. I., & Avolio, B. J. (2000). Opening the black box: An experimental investigation of the mediating effects of trust and value congruence on transformation and transactional leadership. *Journal of Organizational Behavior, 21*(8), 949–964. doi:10.1002/1099-1379(200012)21:8<949::AID-JOB64>3.0.CO;2-F

Kaboli, A., Tabari, M., & Kaboli, E. (2006). *Leadership in virtual teams*. Paper presented at the Sixth International Symposium on Operations Research and Its Applications, Xinjiang, China.

Kagan, S., & Bowman, B. (1997). Leadership in early care and education: Issues and challenges. In S. Kagan & B. Bowman (Eds.), *Leadership in care and education* (Vol. 3-8). Washington, DC: NAEYC.

Kagan, S., & Hallmark, L. (2001). Cultivating leadership in early care and education. *Child Care Information Exchange, 140*, 7–12.

Kahai, S. S., Sosik, J. J., & Avolio, B. J. (2004). Effects of participative and directive leadership in electronic groups. *Group & Organization Management, 29*(1), 67–105. doi:10.1177/1059601103252100

Kanawattanachai, P., & Yoo, Y. (2002). Dynamic nature of trust in virtual teams. *Strategic Information Systems, 11*, 187-213.

Kanawattanachaï, P., & Yoo, Y. (2002). Dynamic nature of trust in virtual teams. *Strategic Information System, 11*, 187–213. doi:10.1016/S0963-8687(02)00019-7

Kaplan, B., & Maxwell, J. A. (1994). Qualitative research methods for evaluating computer information systems. In J. G. Anderson, C. E. Aydin, & S. J. Jay (Eds.), *Evaluating health care information systems: Methods and applications* (pp. 45-68). Thousand Oaks, CA: Sage.

Karlinzing, W., & Patrick, J. (2002). Tap into the power of knowledge collaboration. *Customer Interaction Solutions, 20*(11), 22–26.

Katz, R., & Tushman, M. (1981). An investigation into the managerial roles and career paths of gatekeepers and project supervisors in a major r&d facility. *R & D Management, 11,* 103–110. doi:10.1111/j.1467-9310.1981.tb00458.x

Kayworth, T., & Leidner, D. (2002). Leadership effectiveness in global virtual teams. *Journal of Management Information Systems, 18*(3), 7–40.

Keegan, A. E., & Den Hartog, D. N. (2004). Transformational leadership in a project-based environment: a comparative study of the leadership styles of project managers and line managers. *International Journal of Project Management, 22*(8), 609-618.

Keim, D., & Ward, M. (2003). Visualization. In M. Bertold & D. J. Hand (Eds.), *Intelligent data analysis* (2nd ed., pp. 403-427). Heidelberg, Germany: Springer.

Kelley, H. H., & Thibaut, J. (1978). *Interpersonal relations: A theory of interdependence.* New York: Wiley.

Kelley, L. L., Blackman, D. A., & Hurst, J. P. (2007). An exploration of the relationship between learning organizations and the retention of knowledge workers. *The Learning Organization, 14*(3), 204–221. doi:10.1108/09696470710739390

Kelly, C. (2007). Managing the relationship between knowledge and power in organizations. *Aslib Proceedings: New Information Perspectives, 59*(2), 125–138.

Kember, D., Tak-Shing, H., Bick-Har, L., Lee, A., Ng, S., & Yan, L. (1997). The diverse role of the critical friend in supporting educational action research projects. *Educational Action Research, 5*(3), 463–481. doi:10.1080/09650799700200036

Kerber, K. W., & Buono, A. F. (2004). Leading a team of change agents in a global corporation: Leadership challenges in a virtual world [white paper]. Adapted from K. W. Kerber & A. F. Buono, Intervening in virtual teams: Lessons from practice. In A. F. Buono (Ed.), *Creative consulting: Innovative perspectives on management consulting.* Greenwich, CT: Information Age Publishing.

Kerr, S. (1975). On the folly of rewarding a while hoping for b. *Academy of Management Review, 18,* 769–783. doi:10.2307/255378

Kickul, J., & Neuman, G. (2000). Emergent leadership behaviors: The function of personality and cognitive ability in determining teamwork performance and KSAS. *Journal of Business and Psychology, 15,* 27-51.

Kilduff, M., & Corley, K. G. (2000). Organizational culture from a network perspective. In N. Ashkanasy, C. P. M. Wilderom, & M. F. Peterson (Eds.), *Handbook of organizational culture and climate* (pp. 211-221). New York: Sage.

Kilduff, M., & Tsai, W. (2003). *Social networks and organizations.* London: Sage.

Kim, Y.-G., Yu, S.-H., & Lee, J.-H. (2003). Knowledge strategy planning: Methodology and case. *Expert Systems with Applications, 24*(3), 295–307. doi:10.1016/S0957-4174(02)00158-6

Kimball, L. (1999). Facilitating what you can't see: How to run a cyberspace team. *Technology for Learning, 1/3.*

Kimble, C., & Hildreth, P. (2005). Virtual communities of practice. In M. Khosrow-Pour (Ed.), *Encyclopedia of information science and technology* (pp. 2991-2995). Hershey, PA: Idea Group Reference.

Kimble, C., Hildreth, P., & Wright, P. (2000). Communities of practice: Going virtual. In Y. Malhotra. (Ed.), *Knowledge management and business model innovation* (pp. 220-234). Hershey, PA: Idea Group Publishing.

Kimble, C., Hildreth, P., & Wright, P. (2001). Communities of practice: Going global. In K. P. Mehdi (Ed.), *Knowledge management and business model innovation* (pp. 220-234). Hershey, PA: Idea Group Publishing.

Kirkman, B. L., Rosen, B., Gibson, C. B., Tesluk, P. E., & McPherson, S. O. (2002). Five challenges to virtual team success: Lessons from Sabre, Inc. *The Academy of Management Executive, 16,* 67–79.

Kirkman, L. B., & Mathieu, J. E. (2005). The dimensions and antecedents of team virtuality. *Journal of Management, 31*(5), 700–718. doi:10.1177/0149206305279113

Kirkman, L. B., & Mathieu, J. E. (2005). The dimensions and antecedents of team virtuality. *Journal of Management, 31*(5), 700–718. doi:10.1177/0149206305279113

Kirkpatrick, S. A., & Locke, E. A. (1991). Leadership traits do matter. *Academy of Management Executive,* March, 44-60.

Klauss, R., & Bass, B. M. (1981). *Impact of communication.* New York: Academic Press.

Klein, J. A., & Kleinhanns, A. (2003). Closing the gap in virtual teams. In C. B. Gibson & S. G. Cohen (Eds.), *Virtual teams that work: Creating conditions for virtual teams effectiveness* (pp. 381-400). San Francisco: Jossey-Bass.

Klimoski, R., & Mohammed, S. (1994). Team mental model: Constract or methaphor? *Journal of Management, 20*(2), 403–437. doi:10.1016/0149-2063(94)90021-3

Klimoski, R., & Mohammed, S. (1994). Team mental model: Constract or methaphor? *Journal of Management, 20*(2), 403–437. doi:10.1016/0149-2063(94)90021-3

Kling, R., & Courtright, C. (2003). Group behavior and learning in electronic forums: A sociotechnical approach. *The Information Society, 19,* 221–235. doi:10.1080/01972240309465

Knights, D., & Murray, F. (1994). *Managers divided: Organization politics and information technology management.* Chicester, UK: Wiley.

Kolb, D. A., Rubin, I. M., & McIntyre, J. M. (1984). *Organizational psychology: Readings on human behavior in organizations.* Englewood Cliffs, NJ: Prentice-Hall.

Kolb, D. C. (1999). *Team leadership.* Durango, CO: Lore International Group.

Kotter, J. (2001). What leaders really do. *Harvard Business Review,* (December): 85–96.

Krackhardt, D. (1992). The strength of strong ties: The importance of philos in organizations. In N. Nohria & R. Eccles (Eds.), *Network and organizations: Structure, form and action* (pp. 216-239). Boston: Harvard University Press.

Krackhardt, D. (1999). The ties that torture: Simmelian tie analysis in organizations. *Research in the Sociology of Organizations, 16,* 183-210.

Krackhardt, D., & Brass, D. (1994). Intraorganizational networks. In S. Wasserman & J. Galaskiewicz (Eds.), *The micro side. Advances in social network analysis* (pp. 207-229). Thousand Oaks, CA: Sage.

Krackhardt, D., & Kilduff, M. (2002). Structure, culture and simmelian ties in entrepreneurial firms. *Social Networks, 3*(24), 279-290.

Kramer, R. M., & Cook, K. S. (2004). Trust and distrust in organizations: Dilemmas and approaches. In R. M. Kramer & K. S. Cook (Eds.), *Trust and distrust in organizations. Dilemmas and approaches* (pp. 1-17). New York: Russel Sage Foundation.

Kramer, R. M., & Tyler, T. R. (1996). Whither trust. In R. M. Kramer & T. R. Tyler (Eds.), *Trust in organizations: Frontiers of theory and research.* Thousand Oaks, CA: Sage Publications.

Krauss, R., & Fussell, S. (1990). Mutual knowledge and communicative effectiveness. In J. Galegher, R. Kraut, & C. Egido (Eds.), *Intellectual teamwork: Social and technological foundations of cooperative work* (pp. 111-146). Hillsdale, NJ: Lawrence Erlbaum.

Krauss, R., & Fussell, S. (1990). Mutual knowledge and communicative effectiveness. In J. Galegher, R. Kraut, & C. Egido (Eds.), *Intellectual teamwork: Social and technological foundations of cooperative work* (pp. 111-146). Hillsdale, NJ: Lawrence Erlbaum.

Krech, D., Crutchfield, R. S., & Ballachey, E. L. (1962). *Individual in society.* New York: McGraw-Hill.

Kuan, K., & Chau, P. (2001). A perception-based model of EDI adoption in small businesses using technology-organization-environment framework. *Information & Management, 38,* 507–521. doi:10.1016/S0378-7206(01)00073-8

Kubo, I., & Saka, A. (2002). An inquiry into the motivations of knowledge workers in the Japanese financial industry. *Journal of Knowledge Management, 6*(3), 262–271. doi:10.1108/13673270210434368

Kuhn, T. S. (1996). *The structure of scientific revolutions* (3rd ed.). Chicago: Chicago University Press.

Kurnia, S., & Johnston, R. B. (2000). The need for a processual view of inter-organizational systems adoption. *The Journal of Strategic Information Systems, 9*(4), 295–319. doi:10.1016/S0963-8687(00)00050-0

Lam, W., & Chua, A. (2005). The mismanagement of knowledge management. *Aslib Proceedings: New Information Perspective, 57*(5), 424–433.

Lambert, L. (2003). Shifting conceptions of leadership: Towards a redefinition of leadership for the 21st century. In B. Davies & J. West-Burnham (Eds.), *Handbook of educational leadership and management*. London: Pearson Longman.

Lang, J. C. (2001). Managerial concerns in knowledge management. *Journal of Knowledge Management, 5*(1), 43–57. doi:10.1108/13673270110384392

Latour, B. (1987). *Science in action: How to follow scientists and engineers through society*. Cambridge, MA: Harvard University Press.

Latour, B. (1991). Technology is society made durable. In J. Law (Ed.), *A sociology of monsters: Essays on power, technology and domination*. London: Routledge.

Laub, J. A. (1999). Assessing the servant leadership organization: Development of the Servant Organizational Leadership Assessment (OLA) instrument. *Dissertation Abstracts International, 62*(02), 308. (UMI No. 9921922).

Lave, J., & Wenger, E. (1991). *Situated learning. Legitimate peripheral participation*. Cambridge, UK: Cambridge University Press.

Law, J. (1991). Introduction: Monsters, machines and sociotechnical relations. In J. Law (Ed.), *A sociology of monsters: Essays on power, technology and domination*. London: Routledge.

Law, J. (1992). Notes on the theory of the actor-network: Ordering, strategy and heterogeneity. *Systems Practice, 5*(4), 379–393. doi:10.1007/BF01059830

Law, J. (2000). *Networks, relations, cyborgs: On the social study of technology*. Retrieved December 23, 2003, from http://www.comp.lancs.ac.uk/sociology/soc042jl.html

Lawler, E. E. III, & Finegold, D. (2000). Individualizing the organization: Past, present, and future. *Organizational Dynamics, 29*, 1–15. doi:10.1016/S0090-2616(00)00009-7

Leadbeater, C. (1997). *The rise of the social entrepreneur*. London: Demos.

Ledbetter, D. S. (2004). Law enforcement leaders and servant leadership: A reliability study of the organizational leadership assessment. *Dissertation Abstracts International, 64*(11), 4200. (UMI No. 3110778).

Lee, F., Vogel, D., & Limayem, M. (2002). Virtual community informatics: What we know and what we need to know. In *Proceedings of the 35th Hawaii International Conference on System Sciences*. Hawaii: IEEE.

Leidner, D. E., & Fuller, M. (1997). Improving student learning of conceptual information: GSS supported collaborative learning vs. individual constructive learning. *Decision Support Systems, 20*, 149–163. doi:10.1016/S0167-9236(97)00004-3

Leidner, D. E., & Jarvenpaa, S. L. (1995). The use of information technology to enhance management school education: A theoretical view. *MIS Quarterly, 19*(3), 265–291. doi:10.2307/249596

Leitch, R., & Williams, C. (2006). *Being and having a critical friend*. Paper presented at the CCEAM Conference, Cyprus. Retrieved May 27, 2008, from http://www.toplinisis.com/conference/CCEAM/wib/index

Lertwongsatien, C., & Wongpinunwatana, N. (2003). E-commerce adoption in Thailand: An empirical study of small and medium enterprises (SMEs). *Journal of Global Information Technology Management, 6*(3), 67–83.

Lewicki, R. L., & Bunker, B. B. (1996). Developing and maintaining trust in work relationships. In R. Kramer & T. Tyler (Eds.), *Trust in organizations. Frontiers of theory and research*. Thousand Oaks, CA: Sage.

Lewis Tyran, K., Tyran, C. K., & Shepherd, M. (2003). Exploring emerging leadership in virtual teams. In C. B. Gibson & S. G. Cohen (Eds.), *Virtual teams that work: Creating conditions for virtual teams effectiveness* (pp. 183-195). San Francisco: Jossey-Bass.

Lewis, J. D., & Weigert, A. (1985). Trust as a social reality. Social forces. *Social Forces, 63*(4), 967–985. doi:10.2307/2578601

Lewis, R. J. (2000). An introduction to classification and regression tree (CART) analysis. In *Proceedings of the Annual Meeting of the Society for Academic Emergency Medicine,* San Francisco.

Liebeskind, J. P. (1996). Knowledge, strategy, and the theory of the firm. *Strategic Management Journal, 17*(Winter special issue), 93-107.

Lin, C., & Tseng, S. (2005). The implementation gaps for the knowledge management systems. *Industrial Management & Data Systems, 105*(2), 208–222. doi:10.1108/02635570510583334

Linstone, H. A., & Turoff, M. (Eds.). (1975). *The Delphi method: Techniques and applications.* Reading, MA: Addison-Wesley Publishing Company.

Lipnack, J., & Stamps, J. (1997). *Virtual teams: Reaching across space, time and organizations with technology.* New York: John Wiley and Sons.

Lipnack, J., & Stamps, J. (2000). *Virtual teams: People working across boundaries with technology* (2ⁿᵈ ed.). New York: John Wiley and Sons.

Locke, E. A., & Latham, G. P. (1990). *A theory of goal setting and task performance.* Englewood Cliffs, NJ: Prentice Hall.

Lombard, M., Snyder-Duch, J., & Bracken, C. C. (2002). Content analysis in mass communication: Assessment and reporting of intercoder reliability. *Human Communication Research, 28*(4), 587–604. doi:10.1111/j.1468-2958.2002.tb00826.x

Lucier, C. (2003). When knowledge adds up to nothing: Why knowledge management fails and what you can do about it. *Development and Learning in Organizations, 17*(1), 32–35. doi:10.1108/14777280310795739

Luftman, J. (2003). Assessing IT/business alignment. *Information Systems Management, 20*(4), 9–15. doi:10.1201/1078/43647.20.4.20030901/77287.2

Lurey, J. S., & Raisinghani, M. S. (2001). An empirical study of best practices in virtual teams. *Information & Management, 38*(8), 523–544. doi:10.1016/S0378-7206(01)00074-X

Mabry, E. A. (2002). Group communication and technology: Rethinking the role of communication modality in group work and performance. In L. R. Frey (Ed.), *New directions in group communication* (pp. 285-298). Thousand Oaks, CA: Sage.

MacBeath, J. (1998). 'I didn't know he was ill': The role and value of the critical friend. In L. Stoll & K. Myers (Eds.), *No quick fixes: Perspectives on schools in difficulty.* London: Falmer Press.

Macbeath, J. (1998). *Effective school leadership: Responding to change.* London: Paul Chapman.

Macneil, C. M. (2003). Line managers: Facilitators of knowledge sharing in teams. *Employee Relations, 25*(3), 294–307. doi:10.1108/01425450310475874

Maher, M. L., Simoff, S. J., & Cicognani, A. (2000). *Understanding virtual design studios.* Heidelberg, Germany: Springer.

Maier, R. (2002). *Knowledge management systems: Information and communication technologies for knowledge management.* Berlin, Germany: Springer Verlag.

Majchrzak, A., Malhotra, A., Stamps, J., & Lipnack, J. (2004). Can absence make a team grow stronger? *Harvard Business Review, 82*, 131–137.

Malhotra, A., & Majchrzak, A. (2005). Virtual workspace technologies. *Sloan Management Review, 46*, 11–14.

Malhotra, A., Majchrzak, A., & Rosen, B. (2007). Leading virtual teams. *The Academy of Management Perspectives, 21*, 60–69.

Malhotra, A., Majchrzak, A., & Rosen, B. (2007). Leading virtual teams. *The Academy of Management Perspectives, 21*, 60–70.

Malhotra, Y. (2001). *It is time to cultivate growth.* Retrieved May 5, 2008, from http://www.brint.net/members/01060524/britishtelecom.pdf

Malhotra, Y. (2002). Why knowledge management systems fail? Enablers and constraints of knowledge management in human enterprises. In C. W. Holsapple (Ed.), *Handbook on knowledge management 1: Knowledge matters* (pp. 577-599). Heidelberg, Germany: Springer-Verlag.

Malterud, K. (2001). Qualitative research: Standards, challenges, and guidelines. *Lancet, 358,* 483–488. doi:10.1016/S0140-6736(01)05627-6

Mankin, D., Cohen, S. G., & Bikson, T. K. (1996). *Teams and technology.* Boston: Harvard Business School Press.

Manz, C. C., & Sims, H. P., Jr. (2001). *The new superleadership.* San Francisco: Berrett-Koehler.

Marchington, M., Grimshaw, D. (Eds.). (2005). *Fragmenting work. Blurring organizational boundaries and disordering hierarchies.* Oxford: Oxford University Press.

Marks, M. A., Zaccaro, S. J., & Mathieu, J. E. (2000). Performance implications of leader briefings and team-interaction training for team adaptation to novel environments. *The Journal of Applied Psychology, 85,* 971–986. doi:10.1037/0021-9010.85.6.971

Markus, M. L. (1994). Electronic mail as the medium of managerial choice. *Organization Science, 5*(4), 502–527. doi:10.1287/orsc.5.4.502

Marquardt, M. (2004). *Optimizing the power of action learning.* Mountain View, CA: Davies-Black.

Marquardt, M. (2004). Harnessing the power of action learning . *Training & Development,* (June): 26–32.

Marquardt, M. (2004). *Optimizing the power of action learning.* Mountain View, CA: Davies-Black.

Marshall, P., Sor, R., & McKay, J. (2000). The impacts of electronic commerce in the automobile industry: An empirical study in Western Australia. In [Berlin, Germany: Springer Verlag.]. *Proceedings of the CAiSe, 2000,* 509–521.

Marsick, V., & O'Neil, J. (1999). The many faces of action learning. *Management Learning, 30*(2), 159–176. doi:10.1177/1350507699302004

Mathieu, J. E., Heffner, T. S., Goodwin, G. F., Sala, E., & Cannon-Bowers, J. A. (2000). The influence of shared mental models on team process and performance. *The Journal of Applied Psychology, 85*(2), 273–283. doi:10.1037/0021-9010.85.2.273

Mayer, R. C., Davis, J. H., & Schoorman, F. D. (1995). An integrative model of organizational trust. *Academy of Management Review, 20*(3), 709–734. doi:10.2307/258792

Mayer, R. C., Davis, J. H., et al. (1995). An integrated model of organizational trust. *Academy of Management Review, 3*(20), 709-734.

Maznevski, M. L., & Chudoba, K. M. (2000). Bridging space over time: Global virtual team dynamics and effectiveness. *Organization Science, 11,* 473–492. doi:10.1287/orsc.11.5.473.15200

Maznevski, M. L., & Chudoba, K. M. (2000). Bridging space over time: Global virtual team dynamics and effectiveness. *Organizational Science, 11*(5), 473-492.

McAllister, D. J. (1995). Affect- and cognition-based trust as foundations for interpersonal cooperation in organizations. *Academy of Management Journal, 1*(38), 24-59.

McClelland, D. C., & Burnham, D. (1976). Power is the great motivator. *Harvard Business Review, 54,* 100–110, 159–166.

McCrimmon, M. (1995). Bottom-up leadership. *Executive Development, 8*(5), 6–12. doi:10.1108/09533239510093215

McCroskey, J. C., & Richmond, V. P. (1998). Willingness to communicate. In J. C. McCroskey, J. A. Daly, M. M. Martin, & M. J. Beatty (Eds.), *Communication and personality: Trait perspectives* (pp. 119-131). Cresswell, NJ: Hampton Press.

McDonough, E. F., Kahn, K. B., & Barczak, G. (2001). An investigation of the use of global, virtual, and collocated new product development teams. *Journal of Product Innovation Management, 18*(2), 110–120. doi:10.1016/S0737-6782(00)00073-4

McEvily, B., & Zaheer, A. (2004). Architects of trust: The role of network facilitators in geographical clusters. In R. M. Kramer & K. S. Cook (Eds.), *Trust and distrust in organizations. Dilemmas and approaches* (pp. 189-213). New York: Russel Sage Foundation.

McGill, I., & Brockbank, A. (2004). *The action learning handbook*. London: RoutledgeFalmer.

McGill, I., & Brockbank, A. (2004). *The action learning handbook*. London: RoutledgeFalmer.

McGrath, J. E. (1991). Time, interaction, and performance (TIP): A theory of groups. *Small Group Research, 22*(2), 147–174. doi:10.1177/1046496491222001

McGrath, J. E., & Hollingshead, A. B. (1994). *Groups interacting with technology: Systems, ideas, evidence and an agenda*. Newbury Park, CA: Sage.

McKee, T. W. (2004). *Motivating your very busy volunteers*. Retrieved September 2, 2007, from http://www.worldvolunteerweb.org/getnews/news2.cfm?ArticlesID=572

McKnight, D. H., Cummings, L. L., et al. (1995). *Trust formations in new organizational relationships* (Information and Decision Sciences Workshop). University of Minnesota.

McShane, S. L., & Von Glinow, M. A. (2000). *Organizational behavior*. Boston: Irwin McGraw-Hill.

Meade, A. (2003). *ECE centres of innovation in New Zealand.* Paper presented at the Leadership and Management in the Early Years Conference, Pen Green Leadership Centre, Corby, North Hamptonshire.

Mehra, A., Smith, B. R., Dixon, A. L., & Robertson, B. (2006). Distributed leadership in teams: The network of leadership perceptions and team performance. *The Leadership Quarterly, 17*, 232–245. doi:10.1016/j.leaqua.2006.02.003

Meier, C. (2003). Doing 'groupness' in a spatially distributed work group: The case of videoconferences at Technics. In L. R. Frey (Ed.), *Group communication in context: Studies of bona fide groups* (2nd ed., pp. 367-397). Mahwah, NJ: Lawrence Erlbaum.

Mennecke, B. E., & Valacich, J. S. (1998). Information is what you make of it: The influence of group history and computer support on information sharing, decision quality, and member perceptions. *Journal of Management Information Systems, 15*(2), 173–178.

Mennecke, B., Valacich, J., & Wheeler, B. (2000). The effects of media and task on user performance: A test of the task-media fit hypothesis. *Group Decision and Negotiation, 9*, 507–529. doi:10.1023/A:1008770106779

Meyerson, D., Weick, K. E., & Kramer, R. M. (1996). Swift trust and temporary groups. In R.M. Kramer (Ed.), *Trust in organizations: Frontiers of theory and research* (pp. 166-195). Thousand Oaks, CA: Sage Publications, Inc.

Meyerson, D., Weick, K., et al. (1996). Swift trust and temporary groups. In R. Kramer & R. Tyler (Eds.), *Trust in organizations. Frontiers of research and theory* (pp. 166-195). Thousand Oaks, CA: Sage.

Miears, L. D. (2005). Servant-leadership and job satisfaction: A correlational study in Texas Education Agency Region X public schools. *Dissertation Abstracts International, 65*(09), 3237. (UMI No. 3148083).

Miles, R. E., Snow, C. C., Mathews, J. A., & Miles, G. (1997). Organizing in the knowledge age: Anticipating the cellular form. *The Academy of Management Executive, 11*, 7–24.

Millen, D. R., Fontaine, M. A., & Muller, M. J. (2002). Understanding the benefit and costs of communities of practice. *Communications of the ACM, 45*(4), 69–73. doi:10.1145/505248.505276

Miller, D. (1987). The genesis of configuration. *Academy of Management Review, 12*(4), 686–701. doi:10.2307/258073

Ming Yu, C. (2002). Socializing knowledge management: The influence of the opinion leader. *Journal of Knowledge Management Practice, 3*, 76–83.

Ministry of Education. (2008). *Statement of intent, 2008-2013.* Wellington, New Zealand: Ministry of Education.

Mirchandani, D. A., & Motwani, J. (2001). Understanding small business electronic commerce adoption: An empirical analysis. *Journal of Computer Information Systems,* (Spring): 70–73.

Mishira, A. K. (1996). Organizational response to crisis: The centrality of trust. In R. M. Kramer & T. R. Tyler (Eds.), *Trust in organizations: Frontiers of theory and research* (pp. 261-287). Thousand Oaks, CA: Sage.

Misiolek, N. I. (2005). *Patterns of emergent leadership is ad hoc virtual teams.* Unpublished doctoral dissertation, School of Information Studies, Syracuse University.

Misiolek, N. I., & Heckman, R. (2005). Patterns of emergent leadership in virtual teams. In *Proceedings of the 38th Annual Hawaii International Conference on System Sciences (HICSS'05),* HI.

Mohrman, S. A., Cohen, S. G., & Mohrman, A. M., Jr. (1995). *Designing team-based organizations: New forms for knowledge work.* San Francisco: Jossey-Bass.

Molina, M., & Yoong, P. (2003). Knowledge sharing in a co-opetitive environment: The case of business clusters. *Journal of Information and Knowledge Management, 2*(4), 1–23.

Molnar, D. R. (2007). Serving the world: A cross-cultural study of national culture dimensions and servant leadership. *Dissertation Abstracts International, 68/05,* 139. (UMI No. AAT 3266277).

Monalisa, M., Daim, T., Mirani, F., & Dash, P. (2008). Managing global design teams. *Research Technology Management, 51*(4), 48–59.

Montoya-Weiss, M., Massey, A., & Song, M. (2001). Getting it together: Temporal coordination and conflict management in global virtual teams. *Academy of Management Journal, 44*(6), 1251–1262. doi:10.2307/3069399

Morgan, G. (1997). *What is leadership? Walking around a definition.* Boston: Center for Career Development in Early Care and Education.

Morgan, G., & Smircich, L. (1980). The case for qualitative research. *Academy of Management Review, 5*(4), 491–500. doi:10.2307/257453

Morris, J. (1997). Minding our ps and qs. In M. Pedler (Ed.), *Action learning in practice* (3rd ed., pp. 49-59). Aldershot, UK: Gower.

Mowrer, D. E. (1996). A content analysis of student/instructor communication via computer conferencing. *Higher Education, 32*(2), 217–241. doi:10.1007/BF00138397

Mowshowitz, A. (1997). Virtual organization. *Communications of the ACM, 40*, 30–37. doi:10.1145/260750.260759

Muijs, D., Aubrey, C., Harris, A., & Briggs, M. (2004). How do they manage? *Journal of Early Childhood Research, 2*(2), 157–169. doi:10.1177/1476718X04042974

Mullen, B., Salas, E., & Driskell, J. E. (1989). Salience, motivation and artifact as contributions to the relation between participation rate and leadership. *Journal of Experimental Social Psychology, 25,* 545-559.

Müller, R., & Turner, J. R. (2006). Leadership competences and their successful application in different types of project. In L. Ou & R. Turner (Ed.), *Proceedings of IRNOP VII (International Research Network for Organizing by Projects),* Northwestern Polytechnic University, Xi'an, China.

Müller, R., & Turner, J. R. (2007). Matching the project manager's leadership style to project type. *International Journal of Project Management, 25*(1), 21-32.

Müller, R., & Turner, J. R. (2007b). The influence of project managers on project success criteria and project success by type of project. *European Management Journal, 25*(4), 289-309.

Müller, R., Geraldi, J., & Turner, J. R. (2007, September). *Linking complexity and leadership competences of project managers.* Paper presented at IRNOP VIII Conference

(International Research Network for Organizing by Projects), Brighton, UK.

Mullins, L. J. (1996). *Management and organizational behavior.* London: Pitman.

Munck, G. L. (1998). Canons of research design in qualitative analysis. *Studies in Comparative International Development, 33*(3), 18–45. doi:10.1007/BF02687490

Murphy, P. E. (1999). Character and virtue ethics in international marketing: An agenda for managers, researchers, and educators. *Journal of Business Ethics, 18*(1), 107–124. doi:10.1023/A:1006072413165

Myers, M. R., Slavin, M. J., & Southern, W. T. (1990). Emergence and maintenance of leadership among gifted students in group problem solving. *Roeper Review, 12*(4), 256-260.

Nahapiet, J., & Goshal, S. (1998). Social capital, intellectual capital and the organizational advantage. *Academy of Management Review, 23*(2), 242–266. doi:10.2307/259373

Neuman, G. A., & Wright, J. (1999). Team effectiveness: Beyond skills and cognitive ability. *The Journal of Applied Psychology, 84*(3), 376–389. doi:10.1037/0021-9010.84.3.376

Niederman, F., Beise, C. M., & Beranek, P. M. (1993). Facilitation issues in distributed group support systems. In *Proceedings of the 1993 conference on Computer personnel research* (pp. 299-312).

Nissenbaum, H. (2004). Will security enhance trust online, or supplant it? In R. M. Kramer & K. S. Cook (Eds.), *Trust and distrust in organizations. Dilemmas and approaches* (pp. 155-185). New York: Russel Sage Foundation.

Nonaka, I. (1994). A dynamic theory of organizational knowledge creation. *Organization Science, 5*(1), 14–37. doi:10.1287/orsc.5.1.14

Nonaka, I. (1994). A dynamic theory of organizational knowledge creation. *Organization Science, 5*, 14–38. doi:10.1287/orsc.5.1.14

Nonaka, I. (1998). The knowledge-creating company. In *Harvard Business Review on Knowledge Management.* Boston: Harvard Business School Publishing.

Nonaka, I., & Takaeuchi, N. (1995). *The knowledge creating company: How Japanese companies create the dynamics of innovation.* New York: Oxford University Press.

Nonaka, I., & Takeuchi, H. (1995). *The knowledge-creating company.* New York: Oxford University Press.

Nonaka, I., Toyama, R., & Konno, N. (2001). SECI, Ba and leadership: A unified model of dynamic knowledge creation. In I. Nonaka & D. J. Teece (Eds.), *Managing industrial knowledge: Creation, transfer, and utilization* (pp. 13-43). Thousand Oaks, CA: Sage.

Nordin, M., Pauleen, D., & Gorman, G. (2009). fc). Investigating KM antecedents: KM in the criminal justice system. *Journal of Knowledge Management, 13*(2). doi:10.1108/13673270910942664

Nupponen, H. (2006). Leadership concepts and theories. *Australian Journal of Early Childhood, 31*(1), 43–50.

O'Bannon, D. P., & Pearce, C. L. (1999). A quasi-experiment of gain sharing in service organizations: Implications for organizational citizenship behavior and pay satisfaction. *Journal of Managerial Issues, 11,* 363–378.

O'Connell, M. S., Doverspike, D., & Cober, A. B. (2002). Leadership and semiautonomous work team performance: A field study. *Group & Organization Management, 27*(1), 50–65. doi:10.1177/1059601102027001004

O'Hara-Devereaux, M., & Johansen, R. (1994). *Global work: Bridging distance, culture and time.* San Francisco: Jossey-Bass.

O'Leary, M., Orlikowski, W., et al. (2002). Distributed work over the centuries. Trust and control in the Hudson Bay Company. In P. Hinds & S. Kiesler (Eds.), *Distributed work.* Cambridge, MA: MIT Press.

O'Neil, J. (1997). Set advising: More than just process consultancy. In M. Pedler (Ed.), *Action learning in practice* (3rd ed., pp. 243-255). Aldershot, UK: Gower.

O'Regan, N., & Ghobadian, A. (2004). Testing the homogeneity of SMEs: The impact of size on managerial and organizational processes. *European Business Review, 16*(1), 64–79. doi:10.1108/09555340410512411

O'Reilly, C. A., & Roberts, K. H. (1974). Information filtration in organizations: Three experiments. *Organizational Behavior and Human Performance, 11*, 253–265. doi:10.1016/0030-5073(74)90018-X

OECD. (2002). *Measuring the information economy 2002*. Retrieved August 20, 2004, from http://www.oecd.org

Olson, G. M., & Olson, J. S. (2003). Human-computer interaction: Psychological aspects of human use of computing. *Annual Review of Psychology, 54*, 491–516. doi:10.1146/annurev.psych.54.101601.145044

Oltra, V. (2005). Knowledge management effectiveness factors: The role of HRM. *Journal of Knowledge Management, 9*(4), 70–86. doi:10.1108/13673270510610341

Orlikowski, W. J. (2002). Knowing in practice: Enacting a collective capability in distributed organizing. *Organization Science, 13*(3), 249–274. doi:10.1287/orsc.13.3.249.2776

Oxford Concise Dictionary (1995). 9th edn. UK: Oxford University Press.

Ozaralli, N. (2003). Effects of transformational leadership on empowerment and team effectiveness. *Leadership and Organization Development Journal, 24*(6), 335–344. doi:10.1108/01437730310494301

Page, D., & Wong, P. T. (2000). A conceptual framework for measuring servant-leadership. In S. B.-S. K. Adjibolosoo (Ed.), *The human factor in shaping the course of history and development* (pp. 1-16). Latham, MD: University Press of America.

Palvia, P. C., & Palvia, S. C. (1999). An examination of the IT satisfaction of small-business users. *Information & Management, 35*(3), 127–137. doi:10.1016/S0378-7206(98)00086-X

Panteli, N. (2002). Richness, power cues and email text. *Information & Management, 40*, 75–86. doi:10.1016/S0378-7206(01)00136-7

Panteli, N. (2005). Trust in global virtual teams. *Ariadne 43*. Retrieved April 2007 from http://www.ariadne.ac.uk/issue43/panteli/

Parry, K. (2004). *The seven sins and the seven virtues of leadership: Which path do we follow?* (The Leading Matters Symposium Series). Centre for Leadership & Management in Education, Graduate School of Management, Griffith University, Australia, Griffith University EcoCentre.

Partington, D. A. (2003). Managing and leading. In J. R. Turner (Eds.), *People in project management*. Aldershott, UK: Gower.

Paterson, F., & West-Burnham, J. (2005). Developing beginning leadership. In M. Coles & G. Southworth (Eds.), *Developing leadership: Creating the schools of tomorrow* (pp. 108-126). Maidenhead, Berkshire, UK: Open University Press.

Paul, S., Seetharaman, P., Samarah, I., & Mykytyn, P. P. (2004). Impact of heterogeneity and collaborative conflict management style on the performance of synchronous global virtual teams. *Information & Management, 41*(3), 303–321. doi:10.1016/S0378-7206(03)00076-4

Pauleen, D. (2003). Leadership in a global virtual team: An action learning approach. *Leadership and Organization Development Journal, 24*(3), 153–162. doi:10.1108/01437730310469570

Pauleen, D. F., & Yoong, P. (2001). Facilitating virtual team relationship via Internet and conventional communication channels. *Internet Research: Electronic networking applications and policy, 11*(3), 190-202.

Pauleen, D. F., & Yoong, P. (2001). Relationship building and the use of ICT in boundary-crossing virtual teams: A facilitator's perspective. *Journal of Information Technology, 16*(4), 205–220. doi:10.1080/02683960110100391

Pauleen, D. F., & Yoong, P. (2004). Studying human-centered IT innovation using a grounded action learning approach. *Qualitative Report, 9*(1), 137–160.

Pauleen, D. J. (2003). Leadership in a global virtual team: An action learning approach. *Leadership and*

Organization Development Journal, 24, 153–162. doi:10.1108/01437730310469570

Pauleen, D. J. (2003). Leadership in a global virtual team: An action learning approach. *Leadership and Organization Development Journal, 24*(3), 153-162.

Pauleen, D. J., & Yoong, P. (2001). Facilitating virtual team relationships via Internet and conventional communication channels. *Internet Research: Electronic Networking Applications and Policies, 11,* 190-202.

Pauleen, D. J., & Yoong, P. (2001). Facilitating virtual team relationships via Internet and conventional communication channels. *Internet Research, 11*, 190–202. doi:10.1108/10662240110396450

Pauleen, D. J., & Yoong, P. (2001). Relationship building and the use of ICT in boundary crossing virtual teams: A facilitator's perspective. *Journal of Information Technology, 16*, 205–220. doi:10.1080/02683960110100391

Pavitt, C. (2004). *Small group communication: A theoretical approach* (3rd ed.). Retrieved June 15, 2004, from http://www.udel.edu/communication/pavitt/bookindex.htm

Pawlowski, S., & Robey, D. (2004). Bridging user organizations: Knowledge brokering and the work of information technology professionals. *MIS Quarterly, 28*(4), 645–672.

Pearce, C. L. (2004). The future of leadership: Combining vertical and shared leadership to transform knowledge work. *The Academy of Management Executive, 18*, 47–59.

Pearce, C. L. (2008). Follow the leaders. *Wall Street Journal*, pp. B8, 12.

Pearce, C. L., & Conger, J. A. (Eds.). (2003). *Shared leadership: Reframing the hows and whys of leadership.* Thousand Oaks, CA: Sage.

Pearce, C. L., & Osmond, C. P. (1996). Metaphors for change: The ALPs model of change management. *Organizational Dynamics, 24*, 23–35. doi:10.1016/S0090-2616(96)90003-0

Pearce, C. L., & Osmond, C. P. (1999). From workplace attitudes and values to a global pattern of nations: An application of latent class modeling. *Journal of Management, 25*, 759–778. doi:10.1177/014920639902500507

Pearce, C. L., & Sims, H. P. Jr. (2002). Vertical versus shared leadership as predictors of the effectiveness of change management teams: An examination of aversive, directive, transactional, transformational, and empowering leader behaviors. *Group Dynamics, 6*, 172–197. doi:10.1037/1089-2699.6.2.172

Pearce, C. L., Sims, H. P., Cox, J. F., Ball, G., Schnell, E., Smith, K. A., & Trevino, L. (2003). Transactors, transformers and beyond: A multi-method development of theoretical typology of leadership. *Journal of Management Development, 22*, 273–307. doi:10.1108/02621710310467587

Pedler, M., Burgoyne, J. G., & Boydell, T. (2003). *A manager's guide to leadership.* Maindenhead, UK: McGraw-Hill.

Peek, S. (2002). Virtual networks link entrepreneurs to skills. *RE: THINK Supplement to the Sunday Star Times.*

Peterson, R. R. (2004). Crafting information technology governance. *Information Systems Management, 21*(4), 7–21. doi:10.1201/1078/44705.21.4.20040901/84183.2

Pfeffer, J., & Veiga, J. F. (1999). Putting people first for organizational success. *The Academy of Management Executive, 13*, 37–48.

Piccoli, G., & Ives, B. (2003). Trust and the unintended effects of behavior control in virtual team. *MIS Quarterly, 27*(3), 365–396.

Piccoli, G., & Ives, B. (2003). Trust and the unintended effects of behavior control in virtual teams. *MIS Quarterly, 27*(3), 365-395.

Piccoli, G., Powell, A., & Ives, B. (2004). Virtual teams: Team control structure, work processes, and team effectiveness. *Information Technology & People, 17*(4), 359–379. doi:10.1108/09593840410570258

Podolny, J., & Baron, J. (1997). Resources and relationships, social networks and mobility in the workplace. *American Sociological Review, 62*, 673-693.

Podsakoff, P., MacKenzie, S., Moorman, R., & Fetter, R. (1990). Transformational leader behaviors and their effects on follows' trust in leader, satisfaction, and organizational citizenship behaviors. *The Leadership Quarterly, 1*, 107–142. doi:10.1016/1048-9843(90)90009-7

Politis, J. D. (2001). The relationship of various leadership styles to knowledge management. *Leadership and Organization Development Journal, 22*(8), 354–364. doi:10.1108/01437730110410071

Politis, J. D. (2002). Transformational and transactional leadership enabling (disabling) knowledge acquisition of self-managed teams: The consequences for performance. *Leadership and Organization Development Journal, 23*(4), 186–197. doi:10.1108/01437730210429052

Politis, J. D. (2005). The influence of managerial power and credibility on knowledge acquisition attributest. *Leadership and Organization Development Journal, 26*(3), 197–214. doi:10.1108/01437730510591752

Poon, S., & Swatman, P. M. C. (1999). An exploratory study of small business Internet commerce issues. *Information & Management, 35*(1), 9–18. doi:10.1016/S0378-7206(98)00079-2

Popper, K. (2002). *The logic of scientific discovery* (J. Fried & L. Fried, Trans.). New York: Routledge.

Porterhouse, M., & Dulewicz, V. (2007). *Agile project managers' leadership competencies* (Henley Working Paper Series). Henley Management College, Henley-on-Thames, UK.

Powell, A., Piccoli, G., & Ives, B. (2004). Virtual teams: A review of current literature and directions for future research. *The Data Base for Advances in Information Systems, 35*(1), 6–36.

Powell, J. (2001). *Using learning styles and action learning, over the Internet, to drive learning for innovation in small and medium enterprises - a case study from construction* [Electronic Version]. Retrieved May 15, 2006, from http://www.portlandpress.com/pp/books/online/vu/pdf/vu_ch8.pdf

Preece, J., & Maloney-Krichmar, P. (2003). Online communities. In J. Jacko & A. Sears (Eds.), *Handbook of human-computer interaction* (pp. 596-620). Mahwah, NJ: Lawrence Erlbaum Associates Inc.

Preece, J., & Rogers, Y. (2002). *Interaction design: Beyond human-computer interaction*. New York: John Wiley & Sons.

Premkumar, G., & Ramamurthy, K. (1995). The role of interorganisational and organizational factors on the decision mode for adoption of interorganisational systems. *Decision Sciences, 26*(3), 303–336. doi:10.1111/j.1540-5915.1995.tb01431.x

Prensky, M. (2005-6). Listen to the natives. *Educational Leadership, 63*(4), 8–13.

Prinz, W. (1999). NESSIE: An awareness environment for cooperative settings. In *Proceedings of the Sixth European Conference on Computer Supported Cooperative Work* (pp. 391-410).

Proctor-Thomson, S., & Parry, K. (2001). What the best leaders look like. In K. Parry (Ed.), *Leadership in the antipodes: Findings, implication and a leadership profile* (pp. 166-191). Wellington, New Zealand: Institute of Policy Studies and the Centre for the Study of Leadership, Victoria University of Wellington.

Prusak, L., & Cohen, D. (2001). *In good company: How social capital makes organizations work*. Boston: Harvard Business School Press.

Raelin, J. (2000). *Work-based learning: The new frontier of management development*. Upper Saddle River, NJ: Prentice Hall.

Raelin, J. (2004). Don't bother putting leadership into people. *The Academy of Management Executive, 18*(3), 131–135.

Rafaeli, S., & Sudweeks, F. (1997). Net interactivity. *Journal of Computer-Mediated Communication, 2*(4).

Rafaeli, S., & Sudweeks, F. (1998). Interactivity on the nets. In F. Sudweeks, M. McLaughlin, & S. Rafaeli (Eds.), *Network and Netplay: Virtual groups on the Internet* (pp. 173-190). Cambridge, MA: MIT Press.

Ragin, C. A. (1994). *Constructing social research.* Thousand Oaks, CA: Sage.

Rahim, M. A. (1989). Relationships of leader power to compliance and satisfaction with supervision: Evidence from a national sample of managers. *Journal of Management, 15*, 545–556. doi:10.1177/014920638901500404

Raja, J., Huq, A., & Rosenberg, D. (2006). The role of trust in virtual and co-located communities of practice. In E. Coakes (Ed.), *Encyclopedia of communities of practice in information and knowledge management* (pp. 453-458). Hershey, PA: Idea Group Reference.

Raub, S., & Rüling, C.-C. (2001). The knowledge management tussle - speech communities and rhetorical strategies in the development of knowledge management. *Journal of Information Technology, 16*(2), 113–130. doi:10.1080/02683960110054807

Raven, A. (2003). Team or community of practice: Aligning tasks, structures, and technologies. In C. B. Gibson & S. G. Cohen (Eds.), *Virtual teams that work: Creating conditions for virtual team effectiveness* (pp. 292-306). San Francisco: Jossey Bass.

Raven, B. H. (1965). Social influence and power. In I. D. Steiner & M. Fishbein (Eds.), *Current studies in social psychology* (pp. 371-382). New York: Holt, Rinehart, Winston.

Raven, B. H. (1992). A power/interaction model of interpersonal influence: French and Raven thirty years later. *Journal of Social Behavior and Personality, 7*, 217–244.

Ready, D. (2004). Leading at the enterprise level. *MIT-Sloan Management Review, 45*(3), 87–91.

Reddin, W. J. (1970). *Managerial effectiveness.* New York: McGraw Hill.

Regula, C. R., & Julian, J. W. (1973). The impact of quality and frequency of task contributions on perceived ability. *The Journal of Social Psychology, 89*, 115-122.

Reynolds, T. J., & Gutmann, J. (1988). Laddering theory, method, analysis, and interpretation. *Journal of Advertising Research, 18*(1), 11–31.

Ribiere, V. M., & Sitar, A. S. (2003). Critical role of leadership in nurturing a knowledge-supporting culture. *Knowledge Management Research and Practice, 1*, 39–48. doi:10.1057/palgrave.kmrp.8500004

Richardson, J., Long, G., & Woodley, A. (2003). Academic engagement and perceptions of quality in distance education. *Open Learning, 18*(3), 223–244. doi:10.1080/0268051032000131008

Ridings, C. M., & Gefen, D. (2004). Virtual community attraction: Why people hang out online. *Journal of Computer-Mediated Communication, 10*(1).

Riege, A. (2005). Three dozen knowledge sharing barriers managers must consider. *Journal of Knowledge Management, 9*(3), 18–35. doi:10.1108/13673270510602746

Riege, A. (2007). Actions to overcome knowledge transfer barriers in MNCs. *Journal of Knowledge Management, 11*(1), 48–67. doi:10.1108/13673270710728231

Riva, G., & Galimberti, C. (2001). Complementary explorative multilevel data analysis—CEMDA: A socio-cognitive model of data analysis for Internet research. In G. Riva & C. Galimberti (Eds.), *Towards cyberpsychology: Mind, cognitions and society in the Internet age* (pp. 19-35). Amsterdam: IOS Press.

Robbins, S. P. (1997). *Essentials of organizational behaviour.* Englewood Cliffs, NJ: Prentice Hall.

Robinson, V. (2004). New understandings of educational leadership. *set 2004, 3*, 39-43.

Roche, V., & Vernon, M. (2003). *Developing a virtual learning community of managers in rural and remote health services.* Retrieved May 5, 2006, from http://www.abc.net.au/rural/ruralhealth2003/stories/s799695.htm

Roche, V., & Vernon, M. (2003). Developing a virtual learning community of managers in rural and remote health services, Retrieved May 5, 2006, from http://www.abc.net.au/rural/ruralhealth2003/stories/s799695.htm

Rodd, J. (2001). Building leadership expertise of early childhood professionals. *Journal of Early Childhood Teacher Education, 22*, 9–12.

Rodd, J. (2006). *Leadership in early childhood* (3rd ed.). Crows Nest NSW, Australia: Allen & Unwin.

Rogers, E. (2003). *The diffusion of innovations* (5th ed.). New York: The Free Press.

Rogers, E. M. (1995). *Diffusion of innovations* (4th ed.). New York: The Free Press.

Romano, N. C. J., Nunamaker, J. F. J., Briggs, R. O., & Mittleman, D. D. (1999). Distributed GSS facilitation and participation: Field action research. In *System Sciences, 1999. HICSS-32. Proceedings of the 32nd Annual Hawaii International Conference on* (pp. 1-12).

Rose, J. (1997). Soft systems methodology as a social science research tool. *Systems Research and Behavioral Science, 14*(4), 249–258. doi:10.1002/(SICI)1099-1743(199707/08)14:4<249::AID-SRES119>3.0.CO;2-S

Rose, J., & Truex, D. (2000). Machine agency as perceived autonomy. In R. Baskerville, J. Stage, & J. I. DeGross (Eds.), *Organizational and social perspectives on information technology*. Boston: Kluwer.

Rosen, B., Furst, S., & Blackburn, R. (2006). Training for virtual teams: An investigation of current practices and future needs. *Human Resource Management Journal, 45*, 229–247. doi:10.1002/hrm.20106

Rosen, B., Furst, S., & Blackburn, R. (2007). Overcoming barriers to knowledge sharing in virtual teams. *Organizational Dynamics, 36*, 259–273. doi:10.1016/j.orgdyn.2007.04.007

Rousseau, D. M. (2001). Schema, promise and mutuality: The building blocks of the psychological contract. *Journal of Occupational and Organizational Psychology, 74*(4), 511–542. doi:10.1348/096317901167505

Rovai, A. P. (2002). Sense of community, perceived cognitive learning, and persistence in asynchronous learning networks. *The Internet and Higher Education, 5*(4), 319–332. doi:10.1016/S1096-7516(02)00130-6

Russell, R. F. (2001). The role of values in servant leadership. *Leadership and Organization Development Journal, 22*(2), 76–89. doi:10.1108/01437730110382631

Russell, R. F., & Stone, A. G. (2002). A review of servant leadership attributes: Developing a practical model. *Leadership and Organization Development Journal, 23*(3), 145–157. doi:10.1108/01437730210424

Sabherwal, R., Jeyaraj, A., & Chowa, C. (2006). Information system success: Individual and organizational determinants. *Management Science, 52*(12), 1849–1864. doi:10.1287/mnsc.1060.0583

Sainte-Onge, H., & Wallace, D. (2003). *Leveraging communities of practice for strategic advantage*. Boston: Heineman-Butterworth.

Saint-Onge, H., & Wallace, D. (2003). *Leveraging communities of practice for strategic advantage*. Boston, MA: Butterworth-Heinemann.

Sambamurthy, V., & Zmud, R. W. (1999). Arrangements for information technology governance: A theory of multiple contingencies. *MIS Quarterly, 23*(2), 261–290. doi:10.2307/249754

Sanchez, R. (2005). Knowledge management and organizational learning: Fundamental concepts for theory and practice [Electronic Version]. *Working Paper Series, Lund University, Institute of Economic Research*. Retrieved September 3, 2007, from http://econpapers.repec.org/paper/hhblufewp/2005_5F003.htm

Sarin, S., & McDermott, C. (2003). The effect of team leader characteristics on learning, knowledge application and performance of cross functional new product development teams. *Decision Sciences, 34*(4), 707–740. doi:10.1111/j.1540-5414.2003.02350.x

Saunders, C., Van Slyke, C., & Vogel, D. R. (2004). My time or yours? Managing time visions in global virtual teams. *The Academy of Management Executive, 18*, 19–31.

Saunders, M., Lewis, P., & Thornhill, A. (2007). *Research methods for business students* (4th ed.). Essex, UK: FT Prentice Hall.

Schindler, P. L., & Thomas, C. C. (1993). The structure of interpersonal trust in the workplace. *Psychological Reports, 73*, 563–573.

Schlager, M., & Fusco, J. (2003). Teacher professional development, technology and communities of practice: Are we putting the cart before the horse? *The Information Society, 19*, 203–220. doi:10.1080/01972240309464

Schneider, B. (1990). *Organizational climate and culture.* San Francisco: Jossey-Bass.

Scholtes, P. R. (1988). *The team handbook: How to use teams to improve quality.* Madison, WI: Jointer Associates Inc.

Schomberg, R. (1999). Leadership development in early childhood education. *Journal of Early Childhood Teacher Education*, 215–219.

Schriesheim, C. A., Hinkin, T. R., & Podsakoff, P. M. (1991). Can ipsative and single-item measures produce erroneous results in field studies of French and Raven's (1959) five bases of power? An empirical investigation. *The Journal of Applied Psychology, 76*, 106–114. doi:10.1037/0021-9010.76.1.106

Schroeder, A., & Pauleen, D. (2007). KM governance: Investigating the case of a knowledge intensive research organisation. *Journal of Enterprise Information Management, 20*(4), 414–431. doi:10.1108/17410390710772696

Schroeder, A., Pauleen, D., & Huff, S. (2007). *Towards a framework for understanding KM governance.* Paper presented at the ICIS.

Schultz, W. C. (1955). *FIRO: A three dimensional theory of interpersonal behaviour.* New York: Holt, Rinehart, Winston.

Scott, P. B. (2005). Knowledge workers: Social, task, and semantic network analysis. *Corporate Communications: An International Journal, 10*(3), 257–277. doi:10.1108/13563280510614519

Scrivens, C. (2003). Educational leadership: What might we learn from research in schools? *Early Education, 31*, 29–35.

Scupola, A. (2003). The adoption of Internet commerce by SMEs in the south of Italy: An environmental, technological and organizational perspective. *Journal of Global Information Technology Management, 6*(1), 51–71.

Senge, P. (1990). *The fifth discipline: The art and practice of the learning organisation.* New York: Doubleday.

Senge, P. (2000). Classic work: The leader's new work: Building learning organizations. In D. Morey, M. Maybury, & B. Thuraisingham (Eds.), *Knowledge management: Classics and contemporary works.* Cambridge, MA: The MIT Press.

Shamir, B. (1999). Leadership in boundaryless organizations: Disposable or indispensable? *European Journal of Work and Organizational Psychology, 8*(1), 49–71. doi:10.1080/135943299398438

Shamir, B., House, R. J., & Arthur, M. B. (1993). The motivational effects of charismatic leadership: A self-concept based theory. *Organization Science, 4*(4), 577–594. doi:10.1287/orsc.4.4.577

Sharratt, M., & Usoro, A. (2003). Understanding knowledge-sharing in online communities of practice [Electronic Version] [from http://www.ejkm.com]. *Electronic Journal of Knowledge Management, 1*, 187–196. Retrieved June 16, 2006.

Shekhar, S. (2006). Understanding the virtuality of virtual organizations. *Leadership and Organization Development Journal, 27*(6), 465–483. doi:10.1108/01437730610687755

Shin, J., & McClomb, G. E. (1998). Top executive leadership and organizational innovation: An empirical investigation of nonprofit human service organizations (HSOs). *Administration in Social Work, 22*, 1–21. doi:10.1300/J147v22n03_01

Silbergh, D., & Lennon, K. (2006). Developing leadership skills: Online versus face-to-face. *Journal of European Industrial Training, 30*(7), 498–511. doi:10.1108/03090590610704376

Simoff, S. J., & Biuk-Aghai, R. (2003a). Generation, transfer and utilisation of knowledge: Knowledge discovery and visualisation. In H. Hasan & M. Handzic (Eds.), *Australian studies in knowledge management* (pp. 184-238). Wollongong, Australia: University of Wollongong Press.

Simoff, S. J., & Biuk-Aghai, R. (2003b). Multimedia mining of collaborative virtual workspaces: An integrative framework for extracting and integrating collaborative process knowledge. In O. Zaiane, S. J. Simoff, & C. Djeraba (Eds.), *Mining multimedia and complex data* (pp. 168-186). Heidelberg, Germany: Springer.

Simoff, S. J., & Maher, M. L. (2000). Analyzing participation in collaborative design environments. *Design Studies, 21,* 119-144.

Singleton, V., & Michael, M. (1993). Actor-networks and ambivalence: General practitioners in the UK cervical screening programme. *Social Studies of Science, 23,* 227–264. doi:10.1177/030631293023002001

Skyrme, D. (1997). *Knowledge management: Making sense of an oxymoron.* Retrieved July 5, 2005, from http://www.skyrme.com/insights/22km.htm

Slevin, D. P. (1989). *The Whole Manager.* New York, NY: Amacom.

Slote, M. (2003). Agent-based virtue ethics. In S. Darwall (Ed.), *Blackwell readings in philosophy: Virtue ethics* (pp. 203-226). New York: Oxford University Press.

Smith, G., & Rupp, W. T. (2002). Communication and loyalty among knowledge workers: A resource of the firm theory view. *Journal of Knowledge, 6*(3), 250–261. doi:10.1108/13673270210434359

Smith, G., & Rupp, W. T. (2003). Knowledge workers: Exploring the link among performance rating, pay, and motivational aspects. *Journal of Knowledge, 7*(1), 107–124. doi:10.1108/13673270310463662

Smith, G., Blackman, D., & Good, B. (2003). Knowledge sharing and organizational learning: The impact of social architecture at ordnance survey. *Journal of Information and Knowledge Management Practice, 4.* Retrieved December 20, 2004, from http://www.tlainc.com/articl50.htm

Smith, M. (2005). Strategies for successful fellowships: Nurturing early childhood leaders. *Young Children, 2005*(January), 12–18.

Snow, C. C., Miles, R. E., & Coleman, H. J. (1992). Managing 21st century network organizations. *Organizational Dynamics, 20*(3), 5–20. doi:10.1016/0090-2616(92)90021-E

Solomon, D. (2003). Virtue ethics: Radical or routine? In M. DePaul & L. Zagzebski (Eds.), *Intellectual virtue: Perspectives from ethics and epistemology* (pp. 57-80). New York: Oxford University Press.

Sorrentino, R. M., & Boutillier, R. G. (1975). The effect of quantity and quality of verbal interaction on ratings of leadership ability. *Journal of Experimental Social Psychology, 11,* 403-411.

Southworth, G. (2002). What is important in educational administration: Learning-centred school leadership. *New Zealand Journal of Educational Leadership, 17,* 5–9.

Southworth, G. (2005). Overview and conclusions. In M. Coles & G. Southworth (Eds.), *Developing leadership: Creating the schools of tomorrow* (pp. 158-173). Maidenhead, UK: Open University Press.

Spears, L. C. (2004). The understanding and practice of servant-leadership. In L. C. Spears & M. Lawrence, *Practicing servant leadership: Succeeding through trust, bravery, and forgiveness* (pp. 9-24). San Francisco: Jossey-Bass.

Spillane, J. (2006). *Distributed leadership.* San Francisco: Jossey-Bass.

Spira, J. B. (2005). *In praise of knowledge workers.* Retrieved April 23, 2008, from http://www.kmworld.com/Articles/ReadArticle.aspx?ArticleID=9605

Stanoevska-Slabeva, K., & Schmid, B. F. (2001). *A typology of online communities and community supporting platforms.* Paper presented at the 34th Annual Hawaii International Conference on System Sciences.

Staples, D. S., Hulland, J. S., & Higgins, C. A. (1999). A self-efficacy theory explanation for the management of

304

remote workers in virtual organizations. *Organization Science, 10*(6), 758–776. doi:10.1287/orsc.10.6.758

Star, S. L., & Griesmer, J. (1989). Institutional ecology, "translation" and boundary objects: Amateurs and professionals in Berkley's Museum of Vertebrate Zoology. *Social Studies of Science, 19*, 387-420.

Steiner, I. D. (1972). *Group process and productivity.* New York: Academic.

Stephens, C. S., Ledbetter, W. N., Mitra, A., & Ford, F. N. (1992). Executive or functional manager? The nature of the CIO's job. *MIS Quarterly, 16*(4), 449–467. doi:10.2307/249731

Stevens, J. (1996). *Applied multivariate statistics for the social sciences.* NJ: Mahwah: Lawrence Erlbaum Publishers.

Stewart, K. J. (2006). The impact of ideology on effectiveness in open source software development teams. *MIS Quarterly, 30*(2), 291–314.

Stewart, T. (2001). *The wealth of knowledge: Intellectual capital and the 21th century organisation.* New York: Currency Doubleday.

Stone, A. G., Russell, R. F., & Paterson, K. (2004). Transformational versus servant leadership: A difference in leader focus. *Leadership and Organization Development Journal, 25*(4), 349–361. doi:10.1108/01437730410538671

Storey, J., & Barnett, E. (2000). Knowledge management initiatives: Learning from failure. *Journal of Knowledge Management, 4*(2), 145–156. doi:10.1108/13673270010372279

Suchan, J., & Hayzak, G. (2001). The communication characteristics of virtual teams: A case study. *IEEE Transactions on Professional Communication, 44*(3), 174–186. doi:10.1109/47.946463

Sudweeks, F. (2004). *Development and leadership in computer-mediated collaborative groups.* PhD thesis, Communication Studies, Murdoch University, Australia.

Sudweeks, F., & Simoff, S. (1999). Complementary explorative data analysis: The reconciliation of quantitative and qualitative principles. In S. Jones (Ed.), *Doing Internet research* (pp. 29-55). Thousand Oaks, CA: Sage.

Sudweeks, F., & Simoff, S. J. (2005). Leading conversations: Communication behaviours of emergent leaders in virtual teams. In *Proceedings of the 38th Hawaii International Conference on System Science.*

Swaffield, S. (2005). No sleeping partners: Relationships between head teachers and critical friends. *School Leadership & Management, 25*(1), 43–57. doi:10.1080/1363243052000317082

Swaffield, S. (2007). Light touch critical friendship. *Improving Schools, 10*(3), 205–219. doi:10.1177/1365480207077845

Syed-Ikhsan, S. O. S., & Rowland, F. (2004). Benchmarking knowledge management in a public organization in Malaysia. *Benchmarking: An International Journal, 11*(3), 238–266. doi:10.1108/14635770410538745

Szulanski, G. (2000). The process of knowledge transfer: A diachronic analysis of stickiness. *Organizational Behavior and Human Decision Processes, 82*(1), 9–27. doi:10.1006/obhd.2000.2884

Talisayon, D. (2002). Knowledge and people. *Business World*, p. 1.

Tannenbaum, R. & Schmidt, K. H. (1958). How to choose a leadership style. *Harvard Business Review,* March-April.

Tarmazi, H., de Vreede, G., & Zigurs, I. (2007). Leadership challenges in communities of practice: Supporting facilitators via design and technology. *International Journal of e-Collaboration, 3*(1), 18–39.

Tarmizi, H., & de Vreede, G. J. (2005). A facilitation task taxonomy for communities of practice. In *Proceedings of the Eleventh Americas Conference on Information Systems* (pp. 1-11).

Tatnall, A., & Gilding, A. (1999, January). *Actor-network theory and information systems research.* Paper presented at the ACIS 99 Conference, Wellington, Victoria University of Wellington.

Tavakolian, H. (1989). Linking the information technology structure with organizational competitive strategy: A survey. *MIS Quarterly, 13*(3), 309–318. doi:10.2307/249006

Taylor, F. W. (1998). *The principles of scientific management.* New York: Dover Publications.

Thomas, D. M., Bostrom, R. P., & Gouge, M. (2007). Making knowledge work in virtual teams. *Communications of the ACM, 50*(11), 85–90. doi:10.1145/1297797.1297802

Thompson, C. H. (2006). The public school superintendent and servant leadership. *Dissertation Abstracts International, 66*(09). (UMI No. 3190501).

Thompson, J., Alvy, G., & Lees, A. (2000). Social entrepreneurship: A new look at the people and the potential. *Management Decision, 38*(5), 328–338. doi:10.1108/00251740010340517

Thong, J. Y. L. (1999). An integrated model of information systems adoption in small business. *Journal of Management Information Systems, 15*(4), 187–214.

Thong, J., & Yap, C. (1995). CEO characteristics, organizational characteristics and information technology adoption in small business. *Omega . International Journal of Management Sciences, 23*(4), 429–442.

Thornton, K. (2005). *Courage, commitment and collaboration: Notions of leadership in the New Zealand ECE 'Centres of Innovation'.* Unpublished master's thesis, Victoria University of Wellington, Wellington.

Thornton, K., & Yoong, P. (2008). *The application of online action learning to leadership development: A case study.* Paper presented at 9th European Conference on Knowledge Management, Southampton, Great Britain.

Timperley, H. (2005). Distributed leadership: Developing theory from practice. *Journal of Curriculum Studies, 37*(4), 395–420. doi:10.1080/00220270500038545

Tjosvold, D. (1988). Cooperation and competitive interdependence. *Group Organizational Studies, 13,* 274–289. doi:10.1177/105960118801300303

Tobin, G. A., & Begley, C. M. (2004). Methodological rigor within a qualitative framework. *Methodological Issues in Nursing Research, 48*(4), 388–396.

Tornatzky, L. G., & Fleischer, M. (1990). *The processes of technological innovation.* Lanham, MD: Lexington Books.

Townsend, A. M., DeMarie, S. M., & Hendrickson, A. R. (1998). Virtual teams: Technology and the workplace of the future. *The Academy of Management Executive, 12*(3), 17–29.

Townsend, A. M., DeMarie, S. M., & Hendrickson, A. R. (1998). Virtual teams: Technology and the workplace of the future. *The Academy of Management Executive, 12*(3), 17–29.

Townsend, A. M., DeMarie, S. M., & Hendrickson, A. R. (1998). Virtual teams: Technology and the workplace of the future. *Academy of Management Journal, 12*(3), 17-29.

Turner, J. R. (1999). *The handbook of project-based management: Improving the processes for achieving strategic objectives.* London: McGraw-Hill.

Turner, J. R., & Müller, R. (2006). *Choosing appropriate project managers.* Newton Square, PA: Project Management Institute.

Tushman, M. L. (1977). Special boundary roles in the innovation process. *Administrative Science Quarterly, 22*(4), 587–605. doi:10.2307/2392402

Tyran, K. L., Tyran, C. K., & Shepherd, M. (2003). Exploring emergent leadership in virtual teams. In C. B. Gibson & S. G. Cohen (Eds.), *Virtual teams that work: Creating conditions for virtual team effectiveness* (pp. 183-195). San Francisco, CA: Jossey-Bass.

Un, C. A., & Cuervo-Cazurra, A. (2004). Strategies for knowledge creation in firms. *British Journal of Management, 15,* 27–41. doi:10.1111/j.1467-8551.2004.00404.x

Van Buren, M. (1999). A yardstick for knowledge management. *Training and Development Journal, 53*(5), 71–78.

Van der Smagt, T. (2000). Enhancing virtual teams: Social relations vs. communication technology. *Industrial Management & Data Systems*, *100*(4), 148–156. doi:10.1108/02635570010291766

Van Grembergen, W. (2004). *Strategies for information technology governance*. Hershey, PA: Idea Group Publishing.

Victor, B., & Stephens, C. (1994). The dark side of the new organizational forms: An editorial essay. *Organization Science*, *5*(4), 479–482. doi:10.1287/orsc.5.4.479

Viitala, R. (2004). Towards knowledge leadership. *Leadership and Organization Development Journal*, *25*(6), 528–544. doi:10.1108/01437730410556761

Vogel, D., van Genuchten, M. L. D., Verveen, S., van Eekout, M., & Adams, A. (2001). Exploratory research on the role of national and professional cultures in a distributed learning project. *IEE Transactions on Professional Communication*, *44*(2), 114–125. doi:10.1109/47.925514

volio, B. J., Kahai, S., & Dodge, G. E. (2000). E-leadership: Implications for theory, research, and practice. *The Leadership Quarterly*, *11*(4), 615–668. doi:10.1016/S1048-9843(00)00062-X

Vroom, V. H., & Yetton, P. W. (1973). *Leadership and decision making*. Pittsburgh, PA: University of Pittsburgh Press.

Wagner, C., & Bolloju, N. (2005). Supporting knowledge management in organizations with conversational technologies: Discussion forums, Weblogs and Wikis. *Journal of Database Management*, *16*(2), 1–8.

Walker, A., & Dimmock, C. (2005). Developing leadership in context. In M. Coles & G. Southworth (Eds.), *Developing leadership* (pp. 80-94). Maidenhead, Berkshire, UK: Open University Press.

Wall, J. A., Stark, J. B., & Standifer, R. L. (2001). A current review and theory development. *Journal of Conflict Resolution*, *45*(3), 370-391.

Walsham, G. (1995). The emergence of interpretivism in IS research. *Information Systems Research*, *6*(4), 376–394. doi:10.1287/isre.6.4.376

Walther, J. B., & Tidwell, L. C. (1995). Nonverbal Cues in computer-mediated communication, and the effect of chronemics on relational communication. *Journal of Organizational Computing*, *5*(4), 355–378.

Ware, J. P., & Grantham, C. E. (2007). Knowledge work and knowledge workers. Retrieved April 24, 2008, from http://www.thefutureofwork.net/assets/Knowledge_Work_and_Knowledge_Workers.pdf

Warkentin, M. E., Sayeed, L., & Hightower, R. (1997). Virtual teams versus face-to-face teams: An exploratory study of a Web-based conference system. *Decision Sciences*, *28*(4), 975–996. doi:10.1111/j.1540-5915.1997.tb01338.x

Wasko, M. M. L., & Faraj, S. (2000). "It is what one does": Why people participate and help others in electronic communities of practice. *The Journal of Strategic Information Systems*, *9*(2-3), 155–173. doi:10.1016/S0963-8687(00)00045-7

Wasserman, S., & Faust, K. (1994). *Social network analysis. Methods and applications*. New York: Cambridge University Press.

Weber, M. (1947). *The theory of economic organization* (A. Henderson & T. Parsons, Trans., T. Parsons, Ed.). New York: The Free Press.

Wegge, J. (2006). Communication via videoconference: Emotional and cognitive consequences of affective personality dispositions, seeing one's own picture, and disturbing events. *Human-Computer Interaction*, *21*, 273–318. doi:10.1207/s15327051hci2103_1

Wegge, J., Bipp, T., & Kleinbeck, U. (2007). Goal setting via videoconferencing. *European Journal of Work and Organizational Psychology*, *16*, 169–194. doi:10.1080/13594320601125567

Weill, P. (2004). Don't just lead, govern: How top-performing firms govern IT. *MIS Quarterly Executive*, *3*(1), 1–17.

Weisband, S. (2002). Maintaining awareness in distributed team collaboration: Implication for leadership and performance. In P. Hinds & S. Kiesler (Eds.), *Distributed work* (pp. 311-333). Cambridge, MA: MIT Press.

Weisband, S. (2002). Maintaining awareness in distributed team collaboration: Implication for leadership and performance. In P. Hinds & S. Kiesler (Eds.), *Distributed work* (pp. 311-333). Cambridge, MA: MIT Press.

Wellman, B. (2002). Little boxes, globalization, and networked individualism? In M. Tanabe, P. v. d. Besselaar, & T. Ishida (Eds.), *Digital cities II: Computational and sociological approaches* (pp. 10-25). Berlin: Springer.

Wellman, B., Quan-Haase, A., Boase, J., Chen, W., Hampton, K., Diaz, I., et al. (2003) The social affordances of the internet for networked individualism. *Journal of Computer Mediated Communication, 8*(3). Retrieved April 2007 from http://www.ascusc.org/jcmc/vol8/issue3/wellman.html

Wellman, B., Quan-Haase, A., Witte, J., & Hampton, K. N. (2001). Does the Internet increase, decrease, or supplement social capital? Social networks, participation, and community commitment. *The American Behavioral Scientist, 45*(3), 436–456. doi:10.1177/00027640121957286

Wenger, E. (1998). *Communities of praxis. Learning, meaning and identity.* Cambridge: Cambridge University Press.

Wenger, E. (2006). *Communities of practice: A brief introduction.* Retrieved August 30, 2006, from http://www.ewenger.com/theory/index.htm

Wenger, E. C., & Snyder, W. M. (2000). Communities of practice: The organizational frontier. *Harvard Business Review, 78*(1), 139–145.

Wenger, E., McDermott, R. A., & Snyder, W. (2002). *Cultivating communities of practice: A guide to managing knowledge.* Boston: Harvard Business School Press.

West-Burnham, J. (2003). Learning to lead. In B. Davies & J. West-Burnham (Eds.), *Handbook of educational leadership and management* (pp. 57-59). London: Pearson Education.

Whetstone, J. T. (2001). How virtue fits with business ethics. *Journal of Business Ethics, 33*, 101–114. doi:10.1023/A:1017554318867

Whitley, E. A. (1999). *Habermas and the non-humans: Towards a critical theory for the new collective.* Retrieved December 23, 2003, from http://www.keele.ac.uk/depts/stt/cstt2/papers/whitley.htm

Wickham, K., & Walther, J. (2007). Perceived behaviour of emergent and assigned leaders in virtual groups. *International Journal of e-Collaboration, 3*(1), 1–17.

Wiig, K. (2000). Knowledge management: An emerging discipline rooted in a long history. In D. Charles & D. Chauvel (Eds.), *Knowledge horizons: The present and the promise of knowledge management* (pp. 3-26). Woburn, MA: Butterworth-Heinemann.

Williamson, O. E. (1975). *Market and hierarchies: Analysis and antitrust implications.* New York: Free Press.

Wilson, J. M., Straus, S. G., et al. (2006). All in due time: The development of trust in computer-mediated and face-to-face teams. *Organizational Behavior and Human Decision Processes, 99*, 16-33.

Wilson, S. (2003). Forming virtual teams. *Quality Progress, 36*(6), 36–41.

Withey, M. J. (2003). Development of scale to measure knowledge work. *International Journal of Knowledge, Culture, and Change Management, 3*. Retrieved April 24, 2007, from http://www.management.journal.com

Witmer, D. F. (1997). Communication and recovery: Structuration as an ontological approach to organizational culture. *Communication Monographs, 64*, 324-349.

Witten, I. H., & Frank, E. (2000). *Data mining: Practical machine learning tools and techniques with Java implementations.* San Francisco: Morgan Kaufmann.

Wolff, K. H. (Ed.). (1950). *The sociology of Georg Simmel.* New York: The Free Press.

Wood, W., & Rhodes, N. D. (1992). Sex differences in interaction style in task groups. In C. Ridgeway (Ed.), *Gender, interaction, and inequality* (pp. 97-121). NY: Springer-Verlag.

World Values Survey. (2008). *World values survey: The world's most comprehensive investigation of political and sociocultural change.* Retrieved June 25, 2008, from http://www.worldvaluessurvey.org/

Wright, K. J. T. (1970). Exploring the uniqueness of common complaints. *The British Journal of Medical Psychology, 41*, 221–232.

Yeatts, D. E., & Hyten, C. (1998). *High-performing self-managed work teams: A comparison of theory and practice.* Thousand Oaks, CA: Sage.

Yin, R. K. (2003). *Case study research: Design and methods* (3rd ed.). London: Sage.

Yoo, Y., & Alavi, M. (1996). *Emergence of leadership and its impact on group performance in virtual team environments: A longitudinal field study.* Paper presented at the International conference on information systems, Cleveland, Ohio.

Yoo, Y., & Alavi, M. (2002). *Electronic mail usage patterns of emergent leaders in distributed teams.* Retrieved February 2, 2004, from www.weatherhead.cwru.edu/sprouts/2002/020309.pdf

Yoo, Y., & Alavi, M. (2002, Summer). Electronic mail usage pattern of emergent leaders in distributed teams. *Sprouts: Working Papers on Information Environments. Systems and Organizations, 2.*

Yoo, Y., & Alavi, M. (2004). Emergent leadership in virtual teams: What do emergent leaders do? *Information and Organization, 14*(1), 27–58. doi:10.1016/j.infoandorg.2003.11.001

Yoo, Y., & Alavi, M. (2004). Emergent leadership in virtual teams: What do emergent leaders do? *Information and Organization, 14*, 27–58. doi:10.1016/j.infoandorg.2003.11.001

Yoo, Y., & Alavi, M. (2004). Emergent leadership in virtual teams: What do emergent leaders do? *Information and Organization, 14*, 27–58. doi:10.1016/j.infoandorg.2003.11.001

Yoong, P., & Galluppe, B. (2001). Action learning and groupware technologies: A case study in GSS facilitation research. *Journal of Information Technology and People, 14*(1), 78–90. doi:10.1108/09593840110384780

Young, J. R. (1999). Course for instructors helps keep students. *The Chronicle of Higher Education, 46*(11), A59.

Yukl, G. (1975). Toward a behavioural theory of leadership. In Houghton, et al. (Eds.), *The management of organizations and individuals.* London: Ward Lock Educational.

Yukl, G. (2006). *Leadership in organizations.* Upper Saddle River, NJ: Prentice Hall.

Yukl, G. A., & Falbe, C. (1991). Importance of different power sources in downward and lateral relations. *The Journal of Applied Psychology, 76*, 416–423. doi:10.1037/0021-9010.76.3.416

Yukl, G., Gordon, A., & Taber, T. (2002). A hierarchical taxonomy of leadership behavior: Integrating a half century of behavior research. *Journal of Leadership & Organizational Studies, 9*(1), 15–32. doi:10.1177/107179190200900102

Zaccaro, S. J., & Bader, P. (2003). E-leadership and the challenge of leading e-teams: Minimizing bad and maximizing the good. *Organizational Dynamics, 31*, 377–387. doi:10.1016/S0090-2616(02)00129-8

Zaccaro, S. J., & Bader, P. (2003). E-leadership and the challenges of leading e-teams: Minimizing the bad and maximizing the good. *Organizational Dynamics, 31*(4), 377-387.

Zak, P., Kurzban, R., & Matzner, W. T. (2005). Oxytocin is associated with human trustworthiness. *Hormones and Behavior, 48*, 522–527. doi:10.1016/j.yhbeh.2005.07.009

Zaleznik, A. (2004). Managers and leaders: Are they different? *Harvard Business Review,* (January): 74–97.

Zhang, J., & Faerman, S. (2007). Distributed leadership in the development of a knowledge sharing system. *European Journal of Information Systems, 16*, 479–493. doi:10.1057/palgrave.ejis.3000694

Zigurs, I. (2003). Leadership in virtual teams: Oxymoron or opportunity? *Organizational Dynamics, 31*(4), 339–351. doi:10.1016/S0090-2616(02)00132-8

Zigurs, I., & Buckland, B. (1998). A theory of task/technology fit and group support systems effectiveness. *MIS Quarterly*, *22*(3), 313–334. doi:10.2307/249668

Zolin, R., & Hinds, P. (2002). Trust in context: The development of interpesonal trust in geographically distributed work teams (CIFE Working Paper). S. University. Stanford, Center for Integrated Facility Engineering.

About the Contributors

Pak Yoong is a professor and Director of a PhD programme in Information Systems and E-commerce at the School of Information Management at the Victoria University of Wellington, New Zealand. He teaches in the areas of virtual organisation, research methods and IS leadership. His research, teaching and consulting experience is in the facilitation of virtual meetings, online communities of practice, online knowledge sharing and human resource development in information technology environments. Pak uses action learning and action research methods for many of his research projects and pioneered the use of 'grounded action learning' method (a combination of grounded theory and action learning) in IS research.

* * *

Mahfooz A. Ansari (MA, University of Kansas; PhD, Patna University) is currently on the Faculty of Management, University of Lethbridge. Earlier, he held faculty positions at several institutions, including the University Science Malaysia and the Indian Institute of Technology Kanpur. He has over 30 years of teaching, consultancy, and research experience, and is a recipient of several recognitions and awards, including the Fulbright Hays Award and Academy of Management Best Paper Awards. His current program of research focuses on Leader-Member Exchange (LMX), Social Power and Influence, and Cross-Cultural Aspects of Leadership and Influence. He has published two books and over 65 journal articles, and has delivered about 60 presentations at several professional conferences. He has supervised some 25 doctoral dissertations and 50 master's theses. His work has appeared in such journals as *Organizational Behavior and Human Decision Processes, Journal of International Business Studies,* and *Human Relations.*

John Willy Bakke works as a research scientist at Telenor Business Development and Research, where his primary areas of research are flexible work arrangements, small business studies, and user interpretations and user acceptance of technologies. Recent projects include studies of SMEs in European and Asian markets, the role of ICTs and workplace design for work task execution and collaboration, and trust and social capital in distributed groups. He has published a number of articles and papers in these areas, and is also the editor and co-editor of books on telework, distributed work, and workplace design.

Traci A. Carte is an Associate Professor of MIS in the Michael F. Price College of Business at the University of Oklahoma. She received her Ph.D. in MIS from the University of Georgia. Currently, her research interests include IT support for diverse teams, politics and IT, and research methods. Her research has been published in such journals as *MIS Quarterly, Information Systems Research, Group Decision & Negotiation, Decision Support Systems,* and *Journal of the AIS*. She serves on the editorial board of *MIS Quarterly*.

Petros Chamakiotis teaches at the University of Bath, UK. He gained his (4-year honours) *BSc in Economics* from the University of Piraeus Department of Economics, Greece, while he thereafter proceeded to an *MSc in Management and Strategic Information Systems* at the University of Bath School of Management in the UK. During his postgraduate studies, he was given the chance to explore the phenomenon of 'virtuality' mainly through an inter-university academic project. Barring virtual teams and their various implications among traditional working processes, his research interests embrace computer-mediated communication, and business and marketing prospects afforded by recently emerged arrangements such as social networking websites. He is also an active member of the *IFIP W.G. 9.5 'Virtuality & Society.'*

Charlie C. Chen is an Assistant Professor in the Department of Computer Information Systems at Appalachian State University. He received his Ph.D. in Management Information Systems from Claremont Graduate University in 2003. He has authored more than 30 referred articles and proceedings, presented at many professional conferences and venues. Dr. Chen has published in journals such as *Communications of* the AIS, *Journal of Knowledge Management Research Practice, and Journal of Information Systems Education*. Dr. Chen is a Project Management Professional (PMP) certified by the Project Management Institute. Dr. Chen is working on improving information system solutions infrastructural, managerial and operational perspectives. His current main research areas are online learning, mobile commerce, and supply chain technology.

Jocelyn Cranefield is completing a PhD in Information Systems at Victoria University of Wellington. Her research project is investigating how online communities facilitate the transfer and embedding of knowledge in the context of professional change. Jocelyn holds a TEC Top Achiever Scholarship. She also works part-time as an Information and Web Strategy consultant and as a professional musician. Jocelyn holds a Master of Information Management degree (e-business, distinction) from Victoria University of Wellington and is co-founder of the New Zealand Knowledge Management Network.

Mohamed Daassi is a PhD in Management Information Systems and Assistant Professor at the University of Bretagne Occidentale (France). He holds a B.Sc in Operations Research and an European M.Sc in Management and Technology of Information Systems. His current research and teaching interests include Collaborative Technologies, Virtual Teams, Social aspects of Human-Computer Interaction, and Online Consumer Behavior.

Gert-Jan de Vreede is the Kayser Distinguished Professor at the Department of Information Systems & Quantitative Analysis at the University of Nebraska at Omaha where he is director of the Center for Collaboration Science. He is also affiliated with the Faculty of Technology, Policy and Management of Delft University of Technology in the Netherlands from where he received his PhD. His research focuses on field applications of e-collaboration technologies, the theoretical foundations of (e)-collaboration, Collaboration Engineering, and the facilitation of group meetings. His research has been published in various journals, including *Journal of Management Information Systems, Journal of the AIS, Commu-*

nications of the AIS, Small Group Research, Communications of the ACM, DataBase, Group Decision and Negotiation, International Journal of e-Collaboration, Journal of Decision Systems, Journal of Creativity and Innovation Management, Simulation & Gaming, Simulation, and *Journal of Simulation Practice and Theory.*

Marc Favier, PhD, is Full Professor of Information Systems at the University of Grenoble (France). He is a graduate of Computer Science. He has published 28 articles in scientific journals and eight books or chapters of books. He is directing PhD students and is or was the director of various graduate or PhD programs in IS or MBA. His current research and teaching interests include information management, strategy and IS, E-business, DSS, collaborative technologies and virtual teams.

Albert L. Harris is a Professor of MIS at the Walker College of Business, Appalachian State University, and Editor-in-Chief of the Journal of Information Systems Education. He was a 2006 Fulbright scholar to Portugal. He is a member of the Board of Directors for the Education Special Interest Group (EDSIG) of AITP and serves as Secretary of the International Association of Information Management (IAIM). He previously served for three years as Treasurer of EDSIG. He is a Certified Information Systems Auditor and a Certified Management Consultant. He received his Ph.D. in MIS from Georgia State University, his M.S. in Systems Management from the George Washington University, and his B.S. in Quantitative Business Analysis from Indiana University. Dr. Harris has traveled extensively and has used these experiences in his teaching and research. His research interests include IS education, IS ethics, and global IS/IT issues. He has more than 85 publications as book chapters, in numerous journals, and in international and national conference proceedings. He is a co-Editor of a book titled *Managing Global Information Technology: Strategies and Challenges.*

Julia E. Hoch, Ph.D. works as research and teaching assistant at the Department of Work-, Organizational- and Social Psychology at University of Technology, Dresden, Germany. She studied psychology and business at University of Kiel, and holds a doctor in psychology from the University of Kiel, Germany as well. During her PhD studies she was working as research and teaching assistant at University of Kiel and the Technical University of Munich, Germany. Her research interests include the topics of shared leadership, distributed leadership, virtual team performance and motivation and leadership in teams

Sid Huff is Professor of Information Systems and Head of the School of Information Management at Victoria University of Wellington, New Zealand. His teaching and research focus on IS strategy, IT governance, senior management roles in information systems, and IS management. His work has appeared in numerous academic and practitioner journals, including *MIS Quarterly, Information Systems Research, Journal of MIS, Journal of Strategic Information Systems, Communications of the ACM, CAIS* and others. He has also written over 50 teaching cases for educational use, and was the originator of the IS World web site on Teaching IS with Cases. His most recent book is *Managing IT Professionals in the Internet Age,* co-authored with Dr. Pak Yoong. He holds degrees in Applied Mathematics, Electrical Engineering and Business Administration, from Queens University. He received his Ph.D. in Information Systems from the M.I.T. Sloan School of Management.

Annick Janson is the Microsoft NZ Research Director, 'Partners in Learning' programme. She previously held the positions of inaugural Research Director, New Zealand Leadership Institute, University of Auckland Business School; Researcher in Residence, INSEAD and Visiting Research Associate at the Gallup Leadership Institute and Harvard School of Consulting & Clinical Psychology. As the Principal Investigator of the Leadership Pathway research at the Royal Society of New Zealand she is designing the first electronic New Zealand leadership archive, enabling storytelling analysis and web-based dissemination toward leadership tacit knowledge learning. This work also pioneers a visual research reporting methodology for the Social Sciences. Janson received a Gallup Positive Psychology Award in Sept. 2006 for research in Leadership Formative Experiences and represented New Zealand at the Global Leadership Summit, Gallup Leadership Institute, Washington 2006. She served on several advisory boards and government steering committees and as editor for a number of refereed publications in her areas of expertise. She has a Ph.D., Management Systems, University of Waikato, New Zealand (emergence of online leadership), an M.A. in Clinical Psychology and is a registered Clinical and Educational Psychologist.

Nabila Jawadi is a PhD in Management Information Systems and Assistant Professor at Amiens School of Management (France). Her research experience is in the Virtual team management including leadership, trust and performance management. She also was interested in e-learning adoption in organization. Her overall interest field includes impacts of ICT on organization management. She also teaches in the area of virtual teams, leadership and IS for enterprises.

Sharmila Jayasingam (B.Tech. Management; MBA, University Science Malaysia) has been an academician at various universities in Malaysia including the Universiti Tenaga Nasional, and Multimedia University for about 7 years. Currently, she is a lecturer in leadership and entrepreneurship at the Faculty of Business and Accounting, University of Malaya. Her previous academic position at the Multimedia University created a research interest on knowledge management as well. Therefore, her research is interdisciplinary and addresses entrepreneurship, leadership, and knowledge management issues. She is currently pursuing her Ph.D. research focusing on the topic of social power and influence and knowledge management practices.

Tom Erik Julsrud, PhD, works as a research scientist at Telenor Research and Innovation and is also associated to Sør Trøndelag University College. His research areas of interests include social networks; trust in organizations; organizational change and social capital. He has co-authored books on telework and distributed work, and has published several articles and papers on collaboration in distributed and virtual teams. His latest work focuses in particular on the development of trust in virtual environments and distributed work groups.

Michel Kalika, PhD is full professor of Management Information Systems. He is the director of Strasbourg Management School. He was he director of the Center for research in Management & Organization and the PhD program in Information Systems (e-management) at the University of Paris-Dauphine. His research focus is the use of e-mail by managers and the impact on meetings, IT strategic alignment, the link between IT and performance. He is the author or co-author of books on organizational structure, management, e-management and numerous articles in academic journals.

Heather King is the Houston Managing Director for Gabbard & Company, a management consulting firm founded in 1998 with offices in Oklahoma City, Tulsa and Houston. Heather has expertise in leadership development, instructional design, change management and performance improvement. Heather is dedicated to helping individuals and organisations grow through collaborative planning and effective implementation. She has worked with organisations in the energy, financial services, non-profit, government and tribal sectors. Heather is certified as a Professional Balanced Scorecard Practitioner, holds a certificate in ISO 9000 and a certificate in coaching from the American Society of Training and Development. Heather graduated from the University of New Mexico with Bachelors of Science in Biological Anthropology and Psychology and competed a Master of Business Administration from the University of Oklahoma.

Darin R. Molnar, PhD is CEO of eXcolo Research Group, a leadership and management consulting firm located in Portland, Oregon. Dr Molnar's research interests include explorations of the cross-cultural applicability of servant leadership and examinations of how personal values comprise the fundamental construct of any leadership practice. When he is not busy with his consulting practice or research pursuits, you can find Dir Molnar in on-ground and online classrooms teaching college and graduate school courses in leadership, management and general business. Please send inquiries regarding consulting or research interests to Darin@Molnar.com or call 971-222-7359

Ralf Müller is Associate Professor of Business Administration at Umeå University, Sweden and Adjunct Professor of Project Management at the Norwegian School of Management BI. Furthermore he is Adjunct Professor at ESC Lille, France and visiting faculty member at Tilburg University, The Netherlands, and Managing Director of PM Concepts, a Sweden based management consultancy. He lectures and researches in leadership and governance of project management, as well as in research methodologies. He is the (co-)author of more than 60 publications, including books, book chapters, papers in international management journals, as well as conference papers. He is the author of one of the first books on project governance. Ralf serves at the editorial review board of five academic journals and was awarded the 2009 Emerald reviewer of the year award. He spent 30 years in business, consulting large enterprises in project management and governance (e.g., as worldwide director of project management in NCR Teradata). He is a co-founder of two PMI chapters in Europe and contributor to several PMI standards.

Niki Panteli is a Senior Lecturer in Information Systems and Director for the Centre for Information Management at the University of Bath and the Chair of the IFIP W.G. 9.5 'Virtuality & Society'. Her main research interests lie in the area of IT-enabled transformation, virtual teams and computer-mediated communication. Within this field, she has studied issues of trust, conflict and collaborations in virtual, geographically-dispersed environments. She has published articles in numerous journals including *Communications of ACM, Decision Support Systems, Information & Organization, Information and Management, IEEE Transactions on Professional Communication, Behaviour and Information Technology, European Journal of Information Systems, Futures, New Technology, Work and Employment and the Journal of Business Ethics*. Further, her work has appeared in book chapters and conference proceedings. She is also the co-editor of 'Exploring Virtuality within and beyond Organizations' (Palgrave, 2008).

David J. Pauleen is a Senior Lecturer in the Department of Management and International Business at Massey University, New Zealand. He has researched, taught and published in the areas of knowledge management, virtual teams, cross-cultural management and emerging work practices. His work has appeared in such journals as the Journal of Management Information Systems, Sloan Management Review, Journal of Knowledge Management, Journal of Information Technology, and Internet Research. He is also editor of the books, Virtual Teams: Projects, Protocols and Processes (2004) and Cross-Cultural Perspectives on Knowledge Management (2007) and co-editor of Personal Knowledge Management: Individual and Organizational Perspectives (2009).

Craig L. Pearce is an associate professor of Management at the Peter F. Drucker and Masatoshi Ito School of Management. He received his Ph.D. from the University of Maryland, his MBA from the University of Wisconsin-Madison and his B.S., with honors and distinction, from Pennsylvania State University. He is an active keynote speaker and consultant in the areas of leadership, team and organizational development. He has published more than three-dozen articles and book chapters in such outlets as Strategic Management Journal, Leadership Quarterly, Academy of Management Executive and the Wall Street Journal. His book, *Shared Leadership*, is published by Sage Publications, and he is currently working on a second book on shared leadership, to be published by Stanford University Press. He sits on several editorial boards, including serving as Associate Editor of Leadership Quarterly. His work has been cited more than 700 times and he has won several awards for his research, teaching and service, including a 1997 award from the Center for Creative Leadership, the 2000 Barclays American Award, the 2004 Ascendant Scholar Award and the 2008 Asia Pacific Leadership Award.

Andreas Schroeder is currently working as a rresearch fellow at the Centre for Applied Knowledge and Innovation Management, City University of Hong Kong. His main research interests include the governance of new and innovative organizational initiatives. He has further published on aspects of supply chain management and open collaboration systems.

Ada Scupola is an associate professor at the Department of Communication, Business and Information Technologies, Roskilde University, Denmark. She holds a Ph.D in social sciences from Roskilde University, an MBA from the University of Maryland at College Park, USA and a MSc. from the University of Bari, Italy. She is the editor-in-chief of The International Journal of E-Services and Mobile Applications. Her main research interests are e-services, adoption and diffusion of e-commerce and e-services in SMEs, ICTs in clusters of companies, innovation theory. She is collaborating and has collaborated to several national and international research projects on the above subjects. Her research has been published in several international journals among which *The Information Society, Journal of Enterprise Information Management , Journal of Electronic Commerce in Organizations, The Journal of Information Science, The Journal of Global Information Technology Management, Scandinavian Journal of Information Systems, The Journal of Electronic Commerce in Developing Countries* and in numerous book chapters and international conferences.

Simeon J. Simoff is professor of Information Technology and Head of the School of Computing and Mathematics at the University of Western Sydney. He is also Head of the e-Markets Research Group at the University of Technology, Sydney. He is also a founding co-director of the Institute of Analytic Professionals of Australia. He is known for the unique blend of interdisciplinary scholarship and innovation, which integrates the areas of data mining, design computing, virtual worlds and digital media, with application in the area of electronic trading environments. His work in these fields has resulted in 11 co-authored/edited books and more than 170 research papers, and a number of cross-disciplinary educational programs in information technology and computing. He is co-editor of the CRPIT series "Conferences of Research and Practice in Information Technology". He has initiated and co-chaired several international conference series in the area of data mining, including The Australasian Data Mining series AusDM, and the ACM SIGKDD Multimedia Data Mining and Visual Data Mining series.

Fay Sudweeks is an Emeritus associate professor at Murdoch University and Adjunct Associate Professor at the Australian National University, Australia. She has Bachelor of Arts (Psychology, Sociology), Master of Cognitive Science, PhD (Communication Studies) degrees. Her research interests are social, cultural, and economic aspects of CMC and CSCW, group dynamics, and e-learning. She has published authored book, 5 edited books, 15 edited proceedings, and more than 80 papers in journals, books, and conference proceedings. She is on editorial boards of Journal of Computer-Mediated Communication, New Media and Society, International Journal of e-Learning, Human Communication Research, Open Communication Journal, International Journal of Education and Development using Information and Communication Technologies, Journal of Electronic Commerce Research and Journal of Electronic Commerce in Organizations. With Charles Ess, she has co-chaired six international conferences on Cultural Attitudes towards Technology and Communication (CATaC).

Halbana Tarmizi is an assistant professor in Management Information Systems Department at Abu Dhabi University, United Arab Emirates. He received his Ph.D. in Information Technology from College of Information Science and Technology at the University of Nebraska at Omaha. He holds a Master degree in Telecommunications from Michigan State University and a Dipl.-Ing. in Electrical Engineering from RWTH Aachen, Germany. His research interests include collaboration technology, online communities, virtual teams, and telecommunication and networking. He has published and presented his works in International Journal of e-Collaboration, e-Service Journal as well as conferences such as AMCIS, HICSS and MWAIS.

Kate Thornton is a lecturer and professional development facilitator in the Faculty of Education at Victoria University of Wellington in Wellington, New Zealand. Kate has a teaching background in the secondary, early childhood and tertiary sectors. Her main research interest is leadership and leadership development in the early childhood education sector and she is also interested in the use of mentoring to support leadership development. Kate is currently involved in doctoral study exploring the role of ICT in supporting leadership development in the New Zealand ECE Sector. This study which should be completed in 2009 involves the use of blended action learning groups to encourage leadership learning.

Christina L. Wassenaar is the Academic Program Director at the Peter F. Drucker and Masatoshi Ito School of Management. She has a B.S. in Agricultural Business from California Polytechnic University, Pomona, her MBA from the Drucker School and is currently completing her Ph.D from the Drucker School. Prior to joining the Drucker School she worked in Marketing Research, Management and Business Development for companies like Johnson & Johnson, MGM Home Entertainment (now Sony Home Entertainment), Con Agra, and ACNielsen. Her research interests include shared leadership, culture creation, organizational commitment and team motivation.

Juergen Wegge, Ph.D. is a full professor and chair of the Department of Work-, Organizational- and Social Psychology at the Technical University of Dresden, Germany. He holds a doctor and habilitation in psychology from the University of Dortmund, Germany. He has been working as director of the international masters-program "Psychology of Excellence" at LMU Munich (2005-2007), before that he was working as a professor at the Universities of Konstanz and Bielefeld. He is the vice president of the section of work and organizational psychology of the German society of psychology and member of AOM, SIOP, IAAP, EAWOP. He has worked as reviewer for Journal of Occupational and Organizational Psychology, British Journal of Management, Zeitschrift für Arbeit- und Organisationspsychologie, Zeitschrift für Personalpsychologie and others. His work topics are work motivation, leadership, work and stress and excellent performance in organizations. He has published three books, 31 journal articles and 55 book chapters on these topics.

Jiinpo Wu is associate professor in the Information Management Department at Tamkang University in Taiwan. He received his Ph.D. in Business Computer Information Systems from North Texas University. His research areas are executive information systems, online learning and social network analysis.

Index